The LITERATURE
of
MUSIC BIBLIOGRAPHY

Fallen Leaf Reference Books in Music
ISSN 8755-268X, No. 21

THE LITERATURE
of
MUSIC BIBLIOGRAPHY

An ACCOUNT of the WRITINGS
on the HISTORY of
MUSIC PRINTING & PUBLISHING

D. W. Krummel

Fallen Leaf Press
Berkeley, California

Published by Fallen Leaf Press
P. O. Box 10034
Berkeley, CA 94709 USA

Library of Congress Cataloging in Publication Data

Krummel, Donald William, 1929-
    The literature of music bibliography : an account of the writings on
the history of music printing & publishing / D. W. Krummel.
        p.   cm. — (Fallen Leaf reference books in music, ISSN
8755-268X: no. 21)
    Includes bibliographical references and index.
    ISSN 0-914913-21-2 (alk. paper)
    1. Music printing—History—Bibliography. 2. Music— Publishing—
History— Bibliography.   I. Title.   II. Series.
ML 112.K765 1993
016.0705'794—dc20   92-10492
                                                                              CIP
                                                                              MN

The paper used in this book meets the minimum requirements of the American National Standard for Information
Services—Permanence of Paper for Printed Library Materials, ANSI Z39.48–1984.

CONTENTS

For O. W. Neighbour
and Richard Macnutt

Preface

MUSIC AND PRINTING have been partners since the days of Gutenberg. Although Fust and Schoeffer, Gutenberg's sometime associates, failed to find a way to print musical notation in their marvelous Mainz psalter of 1457, they tacitly acknowledged its importance by leaving room for it to be added in manuscript. Printers ever since have been challenged by notation that is clearly less than accommodating, while music publishers, who soon entered the picture, found themselves challenged by a market that has typically been as exciting as it was inauspicious. The subsequent history has thus rarely been one of great success, although it has clearly been one of abundance. During the late nineteenth century, for instance, the world's printing presses produced nearly as many titles of printed music as of printed books.

As musicians come to learn about the historical backgrounds of their repertory, they discover the engaging and often unsuspected circumstances under which particular works have been presented to the public. Scholars in particular need to understand the early practices of music printers and publishers, while composers and performers often find that historical conditions offer the most useful explanations of the rationales behind current practices. Specialists in other fields, along with general readers, are often fascinated by details about two beloved artifacts of our civilization: our books and our music.

Music printing — the activity of committing musical notation to surfaces appropriate for duplication and then producing multiple copies from the surfaces — and music publishing — the activities of acquiring musical works, editing them for the printer, and then promoting and distributing the copies that were prepared — have been often described. The better the activities are known, the greater the likelihood that imaginative readers will ask even more questions.

Printing technology seems particularly inaccessible, either superficial or opaque, and more curious than pertinent. Printers have described their practices, but usually with the aim of helping readers appreciate "the predicament," while never revealing any trade secrets. (The secrets may not actually be terribly important, but those who depend on them think they are, and feel more secure in their work as a result.) Like most crafts, music printing has entailed extensive training through apprenticeship, so as to develop the skilled hand and of the sensitive eye as much as of the systematic intellect. Printing, rather than publishing, is still what comes to mind first when one thinks of studying musical documents. It is significant that the major precursor of this book is called a "Bibliography of the History of Music Printing."[1]

The literature of music publishing, in contrast, is mostly promotional, when it exists at all. Publishers understandably feel most secure in recalling anecdotes of happy relationships with the great and famous, so as to remind the muse that her handmaidens are indispensable. Few of the writings discuss the particulars of business arrangements, and many of them seem painfully defensive in arguing the ethics of the law and the social function of the marketplace. Since the record of music publishing speaks for itself

---

1. Åke Davidsson, *Bibliographie zur Geschichte des Musikdrucks* (Stockholm: Almquist & Wiksell, 1965). See 963 below.

through its output of printed music, writings on the topic are all too easily seen as answering questions that nobody is asking. One of the goals of the present study is to suggest that the questions, to the extent that they help us understand the role of musical documents and their sponsors in our society, are in fact very important.

Bibliographers, as critics and historians, stand one step removed from the activity that they are studying. As they intellectualize the activities of printers and publishers, bibliographers seek to explain why particular documents look and work the way they do. The relationship between the printer or publisher and the bibliographer is thus one of point of view. Music bibliography as a specialty has emerged slowly but notably over the past sixty years, as earlier writings came to be identified as part of the subject and as new scholarship was added to the canon. The literature is now large and rich enough to require, first, a rigorous definition of scope, so as to clarify the agenda of questions that have and have not been addressed and that might, should, or can never be addressed through bibliographical evidence; and second, a sense of intellectual structure of the domain of music bibliography — tracing its history, rationalizing its agenda, and suggesting its prospects, as it also makes the content of its literature more readily available to readers. I have prepared this book with these goals in mind.

SCOPE

The activities of listing musical editions are different from the activities of studying them, although each activity suffers as it neglects the other. This book is concerned primarily with the activities of studying; lists are included only as they contribute explicitly to the activities of studying. This text covers prose writings *about* music printing and publishing — books and historical or descriptive essays, along with such related printed matter as instructional texts, music type specimens, patent records, exhibition catalogues, and other such peripheral materials.

Specialized lists of musical works are excluded, unless they are conceived specifically with bibliographical study in mind. For the vast world of library catalogues, repertory guides, and other citation sources — in other words the domain of "enumerative music bibliography" — I defer to the coverage (extensive if not as comprehensive as one might wish) in general guides to music reference books. Nor have I covered writings on the practices of music cataloguing and bibliographical citation, except insofar as they relate to the physical examination and study of printed music (see pp. 6-8).

I have also excluded writings on individual printers or publishers — histories, accounts, memoirs, and catalogues. They are numerous, and described in many sources.[2] No survey in this field, to be sure, can lay claim to respectability without recognizing certain landmark works on particular shops or firms. I have included these selectively, mostly under the geographical centers in question in Chapter 6.

Specific editions often emerge as noteworthy in their historical importance, whether by the intent of their pro-

---

2. Including this literature would probably increase this book by about one-third. Most of the 500-odd writings in question, while relevant to one specific printer or publisher and their repertories, are of incidental importance to the study of music bibliography in general.

The "Dictionary of Music Printers and Publishers" (pp. 185-486) in the 1990 Grove handbook on *Music Printing and Publishing* (57 below) is one of several sources that cover the literature relating to particular names. The present book will naturally be seen as either a complement or a sequel to that handbook, although there is very little overlap, either in content or intended function. The handbook may appear to have been conceived as something of a distillation for reference purposes of this work, which is intended more for those who pursue specialized bibliographical studies. In time this may indeed become the effective relationship between the two, although the handbook was planned first and with no thought that the present book would ever exist; nor of course could the present book have been prepared without the contributions of others to the handbook.

ducers or through discovery by later scholars. The most important of these do turn up in the annotations here. More directly pertinent, and also more elusive, are the few that were prepared as examples of fine printing and as paragons of the graphic arts as applicable to music. The most famous of the bibliophilic editions are listed on pp. 338-46. The major bibliographies of printed music with useful printer and publisher indexes are also cited in Chapter 8.

With considerable misgivings I have found it best to exclude writings on several other timely and prolific specialties, most of them as unstable conceptually as they are lively politically. Chapter 3, for instance, stops just short of discussing the literature on computerized music printing, vast and burgeoning — and perhaps best covered in online data bases, at least until parts of the field become stable enough to allow for the retrospective literature to be canonized. Furthermore, I have not always felt comfortable in identifying the point at which the presentation of encoded musical notation should be seen as intended primarily for purposes of preparing of printing surfaces that will lead to formal publication. Some will argue that this purpose now scarcely exists at all, in other words that music publishing is itself a thing of the past: I can't for a minute imagine or wish it. At such time as the goals of computerized presentation of musical notation are sorted out, so that particular functions acquire either an ascendancy or an autonomy, the literature will be ready for a proper historical survey.

Chapter 5 similarly excludes most writings in the equally vast and changing world of performance rights — an activity today the major concern of many of the large music publishers, to the virtual exclusion of music printing. Nor is the recent trade literature listed in any of its fullness. For the national lists of major printers and publishers in Chapter 6, the latest convenient and meaningful dividing line for the establishment of new firms was as painfully distant as 1920. This may be seen either as testimony that the new firms are doing things wrong, or that the old ones are doing things right — or, most likely of all, that bibliographers do their best work when their efforts can be defined historically.

I should not wish to argue that writings on reception history and canon formation are anything but central to this book, although I must draw a line in quickly shifting sands so as to exclude some very impressive recent studies that use the evidence of publication in building larger arguments. The coverage of composer-publisher relationships in Chapter 5 will likely prove to be particularly uneven, no doubt in large part because my thick head has trouble understanding how precisely the concept of "text" fits into the distinction between physical objects and intellectual content. Nor am I at all happy to exclude the study of music manuscripts, on the one hand, and of sound recordings on the other. Paleography and discography, however, each require a special knowledge of materials, techniques, and literatures that are quite different from those studied by bibliographers. Furthermore, the fields overlap with bibliography less than one would expect. In its broadest sense, bibliography is often seen as concerned with all aspects of the dissemination of texts. However attractive such a conception, human limitations force me to retreat into the narrower definition of music bibliography that prevails here. Regretfully I must leave future readers with the pleasure of formulating new definitions of the topic, so as accommodate writings appropriate to the broader scope.

For writings primarily of a historical character, I have tried to extend the coverage into the 1990s, although obviously a number of recent studies will have escaped my notice.

When can a particular writing be said to be *about* music printing and publishing? The question is important to the extent that important facts and perspectives often appear in writings that primarily deal with related topics. I have mentioned some of these writings in passing, in the belief that readers may want to look into the literature on other topics. A few brief and seemingly unimportant writings have been omitted. Some of them — probably unimportant but possibly very interesting — may yet turn up, especially in libraries in continental Europe, which I have not visited in recent years. Under the circumstances, the reader will need to recognize this as a selective rather than a comprehensive bibliography, although I believe the major works will all be present, at least those that address the questions set forth in Chapter 1 and thus contribute to the intellectual identity of the field. Davidsson's list in particular includes several kinds of writings that are excluded here, along the way implying an alternative conception of what does and does not constitute the literature of music bibliography.

No definition of music bibliography will please everyone, partly because music belongs to a world of passionate sentiments, and partly because, as a result, its learning is rich and diffuse. Bibliography can indeed overlap with lexicography, although not all reference works are bibliographical; it may indeed be relevant to citation practices, although much descriptive and almost all subject cataloguing today is concerned with the implementation of other means of access; it may indeed rely on extensive and painstaking source work, although not all scrupulous scholarship should be seen as bibliographical. If delimitations are painful to accept, it is not so much because bibliography has vague boundaries but rather because it is almost instinctively respected.

I have personally inspected all items cited here, except for those specified through bracketed references in the annotations to other sources. Many of these references use the standard abbreviations shown on p. xvii.

Often the same text will be published twice, revised slightly or not at all; or it will reappear in abstracted or excerpted form. I have attempted to gather these variants, so as to direct readers to the preferable presentation or alert them to differences that may or may not be worth further attention. Not all of the variants are conveniently available or even identified. Many decisions on merging entries need to be seen as judgment calls. Older writings may be reissued with only minor addenda and corrigenda; they may appear in a revision that is important to a new audience; or they may be excerpted in ways that develop particular details into new and important topics in their own right. What may be surprising is the extent of the redundancy in the literature from earlier periods. In several instances (at some risk of bruised egos, for which I apologize) I have cited a second writing under another one, mostly for purposes of bringing out a significant intellectual lineage.

STRUCTURE

The classified arrangement, as set forth in the Table of Contents, attempts both to collect related writings ("literary warrant") and to address the special interests of different audiences ("reader warrant"). To the extent that my main goal is to organize and describe the intellectual record, I have generally favored the former.

Of the nine chapters, the first serves to establish the theoretical foundations of music bibliography by identifying the basic kinds of questions that music bibliographers consider. Chapter 2 describes and evaluates the general historical surveys. Chapters 3 and 4 are devoted to music printing, the former emphasizing technology (printing surveys and manuals, music type specimens, presentation) and the latter aesthetics (exhibitions, title pages, and related printed materials of music). Chapter 5 covers music publishing in general (including copyright and relationships between composers and publishers); 6 treats both music printing and publishing as defined geographically. Music bibliography depends on library resources, and thus Chapter 7 is devoted to the institutional and collecting history in general. Chapter 8 identifies the most important general directories and bibliographical sources of importance to music bibliographers, while 9 recapitulates the agenda of Chapter 1 with a view to future scholarship.

Each section proceeds chronologically by imprint date, unless the introductory discussions specify otherwise. A chronological order proves to be particularly instructive when the literature is extensive (as with the first section of Chapters 2), or when major trends can be brought out (as with the first two sections of Chapter 3).

I owe special thanks to the diligence and support of many colleagues. The selected denizens of Treborough House and Ham Farm, to whom this study is dedicated, provided intellectual stimulation as much as patient toleration during oddly depressing times, the latter no doubt a particular imposition. My uncommonly indulgent wife has also paid dearly, and I hope my readers may feel as sorry for her as I do. Numerous librarians have been a special privilege to work with, particularly at St. Bride in London (where James Mosley and Nigel Roche were exceptionally helpful), at the British Library, and over many years at the Newberry Library in Chicago (where Bernard E Wilson has been a particular joy over many years). Mrs Rosemary Poole has kindly provided invaluable access to the papers of the late H. Edmund Poole, whose several essays are a reminder of what has been lost to us for his never being able to complete his comprehensive study of music printing. I owe a good number of citations to the watchful eyes of David Hunter, who, along with Ann Basart, Eva Einstein, Douglas Leedy, and Messrs. Neighbour and Macnutt, have read and commented on several of the early drafts of this text. Ann Basart, my supportive publisher and intimidating editor, has been indispensible in clarifying and reconciling my notions of how the physical book and intellectual book must fit together.

I am also grateful to Lynn Hanson for helping prepare and for solving many of the problems of executing the graphic design of this book through a computer that was always two steps ahead of us and five steps behind us; to C. Martin Rosen and Elaine Walker in locating some deliciously obscure titles, and to Holly Eastman and Patricia Maltby for checking countless odd details; to James Clark for help with the Cyrillic typography; to James Coover and Hans Lenneberg for some useful citations; to Hugh Taylor on behalf of the Anderson Room at the Cambridge University Library; and to Michael Ochs, John Shepard, Terry Belanger, Neil Ratliff and Geraldine Ostrove, for lining up the assistance of Angela Doane in New York, Colum Amory at Harvard, and Russell Girsberger in Washington. In Urbana, a good number of specialists across the university library helped clear up literally hundreds of loose ends, while the interlibrary loan staff has worked diligently. Kent Yates was invaluable both in enabling me punch this text into a computer, and in talking me into agreeing to survive no fewer than three different major disasters (one crash, one total erasure, and an impending typographical black hole); while many colleagues and students over the years have stimulated the assembly of this book through curious particulars, provocative questions, and good will.

Blue Hill, Maine
July 1992

ABBREVIATIONS

Sources cited in short form are listed below, with brief particulars and reference in parenthesis to the fuller citation in this book:

ABHBL	*Annual Bibliography of the History of Books and Libraries*, 1973- . (975)
Bigmore & Wyman	E. C. Bigmore and C. W. H. Wyman, *A Bibliography of Printing*, 1880. (961)
BdMs	*Bibliographie des Musikschrifttums*, 1936- . (972)
Bradley	Carol June Bradley, *Reader in Music Librarianship*, 1973. (965)
Davidsson	Åke Davidsson, *Bibliographie zur Geschichte des Musikdrucks*, 1965. (963)
Grove 6	*The New Grove Dictionary* (6th ed.), 1980. (See 95)
Grove P&P	*Music Printing and Publishing*, 1990. (57)
Plesske	Hans-Martin Plesske, *"Bibliographie des Schrifttums zur Geschichte deutscher und österreichischer Musikverlage,"* 1968. (751)
RILM	*RILM Abstracts*, 1966- . (974)

Scarce materials are located in major collections with these sigla:

ATF	Library of the American Type Founders Corp., Columbia University, New York. (see 971)
BL	British Library (formerly British Museum), London (including the Paul Hirsch collection)
Broxbourne	Broxbourne Library: Collection of A. F. Ehrman, Oxford, now dispersed. (see 294)
Mainz GM	Gutenberg Museum, Mainz
Newberry	Newberry Library, Chicago (see 970 for the John M. Wing collection, 958 for the music holdings)
NYPL	New York Public Library. (See the *Dictionary Catalog of the Music Collection*, 2nd ed., Boston: G. K. Hall, 1982, esp. vol. 33, pp. 49-60, 183-92)
Poole	Working files of the late H. Edmund Poole, Cambridge University Library (Anderson Room)
St. Bride	St. Bride's Foundation, London (see 969)

See also the footnotes on p. 108 for short forms of works cited on pp. 112-35; on p. 152 for works cited on pp. 153-62; and on p. 205 for works cited on pp. 205-07.

LIST OF ILLUSTRATIONS

Figures 1-4 are reproduced at the size
of the originals; figures 5-6 have been
reduced and retouched for reproduction.

The LITERATURE
of
MUSIC BIBLIOGRAPHY

I.

The Theory of Music Bibliography

MUSIC BIBLIOGRAPHY is the study of the printed documents of music. Of these there are many kinds: prose writings about music in books and periodicals, announcements, reviews and notices in newspapers, programs, pictures, posters, contracts, and correspondence. The most important, often regarded as the quintessence of music itself, are those devoted to musical notation for use by performers.

As defined here, music bibliography is concerned mainly with physical objects and only secondarily with musical content. Several theorists of bibliography have been so brave as to add a truculent qualifying phrase: bibliography is the study of physical objects *irrespective of their contents*. To accept this definition is to question the very concept of music bibliography: music is left out in the cold, since many of the peculiar problems of work with musical documents are explained through the musical content. Better to argue that music bibliography is the study of particular documents that are grouped together *because of* their contents.

Historically, most music has been either printed from type (*Notensatz*) or engraved (*Notenstich*). The basic distinction is one of printing, although publishing practices are often determined out of the distinction. Theorists of bibliography come to appreciate the difference: typographic music adapts readily and usefully to the practices of bibliography in general, but engraved music does so with much more difficulty.[1]

Printing entails two activities, first the preparation of printing surfaces, and then the presswork, or the transfer of ink from the printing surfaces to the paper. Typography, along with other kinds of raised surfaces (*Hochdruck*), is printed at the platen press (or letterpress) or its successors, whereas engraving (intaglio, or *Tiefdruck*) works with incised printing surfaces and is executed on the rolling press. A third basic process, which involves the chemically actuated printing surfaces of lithography (*Flachdruck*), has historically functioned as an alternative to engraving, at least where music in concerned. A fourth process, using stencils (*Durchdruck*), is less common but has an interesting history

---

1. The objects in question do want for a term that is both clear and concise. "Music" in English is ambiguous: it refers to the sound, although performers often use it to refer to the document on paper ("watch the music," or "bring your music to the rehearsal"). In German the terms *Noten* or *Musikalien* clearly identify the documents; but there are no counterparts in English, or in French or Italian either. In English, "music publications" and "printed music" can be used, also "musical editions" (but so as to beg a difference between "musical," suggesting God-given talent, and "music," ugly as a noun-qua-adjective). These are all cumbersome; writers come to avoid any term if at all possible, but settle for one of the cumbersome forms when it is absolutely necessary. "Sheet music" is more casual and less verbose, but it rather demeans professional performers; "scores" sounds more professional, although it patronizes songs that become hits and parodies those that do not. Furthermore, "scores" do not subsume "parts," which are their functional partners. "Printed music" (or, when the collective is grammatically awkward, "musical editions") seems to prevail in a weary battle.

A righteous sermon must follow here: the term "prints" needs to be recognized as a barbarism. (It trippeth from the lips—and of Renaissance musicologists most shamelessly, I fear—rather like tabacky from the lips of a St. Louis Cardinal relief pitcher.) There may be some basis for using it in speaking of handsome engravings that aspire to comparison with the masterpieces of Dürer, Rembrandt, or Piranesi; for ordinary letterpress music, however, one has no choice but to use the cumbersome expressions, at least if other bibliographers are expected to take one seriously.

of use with music (see "Stencilled Music," pp. 62-63 below.) Recent improvements in printing technology have made it increasingly difficult to distinguish which one of the four basic processes was employed in a particular text.[2] As for the raised surfaces, these may be either *composite*, as with settings of type, or *holistic*, as in block printing. Composite or typographically assembled surfaces for music, unlike those for literary texts, need to accommodate both continuous staff lines and the different signs on the lines or spaces, which need to appear in various positions relative to the staff lines and spaces. The results can be distinguished as *linear*, *nested*, or *mosaic*, and may involve one, two, or even three press runs. The holistic surfaces are typically blocks, either of wood or metal (and the printed results from the two are often not easily distinguishable). They usually produce black text on white background, although white text on black is not unknown, especially in central-European theory books of the early sixteenth century. Other memorable holistic raised surfaces include the woodblocks used by Andrea Antico, *ca.* 1520; in the 1698 Bay Psalm Book, the first music printed in British North America; and in *The Beggar's Opera* and its counterparts in London around 1730. Stereotyping (castings of type) of music emerged in the nineteenth century, although *clichés* of music type tied together for repeated use through several editions are beginning to be identified in seventeenth-century England.

A distinction between composite and holistic surfaces does not really apply to engraving or lithography: plates are of their very nature holistic. They may change, of course, their text having been intentionally altered or their surfaces dam-

---

2. For historical purposes the distinctions are clear, although there are a few early music books that were executed so flawlessly, or strangely, as to defy assignment. Luther's 1545 *Geystliche Lieder*, the so-called "Bapst'-sches Gesangbuch," may be an example. Sophisticated hybrids today often leave bibliographers arguing over which of the four categories are to be seen as basic.

aged through repeated use or heavy handling. The text on engraved plates may be incised, either entirely *by hand*, so as to produce signs each slightly different, or *with punches* for recurring signs, so as to produce forms that are essentially congruent. Thanks to many nineteenth-century technological improvements, however, transfer processes enable any of the forms of presswork to accept any kind of printing surface, including the handwritten copy from a composer or copyist, or as generated by a computer.

The Agenda of Music Bibliography

What questions do music bibliographers ask in the course of their work with the music they study? Over the past two centuries, their inquiries have come to cluster around nine interrelated questions: description, dating, plate numbers, other internal and external evidence, text, terminology, impact, and motivation. A theoretical literature, including the writings below, has come to identify the subject under consideration, propose and defend the arguments, conceal or concede the limitations and uncertainties, and thereby formulate the conceptual identity of music bibliography. Rather than explicitly ask why the study of musical documents needs to be separated from the study of other kinds of documents, or why music needs to have its documents studied at all, they assume the necessity. By establishing the pedigrees of analytical, textual, descriptive, and historical bibliography as they apply to music, they propose the agenda through which music bibliography comes to be defined and recognized. The questions are these:

1. Description. Publishers list their titles with two goals in mind: inventory and promotion. The same basic goals also guide the practices of compilers of bibliographical lists and library cataloguers. What conventions of citation do musical editions require? How, through formulary statements, can attention be directed to those precise facts that may be important in describing the physical item, to the exclusion of other facts that are likely to be unimportant?

Emphasizing the interdependence between bibliographical study and bibliographical listing will probably seem commonplace to some (mostly those who use or compile lists) and wrong-headed to others (mostly those who do the studying). My argument that the interdependence is both proper and significant is reflected in the annotations to the Schmid series from the 1840s (1), and to Deutsch (4 in particular, but also the later essays, 11-12). "Citing the Score" (39) discusses the history of the interdependence.

Bibliographical lists may fall largely outside the scope of this book; but, in terms of the present emphasis of studying rather than of listing, the loss may not be all that great, since the introductions to most lists, even the best of them, address procedural questions only implicitly in their citations, and very seldom explicitly. Bibliographical citations themselves inevitably beget standards: when we find that they work we imitate their practices. Writings concerned primarily with music citation practice, whether in the name of the descriptive cataloguing or the descriptive bibliography of music, are also not included here.[3]

Three related considerations must still be recognized: (a) standardization of citation practices, consistent for printed music of all kinds, and ideally for documents of all kinds; (b) reconciliation of bibliographical practices with cataloguing practices; and (c) expansion of the concept of bibliography in the practical interests of preserving and providing access to the physical document.

The most important question is whether music bibliography can, and in its best interests should, conform to the practices of general bibliographers, who deal mostly with printed books. Among the writers cited below, Tanselle (39) answers in the affirmative, Fog

---

3. I particularly regret having to omit several writings on the practices of listing music, especially those that explore the intentions behind the special practices. A notable example is Horst Leuchtmann's "Zur Bibliographie von Musikdrucken der zweiten Hälfte des 16. Jahrhunderts," in *Ars Iocundissima: Festschrift für Kurt Dorfmüller zum 60. Geburtstag* (Tutzing: Hans Schneider, 1984), pp. 189-200. What distinguishes such writings is a sensitivity to details of the physical objects, their historical contexts, and the importance of the findings to scholarship. At the same time, writings on the bibliographical listing of music have as their main topic not the findings but their presentation. Stretching the point to include writings of some intellectual distinction would entail consideration of a large number of less important writings, many of them descriptions of local practices.

(34) in the negative; Hopkinson (12, 21) attempts to press forward, respecting both sides at the same time. This is not easy.

The larger questions of conformity to standards are rarely discussed in prose essays. Among the bibliographies cited here that would imply an answer in the affirmative are Day and Murrie (663) and McMillan (886), as well as several on incunabula, including Duggan (133) and three Swiss titles (807-09) — all of them concerned mostly with typographic music. Hunter (672) is among those who have looked for a reconciliation, and with engraved music in mind. Other notable attempts include Iain Fenlon's *Catalogue of the Printed Music* in the Barber Institute of Fine Arts at Birmingham University (London: Mansell, 1976).

Deutsch (11) is among the few who explicitly acknowledge a difference between bibliographical and cataloguing practices. He gives an example of the same work cited differently by each. Among cataloguing manuals, Smiraglia (41), by providing the fullest statement of cataloguing practice appropriate to the needs of bibliographers, suggests that the two may not be all that far apart, at least when cataloguers are not constrained by production schedules — and of course these are very much present, guiding the very conception of our cataloguing codes. If cataloguers often feel awed and disparaged by bibliographers, bibliographers should also recognize the special responsibilities that are expected of them. Instead of being beholden to production schedules, they are of course beholden to nothing less than the awesome but imaginative task of suggesting redefinitions of learning itself.

Schmieder (16, but also 13 and 15) is the major spokesman for those who, viewing the devastation in Germany after World War II and the pressing demands of scholarship, extended the role of bibliography into matters of preservation and access, under the rubric of *Dokumentation*. His concerns are largely taken for granted in libraries today, if often as ideals more than practices.

2. Dating. With the rise of music engraving around 1700 came the practice of excluding the date from imprint statements. How can dates be inferred from extant evidence?

The problem has been approached both by scholars who need specific facts, and by bibliographers and cataloguers who seek to provide the facts for the scholars to use. One might expect scholars to need dates in order to build arguments, and bibliographers to need them mostly because imprint statements look embarrassingly naked without them. In fact the situation is often reversed: scholars often as not find little use for dates but cite them just the same, mostly so as to appear painstakingly scrupulous. Bibliographers, on the other hand, often build interesting arguments from dates, but knowing how limited they are and how misleading they can be, often prefer to omit them from citations altogether.

Probably many more dates have been supplied than users of them identified, and this may bother librarians in particular in an age governed by a spirit of accountability. In defense of the efforts of bibliographers and cataloguers, two arguments are crucial: (1) providing dates is clearly in keeping with the library's mandate to describe its collections so as to be of service to its readers; and (2) establishing dates is most efficiently and authoritatively done by bibliographers (in that it involves matters of context, i.e., the history of music publishing practices) and cataloguers (in that it involves matters of presentation, i.e., cataloguing rules), rather than by the users of bibliographies and catalogues individually.

Schmidt-Phiseldeck (5) in 1927 was not the first to recognize the importance of dates, but probably the first to do so in a separate essay. The IAML *Guide* (30), as placed in perspective by Lenneberg (27), remains the most thorough exploration of the solutions. Dating is complicated, but the complexity can also offer a basis for exploring causal relationships: this is evident in the writings by authors such as Matthäus (24), Fog (33), and Hunter (670), in which the word "dating" appears in their titles and in fact remains the basic objective of their studies, although their texts explore relationships suggested by the evidence.

3. Plate Numbers. In order to organize and provide access to their inventory, publishers of engraved music often identify editions through numbers, presumably assigned sequentially. What do these numbers tell us about individual titles, their dates in particular, and collectively about the publishers' activities in selecting and promoting their catalogue?

The literature falls under three rubrics: (a) prose discussions of plate numbers, which seek to explain the sequences, the forms of statement, and the house practices; (b) summary lists, which indicate a publisher's lowest and highest known numbers from a given year, as a guide for assignments in imprint statements; and (c) numerical inventories, which arrange a publisher's entire catalogue by plate number so as to display the history of the firm's activities.

Barclay Squire (3) issued the first list in 1914, along with an acknowledgement of earlier work by Sonneck and a call for further work. To be sure, others at this time who dealt with musical editions as engravers, publishers, or retailers, must have used plate numbers in their daily work. (The 1857 Ricordi catalogue (720), for instance, is arranged by plate numbers.) Gradually, as scholars and librarians became interested in studying engraved music, their separate interests no doubt merged, and the importance of plate numbers presumably began to dawn on them. Uncovering this prehistory, however unlikely, would be fascinating.

Kossmann (812) may have been the first to respond in print to Squire's call, although by 1928 many music cataloguers were assembling local plate-number indexes. In the nascent world of American music librarianship, Meyer and Christensen (799) and Hill (758) were beginning to find the card files useful, as these writers added to a literature that was to culminate in Deutsch's second 1945 landmark overview (12). Weinmann's Viennese lists began to appear about this same time.

The next few decades were generally ones of disillusionment. Cecil Hopkinson's several French bibliographies (603, 686), as well as the Neighbour-Tyson English list (678), suggest the limitations of extrapolating functionally conjecturable imprint dates out of plate numbers. The state of the art in general is described in Fuld (23) and in the 1974 IAML *Guide* (31), pp. 53-64. Among studies devoted to geographical areas are Fog's lists for Denmark (840), Devriès and Lesure (687) for France, Mona for Hungary (848); and Wolfe's 1963 inventory (871) for the early United States; Krohn's account (880) discusses the American midwest, although its general relevance is wider.

I have not found a convenient way to summarize the discussions that distinguish between plate numbers and publisher's numbers. (To some publishers edition numbers are different still: see 463.)

4. Other Internal Evidence. What do other aspects of the appearance—typography and layout, as well as other manifestations of the tastes and the procedures of printing "house practice"—tell us about the music and its context?

The writings of craftsmen (Sandars, 46, being a nice example) are invaluable to scholars. One longs for more. I have cited the general printing literature mostly in Chapter 3 (see especially the overview on p. 72), and listed the localizations in Chapter 6.

House practices before *ca*. 1700 (the "era of typography") are discussed by Boorman (132), among others. Modern scholarly study of music type faces begins with Steele (660) and Lenz (767), and continues with Davidsson (833, 835-38), Berz (772), Schaefer (774), and the present author (661). Synthesis will be immensely laborious, and will probably always remain selective. (Such, at least, is my impression from experience in surveying the practices of signing gatherings of partbooks, in 32.)

House practices after *ca*. 1700 (the "era of engraving") began to be critically examined, quietly but auspiciously, with Meyer (10). Lenneberg (37) has framed many useful questions. The most detailed scholarly survey is by Wolfe (871). (For others see the text on p. 72.) Specific practices are explored in Poole's study on Forster (671), a work that merits imitation. The study of engravers' punches (something of a counterpart to the study of type faces from the earlier era), which probably begins with my "Graphic Analysis" essay (869), finds its most detailed application to particular musical works in Leicher-Olbricht (597). The design of the printed page is further informed by matters of aesthetics and legibility, as discussed at the end of Chapter 3 (pp. 146-50); see also the IAML *Guide* (30).

5. External Evidence. What do the operational records of music printers, engravers, and publishers—directories, histories, archival records—tell us about the content and function of musical editions, singly and collectively?

Scattered writings, in Chapter 6 in particular, suggest the range of documentary sources and their uses. The Anisson collection, described by Coyecque (685), deserves special respect. Publishers' archival records are central to the work of Meyer (10), Weinmann (800), Slezak (601), and Hilmar (803). The writings about composers and publishers (pp. 212-34) and the directories (pp. 341-49) also suggest the varieties of sources. Lesure-Devriès (which is worth praising whenever possible) can serve as an anthology of different kinds of sources useful to bibliographers.

11

6. Text. In what ways should performers and scholars trust or distrust the statements in printed music as evidence of the composer's or editor's intention? When two editions differ, on what basis should one or the other be preferred?

The pursuit of authenticity, whether by editors or performers, is based on the critical study of sources. This pursuit, which for music largely dates from the revival of ancient music in eighteenth-century England, was no doubt forwarded by nineteenth-century German academic *Denkmälerwesen*. Unfortunately the practices and the theories from past eras have rarely been made explicit, if they were even rationalized at all. The applicability of bibliographical work to the preparation of modern scholarly editions has been assumed, but the theory of textual criticism for music is little described, at least in books and articles. Explicit descriptions of the editorial activities in music publishing, relatively few in number, are discussed at the end of Chapter 5. Fellowes's buffoonery (143) seems to have few counterparts, serious-minded or otherwise, at least in print.

The saga of textual corruption in music is still to be organized. Deutsch's 1927 essay (4) may appear to be among the first to introduce printed editions into the discussion, although surely the origins are much earlier. Tyson's 1963 Beethoven study (595) is clearly a landmark. Its basic aims are seen in later studies, of Beethoven in the work of Leicher-Olbricht (597), among others, and of the music of such diverse composers as Stephen Foster (by Saunders, 617) and Bartók (by several scholars, 587-90); Brahms (also by various hands, 607-08) and Stravinsky (by Cyr, 645); Chopin (by Kallberg (610) and Berg (by Hilmar, 602). Del Mar's anthology (36) suggests that performers have useful things to learn from textual bibliography, while Fuld's reference guide (23) is an indispensable reference source for the major works, at least insofar as the authentic texts are located in or can be extrapolated from the first appearances in print.[4]

---

4. Among the happiest evidence of the growing maturity of music bibliography is the virtual disappearance of the romantic legendry of virtuoso performers, who, wand'ring one day in the archives ("I was weary and ill at ease"), stumbled upon neglected masterworks. An important point needs to be conceded: it is quite correct to say that they did "discover" the music, in the sense that they found it to be something they could bring to life in

7. Terminology. The topic has three aspects. The first is the most basic, and most bibliographers agree to its importance: what vocabulary did early music printers, engravers, and publishers use in the pursuit of their daily work? The second concerns the terminology used by scholarly bibliographers of today.

The third aspect (actually a subdivision of the second) addresses the means through which variants can be distinguished. Indeed this is one of the most troublesome questions of all music bibliography. No two copies of a publication can possibly be exactly alike. The differences are usually of little importance, apart from the fact that multiple copies exist and occupy physical space in two different locations— and the proposal that they are different understandably leaves sensible persons bored, angry, or saddened to think that intelligent scholars should bother with such hair-splitting. But there are also some examples — probably not many, but certainly a dramatic few — of differences that

---

actual performance, even if the document itself was actually called to their attention by someone else who knew it mostly as a bibliographical object. From this circumstance grows the common experience known by all music bibliographers and research librarians, of having their brains picked by hungry performers — the classic inquiry comes from choral conductors in search of a Renaissance motet, SATB, that sounds like Brahms. Such comedy aside, the crucial role of bibliography in musical performance must always be recognized as one of its major justifications in the first place.

Nor dare one overlook the importance of bibliography in composer attribution studies. The choicest examples come from the late eighteenth century, as music publishers found that music attributed to recognized composers sold better than that of less famous ones. The most notorious example is probably the "opus 3" quartets attributed to Haydn, but now generally agreed to be by Roman Hoffstetter. Other controversies involve works by minor composers published under the false attribution to a major composer in hopes of better sales—and occasionally skillful and interesting enough to actually be mistaken for the work of the master. The prevailing consensus all too easily suggests a triumph of objective factual evidence over subjective musical tastes, the vindication of bibliography in the face of stylistic criticism. Far better, of course, to ask whether the music itself is worth listening to, regardless of the composer.

prove to be very significant when they do turn up. It is thus embarrassing when we cannot account for the differences, briefly, clearly, and convincingly; one way to do this is by conceptualizing the kinds, and applying terms to each. In identifying the basic kinds of differences, one looks to terminology. What terms, based on what concepts, are meaningful in explaining the kinds of differences?

The basic conceptual relationships presumably emerged out of the needs for scholars and printers to talk to each other. England's literary scholars naturally talked with typographic printers, so as to come up with the classic edition/impression/issue/state hierarchy. The European origins are more complex. The titles of Deutsch's early essays (4), using terms like *Originalausgabe* and *Erstdrucke*, suggest the influence of Heinrich Schenker's seminars in Vienna, concerned as they were with the master composers. Indeed one respected later inquiry is the essay by another member of Schenker's circle, Anthony van Hoboken (17). Kathi Meyer's "Was sind musikalische Erstausgaben?" (10) is another early contribution to this discussion, although her plate is in fact well-filled with many other important things. Other major chapters in the story include the 1959 IAML conference, summarized by Hopkinson (21), and its 1974 *Guide* (30, pp. 30-48). Significant later contributions come from Fog (33) and Weinhold (598); Tanselle (38) speaks as a theorist of bibliography in general. In 1989 Hunter also entered the fray (672).[5]

Stanley Boorman's "Glossary" in the Grove *Handbook* (57 below) should prove to be the landmark to which future scholars will turn.

8. Impact. In what ways have printed musical documents reflected the various communities for which they were in-

---

5. Special attention should be called to the general use of the German term *Titel*. It should not be seen as an exact counterpart to the English word "title"; nor does its German usage in music bibliography always conform to that in German cataloguing practice, where it identifies either a complete citation or, sometimes the main entry statement only. Instead, to music printers, publishers, and many bibliographers, it specifically identifies the title page. This designation, to be sure, is not always unambiguous. Sometimes it refers to the cover (particularly one that is brightly

tended? Collectively, how have they been a mirror of, and what have they contributed to, Western civilization? What has been the role of printed music as (to use Elizabeth Eisenstein's popular phrase) an "agent of change?"

Almost all of the writings discussed in Chapter 2 attempt, in some way or another, to place the history of music printing and publishing in a social and cultural framework. (Pattison in 1939, 52, also Clercx in 1954, 815 below, are among the impressive examples). Modern reception history, as it involves the evidence of distribution through publication, finds an early example in Bötticher's study of Lassus (631). Other composers may not have enjoyed Lassus's unprecedented popularity in their day, although many of them will likely emerge in a slightly different light after the distribution of editions has been studied.

Admittedly, few authors have said much about historical settings that is not almost self-obvious, however interesting and relevant. As the literature has proliferated, the predicament has become all the more disconcerting. Happily (if not really surprisingly), few of the writings have worked from any of the classic shopping lists of categories (e.g., 1, political; 2, social; 3, economic; 4, religious; 5, artistic, etc.). In an academic environment increasingly attracted to facts that can be manipulated in a computer and "methodologies" that can be used to confound one's colleagues, scholars have moved away from the vague Germanic contemplation of the *Zeitgeist*, attracted in particular by the precision of the French *annales* tradition. Charts, statistics, and a concern for causality are in fashion as a result. Recent writings by Lenneberg (37), Boorman (132), Hortschansky (542-43), Carter (712), Fenlon (40), Devriès (690), and Lewis (42), and also my essay with Crawford on early American music books (875), variously reflect the agenda.

---

colored or of artistic distinction — cf. Chapter 4, pp. 168-80 — but rarely when the cover is a brochure, printed by letterpress on thin paper). It occasionally includes what in English is known as a caption title, which consists of the identifying information, usually with imprint, on the top part of the first page of music. The German concept of *Titelauflage* is derived from this usage, so that its counterpart concept in English is that of the reissue. The counterpart in the study of letterpress books is the cancelled title page; in the production of engraved music, we infer that the sequence usually provided unbound sheets first, to which covers were added later, so as to make the practice of cancellation relatively uncommon.)

The discussion on pp. 358-71 of the "Epilogue" attempts to define the agenda comprehensively, meaningfully, usefully, and critically. This is a topic on which no pronouncement should ever be seen as definitive — which is precisely why the topic is important.

9. Motivation. Why do such questions fascinate us at all? The reasons arise out of two impulses: bibliophilic (particular musical documents having caught our attention, we want to work with them and know more about them); and hermeneutic (questions having been raised, we seek out the documents that may hold the answer, and look for ways to coax it out of them). The two impulses merge rather instinctively, usually but not always: attempts to separate them, in any event, tend to assume either a militancy or a naïveté that may or may not be appropriate.

The bibliophilic literature is covered specifically as book collecting in Chapter 7. Oldman's essay (9) is powerful testimony that the collector and the scholar ultimately work toward the same goals. The *Philobiblon* essays (8) have much the same spirit in mind, as does Ochs (35). My comments on Mendel (20) relate to this topic.

Other evidence is implicit in the writings of the great scholar-collectors, notably Hirsch, Hoboken, Levy, and Fuld. Antiquarian dealers, like Fog, Hopkinson, Macnutt, Rosenthal, and Schneider, have also produced significant studies; their catalogues (as listed in Coover, 927) often deserve high respect in their own right.

Hermeneutic objectives are implicit in all of the texts discussed in this book, except perhaps for those that attempt only to amuse (e.g., the popular accounts on sheet-music covers) or to sell (e.g., the type-specimen books; and one can argue in both instances). Lesure (18) and Duckles (notably in later writings like 22, 29, and 31), probably provide the best argument that the bibliographer's goals and attitudes are essentially those of the scholar.

Finally, some writings fit into none of these categories, mostly because they seek to fit into all of them. These include brief introductions, such as Meyer (7) and La Rue (19); factual miscellanies organized around driving arguments, such as Krohn (25), Sartori (26), my "functions and forms" essay (32), and many by Deutsch from the 1940s; and attempts at first principles, such as Hopkinson (14) and Fog (33).

All the writings cited in this book, and many more not cited here, contribute to the theory of music bibliography, although their main goal often involves the particular specialties of later chapters. The writings below are those that variously address the theoretical questions most specifically.

Anton SCHMID. "Beiträge zur Literatur und Geschichte der Tonkunst," *Cäcilie* [23 contributions to vols. 21-27, 1842-47].   1

This "Sammlung von grösseren und kleineren Aufsätzen in mannichfältiger Form und bunter Mischung" may be proposed as marking the beginning of scholarly descriptive music bibliography. Its author, in connection with his appointment as the first music *Custos* at the Imperial Library in Vienna, had either been assigned or had assumed the task of organizing the music collections. The prospect of preparing these essays offered him the opportunity to show what was notable in his collection, so as to justify his efforts. His text was no doubt of special interest to his editor, Siegfried Wilhelm Dehn, who was his counterpart in the *Musikabteilung* of the Prussian State Library in Berlin, and who no doubt felt similar needs to promote his own collections, which at this time were somewhat less notable than those in Vienna. Schmid's quarterly contributions appeared regularly, with only four lapses, until the journal itself ceased publication:

Band 21 (1842, Heft 82-84), pp. 101-106, 154-72, 231-44;

Band 22 (1843, Heft 85-88), pp. 42-64, 102-28, 179-86, 439-50;

Band 23 (1844, Heft 89, 91-92), pp. 62-72, 199-212, 257-80;

Band 24 (1845, Heft 93-96), pp. 50-64, 119-28, 177-92, 242-56;

Band 25 (1846, Heft 97-100), pp. 43-64, 114-28, 193-200, 27-80;

Band 26 (1847, Heft 102-104), pp. 128-36, 196-200, 261-64;

Band 27 (1848, Heft 106, 108), pp. 126-27, 246-56.

The whole is further conceived in 47 sections, of which the first large opening section is spread over the years 1842-43 and contains about 250 entries, arranged annalistically in groups (2 liturgical music incunabula; 24 sacred music books, 1501-25; 38 books mostly Lutheran, 1526-61; 27 titles, 1561-88; 61 titles, 77 titles, 1693-1823; 23 titles, 1824-40), ending with citations for 64 "Handschriften aus verschiedenen Jahrhunderten."

Sections 2-47 are each devoted to a particular topic; cumulatively their character is essentially miscellaneous. Some are very brief (Heft 98 includes sections 33-35 and part of 36); and the sequence has no order, suggesting that Dehn had pleaded with Schmid to send in whatever he could supply, either because readers liked them or because Dehn needed copy. Some sections are on composers (3 is on Eberlin, 24 on Cimarosa, 40 on Gesualdo, 41 on Paminger); some are on printers (2 deals with the Carpentras books). Others are on manuscripts in particular libraries: 19 is on the *Hofbibliothek*, 20 on other Viennese collections. A few index other sources: 4 to 7 identify the Italian composers in the early parts of Emmanuele Antonio Cicogna's *Inscrizioni veneziane* (1824-53). Three are *Berichtigungen*.

What distinguishes Schmid's work is his eye for details of the object being cited, and his willingness to adjust the nature and extent of citation in order to accommodate what he saw as the significant character of the material and the likely needs of particular scholarly audiences. Many music lists had of course been prepared prior to 1842. Carl Ferdinand Becker in particular had recently been busily at work. (Indeed, Schmid specifies his first section as a "Nachtrag" to Becker's *Systematisch-chronologische Darstellung* of 1836-39.) Previously, however, the descriptive statements were typically brief, suitable to the needs of routine identification, and consistent across the entire range of coverage. A few of the earlier lists also go into impressive detail, but largely with a consistency of statement appropriate to the literature under consideration. Some eighty years earlier, for instance, Friedrich Marpurg, in nine issues of the *Kritische Briefe* (1759-63), had prepared an impressive "Verzeichnis deutscher Odensammlungen mit Melodien," describing 43 titles in fine detail, but limited to works in this one genre. In Schmid's conception of his assignment, one senses the first evidence of a respect for the differences appropriate to scholarly needs, with subsequent adjustment of the formulary to accommodate the differences. No doubt the work of other scholars in Schmid's day— Aloys Fuchs on Mozart, Carl Georg Winterfeld on Giovanni Gabrieli, several on incunabula in general — rationalized his flexibility as it inspired his search for uncommon details.

Thus Schmid often gives full, or at least detailed, title-page transcriptions, often with line endings; colophon statements, even an occasional collational formula; contents notes or listings, along with biographical details and historical background;

and other ostensibly gratuitous observations that he thought scholars might thank him for. One might view Schmid's work as the earliest expression of the argument that bibliography becomes scholarly as it comes to be allowed to search for relevant particulars. Significance is to be determined by the critical eye, uninhibited by arbitrary restrictions, in the interests of consistency of presentation. This first brave attempt to make adjustments within a descriptive system anticipates the ideal of "degressive bibliography", insofar as it seeks to allow for the presentation of different circumstances of detail. Schmid's citations seem naïve and exuberant; even today they evoke the nostalgic joy of discovering treasures in the course of handling them physically. Perhaps Schmid had actually prepared the citations over the period of discovery two decades earlier, and sent them all together for Dehn to filter into his journal as space allowed or demanded.

Schmid's repertory, to be sure, reflects the character of central European archival institutions of the day. Letterpress editions predominated over engraved ones, sacred music over secular or instrumental, early over recent music, even (perhaps particularly) to the exclusion of Haydn, Mozart, and Schubert. Some of the material in these essays is duplicated in Schmid's 1845 book on Petrucci and his successors (114), but surprisingly little.

Maurin NAHUYS. "Bibliographie musicale," *Annales du bibliophile belge*, n.s., 1 (1881), 90-96.   2

A notice of early rarities. The first part ("Recueil musical de chansons diverses du XVIe siècle") describes three songbook fragments. These are today in the Bibliothèque Nationale, Paris, as Rés. Vm^7 504: see Nanie Bridgman, "Christian Egenolff, imprimeur de musique," *Annales musicologiques*, 3 (1955), 77-177. (The RISM citation as [c.1535][14] wrongly implies that these are a single bibliographical unit rather than three separate books, however.) The second part ("Publications musicales inédites imprimées dans les Pays-Bas") cites five rarities, 1531-1774, with careful transcriptions and with deferential respect for Goovaerts (810) in the annotations.

The joys of connoisseurship pervade the journal, with its fertile mixture of detail from amateurs like Count Nahuys and perspectives from scholars like Edmund van der Straeten, who also con-

19

tributed several short essays on Dutch musicians in Italy and Louvain music incunabula.

William Barclay SQUIRE. "Publisher's Numbers," *Sammelbände der Internationalen Musikgesellschaft*, 15 (1914), 420-27.   **3**
The first essay to discuss plate numbers in their own right and to appeal to librarians to collect them. The publishers covered are Walsh in London, Roger in Amsterdam, Schmid in Nuremberg, and the Hummels in Amsterdam and Berlin. Leipzig and Vienna, for whatever reasons, are not in evidence.

Otto Erich DEUTSCH. "Über die bibliographische Aufnahme von Originalausgaben unserer Klassiker," in *Beethoven Zentenarfeier, Wien, 1927: Internationaler Musikhistorischer Kongress* (Wien: Universal, 1927), pp. 268-72.   **4**
The author pleads for lists and bibliographical studies of the editions of the master composers. By 1929 his plea might appear to us to have taken a slight turn: it is for an "Internationale Musikbibliothek der Erstdrucke": see the *Primo Congresso Mondiale delle Biblioteche e di Bibliografia*, vol. 3 (Rome: Libreria dello Stato, 1931), pp. 332-35. At this date Deutsch could assume that *Originalausgaben* and *Erstdrucken* were identical, since the important goal was for guidance in separating corrupt versions from the *Urtext* of the master composers, such as was expected in Heinrich Schenker's seminar. (The method, interestingly, is very much in the spirit of textual bibliography; and the prospect that a printed edition might occasionally actually be preferable to a holograph source seems quietly to be taken for granted). During subsequent decades, as historical studies slowly came to prevail over critical studies, the major objective of music bibliography itself also slowly came to be redefined. The project that resulted a generation later, the *International Inventory of Musical Sources* (RISM), was thus delimited not qualitatively, as Deutsch would have preferred, but chronologically. Deutsch's brief and unhappy tenure as the first editor of the *British Union Catalogue of Early Music* has been explained on the grounds that his perspectives were those not of a cataloguer but of a bibliographer—an explanation that seems plausible in the light of the conception of

music bibliography that is implicit in Deutsch's 1927 and 1931 writings.

Josef SCHMIDT-PHISELDECK. "Datierung der Musikalien," *ibid*, pp. 279-82.   5

A landmark inquiry into the needs and prospects for assigning imprint dates to undated music. The author, a venerable Danish librarian-polymath with great affection for and wide knowledge of music, deserves special honors as one of the few major theorists of music bibliography who was also a theorist of music cataloguing, his *Musikalien-Katalogisierung: Ein Beitrag zur Lösung ihrer Probleme* (Leipzig: Breitkopf & Härtel, 1926) being a landmark essay that first proposes the concept of uniform (conventional, filing) titles.

Fritz ZOBELEY. "Praktische Probleme der Musikbibliographie," *ibid*, pp. 276-78.   6

The term "practical" bears some notice, as a reflection on the prevalent conception of bibliography as an "auxilliary science" (*Hilfswissenschaft*). Bibliography must be practical, which is to say, useful. It should therefore be easy, Zobeley implies; there can be much to gain if it can even be simplistic, little to lose since intelligence is not needed. Its purpose is access, a first but necessary step in scholarly work. Above all, bibliography must be subservient to the work of scholars, which is harder, and theoretical rather than practical: in contrast, bibliography, being practical, cannot be scholarly at all. The idea of bibliographers as *servi a bibliotheca*—Sir Walter Greg's notion of "useful drudges," there to do for scholars "some of the spade-work that they are too lazy or too incompetent to do for themselves"—pervades this brief essay by the librarian of the Musikwissenschaftliches Institut in Heidelberg.

Kathi MEYER. "Über Musikbibliographie," in *Musikwissenschaftliche Beiträge: Festschrift für Johannes Wolf zu seinem 60. Geburtstage* (Berlin: Martin Breslauer, 1929), pp. 118-22.   7

Observations and prescriptions based on the author's work as Paul Hirsch's librarian. The flourishing of scholarship suggests the need for (1) rules for librarians, (2) a survey of early music manuscripts, (3) a plate number index, and (4) specialized bibliographies.

Georg KINSKY. [Essays in *Philobiblon* (Wien, 1931-35)]. **8**
Vienna-Berlin ties from the days of Schmid and Dehn are
recalled here, now with the librarian in Cologne and the guiding
editorial hands in Vienna, notably among them the antiquarian
dealer and publisher Herbert Reichner. Kinsky's essays emphasize the 19th century:

"Beethoven-Erstdrucke bis zum Jahr 1800," 3 (1930), 329-36

"Signierte Schubert Erstdrucke," 4 (1931), 183-88

"Zeitgenößische Goethe-Vertönungen," 5 (1932), 91-99, 133-37

"Die Handbibliothek des Musiksammlers: ein bibliographische
Überblick," 5 (1932), 253-58 (see 916)

"Musikbibliotheken: Ein Überblick über die wichtigsten öffentlichen
und privaten Musiksammlungen," 6 (1933), 55-67

"Richard Wagners Ballade, 'Die beiden Grenadiere,'" 7 (1934), 343-46

"Erstlingsdrucke der deutschen Tonmeister der Klassik und Romantik,"
7 (1934), 347-64. Also issued separately (Wien: Reichner, 1934)

"Die Urschriften Bach und Händels: Ein Beitrag zum Gedenkjahr
1935," 8 (1935), 109-122

"Berühmte Opern: Ihre Handschriften und Erstdrucke," 8 (1935), 363-
94

"Die Erstausgaben und Handschriften der Sinfonien Beethovens," 9
(1936), 339-51

The series also includes Stefan Zweig's description of "Meine
Autographen Sammlung," 3 (1930), 279-89, with illustrations
and a list of the music, also his *Sinn und Schönheit der
Autographen* (917), which first appeared as a *Beilage* to Jahr 8,
Heft 4 (1935). Other collections are described as well: Paul and
Olga Hirsch in 3 (1930), 433-45 (a lengthy, well-illustrated essay,
probably by Kathi Meyer); Joseph Proksch in 7 (1934), 342; and
Jean Auguste Stellfeld in André M. Pols, "Die Musikbibliothek
Stellfeld," 7 (1934), 366-70. Meyer also provides landmark
studies, on the concept of first editions in general (1935; see 10
below) and on music illustration (1938; see 473 below); while
Otto F. Babler discusses "Mozart als Leser" in 3 (1930), 62-65;
and Liesbeth Weinhold reports on an exhibition of "Musiker-
autographen aus fünf Jahrhunderten" in 12 (1940), 52-57.

These essays, coming as they do from a general bibliophilic
journal outside the world of musicology, are a special pleasure
for music bibiographers to discover, since the erudition is im-

pressive, the arguments thoughtful, and the presentation attractive, with many illustrations. Kinsky's survey of early Bach editions (583) also reflects this bibliographical ambience.

Cecil B. OLDMAN. "Collecting Musical First Editions," in John Carter, *New Paths in Book Collecting* (London: Constable, 1934), pp. 107-16. **9**

Music scholars and bibliophiles, as they learn to enjoy knowing and working with their collections, come to admire the author's expertise, developed while Oldman was a librarian and Mozart specialist at the British Museum and colleague of Otto Erich Deutsch, Paul Hirsch, Alfred Loewenberg, and A. Hyatt King.

Also issued separately, London: Constable, [1938], with "Addenda and Corrigenda" on the inside covers, and reprinted (as corrected) in Bradley, pp. 107-16.

Kathi MEYER. "Was sind musikalische Erstausgaben?" *Philobiblon*, 8 (1935), 181-84. **10**

A brief but very important work, worth singling out from among its peers in the *Philobiblon* series. Through recourse to music publishers' archives (in this case those of Schott in Mainz, here specifically documenting the history of the reprinting of Kreutzer's overture to *Lodoiska*), the author considers questions basic to analytical and descriptive music bibliography, suggesting along the way some of the limitations of plate numbers, and presenting evidence of press runs.

The author's translation, "Are There Musical First Editions?" appears in Bradley, pp. 103-06.

Otto Erich DEUTSCH. "Music Bibliography and Catalogues," *The Library*, 4th series, 23 (1943), 151-70. **11**

Observations on the distinctions between general bibliography and music bibliography, and between bibliography and cataloguing, built around commentary on recent publications, notably the Music Library Association's 1941 *Code for Cataloging Music*.

This is probably the most important of the author's essays on music bibliography from his London years: others include "Music and Bibliographical Practice," *Music Review*, 2 (1941), 253-66, and "Theme and Variations," *ibid*, 12 (1951), 68-71.

Reprinted in Bradley, pp. 117-26.

Otto Erich DEUTSCH. "Music Publishers' Numbers: A Selection of 40 Dated Lists, 1710-1900," *Journal of Documentation*, 1 (1945/46), 206-216; 2 (1946/47), 80-91.   **12**
Lists of numbers with their dates for several dozen publishers, mostly 19th-century German firms.

Also issued separately, London: ASLIB, 1946. The new edition, slightly expanded and updated and in German, is now entitled *Musikverlagsnummern: eine Auswahl von 40 datierten Listen 1710-1900* (Berlin: Merseburger, 1961). Deutsch's brief "Nachtrag" appears among the "Berichte und kleine Beiträge" in *Die Musikforschung*, 15 (1962), 155.

Wolfgang SCHMIEDER. "Zur Katalogisierung der Musica Practica," *Zentralblatt für Bibliothekswesen*, 64 (1950), 343-51.   **13**
Address at the International Congress of Music Librarians, Florence, 1949, identifying five areas in need of attention. It is useful to speak to them here in reverse order. The last three deal with the choice and formulation of entries and with practices of collocation—matters that today are the province of cataloguers more than bibliographers. The second matter is dating—which continues to be important to both.

It is the first that explores a matter rarely dealt with elsewhere: the distinctions between *musica theoretica* and *musica practica*. The differences, constantly changing, affect the work of three groups who work with printed music. In the interest of service, librarians learn to work in gray areas that constantly override their classification schemes. (Libretti, hymnology, and folk-song are the most conspicuous of the areas.) Bibliographers delimit their inquiries in the interests of manageability, or expand them in interests of relevance. The book and music trades position their distinctions with a view to wider or more effective marketing. Admittedly Schmieder does not develop arguments relevant to the concerns of each one of these groups; his theoretical observations, however, offer valuable insights for all of them.

Cecil HOPKINSON. "Fundamentals of Music Bibliography," *Journal of Documentation*, 11 (1955), 119-29.   **14**
After surveying recent music reference sources, the author seeks to clarify the aims of scholarly music lists and the practices of

dating, with due cognizance of Richard S. Hill's suggestion that lists were intended primarily for collectors, musicians, or historians. To Hill, Hopkinson was the owner of the First Edition Book Shop, catering to wealthy, precious, gentleman collectors. Hopkinson's earlier efforts in music bibliography — handsomely printed and fastidious in detail to the point of crankiness — had been issued either privately, as had his lavish and ground-breaking Berlioz bibliography, or by the Edinburgh Bibliographical Society, as with the studies on national song (677) and on Domenico Scarlatti and Handel editions in France and England. The 1955 essay is reprinted in *Bradley*, pp. 127-34.

Wolfgang SCHMIEDER. "Musikbibliographie: Ein Beitrag zu ihrer Geschichte und ihrer Problemen," *Archiv für Musikwissenschaft*, 12 (1955), 239-47.   **15**

A brief but densely packed and provocative essay, with useful observations on morphology, a historical overview, and identification of the problems of international coverage, entry practices, and formal presentation.

Schmieder's theoretically minded writings from this period also include "Musikbibliographische Probleme: Ein Beitrag zur Theorie der Verzeichnung von Büchern über Musik," in the *Bericht über den Internationalen Musikwissenschaftlichen Kongress, Bamberg 1953* (Kassel: Bärenreiter, 1954), pp. 282-86. Gradually the concept of documentation is beginning to emerge.

—. "Grenzen und Ziele der Musikdokumentation," in *Bericht über den internationalen musikwissenschaftlichen Kongress Wien, Mozartjahr 1956* (Graz, Köln: Böhlau, 1958), p. 551.   **16**

A summary ("stark gekürzte Zusammenfassung") of an attempt to expand music bibliography into music documentation. Not only does music need to be described; its survival must be assured (important in post-War Germany), and its access enhanced (an activity now subsumed under what is called "document delivery"), so as to suggest and promote an intellectual framework for scholarship itself, as realized through systems of description, indexing, and classification. The goal is at once noble, vague, and provocative, and subject to redefinition.

Schmieder's concepts are sharpened in his "Gedanken über den Begriff, das Wesen und die Aufgaben der Musikdokumentation," in the *Bericht über den internationalen musikwissenschaftlichen Kongress Kassel 1962* (Kassel: Bärenreiter, 1963), pp. 334-36. See also "Aphorismen zur Musik-Dokumentation," in *Hans Albrecht in Memoriam* (Kassel: Bärenreiter, 1962), 285-88, with several dozen paragraphs of observations on the objectives of those activities devoted to the contemplation of the evidence of and facts about music.

Anthony VAN HOBOKEN. "Probleme der musikbibliographischen Terminologie," *Fontes artis musicae*, 5 (1958), 6-15.   17

A discussion of the concepts of first and original editions (*Erstausgaben, Originalausgaben*), other printings (*Nachdrucke, Vorabdrucke, Raubdrucke*), and *Auflage* (also *Titelauflage*) in the light of instances, mostly from the late 18th century. ("If music bibliography is a science, it is above all one based on exceptions.")

François LESURE. "Bibliothécaires et musicologues," *Atti del Congresso internazionale di musiche popolari mediterranee, e Convegno dei bibliotecari musicali, Palermo, 26-30 giugno 1954* (Palermo: Ministerio della pubblica istruzione, 1959), pp. 363-37.   18

A manifesto for librarians: they should provide guidance, their horizons must be wide, and they should engage in scholarship.

Translated by Isabelle Cazeaux as "Librarians and Musicologists," in Bradley, pp. 310-12.

Jan LA RUE. "Musical Exploration: The Tasks of Research Bibliography," *Library Trends*, 8 (1960), 510-18.   19

A summary of the "state of the art," directed to an audience of general librarians.

Arthur MENDEL. "Evidence and Explanation," *Report of the 8th Congress of the International Musicological Society, New York, 1961* (Kassel: Bärenreiter, 1962), vol. 2, pp. 3-18.   20

This esteemed essay brings out a perspective that is crucial to music bibliography, as it focuses on the special affections that draw one to the inquiry in the first place. The basic concern of musicologists may be the "musical works themselves, as individual structures and as objects of delight" (p. 4); but these exist in various forms: as ideal and abstracted conceptions, for instance, or as physical events, be they live performances, manuscript copies, published editions, sound recordings, or recorded statements concerning the works. One may study the ideal work of music with no particular concern for its realization in performance; it is also possible to be concerned with the physical document only as a basis for refining and confirming particulars relating to the work of music. It also often happens that the physical document becomes an object of affection, apart from its function as a necessary statement of the music. Out of this condition music bibliography acquires its identity and inspiration.

I include Mendel's essay in the belief that the critical questions he summarizes are formulated differently, by those who see musical documents merely as means to an end, and by those who develop affinities to them as cultural, often also as aesthetic, artifacts in their own right.

There are occasional music bibliographers whose affection resides wholly in the physical document — bibliomaniacs, typically more innocent than perverse, along with other music bibliographers who, after examining some documents, feel blessed never to need to hear the music they are studying — also the sheet-music collectors who love their collections and love the music, but never learned to read music and never really feel any need to learn, even after they have uncovered significant bibliographical particulars. (There are, of course, an even larger number of discophiles and concert-goers whose membership in the musical community is much welcomed and treasured, although their contribution to our knowledge is limited by their lack of musical literacy—much like the gifted performer who, occasionally for convenience but sometimes of necessity, plays by ear.)

Cecil HOPKINSON. "Towards a Definition of Certain Terms in Musical Bibliography," in *Music, Libraries and Instruments* (London: Hinrichsen, 1961; Hinrichsen's 11th Music Book), pp. 147-55.   **21**

Chairman's report of a Discussion Panel at the 5th Congress of the International Association of Music Libraries, Cambridge, July 1-2, 1959, at which Otto Erich Deutsch, Rudolf Elvers, Yvette Fédoroff, Hans Halm, Albert van der Linden, O. W. Neighbour, Albi Rosenthal, and Liesbeth Weinhold were the official members. Hopkinson's imaginatively conceived example (p. 148) seems to have inspired what was no doubt a bewildering range of observations. These were probably not what Hopkinson expected or wanted, although, re-reading them today, one can see how they do reflect a lack of consensus regarding the basic goals of music bibliography itself.

Vincent H. DUCKLES. "Music Librarian, Bibliographer, Documentalist: Secondary Report," *Fontes artis musicae*, 12 (1965), 138-41.   **22**

Attempts to clarify the role of music librarians (and implicitly of bibliographers) in terms of the elusive distinction between information and knowledge.

Reprinted in Bradley, pp. 313-15.

James J. FULD. *The Book of World-Famous Music*. New York: Crown, 1966.   **23**

A guide to the first published appearances of major musical works. The compiler's distinctly personal notion of "world-famous" is further betrayed by a despairingly dorian title arrangement; but the scrupulous research habits are truly quite what one would expect of a sophisticated and honest lawyer who knows where to find evidence and how to interpret it, and who loves and respects books and music as a bibliophile.

The second edition (1971) expands the coverage from just over 800 titles to nearly a thousand, while the third edition (New York: Dover, 1985) adds a Supplement (pp. 669-93) cued to the main text, with about 120 addenda. The 1985 addenda range from odd facts (e.g., the royalties for "God Bless America" are given to the Boy Scouts and Girl Scouts) to impressive essays of potential scholarly significance. Not to be overlooked is Fuld's introduction, with useful discussions of the special activities of music bibliographers and several valuable displays, notably on Jurgenson and Ricordi.

Wolfgang MATTHÄUS. "Quellen und Fehlerquellen zur Datierung von Musikdrucken aus der Zeit nach 1750," *Fontes artis musicae*, 14 (1967), 37-42.   **24**
Reflections on the problems, based significantly on the author's experience with André editions (789), with proposals for three laudable projects: an archive of photocopies of title pages, a collection of publishers' catalogues, and an extracting of announcements from newspapers and periodicals.

Ernst C. KROHN. "On Classifying Sheet Music," Music Library Association, *Notes*, n.s., 26 (1970), 473-78.   **25**
Concerned not with formal classification schemes so much as with Krohn's bibliographical study of his own notable collection.

Claudio SARTORI. "The Bibliographer's Occupation," Music Library Association, *Notes*, 26 (1970), 705-12.   **26**
"A music bibliographer [is occupied] with the external questions of music . . . important as a framework for more general considerations. . . . [Among an author's works] the one I prefer . . . is a book which discusses . . . real musical matters and draws conclusions." Appended is "A First List of Italian Music Publishers' Catalogues," a precursor of Mischiati (708 below).

Hans LENNEBERG. "Dating Engraved Music: The Present State of the Art," *Library Quarterly*, 41 (1971), 128-40.   **27**
A survey of the different activities, beginning with the provocative notion that the focus on dating grew out of the 1927 Vienna Internationaler Musikhistorischer Kongress, Schmidt-Phiseldeck (5) in particular.

Peter DAVISON. "Science, Method, and the Textual Critic," *Studies in Bibliography*, 25 (1972), 1-28.   **28**
On source work in general as applicable to texts of all kinds. Of interest to music bibliographers for its use of editions of Bizet's Symphony in C in illustrating the sterility of the hypothetico-deductive method.

Vincent H. DUCKLES. "Musicology at the Mirror: A Prospectus for the History of Musical Scholarship," in *Per-*

spectives in Musicology (New York: Norton, 1972), pp. 32-
55.   **29**

Introduces the concept of the "arts of custodianship," practiced
by librarians, collectors, bibliographers, and editors (pp. 47-49).
Their work, "usually regarded as auxiliary," has been essential in
formulating the objectives of musicology.

Duckles's "Some Observations on Music Lexicography," *College Music Symposium*, 11 (1971), 115-22, is in a similar spirit.

*Guide for Dating Early Published Music: A Manual of
Bibliographical Practices*, compiled by D. W. Krummel.
Hackensack, N. J.: Joseph Boonin, 1974.   **30**

The "IAML Guide" essentially outlines a general method for
bibliographical dating, based on contributions to the activity of
the Commission on Bibliographical Research of the International Association of Music Libraries. The introduction attempts to reflect the consensus of the respected members of the
informal and largely self-appointed Commission. Often, however, when consensus was simply not at hand, the compiler opted
for the most sensible compromise, in hopes of making everyone
equally happy, but more often with the result of making everyone equally unhappy. The "National Reports," by specialists on
the publishing history and scholarly resources of particular regions, are less exceptionable. These are complemented by illustrations, selected from the collections at the Newberry Library,
Chicago (cf. 958 for their context).

"Supplement," *ibid.*, 24 (1977), 175-84. See also Linda Solow,
"An Index to Publishers, Engravers and Lithographers and a
Bibliography of the Literature cited in the IAML Guide," *ibid.*,
24 (1977), 81-95. Earlier texts, discussions, and announcements
are cited in *Fontes artis musicae*, as cited on p. 15 of the *Guide*.

Vincent H. DUCKLES. "The Library of the Mind: Observations on the Relationship between Musical Scholarship
and Bibliography," in John W. Grubbs, *Current Thought in
Musicology* (Austin: University of Texas Press, 1976), pp.
277-96.   **31**

The work of early scholars, Brossard and Forkel in particular, suggests how "bibliography can serve as an approach to knowledge in its own right" (p. 281).

D. W. KRUMMEL. "Musical Functions and Bibliographical Forms," *The Library*, 5th series, 32 (1976), 327-50.   **32**
The current state of scholarship is proposed in terms of the suggestion that the task of the bibliographer is one of understanding the ways in which musical documents take the forms they do with utilitarian purposes in mind that derive from their intended musical uses. Includes references to bibliographical writings and prospective studies that may not be as well known as they ought to be; an attempt at a history of house practices for signing the gatherings of early part-books (footnote 32); and suggestions of some conceptual differences between a bibliographer's study of printed music and a discographer's study of sound recordings (pp. 348-50.)

Dan FOG. "Random Thoughts on Music Dating and Terminology," *Fontes artis musicae*, 24 (1977), 141-44.   **33**
Bibliographical practices should be developed appropriate to the characteristics of musical materials and the needs of musicians, and thus unfettered from "conventional, book-infected concepts" (although the alternative circumstances under which music bibliography might function are unfortunately not set forth). The ideas reflect on the compiler's notable authority in studies of 19th-century Danish music in particular (840-41, also 621), and as a music antiquarian in general.

Alexander WEINMANN. "Musikalische Quellenforschung, beginnend mit der Zeit Joseph Haydns," *Fontes artis musicae*, 26 (1979), 5-16.   **34**
Lecture at the Joseph-Haydn Institut, Cologne, May 5, 1979, on source work in general, but obviously drawn from his studies of Viennese publishers (800).

Michael OCHS. *Truth, Beauty, Love, and Music Librarianship*. New York: Columbia University, School of Library Service, 1980.   **35**

A lecture delivered at the inaugural ceremonies in honor of the Ida Rosen prize, at once intensely earnest but one appoggiatura short of being disgustingly maudlin; also often quite clever without being either annoying or cloying.
Reprinted in *Harvard Librarian*, May 1981, pp 2, 6.

Norman DEL MAR. *Orchestral Variations: Confusion and Error in the Orchestral Repertoire*. London: Eulenburg, 1981.   **36**
An anthology of mistakes, unauthentic editorial revisions, and questionable readings, drawn together by the prominent conductor from editions of 45 well-known works, amply attesting to the need for better performance editions.

Hans LENNEBERG. "The Haunted Bibliographer," Music Library Association, *Notes*, 41 (1984), 239-48.   **37**
Observations on important bibliographical matters that are still poorly understood: How did the printing processes really work? What considerations informed the early 19th-century tradesman in making business decisions?

G. Thomas TANSELLE. "The Description of Non-Letterpress Material in Books," *Studies in Bibliography*, 35 (1982), 1-42.   **38**
The pre-eminent theorist of general bibliography argues for the applicability of bibliographical practices to maps and music, the latter as reflected in the 1974 IAML *Guide for Dating Early Music* (30). Basing practice on theory, while clearly desirable, satisfying, and obviously essential, still needs to be addressed. Some problems derive from the awkwardness in using letterpress conceptions in work with engraved plates (which are somewhat analogous to standing type), others from the translation of Anglo-American concepts into the largely incompatible Continental environment of bibliography.

D. W. KRUMMEL. "Citing the Score: Descriptive Bibliography and Printed Music," *The Library*, 6th series, 4 (1987), 329-46.   **39**
The distinctive elements in music citations can be traced to major library catalogues of earlier times: title analytics to Johannes

Müller's 1870 Königsberg catalogue, transcriptions of dedications and the study of musical patronage to Gaetano Gaspari's Bologna catalogue, 1892 *ff.*; incipits to Jules Écorcheville's for the Bibliothèque Nationale, 1910 *ff.*; dating to William Barclay Squire's 1912 British Museum catalogue; and descriptive annotations to Oscar Sonneck's 1914 Library of Congress libretto catalogue. The writings of Deutsch in the 1940s reflect a crisis that resulted from the growing demands on music bibliography.

Iain FENLON. "Production and Distribution of Music in the 16th and 17th Centuries," *Acta musicologica*, 59 (1987), 14-17. **40**

Statement of purpose for Round Table IV at the 14th International Congress of the International Musicological Society, Bologna, August 29-30, 1987. The shift of music reproduction "from the copyist's desk to the printer's workshop" leads to "distinctions between 'centre' and 'periphery' and between centres of 'creation' and 'distribution,'" involving repertory, circulation of texts through patronage and as limited and facilitated by political allegiances, and such concerns for access as are today evidenced in modern collections or in early bibliographical lists.

The papers for the session itself appear as "Produzione e distribuzione di musica nella società europea del XVI e XVII secolo," in the *Atti del XIV Congresso della Società internazionale di musicologica: Trasmissione e recezione delle forme di cultura musicale* (Torino: EDT, 1990), vol. 1, pp. 235-318. Contributed by Kristine Forney, Angelo Pompilio, Margaret Murata, Paolo Fabbri, Tim Carter, Jane A. Bernstein, and Rudolf Rasch, these papers reflect earlier writings by the authors, many of them cited elsewhere here. Some are largely reworkings of earlier ideas with a view to the focus of the Round Table; others explore new topics and present new evidence. Mary S. Lewis provides a formal response on pp. 319-25; the discussion is on pp. 326-36.

In many ways the discussions of music publishing in *The Italian Madrigal in the Early Sixteenth Century: Sources and Interpretation* by Fenlon and James Haar (Cambridge: Cambridge University Press, 1988; especially Chapter 4, "The Diffusion of the Early Madrigal," pp. 70-86) confirm, and, in a somewhat lateral sense, epitomize, the spirit of the Bologna conference papers.

Richard D. SMIRAGLIA. *Music Cataloging: The Biblio-graphical Control of Printed and Recorded Music in Libraries*. Englewood, Colo.: Libraries Unlimited, 1989.   **41**
The separation of bibliographers' practices from cataloguers' practices having grown wider and more complicated over recent decades, one of the strengths of this book lies in its effectiveness in conveying the sense of the catalogue to the bibliographically minded. The author's other recent book, rather confusingly entitled *Cataloging Music* (Lake Crystal, Minn.: Soldier Creek Press, 1986), may be more useful to those who want to learn and interpret rules, but bibliographers should find the 1989 book much more substantial to ponder.

Other perspectives of interest to music bibiographers are set forth in the author's earlier essay, "Theoretical Considerations in the Bibliographic Control of Music Materials in Libraries," *Cataloging and Classification Quarterly*, 5 (1985), 1-16. Bibliographers wishing to appreciate the cataloguer's plight may also savor Brian Redfern, "Dinosaurs to Crush Flies: Computer Catalogues, Classification, and Other Barriers to Library Use," *Brio*, vol. 21, no. 1 (Spring/Summer 1984), pp. 4-8.

Among other writings on music cataloguing, Carol June Bradley's *The Dickinson Classification: A Cataloguing and Classification Manual for Music* (Carlisle, Penn.: Carlisle Books, 1968) nicely emphasizes bibliographical activities as essential background for cataloguing and classification. The scheme itself, as conceived by George Sherman Dickinson for Vassar College, and now alas abandoned there (but still used at the State University of New York at Buffalo), is summarized in Bradley's "The Dickinson Classification Scheme," *Fontes artis musicae*, 19 (1972), 13-21.

Mary S. LEWIS. "The Printed Music Book in Context: Observations on Some Sixteenth-Century Editions," Music Library Association, *Notes*, 46 (1990), 899-918.   **42**
The summary proposals emerge from the author's study of Gardane and mid 16th-century Venetian printing (741 below).

Stanley BOORMAN. "What Bibliography Can Do: Music Printing and the Early Madrigal," *Music and Letters*, 72 (1991), 236-58.   **43**

Observations occasioned by two recent books: *The Italian Madrigal in the Early Sixteenth Century*, by Iain Fenlon and James Haar (Cambridge: Cambridge University Press, 1988), and Mary Lewis's Gardane bibliography (cf. 40 and 42 above).

Contemplating such diffuse writings as these, one is tempted to conclude that there is really no central theoretical focus to the study of music bibliography. Certainly there is no diatonic scale, such as has been basic to the theory of music over the history of western civilization; no conventionalization of printing practices, from type design through presswork to assembly of gatherings to marketing, as for general bibliographers. Instead, music bibliography has been born out of a belief that general principles lie behind specific findings, as discovered in the course of handling materials. What these materials have in common is their musical texts and the shared tradition of Western music to which they belong. The documents in question, however, range from Renaissance partbooks to Ricordi opera arias extracted from vocal scores; from pre-Tridentine liturgical incunabula to authentic Beethoven editions; from *Parthenia*, engraved in order to impress a select audience, to the Breitkopf catalogues, typeset in order to catch the eye of the widest possible audience; from humble Palestrina honoring the Pope in a sumptuous choirbook to raucous Tin Pan Alley insulting the public with cheap amusement on the covers.

One can argue that music bibliography has come into existence mostly by default: it arises from the outside — out of the needs of general bibliographers to defer to specialists for guidance in working with the occasional printed music that passes through their hands, and of musicians who need guidance working with copies in front of them. In response to such cries for assistance, the nine-faceted paradigm acquires its intellectual legitimacy. In fascinating ways the facets come to refract the light from one another — one facet provides partial answers to questions that had been seen as distinctive to another facet — thus enabling the rationale of an intellectual unity to emerge.

Music bibliography nevertheless also often suggests a strange marriage. Music is exciting and pleasurable in its demands, usually in such a pre-emptive way as to suggest that bibliography is unrewarding and unchallenging because it needs so little original thought. One goal of this book is to refine all of these impressions. (It may seem unfortunate and it is clearly ironic, for instance, but one use of bibliography is to call attention to the great quantity of unrewarding music that survives today.)

Conversely, bibliography becomes exciting as it becomes problematical. Music that appears to be hopelessly dull (and its dullness is often conspicuously evident on the printed page) in the capable hands of strong performers actually can become very exciting. What it may lack, however — what modern access technology perhaps forces our tastes to recognize as an essential attribute of the music that deserves to be recognized as significant — is a sustaining power, such as is reflected, for instance, in re-publication. Bibliography, as it points in the directions both of textual analysis and of reception history, becomes far from dull. The weight of its objectives, technologies, and controversies, as evidenced in the literature set forth here, suggests its daunting demands for both meticulous detail and for new perspectives. Because of such demands it becomes all the more rewarding.

II.

Historical Surveys

FOR OVER FIVE CENTURIES the art of music has benefitted from the art of the printer. Some of the events in the
history are important but poorly understood; others are fascinating but of dubious significance. There are also landmark legends that are impossible to verify and that smack of
promotional copy. The story is being told and retold contin-
uously, by some who search for explanations, and by others
who simply enjoy fascinating tales.

Fourteen "Major Scholarly Writings" (Section A) suggest
the changing historical emphasis of the literature. A few
"Brief Historical Surveys" (Section B) are also impressive,
and sometimes extensive as well, but there is little in them
that is new. Notable general and reference books that treat
the subject (Section C) are followed by writings on miscellaneous topics (Section D) that are important in the literature but do not really fit elsewhere in this book.

A. Major Scholarly Writings

The history of music printing seems closer to the history of music
than to the history of printing, perhaps because the writing of
music history (like art history in general) has heretofore attracted
rather more imaginative scholarship than has printing history (like

the history of technology in general).[1] Alfred North Whitehead, in his Norton lectures on *The Aims of Education* (New York: Macmillan, 1929), suggests a model: like learning in general, the history of music printing can be usefully grouped into successive periods of romance, precision, and generalization.

Writings before *ca.* 1900 reflect the buoyancy of adventuresome scholar-librarians as they explored romantic frontiers and uncovered facts of who, when, where, and how. The announcements of their findings convey a delight in the heady excitement of discovery; their arguments with each other suggest instincts of territoriality. The early French polymaths (Fournier, Weckerlin), the later German academics (Vogel, Riemann) and their colleagues in England (Squire, Kidson) and America (Sonneck, Kinkeldey), as well as a host of their doctoral students, all reflect this exuberance.

By the 1920s one detects a growing concern for precision: of all the facts, which ones were *truly* important for a clear understanding of a topic that now seemed as boundless as its experts were myopic? Writings from the period between the two wars are typically brief and discriminating in their choice of facts, and their texts are attractively presented, consistent with the aims of addressing general readers, with clarity and style. Meyer and O'Meara, Guégan, Pattison, and Audin carry on this tradition, as do the best encyclopedia essays. The lists of particulars make Jurgenson's book distinctive, the goal being contextual precision. Selectivity in the name of conciseness characterizes King's 1964 booklet.

An era of generalization is slowly emerging, so far in groping pursuit of vague but basic questions: "Why?" "So what"? The approaches range from the implicit to the explicit. Some writers, like Laaff, are fascinated with technology both physical and intellec-

---

1. Printing history, at least, has yet to see the likes of Warren D. Allen's venerable *Philosophies of Music History* (New York: American Book Co., 1939), along with subsequent reconsiderations, misgivings, theorizing, and historiographical perspectives. The closest printing counterpart is probably Elizabeth L. Eisenstein's *The Printing Press as an Agent of Change* (Cambridge: Cambridge University Press, 1979), although here the intent, however laudable, is quite different. Instead of describing the history of bibliography or of bibliographical thought, Eisenstein surveys the explanations of the impact of printing on Western civilization. Embedded in this text are hopes of suggesting counterparts to these studies in the smaller world of music printing and publishing.

tual. Like Jurgenson, their hope is that new perspectives may emerge out of reference lists. The 1990 Grove handbook also entertains hopes for stimulating the kinds of kaleidoscopic juxtapositions that often emerge from alphabetically organized reference books. Other studies attempt to subsume the whole, mainly so as to suggest new ways to look at music printing in the context of Western civilization as a whole. Przywecka-Samecka aspires to the role of bibliographical polymath *par excellence*, and for this deserves special respect. My Engelhard Lecture proposes a range of *histoire du livre* questions that fall outside classic scholarly perspectives and may thus be overlooked. These writings can never be fully satisfying in their restlessness, although their optimism bears a spirit of romance that, one hopes, may signal the beginnings of a new cycle of interpretation.

Romance, precision, and generalization also variously pervade the specialized writings cited in subsequent chapters. The literature on graphics (Chapter 4), as it aspires to the precision of rigorous scholarship of art history, also seeks to preserve the spirit of romance that is implicit in visual statements of all kinds (sometimes rather too joyfully for the tastes of a scholarly audience); while the literature of publishing (Chapter 5), almost out of desperate necessity and in the interests of self-respect, anticipates the search for generalization. The works cited in Chapter 9 may be seen as an attempt to redefine the classic generalizations of music bibliography itself as proposed in Chapter 1.

Pierre-Simon FOURNIER. *Traité historique et critique sur l'origine et les progrès des caractères de fonte pour l'impression de la musique, avec des épreuves de nouveaux caractères de musique.* Berne, Paris: Barbou, 1765.   **44**
The earliest published history of music printing was undertaken to promote Fournier's own typographical innovations by implying their historic mission. Paris is understandably the center of attention, and engraving is scarcely acknowledged to exist. Fournier's efforts were inspired by his older brother's discovery of the Le Bé "memorandum" of the previous century (308, the first account of music printing technology, although it was not likely meant for publication and was undertaken as a personal reminiscence more than a historical account). Le Bé is our source of Fournier's information on Haultin, Le Bé, du Chemin,

Granjon, and Sanlecque, and his errors have been perpetuated ever since. Fournier confirms his predilections as he acknowledges his contemporaries in terms ranging from generous (Breitkopf), to neutral (Loyseau), to damning (the Ballard family, with its monopoly on typographic music, as well as the Gandos, who founded their type). The Gandos' attack on the *Traité*, and Fournier's response, are cited below (166, 168), since these are essentially entrepreneurial more than historical writings.

Fournier ends his *Traité* with an "Ariette, mise en musique par M. L'Abbé Dugue" (pp. 39-47), set in his new mosaic type.

Reprinted in the Archives de l'édition musicale française, Tome IX (Genève: Minkoff, 1972).

Jean-Baptiste WECKERLIN.* "Histoire de l'impression de la musique, principalement en France jusqu'au dix-neuvième siècle," *Bulletin de la Société des compositeurs de musique*, 2 (1864), 44-75.   **45**

An impressive work, all the more so considering its date. It pays high respect to sources, often transcribing original documents with translations side by side. The three sections cover (1) the beginnings, with only passing mention of the Greeks but more on the origins of musical notation, up to Petrucci; (2) the two major 16th-century typographic innovators, Haultin and Le Bé; and (3) other typographers from this and later periods (Briard, Duchemin, the Ballards, Sanlecque), extending into the 17th century. Well executed facsimiles show several 16th-century music type faces.

The essay also appears in *La chronique musicale*, 6 (1874), 241-50; 7 (1875), 55-64, 170-82, as well as in Weckerlin's *Opuscules sur la chanson populaire et sur la musique* (Paris: Baur, 1874, a limited edition of 50 copies devoted to four of his essays, of which this one is the fourth). The texts are all identical except for minor details: several footnotes are different in the *Bulletin*; the *Opuscules* presentation omits the modern transcription of music by Philippe "Danfrif" [*recte*: Danfrie], which appears on p. 176 in the *Chronique*. (One wonders why the text should have been reprinted after so long, and then twice: might the references to the *Bulletin*, a rather evasive serial, be misdated by precisely one decade? In fact, the dates are apparently correct.)

H. SANDARS [*pseud.* of W. J. Stannard]. "Music and Music Printing," *Printing Times and Lithographer*, n.s., 1 (1875), 81-83, 208-11, 231-33.   46

A brief account of the major technological events, intended for an audience of printers. The first part summarizes the history of music and explains the basic printing processes; the second speaks of specific letterpress and engraving innovations, from Playford's day up to some recent experiments with better alloys, making use of the patent literature for the latter; the third deals with lithography. As the history of the technology of music printing is explored, this text will likely emerge as a landmark, notwithstanding some factual shortcomings.

The author also provides a one-page epitome in "History of Music Printing," *The Practical Magazine*, n. s., 7 (1877), p. 189.

Friedrich CHRYSANDER. "A Sketch of the History of Music-Printing, from the 15th to the 18th Century," *Musical Times*, 18 (1877), 265-68, 324-26, 375-78, 470-75, 524-27, 584-87.   47

The author is not amiss in belittling this work as a "sketch." His high repute as a scholar, *qua* printer of his Handel edition, will continue to make this a respected if not a notably original text.

Also issued later in German as "Abriss einer Geschichte des Musikdruckes vom 15. bis 19. Jahrhundert," *Allgemeine Musikalische Zeitung*, 14 (1879), 161-67, 177-83, 193-200, 209-14, 225-32, 241-48.

Festschrift zur 50-jährigen Jubelfeier des Bestehens der Firma C. G. Röder. Leipzig, 1896.   48

A luxurious jubilee volume, handsomely decorated with wide margins and many appended facsimiles (Tafel I-XXVIII), and further enhanced with Hugo Riemann's 88-page "Notenschrift und Notendruck: Bibliographisch-typographische Studie." Riemann's concerns are predictably more with notation than printing. (He probably saw the two as largely identical, although subsequent scholarship suggests that his major concern was for the shape of the notes more than their typographic execution.)

Robert Eitner corrects some factual details in "Geschichte der Notenschrift," *Monatshefte für Musikgeschichte*, 28 (1896), 166-69, ending by observing that Riemann's suggestion of the need for a definitive music bibliography (p. 39) would soon be answered in his *Quellen-Lexikon.*

Zur Westen's 1921 book (459) was the Röder firm's sequel for its next anniversary.

Борис Петрович ЮРГЕНСОН. Очерк истории нотопечатия. С приложением перечня нотных изд. XV-XVI вв. и кратких сведений о главнейшик нечатниках, граверах и издателях XVI-XVIII вв. Москва, 1928.   **49**

Facing the Russian title page is a German version reading thus: B. Jurgenson. *Abriss der Geschichte des Notendruckes, nebst einer Übersicht der in den 15-16 Jahrhunderten erschienenen Musikalien und der bedeutenden Notendrucker, Notenstecher und Verleger der 15-18 Jahrhunderte.* Moskau: R.S.F.S.R., Musiksektion des Staatsverlages, 1928.

This remarkable *vade mecum* begins with a historical account (pp. 5-70), heavily illustrated and presumably drawn from secondary sources for Western Europe and, for Russia, from Boris Jurgenson's personal experience in his family's music publishing firm. Next follows a list of editions by important 15th- to 19th-century music printers (pp. 71-106), arranged by method: printed books with music added in manuscript (8 titles), woodcut music (subdivided as theoretical, sacred, and secular), typographical (vocal, then instrumental, each divided by country and city), and Russian published music. The directory of about 2,000 15th- to 18th-century music printers and publishers (pp. 109-74) is arranged by country and city. (The index, on pp. 175-88, is in the Cyrillic alphabet, with Roman-alphabet names interfiled, often with the Cyrillic form in parentheses.)

Bertrand GUÉGAN. "Histoire de l'impression de la musique," *Arts et métiers graphiques*, 37 (1933), 26-34; 39 (1934), 16-26; 41 (1934), 39-46; 43 (1934), 15-20.   **50**

Of the four sections in this nicely illustrated survey, the first covers the 15th century, the second French music typography from Haultin to Duverger, the third French engraving in the 17th and 18th centuries, the fourth pewter engraving and lithography.

Kathi MEYER and Eva J. O'MEARA. "The Printing of Music, 1473-1934," *The Dolphin*, 2 (1935), 171-207.   **51**

Highly esteemed for two generations, and of continuing value for the clarity and taste with which it presents technical matters. The 1939 Grolier Club exhibition (431) is presumably a by-product of this text.

Bruce PATTISON. "Notes on Early Music Printing," *The Library*, 4th series, 19 (1939), 389-421.   **52**
Admirably concerned with the social context of music printing.

Ernst LAAFF. *Musik mit Fleiß gedrucket: Grundzüge der Entwicklung des Musiknotendrucks*. Eltville: Wiesbadener Kurier, 1956 (Burgverein Eltville e.V., 9. Sonderdruck). **53**
A conveniently tight "Vortrag," consisting of brief essays on the major events, with many odd particulars; a bibliography of about 50 secondary references; eleven lists of books and names; and 12 illustrations. The presentation serves to remind the reader that preciousness, as it pre-empts much that might have been included, also adds weight to what it does choose to include.

Maria PRZYWECKA-SAMECKA. *Dzieje drukarstwa muzycznego do końca XVIII wieku*. Wroclaw: Biblioteka Uniwersytecka, 1957.   **54**
A general overview of music publishing across 18th-century Europe, complementing and anticipating the author's other studies on early periods and on central Europe.
   Drukarstwo muzyczne w Europie do końca XVIII wieku (Wroclaw: Ossolineum, 1987) updates this study and extends its coverage back to the beginnings.

Alec Hyatt KING. *Four Hundred Years of Music Printing*. London: British Museum, 1964.   **55**
One of the most scholarly and readable of the brief surveys, prepared in conjuction with a standing exhibit in the King's Library.
   Reprinted with minor revisions, 1968.

D. W. KRUMMEL. *The Memory of Sound: Observations on the History of Music on Paper*. Washington: Library of Congress, 1988.   **56**
Text of an Engelhard lecture for the Center for the Book, October 29, 1987. The conceptualization of music itself has changed

over the course of history, as music came to be committed to a printed form so as to be not only replicable but also widely disseminated (i.e., across space). The replicability (i.e., over time) is essential to but deceptive in its permanence.

Music Printing and Publishing, edited by D. W. Krummel and Stanley Sadie. London: Macmillan; New York: Norton, 1990 (New Grove Handbooks in Music). **57**

The ten chapters are derived from articles by H. Edmund Poole and the present author in the *New Grove Dictionary of Music and Musicians* (London: Macmillan, 1980) and in *The New Grove Dictionary of American Music* (*ibid.*, 1986), updated and supplemented with Richard Vendome's survey of computerized music printing (pp. 66-78). Of the 700 entries that follow in the "Dictionary of Music Printers and Publishers" (pp. 135-486), about 150 are new to this volume, many of them for names from outside Western Europe and the United States. The rest are updated, particularly with bibliographical references from the two earlier Grove sets. The strength of Stanley Boorman's "Glossary" (pp. 489-550) lies in its perspectives on early letterpress printers more than those of engravers or publishers, while the "Bibliography" is essentially an epitome of (*qua* startingplace for) the present book. The index is useful in tracing the names of imprints for particular composers, and of minor publishers and affiliates. See also p. x*n* above.

B. Brief Historical Surveys

Here are many of the essays that tell the basic story — usually interestingly, often with pictures. Frequently the authors are quite eminent but in specialties other than music printing. The German literature seems prone to discussing the convenience of engraving plates with recourse to a formulaic statement: "Kein Geringerer als der große Meister Johann Sebastian Bach hat . . . seine eigenen Werke teilweise selbst in Kupferplatten eingraviert" ("No less inconsiderable a composer than J. S. Bach engraved some of his own plates " — an idea now discredited).

"Der Musiknotendruck," *Journal für Buchdruckerkunst, Schriftgießerei und die verwandten Fächer*, 11 (1844), cols. 135-39, 145-150. **58**

A brief summary, probably by the journal's editor, Johann Heinrich Meyer.

William H. CUMMINGS. "Music Printing," *Proceedings of the Musical Association*, 11 (1884-85), 99-116.   **59**

A meandering lecture, presumably complemented by a display of the treasures of Cummings's fine personal library. The concluding observations, on contemporary music printing, pay respect to a paper given by Brudenell Carter at the Society of Arts, on "The Influence on Civilisation of Eyesight." The ensuing discussion is really more interesting than the lecture itself. A. H. Littleton of Novello saw Cummings's comments on legibility as "very like a libel of our popular octavo editions" (perhaps quite correctly). He was quick to defend his products: they "have always been accepted as specimens of neatness and cheapness." Others from the audience added critical comments, often on the musical page size. One wishes that the spirit of the confrontation had been captured more precisely.

Robert EITNER. "Der Musiknotendruck und seine Entwicklung," *Zeitschrift für Bücherfreunde*, 1 (1898), 630-36.

Mostly on the 15th and early 16th centuries, with cursory but thoughtful comments on later periods.   **60**

Carl HERRMANN. "Zur Urgeschichte des Notendruckes," *Archiv für Buchgewerbe*, 38 (1901), 13-14, 89-91.   **61**

Based on Riemann; a two-page *Beilage* includes a portrait of J. G. I. Breitkopf and facsimiles of his work.

Theodor KROYER. "Ein Jubiläum des Notendruckes," *Allgemeine Zeitung*, 112 (1901), 6-7.   **62**
[Davidsson 273]

K. JENDROSSEK. "Die Entwicklung des Notendruckes," *Sängerhalle*, 41 (1901), 265-66, 282-83.   **63**
[Davidsson 233]

Karl WESTERMEYER. "Die Entwicklung des Notendrucks," *Signale für die musikalische Welt*, 80 (1922), 1395-99.   **64**
Tidy and competent.

T. REHMANN. "Etwas über Notenschrift und Notendruck," *Gregorius-Bote*, 44 (1928), 70-75. **65**
[Davidsson 408]

Adolf ABER. *Eine Stunde an der Wiege der Musik*. Leipzig: Röder, 1931 (Reclamsbroschüre). **66**
A popular illustrated account, also issued as a *Beilage* to vol. 71, no. 21, of the *Schweizerische Musikzeitung* (Zurich, 1931).

Desmond FLOWER. "On Music Printing, 1473-1701," *Book-Collector's Quarterly*, 4 (1931), 76-92. **67**
With qualifications as a fine printer (e.g., as editor of this journal), the author recognizes some major events that were not well appreciated in his day. Unfortunately his imaginative conjectures also miss the target more often than one would wish. A critical reading of the essay can therefore be highly provocative.

Eli CANTOR. "The Printing of Music," *PM*, vol. 1, no. 12 (August, 1935), pp. 12-15, 24, 26. **68**
In this "intimate journal for production managers, art directors and their associates," edited by Percy Seitlin and Robert L. Leslie, the author calls on the 1935 Meyer-O'Meara essay in *The Dolphin*, and on advice from Peter Verburg of the Schirmer printing plant. Page 12 shows a specimen of music type.

IRASCH. "Aus der Frühgeschichte des Musiknotensatzes," *Graphische Jahrbücher*, 56 (1935), 263*ff*. **69**
[Davidsson 232]

K. J. LÜTHI. "Notizen zur Geschichte des Musiknotensatzes," *Schweizerisches Gutenbergmuseum*, 22 (1936), 234-35.
[Davidsson 314] **70**

"Der Notensatz und seine Geschichte," *Der Buchdrucker*, 5 (1938), 106-08, 138-40. **71**
[Davidsson 371]

Wolfgang SCHMIEDER. "Zur Geschichte des Notendruckes," *Allgemeine Musikzeitung*, 67 (1940), 217-18. **72**
[Davidsson 459]

W. BAUR. "Die Entstehung der Musiknote und die Herstellung von Musikalien in alter und neuer Zeit," *Schweizerische Musiker-Revue*, vol. 17, no. 3 (1941). **73** [Davidsson 23]

Denis ANTONIAZZI. "Musique typographique (origines)," *Schweizerisches Gutenbergmuseum*, 30 (1944), 121-27. **74** On music printing in the Renaissance.

"Von der Entwicklung und dem Wert des Notendrucks," *Der graphische Markt* [Bielefeld], vol. 2, no. 39 (1947). **75** [Davidsson 540]

H. Wolfgang PHILIPP. "Musiknotendruck," *SGM / Schweizer graphische Mitteilungen*, 68 (1949), 165-67. **76** General comments on engraving and layout in the April issue, in anticipation of the special issue on music printing (below).

Hermann STREHLER. "Zur Geschichte des Musiknotendrucks," *ibid*, pp. 283-90. **77** A brief essay by the journal's editor, introducing a handsomely illustrated July *Sondernummer* on "Die Musiknote in der Reproduktion," which also includes Johannes Duft's "Musiknoten in tausendjährigen Handschriften" (pp. 291-93), Ernest Zahler's "Der Musiknotensatz" (pp. 306-09), and essays by Cherbuliez (399 below) and Hader (262 below).

H. BOLTE. "Musiknotendruck," *Der graphische Markt*, 5, (1950), 371-73. **78** [Davidsson 45]

Franz GIEGLING. "Über die Entwicklung des Notendrucks," *Stultifera navis*, 11 (1954), 80-88. **79** A summary overview, drawn from respected sources and ending with smugly positivistic sentiments ("Der Notendruck bietet heute kaum mehr Schwierigkeiten").

"Zwei Jahrhunderte moderner typographischer Musikaliendruck," *Form und Technik*, 5 (1954), 390-92. **80** Historical recollections honoring the Breitkopf bicentenary.

Mable I. HERSHBERGER. *The History and Development of the Processes of Music Printing*. Kent, Ohio, 1958 (Kentucky Microcards, Series B. Library Series, no. 36).   **81**
A Library Science master's thesis, diligently executed.

Paul MIES. "Musikalien einmal von Aussen gesehen," *Musikalienhandel*, 13 (1962), 15-16, 61-63.   **82**
[Davidsson 344].

Allan KOZINN. "Music Printing," *American Music Teacher*, vol. 27, no. 5 (May 1978), pp. 16-17.   **83**
A brief survey, with a few conspicuous errors but still useful.

J. Evan KREIDER. *The Printing of Music, 1480-1680*. Vancouver: Alcuin Society, 1980.   **84**
An appreciative keepsake, with nine illustrations.

Richard TARUSKIN. "Renaissance Favorites: Legacy of the Printer's Art," in *Renaissance Favorites*, vol. 1, no. 1 (1985), 2-6.   **85**
Appropriately casual but learned commentary to accompany program notes for the Waverly Consort, citing 16th-century appearances in print of their repertory.

M. Elisabeth Corrêa NORI and Paulo Alexandre C. VASCONCELOS. *A Arte de música impressa*. São Paulo: Prefeitura do Municípao de São Paulo, [198-].   **86**
[Cited in *Notes*, December 1990, p. 426; LC 90-127511]

Ros JOHNSTON. *The History of Music Printing: Some Ideas and Innovations*. Wellington, N. Z.: University of Victoria, Department of Library and Information Studies, [1990?] (Occasional Papers, 10).   **87**
[Not examined].

Franz ZAMAZAL. "Aus der Geschichte des Musiknotendrucks: II. Teil," pp. 126-32.   **88**
A photocopy, from an unlocated journal, is in the Poole papers. I have not found the source; my guess at a date is 1965.

C.   Coverage in General Sources

Music printing is often acknowledged briefly in reference books and general histories of music, as well as in histories of printing and of libraries in general. Typically, the statements are derivative and perfunctory. The essays below are of special significance, whether for particular details and emphases or because of the author's reputation, as noted in the annotations.

A number of early printers' manuals, discussed in the next chapter, include serious historical essays, among them Castro (1765), Momoro (1773), Krünitz (1806), Fétis on Duverger (1832, 1834), Laborde (1840), Bouchez and Henri Fournier (both 1854).

Charles BURNEY. *A General History of Music, from the Earliest Ages to the Present Period.* London: Printed for the Author, 1776-89.   **89**

Modern edition by Frank Mercer, London: Foulis Press; New York: Harcourt, Brace, 1935; reprinted New York: Dover, 1957.

Includes (*pace* Mercer's index) about thirty references to Walsh, mostly in connection with his editions of Italian opera, and a dozen more to other publishers from "Petruccio" forward. Burney may be generally less meticulous in his descriptions than Hawkins, and less astute in perceiving their relationships, but what events he noticed he described with sympathetic sensitivity.

John HAWKINS. *A General History of the Science and Practice of Music.* London: T. Payne, 1776.   **90**

New edition, London: Novello, Ewer, 1875, reprinted New York: Dover, 1963. (Page numbers are cited from this edition.)

Events in the history of music printing are introduced: i.e., the origins (pp. 379-80), sacred music from Petrucci through Phalèse (pp. 422-233, based mostly on Adami), the madrigal books (p. 448), the Tallis-Byrd monopoly (pp. 455-56, with a transcription of the privilege), Playford and the "new tied note" (pp. 733-37), and the major 18th-century innovations, notably engraving, traced back to the 17th century and *Parthenia*, with passing mention of Fougt (pp. 800-802).

Karl FALKENSTEIN. *Geschichte der Buchdruckerkunst in ihrer Entstehung und Ausbildung.* Leipzig: B. G. Teubner, 1840. **91**

Issued for the Gutenberg centenary ("Ein Denkmal zur vierten Säcular-Feier der Erfindung der Typographie"), with a brief discussion of "Notendruck" (pp. 376-77) and two inserted leaves of music for C. G. Reißiger's accompanied four-part *Lied mit Chor* ("als Probe des typographischen Notendruckes", with two typographical errors in the very first measure, as seen at the right). Verse 4 begins (with earnestly intended words but badly cadenced syllables): "Heil, Gutenberg!"

FIGURE 1: Vocal parts for the passage at left.

Antoine VIDAL. "Typographie et gravure musicales," in *Les instruments à archet*, vol. 3 (Paris: J. Claye, 1878), pp. 1-30.

A lavish display of miscellaneous facts, mostly on the 16th century but extending into the 19th, with seven copiously hand-drawn reconceptions of pages from early musical editions that need to be inspected closely to be appreciated. **92**

Karl FAULMANN. *Illustrierte Geschichte der Buchdruckerkunst.* Wien: A. Hartleben, 1882. **93**

"Der Musiknotendruck" (pp. 297-302) deals with 16th- and 17th-century events and ends with a list of major printers. "Der Musiknotensatz" (pp. 508-14) discusses Breitkopf and later practices. An impressive book.

Carl B. LORCK. *Handbuch der Geschichte der Buchdrucker-kunst*. Leipzig: J. J. Weber, 1882-83.   **94**
Fournier, Gando, and Duverger are discussed on pp. 147-48 of vol. 2, Breitkopf and others on pp. 321-26. Lorck does not intro-duce music printing in his more respected book, *Die Herstellung von Druckwerken* (1868), although he does so in his report on the 1873 Vienna world's exhibition (411 below).

Victor de PONTIGNY.   "Music-Printing," in Sir George Grove, *Dictionary of Music and Musicians* (London: Mac-millan, 1894), vol. 2, pp. 433-37.   **95**
Slightly expanded in the 2nd ed. (1904-10), vol. 3, pp. 323-28. "Printing of Music" is by Frank Kidson in the 3rd ed. (1927; vol. 4, pp. 253-56; also on the same pages in the 4th ed. 1940). In the 5th ed. (1954), William C. Smith covers "Engraving" (vol. 2, pp. 952-53) and Hubert J. Foss "Printing" (vol. 6, pp. 928-34). In the 6th ed. the texts by H. Edmund Poole and the present author, on "Printing and Publishing of Music" (vol. 15, pp. 232-74), are the basis for the 1990 *Music Printing and Publishing* handbook (57 above).

Franz DIETTRICH-KALKHOFF.   "Notendruck," in his *Ge-schichte der Notenschrift* (Jauer in Schlesien: Oskar Hellann, 1907), pp. 114-16.   **96**
Unlike the provocative discussion of "Notenkalligraphie" (pp. 104-13) just preceding, this one is unfortunately superficial.

"La estampación musical," *Enciclopedia universal ilustrada europeo-americana* (Barcelona: J. Espasa, [*ca*.1915]), vol. 37, pp. 731-43.   **97**
Impressively strong on Spanish and liturgical matters.

Johannes WOLF.   "Der Musikdruck," *Handbuch der Nota-tionskunde* (Leipzig: Breitkopf & Härtel, 1919), vol. 2, pp. 475-87.   **98**
A densely packed factual account, solidly based on scholarly authority as cited.

Karl SCHOTTENLOHER.   "Der Musiknotendruck," in his *Das alte Buch* (Berlin: Schmidt, 1921), pp. 224-37.   **99**

A chapter in one of the most respected and imaginative cultural histories of printing, unfortunately limited mostly to the 15th and 16th centuries. The same text appears in later editions, e.g., on pp. 242-56 of the "Dritte Auflage" (Braunschweig: Klinkhardt & Biermann, 1956).

Hanns BOHATTA. "Notenschrift und Notendruck," in his *Einführung in die Buchkunde* (Vienna: Gilhofer & Ranschburg, 1927), pp. 172-77.   **100**
A summary by a respected incunabulist, built around references to secondary sources.

Johannes WOLF. "Der Musikdruck," in *Handbuch der Bibliothekswissenschaft* (Leipzig: Harrassowitz, 1933) vol. 2, pp. 503-05.   **101**
In this edition of a standard German library science handbook, most of Wolf's discussion is given over to music printing. The post-war edition, in contrast, covers the topic in an essay by Alfons Ott, who was no less knowledgeable in music bibliography, but addresses matters mostly of music library management.

J. POORTENAAR. "Music-Printing," in his *The Art of the Book and Its Illustration* (London: G. G. Harrap; Philadelphia: J. B. Lippincott, 1935), pp. 169-71.   **102**
A summary of basic facts in a handsome collector's volume (also issued by the author in a Dutch edition, which I have not seen).

Lexikon des gesamten Buchwesens, edited by Karl Löffler and Joachim Kirchner. Leipzig: Hiersemann, 1936.   **103**
The 12 music entries (vol. 2, pp. 499-509) include "Musikalienhandel" by "Mz.," "Musiker-Erstausgaben" by Georg Kinsky, "Musiknotendruck" by F. Schröder, and "Musikverlag" by Constantin Schneider.
    Some entries are abridged and updated in Kirchner's *Lexikon des Buchwesens* (Stuttgart: Hiersemann, 1953), pp. 505-11.

Gustave REESE. "Printing and Engraving of Music," in Oscar Thompson, *The International Cyclopedia of Music and Musicians* (New York: Dodd, Mead, 1939), pp. 1441-43.   **104**

Masterful, as one would expect, but surprisingly dated. The same text appears in later editions through the 11th (1964), often on different pages.

Franco ABBIATI. *Storia della musica*, Milan: S. A. Fratelli Treves, 1939*ff.*   **105**
"L'invenzione della stampa nei trattati e nelle musiche" (vol. 1, pp. 327-37) is well illustrated, and strong on Petrucci.

Jos. SMITS VAN WAESBERGHE. "Muziekdruk," *Encyclopedie van de muziek*, (Amsterdam, Brussels: Elzevier, 1957) vol. 2, pp. 15-16.   **106**
A brief essay, the major surprise being attribution of single-impression typography to John Rastell in 1516 (see 128 below).

Albi ROSENTHAL. "Édition," in *Encyclopédie de la musique*, edited by François Lesure, Vladimir Fédorov, *et al.* (Paris: Fasquelle, 1958), vol. 1, pp. 684-87.   **107**
Complemented by Lesure's lists of "Éditeurs et antiquaires de musique" (vol. 1, pp. 141-52).
   The Rosenthal text also appears as "Édition musicale" in Marc Honegger's *Dictionnaire de la musique* (Paris: Bordas, 1976), part 2 ("Science de la musique: Formes, Technique, Instruments"), vol. 1, pp. 327-29.

Wilhelm Martin LUTHER and Richard SCHAAL. "Notendruck," *Die Musik in Geschichte und Gegenwart*, vol. 9 (Kassel: Bärenreiter, 1960-61), cols. 1667-95.   **108**
Luther's essay on incunabula (cols. 1667-79) and Schaal's on events after 1500 (cols. 1679*ff.*) are complemented by Schaal's text on publishing (538 below).

J. van VOORTHUYSEN. "Muziekdruk," *Algemene muziekencyclopedie* (Antwerp; Amsterdam: Zuid-Nederlandse Uitgeverij, 1961), vol. 5, pp. 83-90.   **109**
The summary chronology is particularly effective.

Claudio SARTORI. "Stampa musicale," in *La Musica (Enciclopedia storica, IV)*, edited by Guido M. Gatti and

Alberto Basso (Torino: Unione Tipografico-Editrice
Torinese, 1966), pp. 469-81.   **110**
"UTET" deserves respect for one of the finest of the encyclopedia surveys. Sartori's essay is in three sections: (1) "L'invenzione
della stampa musicale," (2) "L'opera del Petrucci e l'arte della
stampa nel XVI secolo," (3) "L'attività editoriali nei secoli se-
guenti." At the end is an extensive list of "Editori e stampatori"
(pp. 481-90), with dates of activity, arranged geographically (including entries under such areas as Cuba, India, Turkey, Japan,
and New Zealand).

W. Turner BERRY and H. Edmund POOLE. *Annals of
Printing: A Chronological Encyclopædia from the Earliest
Times to 1950*. London: Blandford, 1966.   **111**
Description of major events, with respectful attention to sources
and (as one would expect of the second author) an authoritative
placement of music in the context of the whole.

Henry RAYNOR. *A Social History of Music from the Middle
Ages to Beethoven*. London: Barrie & Jenkins, 1972.   **111a**
Chapter 19 ("Composer and Publisher," pp. 331-49) is especially
useful in its carefully conceived focus on the period around
1800. Chapter 8 (pp. 99-108) is on Petrucci and his successors.
Several other references may be traced through the index, in this
volume and in its sequel (*Music and Society since 1815*, ibid.).

Patrick MARCLAND. "Édition musicale," in *Larousse de la
musique*, edited by Antoine Goléa and Marc Vignal (Paris:
Larousse, 1982), vol. 1, pp. 506-07.   **112**
An overview, emphasizing music publishing, with details on the
Société des Auteurs, Compositeurs, et Éditeurs de Musique
(SACEM), division of royalties, and other business matters
(under "Les contrats"), as well as a section on "L'aspect com-
mercial," with a brief list of American and European publishers.

D. Special Topics

Parts of the historical literature of music bibliography also cohere
around several specific topics, among them incunabula and post-
incunabula, early engraving, stencilled music, and mosaic typogra-

phy. Other writings frustrate placement anywhere but under a heading called "miscellaneous."

Incunabula and Post-Incunabula

The topic has attracted specialists in early printing or in Renaissance music, whose work is generally respected in both communities. Its literature also includes the work of others who set out to survey the entire history but who, occasionally to our benefit, never get beyond the early years. Often an essay that emphasizes the fifteenth century will end with a hurried coda extending through the sixteenth or seventeenth, or on a few occasions into even later periods. See also Severin Corsten, *Der Buchdruck im 15. Jahrhundert: Eine Bibliographie* (Stuttgart: Hiersemann, 1988), pp. 124-25 ("Noten- und Musikdruck").

Johann Georg MEUSEL. "Beytrag zur Litterargeschichte der ersten Drucke mit musikalischen Noten," *Historisch-litterarisch-bibliographisches Magazin*, 2 (Zürich, 1790), 136-47. **113**

Printing music becomes particularly laborious when it requires both red and black ink: but who printed the first music and when? Meusel's search led him, alas, not to Italy for a visit to Padre Martini's library, nor to England to talk with Burney or Hawkins, but to a Bamberg missal of 1499, printed by Pfeyl (Meyer-Baer 43) and to a gradual printed in Basel by Jacob of Pforzheim (there are several extant candidates), both of which he describes briefly and quotes extensively.

Anton SCHMID. *Ottaviano dei Petrucci da Fossombrone, der erste Erfinder des Musiknotendruckes mit beweglichen Metalltypen, und seine Nachfolger im sechzehnten Jahrhunderte.* Wien: P. Röhrmann, 1845. **114**

A 27-page essay, followed by a brief synopsis of and transcriptions for about 50 editions, with commentary. Next come brief essays on about 60 16th-century music printers, with detailed citations of their books (pp. 112-308). Most of these are not duplicated in Schmid's *Cäcilie* series (1 above), which dates from these same years. The 21 facsimiles at the end ("Lithographirte Beilagen") are meticulously redrawn by hand.

Reprinted, Amsterdam: Grüner, 1968.

Another attempt to answer questions of what exactly came first and who did exactly what, mostly during the 15th century but extending briefly up to the 18th.

Robert Eitner comments on this book in his *Monatshefte für Musikgeschichte*, 32 (1900), 219-20 and 33 (1901), 159-60.

I have not seen Mantuani's earlier essay, "Über Notendrucke und ältesten Notendruck," *Litteraturblatt der Neuen Freien Presse* (Vienna, October 28, 1900).

Carl WENDEL. "Aus der Wiegenzeit des Notendruckes: ein Bericht über die Geschichte und die Hauptergebnisse der Noteninkunabel-Forschung," *Zentralblatt für Bibliothekswesen*, 19 (1902), 569-81.   **121**

A critical essay on the early scholarly literature on music printing, with comments on Schmid (both the Petrucci studies and the *Cäcilia* "Beiträge"), Chrysander, Weckerlin, Goovaerts, Vernarecci, Thürlings, Riemann, and Molitor.

Hermann SPRINGER. "Zur Musiktypographie in der Inkunabelzeit," in *Beiträge zur Bücherkunde und Philologie: August Wilmanns zum 25. März 1903 gewidmet* (Leipzig: Harrassowitz, 1903), pp. 173-80.   **122**

Concerned mostly with a 1482 Mainz missal printed by Reyser, a 1488 gradual by Wenßler and Kilchen, and the music printed by the younger Peter Schoeffer.

—. "Die musikalischen Blockdrucke des 15. und 16. Jahrhunderts," *Bericht über den zweiten Kongress der Internationalen Musikgesellschaft, Basel, 1906* (Leipzig: Breitkopf & Härtel, 1907), pp. 37-46.   **123**

A complementary study to the above, concerned with determining the exact process and surfaces used for printing the music in a selection of books from Gafurius (1480) to the 18th century.

Marius AUDIN. "Les origines de la typographie musicale," *Le bibliophile*, 1 (1931), 142-48, 223-29; 2 (1932), 13-19.

The Lyons printing historian surveys the early activity, inspired by two important new antiquarian music catalogues: Baer [Frankfurt] no. 585 and Maggs [London] no. 512. The parts cover (1) the beginnings, up to Wynkyn de Worde; (2) movable type, from the liturgical incunabula through Haultin; and (3) the Ballard monopoly and the round-note typography of the French Renaissance; 197 and 252 below are complementary studies. **124**

Otto KINKELDEY. "Music and Music Printing in Incunabula," *Papers of the Bibliographical Society of America*, 26 (1932), 89-118.   **125**
Always with special acknowledgement of earlier scholarship, the distinguished scholar-librarian and pioneer of American musicology begins with the treatises about music, continues with the printing processes, and ends with liturgical books. One admires the careful but incisive assertions; and as one senses the author's apology that he himself would never have the time to do the work, one also admires his aim of challenging his successors.

Julien TIERSOT. "Les incunables de la musique," *Bulletin du Bibliophile et du Bibliothècaire*, n. s., 13 (1934), 110-16.
Comments on the incunabula shown in a major Bibliothèque Nationale exhibition. (The exhibition, which also included manuscripts, paintings, and ephemera, is catalogued in *La Musique française du Moyen Âge à la Révolution*, Paris, 1934.)   **126**

Kathi MEYER-BAER. *Liturgical Music Incunabula: A Descriptive Catalogue.* London: The Bibliographical Society, 1962.   **127**
An attempt to provide an overview through the study of printing practices, as reflected in 257 titles that are cited briefly with details on their notational conception.

The structure of the work, and the constraint with which particulars are presented, make this a frustrating work to use. (Admittedly, the prospect of a full bibliography, with descriptive citations so as to identify the known variants, would have been a Herculean labor indeed, and not necessarily much more useful than what is seen here. The thought of how this book might have been better conceived leaves one concluding that there was probably no way that would have been both useful and convincing.) For happier evidence of the author's scholarship one must look instead to several preliminary essays, among them "Musikdruck in den liturgischen Inkunabeln von Wenssler und Kilchen," *Gutenberg Jahrbuch 1935*, pp. 117-26, and "New Facts on the Printing of Music Incunabula," *Papers of the American Musicological Society, 1940* (1948), pp. 80-87; also (and perhaps especially) "Der Musikdruck in Inkunabeln: ein übersehenes Hilfsmittel zur Beschreibung," *Libri*, 10 (1960), 105-10.

Alec Hyatt KING. "The Significance of John Rastell in Early Music Printing," *The Library*, 6th series, 26 (1971), 197-214. **128**

This cautiously constructed argument, based on a wide range of details, makes a convincing case for Rastell's development of single-impression music typography before Attaingnant, even if it never does establish an exact date for his activity. The red herring turns out to be poor Haultin, leaving us to wonder why Le Bé said what he did. Even more curious is why at least two modern writers, in widely scattered settings — Smits van Waesberghe (106) in Holland in 1957 and Darch (275) in Canada in 1972, neither one with a notable reputation as a scholarly music bibliographer and neither of whom reveals his sources — should have stumbled across the right answer without knowing what they were saying, when the consensus among experts was still to repeat the misconstrued assignment to an unlocated Haultin.

—. "The 500th Anniversary of Music Printing," *Musical Times*, 114 (1973), 1220-23. **129**

Celebrates a Gradual, undated but printed in the early 1470s in south Germany (the evidence for calling it a "Constance Gradual" is inconclusive), which may predate Ulrich Han's 1476 Roman Missal (Hain 11366) as the first music printed from movable type.

Domenico MASSEO. *La stampa musicale nel periodo degli incunaboli: Catalogo degli incunaboli musicali non liturgici.* Dissertation, University of Pavia, 1976-77. **130**

Devoted to the treatises only, not the service books. [*RILM*, 1977, no. 6103].

Maria PRZYWECKA-SAMECKA. *Początki drukarstwa muzycznego w Europie wiek XV.* Wrocław: Ossolineum, 1981 (Prace Wrocławskiego towarszystewa naukowego, seria A, nr. 221). **131**

An overview of music incunabula, with a list of editions by country and city. A preliminary survey of Germany and Switzerland appears as "Początki drukarstwa muzycznego w Niemcych i Szwajcarii," *Roczniki Biblioteczne*, 21 (1977), 91-113. See also her "Problematik des Musiknotendruckes in der Inkunabelzeit," *Gutenberg Jahrbuch 1978*, pp. 51-56.

Stanley BOORMAN. "Early Music Printing: Working for a Specialized Market," in Gerald P. Tyson and Sylvia S. Wagonheim, *Print and Culture in the Renaissance: Essays on the Advent of Printing in Europe* (Newark: University of Delaware Press, 1986), pp. 222-45.   **132**
Complementing Boorman's other studies of the great printer (737), this study explores Petrucci's contribution to the rise of music publishing, as it hypothesizes the operation of the early music press in its economic and cultural settings and suggests a basic "theory of the press" for early music.

The cultural setting of the music printer is emphasized in the author's "Early Music Printing: An Indirect Contact with the Raphael Circle," in *Renaissance Studies in Honor of Craig Hugh Smith* (Florence: Barbèra, 1985), pp. 533-54.

Mary Kay DUGGAN. *Italian Music Incunabula: Printers and Type*. Berkeley: University of California Press, 1992.   **133**
The first of a projected three-volume study of music incunabula, with descriptive bibliographical citations, concordances, and other reference guides. Based on a doctoral dissertation, "Italian Music Incunabula: Printers and Typefonts" (University of California, Berkeley, 1981).

The author also explains her analytical practices in "A System for Describing Fifteenth-Century Music Type," *Gutenberg Jahrbuch 1984*, pp. 67-76.

In addition, Heartz's Attaingnant study (697) includes a valuable summary of early 16th-century music printing in general, in chapters 4 and 5 ("Music and the Book Trade" and "Final Years: Followers," pp. 105-168). Among the writings cited in Chapter 6, specific mention should be made of Pogue (698, 705) on Lyons; for Italy, Bautier-Regnier (709), Haar (710), Cardamone (711), Cusick (729), and almost all of the writings under Venice (734-41); Kittel (804) for Germany, among others that deal mostly with later periods, as well as Refardt and Pfister under Basel (806-07); several under the Low Countries (pp. 289-93), Møller (830) and Davidsson (833, 835-38) for Scandinavia; Przywecka-Samecka for Poland (843) and Hungary (844); and Barris Muños, Anglès, Madurell, and Odriozola, (856-60) for Spain.[2] Note also Eitner (60), Antoniazzi (74), Taruskin (85), Wolf (98), Bohatta (100), Reese (104), and Abbiati (105) above.

Eduard Bernoulli's *Aus Liederbüchern der Humanistenzeit* (Leipzig: Breitkopf & Härtel, 1910) may be subtitled, "Eine bibliographische und Notentypographische Studie," but it is bibliographical only in its concern for transmission of early 16th-century German song texts, and typographical only in its concern for notational intent: layout and compositorial practice are not considered.

The question arises: when does the "early" period of music printing *really* end? For three centuries general incunabulists have used 1500, so as to make their work both finite and perfectable. There is widespread sentiment that 1540 or 1550 would be more appropriate, although for music bibliography, 1500, thanks to Petrucci, is very convenient. After 1500, what is the next landmark? While 1525 (which is a rounded year at the end of a quiescent period) or 1526 (or 1527 for those who may wish to argue calendars) would reflect Attaingnant's innovations, they would reflect on nothing else, so as to imply that his greatness lies in his exclusive domination of the field over the next fifteen years; 1530 recognizes Egenolff in Frankfurt and Moderne and Briand in southern France, these however being more curious than profound events; 1540 is more momentous, thanks to the advent of music printing in major commercial centers, although Venice and Nürnberg actually entered the picture a few years earlier and Antwerp a few years later. The rounded date of 1550 is perhaps the handiest. By this date the major commercial models and technological practices were "in place," and would continue with very few changes until 1700. The few important developments still seem scattered

---

2. This is the era of multiple-impression printing, and a perennial question about this method involves registration of the two press runs. Usually the press work is so accurate as to be virtually flawless. For an example of registration so faulty as to produce a wondrous strange modal transposition, see J. Eric Hunt, *Cranmer's First Litany, 1544, and Merbecke's Book of Common Prayer Noted, 1550* (London: Society for Promoting Christian Knowledge; New York: Macmillan, 1939), pp. 60-63.

and cumulative, especially in contrast to the more definitive events that took place within roughly a decade around 1700 with the advent of engraving, and just after 1900 with the advent of sound recordings.

Early Engraving

Theodor BÖTTCHER. "Musiknoten auf Kupferstichen," *Monatshefte für Musikgeschichte*, 8 (1876), 121-25.   **134**
On the late 16th-century Flemish-Italian *Bildmotetten* and early 17th-century music engravings, most of them Bavarian.

Max SEIFFERT. *Wat leeren ons de schilderijen en prenten der zestiende eeuw over de instrumentale begeleiding van den zang en den oorsprong van de muziekgravure.* Leipzig: C. F. W. Siegel; Amsterdam: G. Alsbach, 1920 (Vereeniging voor Nederlandsche Muziekgeschiedenis, 39).   **135**
Discusses 13 of the *Bildmotetten*, with elegant scholarship but grubby halftone reproductions.

Further studies of the history of music engraving in the sixteenth century may represent one of the most promising topics of future scholarship. What was the precise date and place of printing for the Vienna lute book of Francesco da Milano; or of the *Bildmotetten* from a half-century later? How much music is unrecorded in the bibliographical records of music? What inspired Verovio, or Sadelar, or William Hole, or Nicolas Vallet, to work on copper? Music bibliographers have fascinating questions to ask, even if the answers promise to be more superficial than the events deserve.

Stencilled Music

Eva J. O'MEARA. "Notes on Stencilled Choir-Books," *Gutenberg Jahrbuch 1933*, pp. 169-85.   **136**
Essay on books, mostly from 18th-century France.

Adam GOTTRON. "Beiträge zur Geschichte der kirchenmusikalischen Schablonendrucke in Mainz," *Gutenberg Jahrbuch 1938*, pp. 187-93.   **137**
Complements the O'Meara study.

Albert RODRIGUES. "Die Schablonendrucke des Paters Thomas Bauer in der Stadtbibliothek Mainz," *Gutenberg Jahrbuch 1973*, pp. 85-99.   **138**

Useful as an updating of the two earlier works, but especially for two color illustrations (pp. 88-89) that show how stunningly beautiful these books really are. A context for this essay is provided in Hellmut Rosenfeld, "Der Gebrauch der Schablone für Schrift und Kunst seit der Antike und das Schablonierte Buch des 18. Jahrhunderts," *ibid.*, pp. 71-84.

Mosaic Typography

The story of Breitkopf, Fournier, and their associates is exciting, partly because the personalities were so strong and the challenges they faced were so great, partly because it is hard to imagine their processes ever being very successful. Modern scholars, quick to justify most innovations on grounds that they were less labor-intensive, are no doubt correct in wondering whether the compositor's work with this type could possibly have been less cumbersome than the presswork needed to run off copies from engraved plates. The attractiveness of the new method really lay elsewhere: the music, conceived to resemble the literary texts in printed books, would appeal to music lovers with bibliophilic tastes; and the bibliophiles usually had more money to spend than the musicians, who found engraved editions more suitable to their tastes. The miscalculation of the typographers perhaps failed to recognize that their intended audience of cultivated readers usually interacted with these same musicians in the course of taking lessons, playing chamber music, and presenting concerts.

In addition to the collective essays below, see also the type specimens of the innovators themselves (for Breitkopf 327 below, for Fournier 328, for Fleischman 324, and for Rosart 331).

Ludwig VOLKMANN. "J. G. I. Breitkopf und P. S. Fournier le jeune: Ein Beitrag zur Geschichte des Notendrucks und der Schriftgießerei im 18. Jahrhundert," *Gutenberg Jahrbuch 1928*, pp. 118-41, and *Gutenberg Jahrbuch 1929*, pp. 312-14.   **139**

A summary of the working relationship reflected in the development of mosaic types.

Marius AUDIN.   "Gottlob Breitkopf et la typographie musicale," *Gutenberg Jahrbuch 1950,* pp. 245-54.   **140**
The account of Breitkopf repeats well-known facts, but the comments on his successors (pp. 252-54) are notable.

H. Edmund POOLE. "New Music Types in the Eighteenth Century," *Journal of the Printing Historical Society,* 1 (1965), 21-38; 2 (1966), 23-44.   **141**
A discussion of the mid 18th-century inventions of mosaic music typography of Fleischman, Rosart, Breitkopf, Fournier, and Fougt. Here, perhaps more than in any other of his studies, one is impressed by Poole's painstaking research practices and wide perspectives as a printer, musician, and scholar.

Miscellaneous Topics

A. G. CAMUS. *Histoire et procédés du polytypage* . . . Paris, 1801.   **141a**
In the mid-1780s the Paris firm of Hoffman prepared music using this process, as discussed on pp. 38-52.
   Archival records of this activity, including music proofs, are in the Newberry Library (Case Wing MS fZ 311 .H673).

Frank J. METCALF. "Cut Hymn Books," *American Collector,* 3 (1926-27), 159-61.   **142**
Discussion of one of the curiosities of music printing, the so-called "Dutch door" hymnals, with pages sliced horizontally so as to allow users to match any setting of the words above with any tune below. The practice was not widespread, although its history is yet to be traced. Metcalf identifies books printed in Exeter, New Hampshire, between 1818 and 1825, and shows an example in which the slice produces a larger upper part with the words, almost square in shape and with its own title page, and an oblong lower part with the music. He also refers to such books printed in Chicago in 1880, and in London in 1888. I have also seen several tall octavo hymnals with cut pages published in Sweden around 1800, as well as several others in Swedish for Lutheran congregations published in the American midwest toward the end of the century.

Edmund H. FELLOWES. "Misprints and Errors," *Music and Letters*, 17 (1936), 371-73. **143**
An eminent scholar shares his mischievous delight on discovering the odd musical effects that early compositors produced by setting music type upside down.

Karl Gustav FELLERER. "Opernbearbeitungen im Musikverlag um die Wende des 18./19. Jahrhunderts," in *Musik und Verlag: Karl Vötterle zum 65. Geburtstag* (Kassel: Bärenreiter, 1968), 279-88. **144**
On the advent of the published "Klavierauszug" and its impact on operatic tastes and activities.

Jens Peter LARSEN. "Der musikalische Stilwandel um 1750 im Spiegel der zeitgenössischen Pariser Verlagskataloge," in *Musik und Verlag: Karl Vötterle zum 65. Geburtstag* (Kassel: Bärenreiter, 1968), 410-23. **145**
Reflections on the impact on taste of published music newly available throughout Europe.

D. W. KRUMMEL. "Oblong Format in Early Music Books," *The Library*, 5th series, 26 (1971), 312-24. **146**
The formats described in early printer's manuals may be seen in a large proportion of the partbooks from the 16th century. Musicians' preference for oblong pages has persisted, so that at times all oblong formats, whether quarto, sexto (occasionally), and octavo, are often referred to as "music format." (The distinction between upright and oblong is analogous to the distinction between "portrait" amd "landscape" images among historians of the pictorial arts, and recently in the parlance of computerized printing, although these latter terms are not commonly used among bibliographers.)

Cecil HOPKINSON. "The Earliest Miniature Scores," *Music Review*, 33 (1972), 138-44. **147**
Traces the origins to Pleyel's edition of Haydn soon after 1800, mentioning the later editions of Carli and Heckel.
The topic is explored further in Rita Benton, "Pleyel's *Bibliothèque Musicale*," ibid., 37 (1975), 1-4, and Hans Lenneberg,

"Revising the History of the Miniature Score," Music Library Association, *Notes*, 42 (1988), 258-61.

Mary WEDGEWOOD. "Avant-garde Music: Some Publication Problems," *Library Quarterly*, 46 (1976), 136-52. **148**
Avant-garde music creates problems involving the physical object, graphic details, and commercial distribution. Solutions involve computerization, periodicalization, and self-publishing.

Geoffrey Richard HILL. *Music Printing and Publishing: The Transition from Movable Type to Copper- and Pewter-Plate Engraving.* M. Litt. thesis (Graphics), Newcastle-upon-Tyne, 1978. **149**
[*Doctoral Dissertations in Musicology*, 1984, p. 113.]

Günther BROSCHE. "Das musikalische Verlagswesen zur Zeit Joseph Haydns," in *Joseph Haydn in seiner Zeit* (Eisenstadt: Burgenländische Landesregierung, 1982), pp. 270-75. **150**
An overview of 18th-century music publishing in general, focused on Vienna.

B. C. STYLES. *Music Typesetting.* Ph.D. dissertation, Cambridge University, 1984/85. **151**
[Cited in *Doctoral Dissertations in Musicology*, May 1984-November 1985 (1986).]

Andreas BALLSTÄDT and Tobias WIDMAIER. *Salonmusik: Zur Geschichte und Funktion einer bürgerlichen Musikpraxis.* Wiesbaden, Stuttgart: Franz Steiner, 1989 (*Archiv für Musikwissenschaft*, Beiheft 38). **152**
A detailed analysis of a topic as vast as it is ill-defined. The summary of activities in Paris in the 1830s and 1840s (pp. 28-69) touches on the importance of the publishers. The larger discussion, of German salon music in the last half of the century, also includes Widmaier's valuable essay on "Musikverlag und Musikaliendistribution" (pp. 79-124). Also pertinent are Anhang II ("Musikalien-Leihanstalten im Deutschen Sprachgebiet," pp. 372-76), with names of 56 shops and valuable notes on sources; Anhang IV ("Salonmusiktitel," pp. 382-83), with statistical anal-

yses of the album repertory ("Verzeichnis der Salonalben," pp. 390-95); and the illustrations at the end, many of which show music covers for series and for individual titles.

Katherine BERGERON. *Representation, Reproduction, and the Revival of Gregorian Chant at Solesmes*. Ph.D. dissertation, Cornell University, 1989. **153**

An interpretive study of the notational innovations and, notably in Chapter 2 (pp. 62-105), their realization in typographic letter forms. The ideas of Walter Benjamin and Roland Barthes are crucial to the viewpoints. The argument that the aesthetic of William Morris was a causal as well as a contemporaneous event is explored.

Michael TWYMAN. "Music Method Books," in his *Early Lithographed Books: A Study of the Design and Production of Improper Books in the Age of the Hand Press* (London: Farrand Press, Private Libraries Association, 1990), pp. 103-25. **154**

An extended survey of the early production with pertinent observations on the graphic design, richly illustrated with both overviews of layout and details of calligraphic execution. Several footnotes mention the author's forthcoming specialized study on *Lithographed Music: The First Fifty Years*, to include discussions of particular major publishers. Both texts presumably make special use of the collection of early music lithography assembled by the late Hermann Baron, which the author subsequently acquired for the University of Reading.

In quantitative terms, what is the magnitude of the output of printed music since Gutenberg's day? Any simple answer is sure to be as arguable as it is stupefying. For all the evidence that speaks to the basic question itself (mostly extant copies and bibliographical citations) there is also, perhaps understandably, little evidence that anyone has been so perverse as to wish to address it. It is useful and important insofar as it stimulates questions that are more manageable and more interesting.

It should be apparent from the outset that we can never agree on what to count, because what we choose to ignore is what particularly fascinates us. If we count anthologies rather than the titles in them (as library cataloguing practice does, almost of necessity), we ignore the fact that we use these books mostly for their convenient access to their individual titles. If we count editions rather than bibliographical variants (only a small proportion of which has ever been identified), we ignore the very event that scholarly bibliographers find invariably fascinating and often textually or historically significant. If we work at the national level and attempt to exclude imported music (which is harder to do than one might expect), we ignore the basic importance of publication itself in expanding musical demands to wider audiences. Furthermore, if we attempt to place all of these data in a historical perspective with the intention of discovering trends and suggesting causes, we are encumbered by the fact that most all of the music after 1700 is undated. And how much music from earlier periods has been lost over the course of history?[3]

The *International Inventory of Musical Sources* (RISM: 951 below), purports to cover the output prior to *ca*. 1800. To its total of about 80,000 entries in its "A-1" series, anthologies and printed liturgica can be added, as well as a factor for items no longer extant, so as to suggest a total of 100,000 titles from this period. Of these, perhaps 90,000 date from after 1700. The growth curve is implied by the successive major bibliographies of music imprints: 300 incunabula; 100 from the period 1501-1525 (60 from Petrucci, 40 from others); 300 from 1526-40 (200 of these from Attaingnant); 4,000 from 1540-1600 (estimating becomes increasingly conspicuous); 5,000 from the seventeenth century.

The nineteenth-century output is even more conjectural. Pazdirek (944 below) lists about a million music titles in print in 1800, although the frequency with which one finds titles he missed suggests a total probably several times as great. At the national and regional level, I have estimated the British production between 1800 and 1914 at nearly a million items, as reflected in

---

3. The classic rule of thumb (never tested, to my knowledge) holds that for every four extant titles there is one title lost. The rate of survival is presumed to be higher for books that were intended to be cherished, and lower for ephemera (such as musical broadside ballads), and material that was intended to be heavily used (such as chamber music parts, as well as songs and piano solos issued as sheet music, except when these were fortunate enough to be collected in binders' volumes).

specific totals of registrations at Stationers Hall that rise from 150 to 11,436 a year, to which one must add an indeterminate number for other titles that were not registered; see my essay in the Athlone History for *The Romantic Age* (680 below), pp. 47-50. For the United States, an estimate of 1,652,100 musical editions issued prior to 1951 is similarly based mostly on copyright figures: see "Counting Every Star," *Yearbook of Inter-American Musical Research*, 10 (1974), p. 186. The production from France is probably somewhat greater, that from Germany considerably greater still. The production from the rest of the world can only wildly be guessed at. The proliferation over the twentieth century may slowly have tapered off, for better or worse. For purposes of a rough estimate, a comprehensive database of printed music since Gutenberg's day would include perhaps ten million titles. The figure seems safe to accept until anyone should come up with evidence that would question it.

These totals no doubt show many biases, not the least of them being the increasing production of single short works at the expense of anthologies, beginning around 1700 with the rise of music engraving. A useful way to describe this change is through totals for the most prolific composers, as seen in the *International Inventory of Musical Sources*. The RISM "charts" are as follows:

1. Mozart 3,444	14. Paisiello 534	27. Arnold 283
2. Pleyel 2,285	15. Hoffmeister 452	28. Lasso 281
3. Haydn 2,262	16. Kozeluch ... 448	29. Gluck 273
4. Handel 1,580	17. Clementi 437	30. Sterkel 265
5. Steibelt 948	18. Shield 431	31. Cambini 262
6. Hook 940	19. Méhul 414	32. Devienne ... 259
7. Dibdin 696	20. Viotti 401	33. Zumsteeg .. 254
8. Grétry 684	21. Gyrowetz ... 387	34. J. C. Bach .. 249
9. Vanhal 683	22. Krommer ... 355	35. Giordani 246
10. Dalayrac ... 659	23. Winter 302	36. Cimarosa ... 243
11. Dussek 650	24. Himmel 288	" Corelli 243
12. Arne 592	25. Purcell 284	
13. Gelinek 589	" Storace 284	

The figures for particular composers show only a few surprises: the important reason for including them here is to illustrate a basic change in the nature of the musical publication around 1700.

Of the 37 composers, all but four date from the late eighteenth century: Handel (3) from the early eighteenth, Purcell (25) and Corelli (36) from the turn of the eighteenth, and Lasso (28) from the sixteenth.

The ascendancy of music engraving marks the beginning of the concept of "sheet music," in the sense of publications of only a few pages. Many broadsides were issued before 1700, and many thick books after 1700. The typical musical edition from earlier periods, however, was expected to be bound and placed on a library shelf; the typical edition from later periods was intended to be used on a music rack. The totals are still very approximate,[4] and corrections upwards and downwards are surely in order, but so as perhaps to cancel each other: the early material is less likely to survive because of the ravages of time, but more likely to survive because it looks and functions more like other printed books than does music from later periods, and because it was printed on more durable paper.

---

4. They represent in fact the simple subtraction of a composer's first entry number from the last. I have not taken cancelled or interpolated numbers into account. The figures become even more questionable (and the simplistic process of calculating them all the more justifiable) when one recalls that British and American libraries mostly held fast to a terminal date of 1800, whereas continental libraries often included post-1800 holdings selectively by composer. (Albrechtsberger probably belongs in the above list as well, for instance.) Furthermore, the RISM list is based primarily on library reports, with only occasional checking to reconcile variant information.

III.

The Technology of Music Printing

THE PRACTICES OF MUSIC PRINTING are described in several different kinds of writings. First are the technical manuals for aspiring music printers, who must know both the skills and the tastes, along with the popular accounts for the general public, curious to learn about the tastes but not the skills. The two may be different in spirit, but they are combined here (section A), since they often prove to be indistinguishable. This may seem surprising, although in truth most writings, as they address one audience or the other, do justice to neither. No manual can supplant the guidance of a master printer, and no popular account will be as romantic or as informative as a visit to the premises.

Writings for printing specialists themselves — type specimens, reports of trade organizations, and patent records — come next (section B), followed by writings on the aesthetics and legibility of printed music (section C).

A fourth literature includes modern reconstructions of early practices, by scholars whose knowledge of the specialty usually comes at second hand. The goal is to understand and respect historical artifacts and processes, as evidence of the music that it embodies and the society that saw its creation. Skill and, to a degree even taste, are objective and depersonalized. Writings of this fourth kind are dispersed through the other chapters of this book.

A.   Descriptive and Instructional Literature

Skilled printers (mostly craftsmen, but often craftswomen, notably in late eighteenth-century France: cf. 170 below) have been understandably reluctant to share the secrets of what they actually do. Nor perhaps could they even if they wanted to: years of apprenticeship, involving private instruction and personal criticism, are the best way to train the eye and the hands, and produce the skills and tastes. Reading an instruction book about music engraving, typesetting, and presswork is like reading a book on how to play the violin. This may explain why the technical and the popular literature are inseparable: the best of the former is mostly a more rigorous and less patronizing version of the latter.

Scattered through the literature are a few titles that deserve special respect, landmarks that provide some of our best evidence of historical practices. Honors should be paid to Moxon (1683-84), even if he makes precious little specific mention of music; the Fournier *Traité* (1765), as a first attempt to view present practice in its historical context; the D'Almaine pamphlet (1840s?), which gives us our best picture of the operation of a nineteenth-century music shop; and the detailed manuals by Marahrens (1870), Robert (1902, 1926), Witten (1925), Hader (1948), Ross (1971), and Chlapik (1987), trained craftsmen who by sharing their experience also suggest the respect their critical judgment deserves.

Substantial works for the specialist music engraver or compositor assume a considerable degree of musical literacy. In contrast, the brief sections in many of the general printer's manuals often begin with an explanation of the rudiments of musical notation itself. Even in the most patronizing discussions one occasionally spots the odd fact or perspective that the specialized writings had taken for granted. For the most part, however, the general writings are useful mostly as a reminder that those who prepare the printing surfaces are not necessarily able to read the text that they are setting. A few, to be sure, are mostly recitations of well-known facts, slanted, if not perhaps so as to divert the discussion away from any crucial trade secrets, at least to promote a greater appreciation of the craft heritage.

Bibliographies of Printers' Manuals

Philip GASKELL, Giles BARBER, and Georgina WARRI-LOW. "An Annotated List of Printers' Manuals to 1850," *Journal of the Printing Historical Society*, 4 (1968), 11-31.
The landmark list, with 23 titles in English, 19 in French, 23 in German, and one in Spanish. Its models are the list of twelve titles in Appendix VII (pp. 442-44) of the 1962 edition of Moxon (160), and Herbert Davis, "The Art of Printing: Joseph Moxon and his Successors," *Printing and Graphic Arts*, 5 (1957), 17-33. Gaskell's contribution, devoted to English-language titles and with several American imprints, is the only one that is not superseded in the two works below.   **155**

Giles BARBER. *French Letterpress Printing: A List of French Printing Manuals . . . , 1567-1900.* Oxford: Oxford Bibliographical Society, 1969 (Occasional Papers, 5).   **156**
Successor to the author's section of the above.

Martin BOGHARDT. " 'Der in der Buchdruckerei wohl unterrichtete Lehr-Junge': Bibliographische Beschreibung der im deutschsprachigen Raum zwischen 1608 und 1847 erschienenen typographischen Lehrbücher," *Philobiblon*, 27 (1983), 5-57.   **157**
Successor to the Warrilow section in 155 above.

Bigmore & Wyman (961 below) is also a rich source for technical writings on printing of all kinds.

Hieronymus HORNSCHUH. Ορθοτυπογραφια: *hoc est, Instructio typographicas correcturis.* Leipzig: Michaël Lantzenberger, 1608.   **158**
The *Orthotypographia*, one of the most important manuals before Moxon, mentions music only briefly but shows a specimen of Robert Granjon's music type (7 mm. staff), designated as "Welsche Noten" (p. 44).
Reprinted with a new introduction by Martin Boghardt, Darmstadt: Renata Raecke, 1983.

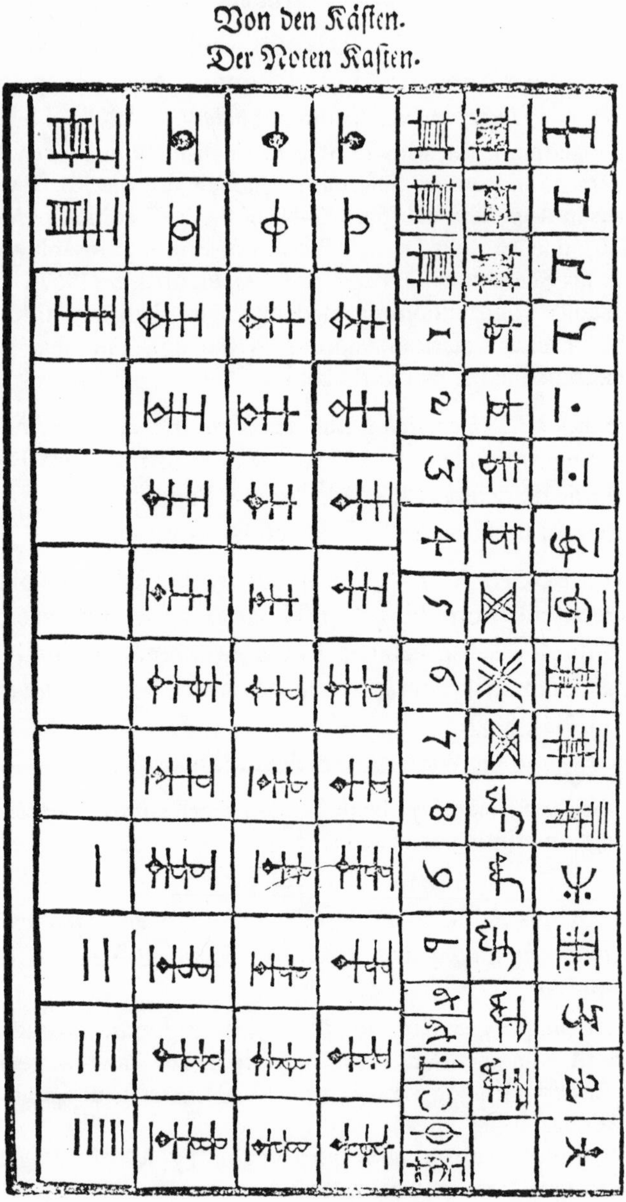

Von den Kästen.
Der Noten Kasten.

FIGURE 2. Music case layout in Veitor's *Formatbüchlein* (159).

Johann Ludwig VEITOR. *Neuauffgesetztes Format-Büchlein*, in Druck verfertiget von Jacob Redinger. Frankfurt: Johann Georg Drullmann, 1679. **159**

Page 66 (at left) shows the earliest illustration I know of a music case layout, for a font of nested type with 93 sorts.

Reprinted with a new introduction by Martin Boghardt, Darmstadt: Renata Raecke, 1983.

Often appended to this 1679 book is the edition with music for Johann Rist's version of the *Depositio cornuti typographici*. The imprint reads, Frankfurt: Johann-Georg Drullmann, 1677; the music is on b2^v, d3^v, d4^v, and d5^v.

Joseph MOXON. *Mechanick Exercises, Or the Doctrine of Handy-Works Applied to the Art of Printing*. London: Moxon, 1683-84. **160**

Bibliographers of all subjects need to know this book; unfortunately it contains only a few references specifically on music.

Of the several reprints and new editions, of special importance is *Mechanick Exercises, Or the Whole Art of Printing*, edited with extensive and invaluable notes by Herbert Davis and Harry Carter (London: Oxford University Press, 1958, 1962; reprinted New York: Dover, 1978).

Jacques JAUGEON. *Description et perfection des arts et mestiers: Des arts, de construire les caractères, de graver les poinçons de lettres, de fondre les lettres, d'imprimer les lettres et de relier les livres, Tome Premier*. Paris, 1704. **161**

A manuscript, the original of which is in the Bibliothèque de l'Institut de France, MS. 2741; two early copies are in the Bibliothèque Nationale. The study on printing was the first part of a projected series of descriptive reports on all of the crafts, undertaken by the Académie Royale des Sciences. This part was completed but never published, although its engraved plates ("*Planches*") are known through extant copies, some of them pulled separately and now scattered through several collections, others seen in the *Médailles sur les principaux événements du Règne de Louis le Grand* (Paris, 1702). Fournier almost certainly used the text in his *Encyclopédie* article on typography (166) and in his other writings. For background see André Jammes, *La réforme de la typographie royale sous Louis XIV: le Grandjean*

(Paris: Paul Jammes, 1961), and his "Académisme et typographie: The Making of the Romain du Roi," *Journal of the Printing Historical Society*, 1 (1965), 71-97.

Music printing is discussed in chapter 9 ("Des caractères de musique," pp. 207-15, with a full-page chart before p. 209). In the *Livre second*, p. 213, a paragraph is devoted to the special mould needed for casting music type ("Du moule à notes de musique"), a matter of special interest to Harry Carter in his modern translation of Fournier's *Manuel* (165).

Johann Heinrich Gottfried ERNESTI. *Die Woleingerichtete Buchdruckerey*. Nürnberg: J. A. Endters Erben, 1721. **162**
One of the first manuals to discuss page layout for music. The opening "Summarische Nachricht" includes biographies and portraits of early Nuremberg printers (Petreius among them). Later sections show "Choral und Figural-Noten" (pp. 38-39), "Ein Noten-Kasten" and "Ein Kasten mit geschriebenen Noten" (the case layout, for diamond notes on p. 54, for rounded notes on p. 55), "Unterricht von den Noten" (explaining signs and note names, p. 136), and oblong formats (pp. 66-75).

The same text also appears in the 1733 edition.

Die so nöthig als nützliche Buchdruckerkunst und Schriftgiesserey. Leipzig: Christian Friedrich Geßner, 1740.   **163**
Geßner and Johan Georg Hager explain musical signs and pitch levels in "Unterricht für einen Setzer, so viel ihm von der Music zu wissen nöthig ist" ("Instructions for a compositor, as much as one really needs to know about music," vol. 1, pp. 142-43).

Reprinted, Hannover: Schlüter, 1981.

A second manual by the authors, entitled *Der in der Buchdruckerei wohl unterrichtete Lehr-Junge, oder: bey der Löblichen Buchdruckerkunst nöthige und nützliche Anfangsgründe* (Leipzig: Geßner, 1743), includes "Kleine Canon Noten" and "Tertia Noten" (f. 7ᵛ) as part of an "Abdruck, oder Verzeichniß derjenigen Teutschen Schriften, welche in der Ehrhardtischen Schriftgießerey allhier befindlich sind. Leipzig, 1743."

Jacob CREED. "A Demonstration of the Possibility of Making a Machine that shall Write Extempore Voluntaries, or other Pieces of Music, as Fast as Any Master shall be Able

to Play Them upon an Organ, Harpsichord, &c.," *Philosophical Transactions*, vol. 44/ii, no. 483 (1747), p. 446.   **164**
The Rev. Mr. Creed's early attempt to link music printing and music automation is also described in Johann Beckmann, *A History of Inventions, Discoveries, and Origins*, translated by William Johnston, 4th revised ed. (London: Henry Bohn, 1846), p. 12.

Pierre-Simon FOURNIER. *Manuel typographique, utile aux gens de lettres, & à ceux qui exercent les différentes parties de l'Art de l'Imprimerie.* Paris: Barbou, 1764-66.   **165**
A general printer's manual, in which vol. 1 (1764), "De la taille," includes the discussions "Du pleinchant" (pp. 28-39), "Du pleinchant, rouge et noir" (pp. 40-43), "De la musique: Caractères anciens" (pp. 45-48), and "De la musique: Caractères nouveaux" (pp. 49-61), with illustrations of the type (pp. 280-91).

Vol. 2 (1766) appeared after the publication of Fournier's general history of music printing (44 above), and the Gandos' response (168 below). It includes Fournier's "Réponse à une mémoire publié en 1766 per MM. Gando, au sujet des caractères de fonte pour la musique" (pp. 289-306; see also pp. 28-63).

In the English translation, *Fournier on Typefounding*, with notes by Harry Carter (London: Soncino Press, 1930; new ed., with Carter's new foreword and supplementary bibliography, New York: Burt Franklin, 1957) see Chapters 6 ("Cutting Plain-Chant," pp. 48-56), 7 ("Cutting Red and Black Plain-Chant," pp. 57-60), 8 ("Cutting Old-Fashioned Music," pp. 61-63), 9 ("Cutting the New Music" [i.e., Fournier's new mosaic type], pp. 64-76), and 27 ("Founding Music Types," pp. 186-88) as well as the introduction and pp. 156, 231, and 239-44.

The "Réponse" (pp. 289-306) is reprinted in the Archives de l'édition musicale française, Tome IX (Genève: Minkoff, 1972).

Fournier's several letters in the *Mercure de France* (May 1756, pp. 121-26; January 1757, pp. 85-95; and January 1759, pp. 179-88 among them) deal primarily with the history of printing in general, and only tangentially with music.

"Procédés de la gravure . . . en musique . . . ," in the *Recueil de planches, sur les sciences, les arts libéraux, et les arts méchaniques, avec leur explication . . .* , 4e livraison (Paris: Brasson, David, le Breton, Durand, 1765), pp. 227-31.   **166**

Justly famous as the first extended and published description of music engraving. The explanatory text appears on pp. 227-29; pp. 230-31 are headed "Gravure en lettres, en géographie et en la musique." The illustration on p. 231 ("Defehrt fecit. Musique grav. par Mad. de Lusse") is widely reproduced. (It is usually in the fifth volume of the *Planches*, the 2e livraison being customarily bound in two parts.)

Denis Diderot originally conceived of the *Planches* series as an integrated counterpart to the literary text in the *Encyclopédie, ou dictionnaire raisonné des sciences, des arts et des métiers.* In fact, there is no discussion of music engraving in the text of the *Encyclopédie* itself — unfortunately, but not surprisingly. Over the nearly two decades of publication, beginning in 1751, often involving clandestine circumstances, the coordination soon lapsed, so that in using the set today, "it is far from easy to find a relevant article for a given plate; in fact it is almost as difficult as it is to find the relevant plate for a given article. . . . the coordination between the two had broken down gravely; in fact the whole system had come close to disintegrating," according to Richard N. Schwab (*Inventory of Diderot's Encyclopédie, VII: Inventory of the Plates*, Oxford: Taylor Institution, Voltaire Foundation, 1984, pp. 5-6. See also John Lough, *Essay on the Encyclopédie of Diderot and d'Alembert*, London: Oxford University Press, 1768. These sources also summarize the early history of the *Encyclopédie*). The *Planches* were conceived as a complement to the original (i.e., "Paris-Neuchâtel") folio edition, although they often appear with others as well, notably the "Geneva" edition, in which the "Gravure" *Planches* are in what is now designated as vol. 5.

The *Encyclopédie*'s typography article (Pierre-Simon Fournier's "Caractères d'imprimerie," vol. 2, pp. 650-66) mentions plainsong type and shows a brief example, but the *Planches* counterpart ("Fonderies en caractères d'imprimerie") does not illustrate music fonts and their use.

The articles on printing and other aspects of the book arts and typography are reproduced and discussed in *Book Making in Diderot's Encyclopédie*, with an introduction by Giles Barber (Westmead: Gregg, 1973. The text and *Planches* from the "Gravure" sections on cutting punches for type are included, but unfortunately the maps and music *Planches* are not; nor are they among those selected in Charles Coulston Gillespie's *Pictorial Encyclopedia of Trades and Industry* (New York: Dover, 1959). Numerous commentators have seen the *Planches* as evidence that the *Encyclopédie* itself was intended for a bourgeois readership. Roland Barthes compares their imagery to that in the 19th-century world's fairs, discussed in the next chapter. See "The Plates of the *Encyclopedia*," on pp. 28-39 in the *New Critical Essays* (New York: Farrar, Straus, and Giroux, 1980; a translation of *Le degré zéro*, Paris: Éditions du Seuil, 1972).

Manifesto d'una nuova impresa di stampare la musica in caratteri gettati nel modo stesso como si scrive. Venezia: Antonio di Castro, 1765. **167**

A brief introduction describes the "Origine," "Necessità," "Variazioni," and "Stabilimento" of the new plan. However brief, it also aspires to high scholarship, with footnote references to about 50 names. Next come two pages of a "Duetto," "inciso e gettato del M. Rev. Sig. D. Giacomo Falconi."

For an actual edition using the punches see the Castro edition of Giuseppe Paolucci's *Preces octo vocibus concinendae . . . horarum* (1767).

Nicolas and Pierre François GANDO. *Observations sur le Traité historique et critique de monsieur Fournier le jeune, sur l'origine et les progrès des caractères de fonte, pour l'impression de la musique.* Berne, et se trouvent à Paris: Moreau, 1766. **168**

An extended (27-page) polemic responding to Fournier's *Traité historique* (44 above), followed by a specimen of the Le Bé typography (now managed by the Gandos for the Ballard heirs), and a specimen printing of Abbé Roussier's "Petit motet" (a setting of Psalm 150), also in some copies a "Vaudeville sur la Rétablissement de la Santé du Roy."

Reprinted in the Archives de l'édition musicale française, Tome IX (Genève: Minkoff, 1972).

Philip LUCKOMBE. *The History and Art of Printing.* London: W. Adlard and J. Browne, for J. Johnson, 1771. **169**

First published anonymously in 1770 as *A Concise History of the Origin and Progress of Printing with Practical Instructions.* A brief discussion of musical notation appears on pp. 163-64, a chart of "Musical Signs" on pp. 475-76, all using Caslon's music type.

Nicolas Étienne FRAMERY. "Graver la musique," and "Graveur, Graveuse," in *Encyclopédie méthodique: musique* (Paris: Panckoucke, 1791), pp. 699-701.   **170**
Brief descriptions of current practices as part of the set prepared by Framery in cooperation with Pierre Louis Ginguené.
The recognition of both masculine and feminine forms should not pass unnoticed.

Christian Gottlob TÄUBEL. *Orthotypographisches Handbuch, oder Anleitung zur gründlichen Kenntniß derjenigen Theile der Buchdruckerkunst.* Halle, Leipzig, 1785.   **171**
The earliest of Täubel's manuals includes occasional music references on pp. 225-31, and a specimen of Breitkopf music type in the "Zweyte Tabelle" following p. 252, as well as an inserted leaf after p. 306 (p. 308 in the 1788 edition) on correcting music proof ("Noten-Correctur"), with an explanation on the verso.
Reprinted Leipzig: Georg Emanuel Beer, 1788; modern reprint of the 1785 ed., with a new introduction by Martin Boghardt, Darmstadt: Renata Raecke, 1984.
Täubel's second manual is the *Praktisches Handbuch der Buchdruckerkunst für Anfänger* (Leipzig: J. G. Müller, 1791; reprinted with a new introduction by Frans A. Janssen and Walter Wilkes, Darmstadt: Renata Raecke, 1982). In it, chapter 6 of Theil 1 ("Von dem, was einem Schriftsetzer von der Musik zu Wissen nöthig ist"; pp. 147-64) begins with the rudiments of notation and ends with a foldout chart entitled "Vorstellung einer Noten-Correctur." Another foldout chart ("Zweyte Tabell," after p. 245) shows "Musikalische Notenschrift." An eight-leaf gathering on proofreading is also inserted after p. 308, with red correction symbols printed on a black text. The last leaf folds out to illustrate "Noten Correctur."
The *Allgemeines theoretisch-practisches Wörterbuch der Buchdruckerkunst und Schriftgießerey* (Wien, 1805-09; reprinted with a new introduction by Martin Boghardt, Darmstadt: Renata Raecke, 1986) is arranged as a dictionary, in which "Musiknotendruck und Satz," (pp. 73-75) speaks to basic needs in just under 1,000 words. Several unpaginated features are added at

the end of vol. 2, includung a four-page "Lob der Buchdrucker-kunst" (words only), the second chorus of which runs thus:
Stille, wenn die Ballen pochen!
Stille, wenn der Deckel fällt!
Horcht! es wird zur ganzen Welt
Hier ein großes Wort gesprochen!
("Be quiet during the inking, and as the platen is lowered: a great word is now being uttered for the whole world to hear.")

Täubel's *Neues Theoretischpractisches Lehrbuch der Buchdru-ckerkunst* (Wien: Binz, 1810; reprinted with a new introduction by Walter Wilkes, Darmstadt: Renata Raecke, 1984) is in 8° rather than 4° format. "Vom Musiknoten-Drucke" (pp. 209-12) is derived from the earlier text but with a few re-wordings.

In the Swedish translation, *Boktryckarekonstens practiska hand-bok för nybegynnare* (Gothenberg: Samuel Norberg, 1823), "Om det, som för en stilsättare kan wara nödigt att weta, rörande musiquen" (vol. 1, pp. 152-66), is derived from the 1791 *Prakti-sches Handbuch*, the major difference being the placement of the musical examples, interspersed in the German text, at the end of the section in the Swedish text.

Antoine François MOMORO. *Traité élémentaire de l'im-primerie.* Paris: Tilliard, 1793.   **172**
A brief music entry (just over 100 words, on pp. 241-42) dis-cusses Ballard and Fournier. The same text appears in the editions of 1796 and of *ca.* 1810.

"Über die neuesten Erfindungen und Verbesserungen im Musikdruck," *Allgemeine musikalische Zeitung*, 6 (1803-04), 747-58.   **173**
Noteworthy is the early date (August 8, 1804) of this comparison of lithography with engraving and typography.

Johann Georg KRÜNITZ. *Ökonomisch-technologische Encyclopädie.* Berlin: Joachim Pauli, 1805-06.   **174**
"Musikstich" ("Die Kunst, Noten in Metallplatten zu graviren," vol. 98, pp. 645-48) and "Notendruck" ("Die Vervielfältigung eines in Noten gesetzten musikalischen Werkes," vol. 102, pp. 686-91) are discussed briefly (in about 700 words each), but with careful and interesting particulars, even footnotes. The latter,

for instance, mentions the music lithography of Anton Nieder-mayr (Regensburg, 1802) and the *Magazin aller neuen Er-findungen* of 1804 (possibly a garbled citation of the item above).

B. VINCARD. *L'Art du typographie: ouvrage utile à MM. les hommes de lettres, bibliographes, et typographes.*   Paris, 1806.   **175**

An added leaf after p. 118 shows mensural and plainchant music. (This text does not appear in the 1823 edition.)

Charles Guillaume RIEBESTHAL. *Nouvelle méthode pour noter la musique et pour l'imprimer avec des caractères mobiles.* Strasbourg: Levrault, 1810.   **176**

One of several publicized attempts at notational reform in which the recourse to solfège is justified as an expedient of printing: cumbersome staff lines are not needed.

The method may be what is described in two other writings that I have not seen: the "Nouvelle manière d'imprimer la musique," *Mémoires de la Société des sciences de Strasbourg*, 1 (1811), p. 1; and B. F. Reinhard, "Extrait d'un mémoire sur le stéréotypage de la musique," *ibid.*, 2 (1812), 28-97. [Davidsson 377, 409]

Godefroy ENGELMANN. *Rapport sur la lithographie intro-duite en France: Adressé à la Société d'Encouragement de Paris* [sic] . . . *le 20 octobre 1815.* Mulhouse: Jean Risler, [1815].   **177**

Valuable for its discussion of the processes for preparing the printing surfaces, with a specimen music page at the end.

Reproduced in Leon Lang, *Godefroy Engelmann, imprimeur lithographique: Les incunables, 1814-1817* (Colmar: Éditions Al-satia, 1977), which also discusses Engelmann's music lithography and cites three examples in the catalogue (see pp. 124, 137).

Alois SENEFELDER. *Vollständiges Lehrbuch der Steindruck-erei.* München: Thienemann; Vienna: Gerold, 1818.   **178**

The English translation, as *A Complete Course of Lithography* (London: Rudolf Ackermann, 1819), includes further details on music. See Michael Twyman, *Lithography, 1800-1850* (London: Oxford University Press, 1970), pp. 96-108 and 257-71 (on the relationships between the editions) and elsewhere (see the index, p. 293); also the reprint of the English edition with a new introduction by A. Hyatt Mayor (New York: Da Capo, 1968).

John JOHNSON. *Typographia; or, The Printer's Instructor*. London: Longman, Hurst, Rees, Orme, Brown, & Green, 1824. **179**

This respected text unfortunately says very little about music, apart from a brief explanation of the "Musical Characters" (vol. 2, pp. 243-45), and, in a report on the "Trade Scale of Prices for Composition and Pressmen" (1810), the detail that "Music [is] to be paid double the body of the sonnet type" (vol. 2, p. 581).
   Reprinted, London: Gregg, 1966.

Thomas Curson HANSARD. *Typographia: An Historical Sketch . . . of the Art of Printing . . . , with Practical Directions*. London: Baldwin, Cradock, & Joy, 1825. **180**

Johnson's counterpart, again with the detail on the compositor's price scale (p. 783).
   Also reprinted, London: Gregg, 1966.

Edward COWPER. "On the Recent Improvements in Music Printing," *Quarterly Journal of Science, Literature, and Art*, 1828, p. 183. **181**

Abstract of a lecture at the Royal Institution on February 22nd, describing his new method of music printing. William Ayrton also reports on the lecture in "Improvements in Music Printing," *The Harmonicon*, 6 (1828), 60. See Leanne Langley, "The Life and Death of the *Harmonicon*: An Analysis," Royal Musical Association, *Research Chronicle*, 22 (1989), pp. 138-63.

J. T. RICHOMME. *Leçons sur la manière de graver la musique*. Paris: Librairie Industrielle, 1829. **182**

Nine lessons, in useful detail with accompanying charts, touching on both planning the design and executing it.

"Rapport de M. DELESTRE sur la musique imprimée en caractères mobiles par M. Duguet," *Athénée des arts de Paris* (1833), 33-35. **183**

On behalf of an appointed committee of Messrs. Taskin, Marchant, and himself, the author proposes that the new system has great potential.

Eugène DUVERGER. *Specimen des caractères de musique gravés, fondus, composés et stéréotypés par les procédés de E. Duverger. Precédé d'une notice sur la typographie musicale par M. Fétis.* Paris, 1834.   **184**

Few music printing innovations have been as well promoted as Duverger's. The present book is a large (13 × 10") folio, with an eight-page specimen at the end: two pages open to a size of 13 × 20". Preceding these is an extended essay by François-Joseph Fétis, "De la typographie musicale," which traces the history of music printing back to 1480 and ends with a comparison of Duverger's system with others of the day. Fétis's text had appeared earlier as "De la typographie musicale, et des nouveaux procédés de M. E. Duverger," *Revue musicale*, 5 (1832), 381-86, with several details near the end that were omitted from the 1834 presentation. For another Fétis essay see 407 below.

Duverger's new typography was also announced in M. Francoeur, "Arts, mécaniques, Rapport . . . ," *Bulletin de la Société d'Encouragement pour l'Industrie Nationale*, 33 (1834), pp. 364-70; and in M. Lagarde, "Rapport sur les nouveaux procédés du typographie musicale de M. Duverger," *Mémoires de la Société Royale et Centrale d'Agriculture, Science et Arts du Département du Nord, séant a Douai*, 1835-36, pp. 317-26. Comparisons with the Breitkopf music typography are seen in "Über die neuen Musik-Notentypen des Hrn. E. Duverger zu Paris," *Journal für Buchdruckerkunst, Schriftgießerei, und die verwandten Fächer*, 6 (1835), cols. 83-87. The type was soon used in England, for instance as early as 1836 in J. Alfred Novello's *The Musical World*. See also the title below, also nos. 197-98, 352, and the patent registration in 380.

Anik Devriès describes the process and its impact in "La stéréomelotypie, procédé d'impression musicale," *Gutenberg Jahrbuch 1983*, pp. 105-11.

"On the Various Processes Applied to Printing Music," *Musical Library*, 1 (1834), Monthly Supplement, pp. 1-4.

William Ayrton assures readers of the serious intent of Charles Knight's new journal, by tracing the history of music printing to its origins, with several well-executed facsimiles and an example of the Duverger typography that Knight was using. **185**

A. FREY. *Manual nouveau de typographie, imprimerie.* Paris: Roret, 1835. **186**

In this "Manuels-Roret" volume a brief "Musique" entry on pp. 319-20 comments on Fournier and Duverger.

For later editions, with different music texts, by E. Bouchez (1857) and Emile LeClerc (1897), see 200 and 218 below.

Wilhelm HASPER. *Handbuch der Buchdruckerkunst.* Carlsruhe, Baden: D. R. Marx, 1835. **187**

"Satz und Druck von Musiknoten" is discussed on pp. 322-23, with examples on pp. 324-25.

Thomas ADAMS. *Typographia: or the Printer's Instructor.* Philadelphia: The Compiler, 1837. **188**

Based largely on Johnson's *Typographia* (1824), with an explanation of the rudiments of music (vol. 2, pp. 243-45). A "Music Upper Case" and "Music Lower Case" are seen on pp. 258-59.

The 4th ed. (Philadelphia: Peck & Bliss, 1853), also the 6th ed., (1856) substitutes on p. 210 a specimen of music type ("Cast at the foundry of L. Johnson & Co., Philadelphia"). The text also suggests the influence of Lawrence Johnson: "any intelligent workman may learn to compose it with facility. A plan of the cases accompanies every fount."

MM. BERTHIAUD and BOITARD. *Nouveau manuel complet de l'imprimeur en taille-douce.* Paris: Roret, 1837. **189**

A revised edition of another of the Manuels-Roret. According to Poole (*Grove P&P*, p. 47), the discussion of "Impression de la musique" (pp. 128-36) is "the first comprehensive account of the printing of music from engraved plates."

Reprinted Paris: Leonce Laget, 1978.

Godefroy ENGELMANN. *Traité théorique et pratique de lithographie.* Mulhouse, 1839-40. **190**

This edition, completed by A. Penot after the author's death, shows tools for writing identical noteheads in rapid succession.

Léon de LABORDE. "De l'art typographique appliqué à l'impression de la musique," *Artiste*, 1840, pp. 285-90.   **191**
The Marquis describes the historical succession, which he sees as culminating in the work of Derriey (cf. 360, 380 below).

William SAVAGE. *A Dictionary of the Art of Printing.* London: Longman, Brown, Green, and Longmans, 1841.   **192**
A respected source, in which "Music" (pp. 487-90) includes a brief text, with two case layouts and a setting of "The National Anthem," using Hugh Hughes's type (see 351 below).
Reprinted, London: Gregg, 1966.

A Day at a Music Publishers: A Description of the Establishment of D'Almaine & Co. London, [1840s].   **193**
A tour of the premises, slightly patronizing but also invaluable as our best first-hand description of an early music engraving shop.
Reproduced with commentary by H. Edmund Poole, *Journal of the Printing Historical Society*, 14 (1979/80), 59-81.

Bartolomeo MONTANELLO. *Di un modo facile ed economico per istampare la musica.* Milano: Ricordi, 1844.   **194**
A "Lettera . . . a Giovanni Ricordi," inspired by Giuseppe Raymond's *Essai de simplification musicographique*, on reforms in music notation more than in music printing. The author's earlier *Intorno alla scrivere la musica: lettera . . . a Marco Beccafichi* (Milano: G. Ricordi, 1843) also deals mostly with notation.

Carl SCHMIED. *Die leichteste Erlernung des Notensatzes mit Typen. Nebst Anweisung, wie die fünf Linien durchlaufend und überhaupt die Stückelungen vermieden werden können* .... Weimar: B. F. Voigt, 1844.   **195**
The British Museum copy (shelf mark 7897.bb.39) was destroyed in World War II. The rewards of further searching promise to be at once less authoritative and more fascinating when one notes that Herr Schmied also prepared monographs on making umbrellas, straw hats, and plaster-of-paris objects.

Some Account of the Methods of Musick Printing, with Specimens of the Various Sizes of Moveable Types, and of Other Matters. London: Novello, 1847.   **196**

A brief announcement, signed by J. Alfred Novello, proposing his availability as a typographic music printer, with specimens of his fonts. Appended is a brief but important statement on "The Economics of Musick Printing": type is cheaper for long runs, especially when stereotypes are in order.

A. BOUCHET. "Études sur l'impression de la musique par les procédés typographiques," *Société Fraternelle des Protés des Imprimeries Typographiques de Paris,* 3. Cahier, 1854.   **197**

An account of music typography, which talks of Hutin [*sic*] and Le Bé, and ends with notes contributed by "M. Alkan, le plus habile collecteur typographique que nous connaissons."

The text is likely to be most readily available in the 1925 reprint in the Union Syndicale et Fédération des Syndicates des Maître Imprimeurs de France, *Bulletin Officiel,* pp. 19-23 (January, covering from the beginnings to 1700), 43-46 (February, on Breitkopf, Fournier, Ollivier, and Duverger), and 67-70 (on recent innovations). Critical notes by Marius Audin suggest that he was also responsible for turning up the 1854 original and recommending it as part of a reprint series of early typographical texts (none of which otherwise concerns music).

Henri FOURNIER. *Traité de typographie.* 2. éd., Tours: Alfred Maine, 1854.   **198**

The title needs to be read precisely: this is a treatise, not a manual. The rationale proposed in "Musique et plain-chant" (pp. 370-74), however brief, is noteworthy: the problem began with "les rapides progrès de science musicale" in the time of Bach, Haydn, and Mozart. Engraving, typography, and lithography (Breitkopf in Leipzig, Reinhardt in Strasbourg, and "Godefroy" [i.e., Engelmann] in Paris are singled out) helped, but an effective solution is seen only with Duverger, although his method "demeurée très-coûteuse." Plainchant receives a mere two lines at the end.

The 3. éd. (1870, pp. 450-54) has a few significant rewordings: no attempts have proven truly advantageous or definitive, but let us hope that the problems will be solved, and by typography.

The first edition (Paris: Fournier, 1825; reprinted Westmead: Gregg, 1979) does not discuss music.

Théotiste LEFEBVRE. *Guide pratique du compositeur d'imprimerie*. Paris: Firmin Didot, 1855.   **199**
Typographic plainchant is discussed in good detail (Chapter 4, section 7, pp. 157-67, with a case layout on p. 168), but not mensural music.

Reprinted 1873 (so as to be available to complement a sequel volume), again in 1880 (reprinted Westmead: Gregg, 1972). In the 4th ed. (1883) the music coverage is still the same as in 1855, but is now on pp. 170-81.

E. BOUCHEZ. *Nouveau manuel complet de typographie*. Paris: Roret, 1857.   **200**
A successor to Frey's 1835 Manuel-Roret, its music coverage (pp. 283-87) expanded to mention Tantenstein, Derriey, and Curmer. (The 1897 successor is by Émile Leclerc, 218 below.)
Reprinted, Paris: Leonce Laget, 1979.

Jean-Marie Herman HAMMANN. *Des arts graphiques destinés à multiplier par l'impression*. Genève: Joel Cherbuliez, 1857.   **201**
One of the earliest attempts to differentiate the printing processes systematically. Unfortunately the historical section treats "Impression de la musique" only briefly (pp. 126-28); the practical section includes only a paragraph (p. 256).

Thomas MACKELLAR. *The American Printer: A Manual of Typography*. Philadelphia: L. Johnson, 1866.   **202**
The discussion of music typography (pp. 98-102) shows four specimens, with layouts for the upper, lower, and side cases.

MacKellar (later partner in the firm of MacKellar, Smiths, and Jordan) saw his book through at least 17 editions by 1889. The cases are occasionally reorganized, but the prose (usually on pp. 114-19) is much the same. Beginning in 1876 a "Comparative Table of Bodies" is shown, along with seven music faces.

See also 359 below.

J. H. BACHMANN. *Die Schule des Musiknoten-Satzes: Ein praktischer Leitfaden zum Selbstunterricht*. Leipzig: Alexander Waldow, 1865.   **203**

In 78 columns, one of the most detailed (and verbose) of the instruction manuals. Cols. 51-52 show a "Musik-Noten-Kasten" from Gronau in Berlin, with 307 music sorts. This work may be dedicated to J. G. I. Breitkopf, but it is stilll a training manual that covers the history very superficially.

First issued separately as "Der Musiknoten-Satz," in Waldow's *Archiv für Buchdruckerkunst*, 1 (1864), cols. 1-16, 77-100, 127-44, 177-82, 209-12; a "2. Auflage" appeared in 1875. An abridged version appears in the *Neues Handbuch der Buchdruckerkunst* (Weimar: Bernhard-Friedrich Voigt, 1876) as Chapter 15 ("Der Musiknotensatz"), pp. 171-81.

August MARAHRENS. *Vollständiges theoretisch-praktisches Handbuch der Typographie.* Leipzig: Verlag der Leipziger Vereinsbuchdruckerei, 1870.   **204**
"Der Musiknoten-Satz" (vol. 1, pp. 512-34) begins with a brief history of music printing; continues with "Der Kegel" (dimensions of type), notational symbols, "Der Musiknoten-Kasten" (showing the lay of the case), "Die Technik des Satzes" (introducing musical layout), and other topics; and ends with a list of music printing abbreviations.

Robert DITTRICH. *Anleitung zum Satz der Musiknoten-Typen.* Leipzig: Alexander Waldow, 1872.   **205**
An extended manual detailing the compositorial practice of music typography. Issued both as part of Waldow's *Lehrbuch der Buchdruckerkunst*, 1870-75, and separately as Heft 12 of *Waldow's Typographische Bibliothek*.

Carl LIPPMANN. "Om sättning af musiknoter," *Nordisk Boktryckeri-Tidning*, (1872) 11-12, 16-17, 21, 25, 33, 36-37, 41, 44; (1873) 3, 7-8, 15, 19, 26, 45-47; (1874) 37-38.   **206**
A general account, beginning with musical notation and extending into details on mosaic type-setting.

Also issued separately by the author, Stockholm, 1872.

Joseph GOULD. *The Letter-Press Printer: A Complete Guide to the Art of Printing.* London: Farrington, 1876.   **207**
"Music composition" is summarized on pp. 108-09. According to Poole (*Grove 6*, vol. 15, p. 240), the illustrations of oblong for-

mat are among the last to be seen in any of the printers' manuals specially designated for the imposition of music.

2nd edition, 1881; 3rd edition, 1884; later editions from the 1890s published by F. Marlborough, undated, all with the same text on the same pages, as late as the 1927 reprint of the sixth edition. The 2nd and later editions include John Southward's "Historical Introduction."

J. C. NØRDIN. *Handbok i boktryckarekonsten.* Stockholm: P. A. Norstedt, 1881.   **208**

The discussion of "Sättning af musiknoter" (pp. 195-213) moves quickly into complex topics and includes a layout of the music case ("Notenkasten").

John SOUTHWARD. *Practical Printing: A Handbook of the Art of Typography.* London: Printer's Register Office, 1882.   **209**

General printers are advised to subcontract their music printing to specialists. Nevertheless, Chapter 35 ("Music Printing," pp. 342-62) goes into considerable useful detail, in a text by "Mr. George Wilson, of Turnmill-street, one of the best and most extensive music printers in London." It also shows a chart of "Messrs. Shanks, Revell, & Co.'s Music Cases" [i.e., those of the Patent Type Founding Company: see 762 below]. See Bigmore & Wyman, pp. 378-80, for background on this work and its relationship to the author's *Dictionary of Typography* (1871).

The book had first appeared serially in 1878 in the issues of *The Printer's Register*, where "Music Printing" is chapter 34 (vol. 18, pp. 45-47, 64-66, 84-86), paragraphs 1171-1228. (The paragraph numbering is confused: nos. 1221-27 are duplicated in the 1878 serialization; in the 1882 book 1341 is duplicated and 1351 is omitted. So much for the legendary proofreading of yore: after 1882 the paragraphs were wisely left unnumbered. The texts themselves, to be sure, are essentially identical.)

Over the years, Chapter 35 shows slight but timely revisions. Those in the 2nd edition (1884) are minor, as are those in the 3rd (1887), although the latter adds discussions of "Gregorian or Chant Music" and "Tonic Sol-Fa Music" (pp. 304-06). The 4th and 5th editions (1900) are repaginated. By this time, however, Southward's *Modern Printing* (221) was coming to dominate the market. A 6th edition was nevertheless prepared by George Jaeger (1911), its main updating being the recognition of "photozinco" reproduction as a fourth basic music-printing process, with no explanations .

G. BOEHM. "A Brief History of Music Composition," *Inland Printer*, 5 (1887-88), 399-400. **210**
Based largely on Faulmann's history (93 above).

"Music Type-Setting," and "The Composition of Music Types," *British Printer*, 4-5 (1891-92). **211**
Brief statements reprinted from unnamed sources.

"La musique typographique," *La Typologie-Tucker: recueil de l'impression et de la lithographie: Revue bibliographique*, 5 (1891), 509-11. **212**
On improvements developed by Henri Chossefoin, used in the Paul Dupont printing shop. (Tucker was the French agency for the Caslon foundry in London.)

Théophile BEAUDOIRE. *Manuel de typographie musicale*. Paris: [The Author], Rue Duguay-Trouin 13, 1891-94. **213**
A detailed technical essay, of which the first half of the first part is devoted to mensural music, the second half (pp. 37-57) to plainchant. The "deuxième partie" (1894; pp. 61-76, also issued as a separate fascicle with unnumbered pages) covers further particulars of mensural practice, while the "troisième partie" (1894; pp. 78-87, with 5 pp. of added examples) is entitled "Musique pour la Liturgie Notée." I have not seen Beaudoire's *Méthode pour la fonte & l'entretien des rouleaux typographiques*, advertised at the end of the first part.

Beaudoire was a noted typefounder whose music fonts ended up in the possession of Deberny & Peignot. (For the specimen books see 363 below.) His essay on "La musique pour la liturgie notée," in the *Revue du Clergé français*, prompted a response by "Schmidt" entitled "La Typographie et le Plain-Chant," *Revue du chant grégorien*, 4 (1895-96), 36-39, 59-62. Beaudoire speaks of his type as "avec les caractères ordinaires de la musique" and acknowledges as his models the forms invented in Paris by "Berchtoldus" in 1494 and adapted over the years by the Giuntas, Plantin, and Lyons printers in 1729 (p. 37). Schmidt's florid polemic was probably occasioned by Beaudoire's failure to recognize the Solesmes notational reforms.

Em. SØRENSEN. *Grundregler for Nodesatsens Teknik.* Copenhagen: R. Helmer, 1892.   **214**
[Davidsson 485. The 1881-92 *Dansk Bogfortegnelse*, p. 239, reports this as "Tillæg til Ny typog. Tidende."]

Joseph DUMOND. *Vade-mecum du typographie.* 2. éd., Bruxelles: P. Weissenbruch, 1894.   **215**
"Musique" (pp. 243-57) describes typesetting with a font from A. & F. Vanderborght, showing how the musical staff is built up; a "Plan de casse" for music; a list of Italian terms; and instructions for numerical notation (Rousseau's "Musique chiffrée") and plainchant, with case layouts for each.

I have not seen the first edition, which Barber dates 1891.

W. H. DRIFFIELD. "Music Printing: Its History and Practice," *The Art Printer,* 1 (1895), 78-79, 151-55, 231-32.   **216**
The three parts are "An Epitomized History of Music Printing by Moveable Types," "Music Composing: How it is Done," and "Music Printing by Lithography and from Plates." Weak on history but perhaps more authoritative on practice; Driffield's 1898-99 series below is more convincing.

"Der Musiknotendruck," in Theodor Goebel, *Die graphischen Künste der Gegenwart: Ein Führer durch das Buchgewerbe* (Stuttgart: Felix Krais, 1895), pp. 130-33.   **217**
A splendid display of the work of German printers, in a book presumably intended for the Biedermeier coffee table (and, this being the first of three volumes in the set, each approaching 4" thickness and on heavy coated stock, the coffee table would have needed to be very substantial). Music printing is in the section "Von Lithographie und Steindruck." Of special interest are two *Beilagen* from Leipzig printers following p. 136 (described on pp. 134-35), one a handsome color announcement followed by three pages of printed music from Oscar Brandstetter, the other a set of three color plates followed by four Röder music pages.

A sequel ("neue Folge") volume from 1902 has no essay on music printing, but shows examples of the work of both Brandstetter and Röder. For volume 3, see 226 below.

Émile LECLERC. *Nouveau manuel complet de typographie.*
Paris: L. Mulo, 1897.   **218**
A third of the Manuels-Roret typography tutors (others, cited
above, are by Frey in 1835 and Bouchez in 1857), in which
chapter 14 ("Musique," pp. 475-504) is entirely new, with a
historical introduction and useful illustrations.
Reprinted, Paris: Leonce Laget, 1979.

Max WITTIG. "Praktische Anleitung für den Musiknotensatz," *Schweizer graphische Mitteilungen,* [1890s?].   **219**
[I have not seen this article, cited in *NYPL*, vol. 33, p. 54]

W. H. DRIFFIELD. "Music Printing," *Inland Printer,* 22
(1898-99), 43, 179, 291, 429, 552.   **220**
Brief summaries, (1) "Historical"; (2) on the elements of musical
notation and an introduction to the type sorts in a music case;
(3) "Combinations," on compositorial layout; (4) "Points worth
Remembering," on compositorial planning; and (5) "Lithographed Music" and "Engraved Music," on the basic processes.
See also the author's 1895 series (216 above).

John SOUTHWARD. *Modern Printing: A Handbook of the
Principles and Practice of Typography and the Auxilliary
Arts.* London: Rathby, Lawrence, 1899.   **221**
A tighter, more demanding essay than that in Southward's *Practical Printing* (1882, later editions to 1911; cf. 209 above, also
207). "Composing Music Types" (pp. 51-66) begins by compar-
ing typography with engraving, and continues with "Distribution," with rudiments of musical notation, showing the lay of the
music case, and with "Composing," on page design and spacing.
   The original four-volume set was also issued in one volume in
1900, the word *Handbook* now changed to *Treatise,* the music
chapter now on pp. 319-34. This same text is also seen in later
editions, e.g. on pp. 312-27 in the 3rd ed. (1912), and in the 5th
ed. (1921) of the *Handbook.*

Henri ROBERT. *Traité de gravure de musique sur planches
d'étain et d'autographie ou similigravure, précédé de
l'historique abrégé de l'impression et de la gravure de
musique.* Paris: Chez L'Auteur, 1902.   **222**

The major contemporary account of music engraving at its period of greatest productivity. The illustrated particulars on music layout are very useful, as is the "Vocabulaire des termes techniques de la gravure de musique."

A considerably enlarged version (1926), now entitled *Traité de gravure de musique sur planches d'étain et des divers procédés de simili-gravure de musique . . . précédé de l'historique du signe, de l'impression et de la gravure de musique*, has 151 rather than 82 pages, expanded about evenly over the topics covered.

A set of 250 music engraver's punches by Robert, sold at Sotheby's in London on May 10, 1984 (lot 132), is now at Northwestern University, Evanston, Illinois.

Friedrich BAUER. *Handbuch für Schriftsetzer*. Frankfurt: Klimsch, 1904.   **223**

In chapter 10 ("Besondere Arten des Werksatzes"), section 7 (pp. 199-203) is devoted to "Der Satz von Musiknoten," with a case layout.

Theodore Low DE VINNE. *Modern Methods of Book Composition*. New York: Century, 1904.   **224**

The section on "Music" (pp. 207-25) includes a case layout and explanation of the sorts for conventional music (pp. 220-23) and tonic sol-fa (pp. 224-25). Among the imposition schemes are "Music or oblong way" (p. 348).

The book is designated as an "intended supplement" to De Vinne's *Correct Composition* (ibid., 1901), which mentions music in passing only once. Both volumes are part of De Vinne's series called "The Practice of Typography," other volumes of which (*The Practice of Type-Making* and *A Treatise on Title-Pages*) also make no significant mention of music. Nor do their later editions: the 1925 *Modern Methods* has the same text as in 1904.

"The Largest Music Printers in the World," *The Modern Lithographer*, 4 (1908), 151-54.   **225**

A description of the industrial premises of C. G. Röder in the Willesden Junction area of London, citing the authority of Dr. Otto Strecker and showing six photographs. This is followed by a brief notice on "Music Engraving and Printing," pp. 154-55.

Otto SÄUBERLICH. "Der Musikaliendruck," in *Das moderne Buch* (Stuttgart: Felix Krais, 1909; *Die graphischen Künste der Gegenwart*, 3. Band), pp. 207-16. 226
A brief, handsomely illustrated essay by a leading engraver of the Oscar Brandstetter firm, in the third and last of a series of luxurious displays of the art of the printer (see 217 for the two predecessors). Following the text are four specimen pages by Brandstetter, one by Röder, and two by Breitkopf & Härtel.

Franz Paul FÖLCK. "Musik-notensatz einst und jetzt," *Archiv für Buchgewerbe*, 48 (1911), 135-38. 227
Comments on the history and practice of music typography.

K. S. C. "Course of a Melody from a Composer's Mind to the Music on Your Piano," *Musical America* (June 1, 1912), p. 3. 228
Aims to make music teachers more respectful of music printing.

Ernest AUSTIN. *The Story of the Art of Music Printing.* London: Lowe & Brydone, 1913, [1925?]. 229
The leading London music engraving firm issued this booklet at least twice. The first was "Published as a Souvenir of the British Music Exhibition, Olympia, September 6th to 20th, 1913"; the other mentions events of 1924.
  Both texts begin with "The Story of Music Printing," drawn from secondary sources. The earlier version continues with "Lowe & Brydone, 1892-1913" (pp. 21-23), while the later adds "Music-Engraving & Printing as seen by a Composer" (pp. 21-26), by Austin himself with his mouth agape at the awesome wonders of music printing that he is witnessing; and "Lowe & Brydone Printers, Ltd., 1892-1924" (pp. 27-31), which adds a few historical details in praise of the firm and ends with "Some Interesting Photographs" (18 in all) of the shop and the staff.

Emil SELMAR. *Typografi for Sættere, Korrektører, Forfattere og Forlæggere.* Kjøbenhavn: Gyldendal, 1913. 230
Instructions for music compositors, with a case layout.

"Music Plate-Making and Printing," *The Gospel Choir*, vol. 1, no. 9 (October 1915), pp. 9-10. 231

A brief note, of interest as a reflection of practices for Homer Rodeheaver's market of revival-meeting songbooks.

Giuseppe Isidoro ARNEUDO. *Dizionario esegetico, tecnico e storico per le arti grafiche* . . . . Torino: R. Scuola tipografica e di arte affini, [1917].   **232**
A brief historical note with particulars on recent Italian music typography appears in vol. 2, pp. 1534-36. A supplementary chart shows a music case layout.

"Music on the 'Monotype,'" *British Printer*, 30 (1917), 109-11.   **233**
Selected texts on tonic sol-fa from the *Monotype Recorder*, with a case layout and suggested solutions to some of the compositorial problems in work with music.

Carl REICHMANN. "Was niemand weiß und alle wissen sollten: Wie eine Notenseite entsteht," *Zeitschrift für Musik*, 87 (1920), 29-31.   **234**
Illustrated with a synopsis of a 360-sort font, and a copy-edited Liszt manuscript alongside the engraved plate prepared from it.

Charles W. HACKLEMAN. *Commercial Engraving and Printing: A Manual.* Indianapolis: Commercial Engraving Publishing Co., 1921.   **235**
"Music Engraving" (pp. 608-11), however brief, is one of the few American writings on the subject.

Francis THIBAUDEAU. *La lettre d'imprimerie.* Paris: Au Bureau de l'édition, 1921.   **236**
"La gravure & l'impression de la musique" (vol. 2, pp. 603-09) includes brief but intelligent and original observations, along with well-selected illustrations.
   This music section does not appear in the author's *Manuel français de typographie moderne* (Paris, 1924).

Stephen H. HORGAN. "Music Engraving and Printing," *The Inland Printer*, 69 (1922), 856.   **237**
A brief commentary. The value of this journal, and other less famous counterparts, in tracing the history of American music printing, is further suggested in passing in Maurice Annenberg's

A Typographical Journey through the Inland Printer, 1883-1900 (Baltimore: Maran Press, 1977), p. 563.

"Notensatz und Notenstich," *Gregorius-Blatt für katholische Kirchenmusik*, 47 (1922), 16-18.   **238**
Fitting together of the text in mosaic type and reconception of a complicated manuscript onto an engraved plate, based largely on the counsel of Otto Säuberlich.

Hubert J. FOSS. "Modern Music Printing," *Music and Letters*, 4 (1923), 340-47.   **239**
The basic printing processes (letterpress, engraving, lithography) are explained for musicians, whose needs will be better served when the processes and their limitations are understood.

Foss's "Romance of Music Printing," *Penguin Music Magazine*, 5 (1948), 13-18, is mostly a simplified updating of this essay.

William GAMBLE. *Music Engraving and Printing: Historical and Technical Treatise*. London: Pitman, 1923.   **240**
A study by a respected authority in the byways more than the main lines of printing (see, for instance, the list of his writings in the 1919 St. Bride catalogue), ostensibly motivated by events of World War I, when British music publishers found themselves without recourse to the Leipzig engraving firms who kept their plates and ran off copies as ordered. (To be sure, the argument becomes a bit clouded by the 1908 article on "The Largest Music Printers in the World," describing the Röder premises in Willesden: see 225 above).

Gamble's historical facts are often flawed, so as to cast doubts on his technical discussions, perhaps inappropriately. Many details on printing practice are unverifiable, but also plausible; the book is of continuing interest.

Reprinted, New York: Da Capo, 1971.

Rudolf WITTEN. *Die Lehre vom Musiknotensatz, seine Einteilung, Auszählung und Berechnung nebst einem geschichtlichen Rückblick über die Entwicklung der Notenschrift und des Notensatzes . . . .* Leipzig, Berlin: Bildungsverband der Deutschen Buchdrucker, 1925 (Buchdrucker-Fachbücher, 11).   **241**

Mentioned with high respect by several contemporaries. I have not seen the author's "Der Musiknotensatz," *Typographische Mitteilungen*, 22 (1925), 61-64 (Davidsson 569); nor have I verified a text by Witten, casually cited in several sources as *Praktikum des Stein- und Zinkdrucks* (1926).

K. GIRNATIS. "Musiknoten: Ihr Werdegang und die heutige Art ihrer Vervielfältigung," *Buch und Kunstdruck*, 26 (1926), 83-90.   **242**
[Davidsson 172]

John STÉPHAN, O. S. B. "The Isotonic Notation," *Penrose Annual*, 29 (1927), 33-36.   **243**
Dom John's system is of interest as music printing mostly because its notation was the work of Paul Woodroffe, and its announcement appeared in a leading British graphic arts journal.
    The system itself is described more fully in a trilingual 34-page booklet, *The Isotonic Notation* (Exeter: S. Lee, [1927]).

Rudolf BECKER. *Der Werdegang der Musiknoten: eine kurze Einführung in das Wesen des Notenstichs und Notensatzes*. Leipzig: Becker, 1928.   **244**
Eight useful illustrated charts, followed by two pages of credits and commentary.

James N. GREEN. "Music Engraving and Printing," in the Stationers' Company and Printing Industry Technical Board, *Annual Craft Lectures for 1927-1928* (London: London School of Printing, [1928]), pp. 79-101.   **245**
Delivered on December 9th, 1927, and introduced by James E. Brydone, the paper, along with the questions it elicited from the floor, reflects the English workmanship of the day.

Fritz RÖDER. "Der Notenstich, Notensatz und Musikaliendruck," *Archiv für Buchgewerbe und Gebrauchsgraphik*, 66 (1929), 541-44.   **246**
Expert observations on the different processes, with particulars on music layout.

Die Entstehung eines Liederbuches, in der Musikalien-druckerei Oscar Brandstetter. Leipzig, [*ca.*1930]. **247**
A nicely illustrated booklet showing the steps in the processes of engraving and printing.

Hubert J. FOSS. "The Printing of Music: Some Problems of Today," *Gutenberg Jahrbuch 1931*, pp. 293-300. **248**
Foss explains the rationale of music printing, in a text comparable in importance to the 1924 *Fleuron* essay (396 below).

Max WITTIG. *Vom Musiknotendruck: Satz und Stich.* Dresden: W. & B. v. Baenisch Stiftung, 1933 (Graphische Hilfsbücher für den Buchhersteller, 7). **249**
An attractive pamphlet, with useful illustrations.

"Der Notenstecher," *Die Musik*, 26 (1933), 71-72. **250**
Brief astonishment at the wonder of it all.

"MUSIKUS." "Schrift, Satz und Drucktechnik der Musiknoten," *Graphische Nachrichten*, 13 (1934), 237-46. **251**
The gaudy cover with Nazi banners, together with a steely arrogance in the typographic design of the text, may tempt one to ignore this essay. This would be wrong: the text includes details not often reported elsewhere (e.g., the names of the main type distributors, although several French names are misspelt), and there are well-conceived charts and illustrations.

Marius AUDIN. "La musique typographique," in Union Syndicale et Fédération des Syndicats des Maîtres Imprimeurs de France, *Bulletin officiel*, 1935, 137-43. **252**
By way of complementing his 1931 essay (124 above) and recalling the reprint of Bouchet's 1854 essays (197), the respected Lyons typographic historian mentions important books, gives evidence of sound habits with secondary sources, and adds perceptive personal observations.

S. DE JONGH. "De typografische muziekdruk," *De tampon*, 16 (1935), 17-34. **253**
The explanation of the rudiments of music is especially serious.

A. von ANDREEVSKY. "Vom Notenschreiben zum Musikalienhandel," *Propyläen*, 34 (1937), 413-14.   **254**
[Davidsson 8]

Kurt SÄUBERLICH. "Die Kunst des Notenstechers," *Deutsche Musikkultur*, 2 (1937/38), 285-91.   **255**
In gothic typography and with the heading, "Träger deutscher Musikkultur," the brief essay also includes illustrations, presumably drawn from the Bärenreiter shop.

"Notenstecher gestern, heute und morgen," *Der Musikalienhandel*, 41 (1939), 5-6, 16.   **256**
[Davidsson 373]

"Notenstich in Geschichte und Technik," *Graphische Technik*, 7 (1939), 95-100.   **257**
[Davidsson 374]

F. K. POPP. "Von der Entstehung der Notenschrift zum Musikalienhandel," *Schweizerische Instrumentalmusik*, 28 (1939), 413.   **258**
[Davidsson 395]

Joseph A. FISCHER. "Engraving and Printing that New Sonata," *American Organist*, 23 (1940), 107-08.   **259**
A brief account for performers.

Hubert J. FOSS. "The Plight of Music Printing," *The Music Review*, 2 (1941), 215-219.   **260**
Admirable mainly for its sensitivity to the attitudes of musicians.

La composición tipográfica de música. Barcelona: Fundición tipográfica Neufville, S.A. [1940s?].   **261**
An extended (29-page) booklet on effective musical layout.

Karl HADER. *Aus der Werkstatt eines Notenstechers*. Wien: Waldheim-Eberle Verlag, 1948.   **262**
Particularly valuable for its illustrations and commentary on the nuances of music layout, from the major printer for Universal Edition. The illustrations have been widely reprinted.

The main points also appear in Hader's "Die 'Tönende schwarze Kunst,'" *Schweizer graphische Mitteilungen*, 68 (1949), 300-03. Leicher-Olbricht (597 below) cites an even more promising unpublished manuscript by Hader, "Die Musikalische Notation: Geschichte, Drucktechnik, und Rechtschreibung."

R. R. VOORHEES. "Music: How it is Printed" [four short articles in *Printing Equipment, Engineer*, 1949-50].   **263**
1: Zinc Plates (October 1949, pp. 21-24); 2: Music type (November 1949, p. 25); 3: Musicktype (December 1949, pp. 73-75); 4: Typemusic (January 1950, p. 46). The latter two are names of specific music printing processes.

George NEWMAN. "Music Engraving," *Typographica*, 4 (1951), 21-29.   **264**
An account for general readers that makes good points very effectively and supports them with useful illustrations.

Hans BUCHDRUCKER. "Der Musiknotensatz: Ein guter Setzer sollte auch darin Bescheid wissen," *Der Druckspiegel*, 7 (1952), 431-39 [also designated as pp. 7-15].   **265**
Serious-minded in its injunctions: it is essential to know and respect the history of written music, and be sensitive to detail and imaginative. Witten (241) is awarded special respect.
    Another essay by this well-named (and perhaps eponymous) author is "Der Musiknotensatz," *Form und Technik*, 5 (1954), 393-95.

Anton MÜLLER. "Vom Notenstich," *Das Musikleben*, 5 (1952), 207-11.   **266**
A brief essay in Ernst Laaff's journal, with photographs.

Norman GRAY. *A Note on Music Engraving and Printing.* London, New York: Boosey & Hawkes, 1952.   **267**
A pamphlet describing music printing techniques, mostly for those who submit copy for publication.

Hans STAHL. "Der Notenstich," *Der Druckspiegel*, 7 (1952), 294-99.   **268**
Subtitled "Der Werdegang eines speziellen Druckerzeugnisses," with helpful illustrations.

The author's "Altes und Neues über den Musiknotendruck," *Form und Technik*, 5 (1954), 396-98, is more patronizing.

"SGL." "Notenstecher bei der Arbeit: Wie Musiknoten vervielfältigt werden; Leipzig, die Wiege des Notendrucks," *Musik und Gesellschaft*, 5 (1955), 324-26.   **269**
Mostly an illustrated description of the Röder plant.

"Music Printing: An Ancient Craft Successfully Adopts Modern Techniques," *British Printer*, vol. 70, no. 11 (Nov. 1957), pp. 56-63.   **270**
Part of a series on "This Surprising World of Print," describing classic methods, with photographs from the Lowe & Brydone shop and comments on recent technological innovations.

Max WITTIG. "Druckformenherstellung für den Musiknotendruck," *Der Polygraph*, 2 (1958), 70-72.   **271**
[Davidsson 571]

P. SCHÖNBERG. "Notenstich und Notensatz," *Kontakte*, 1960, 256-58.   **272**
[Davidsson 460]

"Was man vom 'Notenstich' wissen muss," *Musikalienhandel*, 2 (1960), 409-10.   **273**
[Davidsson 549]

H. ZERASCHI. "Der Musikaliendruck," *Börsenblatt für den deutschen Buchhandel, Beilage: Der Musikalienhandel*, 6 (1960), 12, 16, 20, 24, 28, 32, 36.   **274**
[Davidsson 590]

Bob DARCH. *Music and Paper.* Toronto: Provincial Paper, Ltd., 1962.   **275**
Special issue of *Provincial's Paper*, vol. 27, no. 3. "Ragtime Bob" appropriately begins his account with Scott Joplin, and shows some nice Canadian music covers. Unfortunately he says next to nothing about music paper. Among the curiosities of this article is the statement that "Petrucci's method was modified to a one-impression run by a Londoner, John Rastell" (p. 11). This fact is thought not to have been discovered until Alec Hyatt King's

1971 essay (128 above): in 1962 the reliable sources were still attributing the invention to Haultin. What, now, did "Ragtime Bob" know, and when and how did he come to know it?

R. PYNE. "Music Engraving," *Music Teacher*, April 1963, 172. **276**

Patronizing observations in response to an earlier announcement of a new music typewriter.

Heinz SCHMIDT. "Notenstich und Offsetdruck im Dienste der Musik," *Polygraph Jahrbuch 1964*, pp. 273-79. **277**

A brief illustrated summary of the layout, engraving, and presswork practices at Möseler-Verlag.

Standard Music Engraving Practice. [Washington]: Music Publisher's Association, Music Educators National Conference, 1966. **278**

A statement of music notation and engraving standards, prepared by Maxwell Weaner ("the autographer and graphic arts expert") with help from the respected music engraver-publisher Walter Boelke and at the request of the Production Committee of the Music Publishers' Association (Arnold Broido, chair).

The statement also appears in the *Music Educators Journal*, February-March, 1965, pp. 52-56, 213.

Peter ZINOVIEFF. "The Special Case of Inspirational Computer Music Scores," *London Magazine*, n.s., 100 (July/-August 1969), pp. 165-76. **279**

"Stave notation is especially efficient for what does not need to be written." Other profundities, bibliographical and existential, are tossed into the pot, with a view to PMMABC, i.e., asking a computer, "Please make me a beautiful composition."

Roy BREWER. "Music and Print," *Penrose Annual*, 64 (1971), 144-52. **280**

A perfunctory summary of the technology.

Ted ROSS. *The Art of Music Engraving and Processing.* Miami: Charles Hansen, 1971. **281**

An extensive account of the practices of the music engraver, valuable for its numerous particulars on the layout of music on the page so as to convey the sense of the sound. Some experts have reportedly questioned several of its recommended practices; but until they have done so in print and with a view to dialogue, this book should be seen as a definitive statement.

Ulver FORSCHHAMMER. "Nodetryken gammel kunst i den ny tid," *De grafiske tag*, 71 (1975), pp. 78-82. **282**
"Music Printing: An Old Trade in Modern Times," describing the Wilhelm Hansen firm in Copenhagen.

Hank KASS. *What the New Arranger Should Know about Engraving*. New York: Charles Hansen, 1975 (Commercial Music Bulletin, 2). **283**
Information on the basic processes, drawn mostly from Ross (1971), with several updatings but also much simplification.

Kass's *Tips on Music Engraving, for Everyone who Reads and Writes Music* (Commercial Music Bulletin, 7; 1975), also drawn from Ross, consists of suggestions for amateur composers, mostly dealing with layout. Other titles in the series are concerned more with the business knowledge useful for aspiring song composers (cf. 548 below).

Eckart MORAT. "Notenstecher — ein aussterbender Beruf?" *Das Orchester*, 29 (1981), 117-21. **284**
The brief answer to the question: not with computers today.

Tim KIRBY. "Setting the Right Note," *British Printer*, January 1982, pp. 13-17. **285**
The "dying art" of the engraver; the historic high-spots; and the future, with composers as marvelous as the computers.

Sister Valerie CRYER. "The Setting of Plainchant," *Matrix*, 4 (Winter 1984), pp. 117-21. **286**
An account of music printing at St Mary's Press, Wantage, beginning in 1890, with details on the typesetting activity.

Eckart MORAT. "Die Entwicklung der Herstellung von Druckvorlagen für den Druck von Musiknoten seit 1945," *Gutenberg Jahrbuch 1984*, pp. 77-82. **287**
On the different kinds of printing, with concern for their special prospects for technological innovation.

Herbert CHLAPIK. *Die Praxis des Notengraphikers*. Wien: Doblinger, 1987. **288**

The brief historical introduction summarizes the applicability of the different basic printing processes to music. This is followed by a detailed discussion of how the different musical symbols are most effectively presented. Most of the recommendations agree with Ross: the differences are minor, but interesting to uncover and contemplate.

James PALTRIDGE. "The Page Placed Before the Player," *MadAminA*, vol. 8, no. 1 (Spring 1987), pp. 20-22. **289**

Argues that, "far from having 'died out,' the writing and copying of music is part of the very fabric of our musical culture." (Indeed, this point is one of the arguments in the present book.)

Christopher SMITH. "The Art of Music Printing," *R. S. A. Journal*, vol. 137, no. 5393 (April 1989), pp. 279-88. **290**

A lecture before the Royal Society of Arts, London, November 9th, 1988, on the fifth anniversary of the R.S.A.-Radcliffe Awards for Graphic Excellence in Music Printing.

The author, president of Halstan & Co., Ltd., and descendant of its founders, identifies major events in the history of music notation and printing and speaks with authority about the present, also with an unassailable ambiguity about the future. Predictably, the subsequent discussion (pp. 288-91) is broad and often provocative, with perspicacious responses from the speaker.

"Pictorial History of Music Printing." [n.p., n.d.] **291**

An illustrated pamphlet that, in four pages, shows some sensitivity to graphic matters. *The* [Selmer] *Bandwagon*, vol. 10, no. 4 (October 1962) is cited in the discussion of computerization.

I have not included writings specifically on the use of computers for printing music, with obvious great misgivings. One may argue that the applications are concerned with the preparation of printing surfaces, and hence analogous to music manuscripts and typescripts, which I have also excluded. The argument may not be attractive: more persuasive is the prolific growth of the published record on computer music, and its dispersal through many kinds of writings (some of them, appropriately, most readily accessible today in machine-readable bibliographical data bases). A separate study of the literature in its own right is really needed.

Even now, however, it seems safe to predict that one of the landmarks will be Michael Kassler, "An Essay toward Specification of a Music-Reading Machine," prepared for Project 295-D, Technical Report no. 2, October, 1963; Report on National Science Foundation, Institutional Grant C-248, to Princeton University, also published in *Musicology and the Computer* (New York: City University of New York Press, 1970), pp. 151-75. Not the least of Kassler's strengths is his clear sense of the history of music printing practice and its relevance to the task at hand.

As for the continuing history, its events are well documented in the extended critical discussions in Walter B. Hewlett and Eleanor Selfridge-Field, *Computing in Musicology* (Menlo Park, Cal.: Center for Computer Assisted Research in the Humanities, 1986-). "Music printing" (i.e., mostly the creation of printing surfaces devoted to musical notation) is a regular feature in the successive annual issues; the 1987 issue also includes an inventory of musical characters. An unannotated list of 179 titles on "Music Printing and Transcription" (pp. 145-59) is also found in Deta S. Davis, *Computer Applications in Music: A Bibliography* (Madison, Wis.: A-R Editions, 1988).

B.   Technical and Trade Literature

Included here are, first, bibliographies of type specimens and other major secondary accounts, arranged geographically; next, specimen books themselves, arranged chronologically, along with other materials on particular music type fonts; and finally, miscellaneous technical literature for the music printing trades.

Type specimens, in W. Turner Berry's definition, are "books and sheets . . . printed by, or for, typefounders to send to printers who set type; or, they are produced by printers to show the type faces they have available." Typefounders' specimens are more common where music is concerned. Specimen sheets will predominate in early periods, specimen books in later periods. (But cf. pp. 127-28.)

Music typography is documented in sources both primary — contemporary announcements of new type faces — and secondary — discussions of any aspects of the preparation of printing surfaces, including both the design and the setting of type and the design and use of engraving punches. Of special interest are the several announcements of new music type faces that themselves evoked historical scholarship in their promotional programs. Fournier (44), Duverger (184), and Aird & Coghill (376) are examples. Similarly, the scholarship of music typography is often subsumed in general histories (as in Chapter 2) and occasionally in writings on graphic aesthetics (as in the section that follows).

The specimen literature of music engraving is more modest, confirming the general assumption that punches were prepared mostly by individual artisans. Ties to the world of goldsmiths, implied by the generally high quality of the workmanship, is documented only rarely in archival sources. Special patterns of capitalization and dispersal are also plausible to imagine. For the music engraver, the costs of a set of punches must have represented a major commitment: the burden of the investment was on the engravers, the evidence of use of the punches was in the editions that they themselves produced. Foundries, in contrast, presumably sold music type, or expected to sell it, to many printers: the weight of the investment was on the foundry, while the evidence of actual use of the type is spread across the universe of printer who used or may have used the type. The music type, of course, may have been made available but never sold, or sold but never used.

BIBLIOGRAPHIES OF SPECIMEN BOOKS AND HISTORIES OF TYPOGRAPHY

General

Peter SOHM. *Museum typographicum Sohmiarum, eller Förteckning på de Böcker och Skrifter* .... Stockholm, 1815. **292** A valuable list, with the minimal citations typical of its day. The collection, now in the Kungl. Biblioteket in Stockholm, is further described in Carl Björkbom, "Kungl. Fältboktryckaren Peter Sohm och den Sohmska Samlingen på Kungl. Biblioteket," *Nordisk Boktrycharekonst 1930*, pp. 149-51, and Udo Willers, "Det Svenska Fältboktryckeriet, 1805-1808," *Nordisk tidskrift för bibliotekswesen*, 38 (1944), 163-67. Lacking a more recent published catalogue, the minimal citations here are still useful.

Daniel Berkeley UPDIKE. *Printing Types: Their History, Forms, and Use: A Study in Survivals.* Cambridge, Mass.: Harvard University Press, 1922. **293**

Esteemed mainly because Updike was one of the respected typographers and book designers of the day. His discussion of
music typography, however, is impressionistic, and facts from
the Fournier essay (44 above) are misread, as Stanley Morison
points out in *The Fleuron*, 1 (1923), 123-24. (The questioned
passages are unchanged, however, in the 1927 reprint, as well as
in the 2nd edition (1937; reprinted 1951).

Alan M. FERN. "Typographical Specimen Books: A Check-
List of the Broxbourne Collection," *The Book Collector*, 5
(1956), 256-72.   **294**
A chronological list of materials in the collection assembled by
Albert Ehrman. (The collection is now dispersed; the type specimen books are at Cambridge University Library.) Broxbourne
references in this book identify Ehrman's inventory numbers;
several titles cited below are not listed by Fern, most of them
presumably having been acquired after the early 1950s.

John DREYFUS, et al. *Type Specimen Facsimiles*. London:
Bowes & Bowes Putnam, 1963 (nos. 1-16); London: The
Bodley Head, 1972 (no. 17).   **295**
Full-size facsimiles, mostly of broadsides that are both very large
and very scarce. A number of other early specimens are yet to be
reproduced, but many of the important ones are here.[1]

Great Britain

Edward Rowe MORES. *A Dissertation upon English Typographical Founders and Foundries*. London, 1788.   **296**
Invaluable for the 18th-century lore, most of it unverifiable,
although much (but not all) of it in time proves to be correct.

---

1. As this book goes to press, my attention is called to an announcement
that *Printing History*, in double issue nos. 26/27, will include an article by
Alastair Johnston on the literature of type specimens.
The works on pp. 107-11 are cited with short titles thus on pp. 112-35:

Annenberg (1975): 305	Dreyfus (1963-71): 295	Mosley (1984): 298
Audin (1933): 299	Enschedé (1908): 303	Reed-Johnson
Berry-Johnson	Howe (1951): 299	(1952 ed.): 297
(1935 ed.): 298	Jolles (1925): 300	Sohm (1815): 292
Broxbourne (1956): 294	Mores (1788): 296	Vervliet (1968): 304
Bruckner (1943): 306	Mori (1955): 302	

A modern edition, together with *A Catalogue and Specimen of the Typefoundry of John James* (*1872*), was prepared with an introduction and notes by Harry Carter and Christopher Ricks (Oxford: Oxford Bibliographical Society, 1961).

Talbot Baines REED. *A History of the Old English Letter Foundries*. London: E. Stock, 1887.   **297**
Based on Mores but with much fuller detail.
The new edition, extensively revised and enlarged by A. F. Johnson (London: Faber & Faber, 1952), is even more valuable; for studies of English typography it is indispensable.

W. Turner BERRY and A. F. JOHNSON. *Catalogue of Specimens of Printing Types by English and Scottish Printers and Founders, 1665-1830*. London: Oxford University Press, 1935.   **298**
The authors' supplement appears in "A Note on the Literature of British Type Specimens," *Signature*, n.s., 16 (1952), 29-40.
Reprinted, with the supplement and a new introduction by James Mosley, New York: Garland, 1983. Still further addenda, corrigenda, amplifications of bibliographical particulars, and additional locations appear in Mosley's *British Type Specimens before 1831: A Hand-List*. Oxford: Bodleian Library, 1984 (Oxford Bibliographical Society, Occasional Publications, 14).

France

Marius AUDIN. *Les livrets typographiques des fonderies françaises créées avant 1800: étude historique et bibliographique*. Paris: A l'enseigne de Pégase, 1933.   **299**
A useful directory, supplemented by Ellic Howe, "French Type Specimen Books," *The Library*, 5th series, 6 (1951), 28-41.
Reprinted together, Amsterdam: Gérard Th. van Heusden, 1984.

Germany

Oscar JOLLES. *Die deutsche Schriftgießerei: eine gewerbliche Bibliographie*, von Lothar von Biedermann [et al]. Berlin: H. Berthold, [1923?; 1925].   **300**
"Musiknotentypen" are discussed on pp. 108-09, with 11 references. A valuable inventory of over 1,200 "Schriftproben"

(pp. 177-267) is arranged by city, with "Privatdrucke" listed at the end.

Gustav MORI. *Das Schriftgießergewerbe in Süddeutschland und den angrenzenden Ländern.* Stuttgart: Bauer, 1924. **301**
Based on Mori's collection, which is today in the Staats- und Universitätsbibliothek, Frankfurt, and is sometimes cited (so as to be confused with a book) as *Schriftproben deutscher Schriftgießereien und Buchdruckereien aus den Jahren 1479 bis 1840.*

———. *Frankfurter Schriftproben aus dem 16. bis 18. Jahrhundert: Eine Entwicklung in ausgewählten Beispielen.* Frankfurt: D. Stempel, 1955. **302**
Facsimiles, several of which include music.

Holland and Belgium

Charles ENSCHEDÉ. *Fonderies de caractères et leur matériel dans les Pays-Bas du XVe au XIXe siècle: Notice historique, principalement d'après les données de la Collection typographique de Joh. Enschedé en Zonen à Haarlem.* Haarlem: F. Bohn, 1908. **303**
A fastidious study, devoted mostly to the Enschedé firm but also covering other shops so as to be essential to work with 18th-century typography in general. (Admittedly, the illustrations of very small psalm-book fonts are too meticulous to be reconcilable with originals usually executed with much less care.)

The translation, *Typefoundries in the Netherlands from the Fifteenth to the Nineteenth Century*, prepared by Harry Carter, assisted in the translation by Netty Hoeflake and edited by Lotte Hellinga (Haarlem: Stichting Museum Enschede, 1978), lends the authority of recent scholarship. It also adds several valuable features, most notably a "List of Type-Specimens" (pp. 437-54), which supersedes Hoeflake's "Type Specimens before 1800," in Wytze Gs Hellinga, *Copy and Print in the Netherlands: An Atlas of Historical Bibliography* (Amsterdam: North-Holland Publishing Co., 1962), pp. 124-32.

The Enschedé specimens themselves are cited in 324 below.

H. D. L. VERVLIET. *Sixteenth-Century Printing Types of the Low Countries.* Amsterdam: Hertzberger, 1968. **304**

Beautiful as a summary of scholarship and as a physical book. The music type is mostly from the Plantin shop (See 309 below).

United States

Maurice ANNENBERG. *Type Foundries of America and their Catalogs.* Baltimore and Washington: Maran Printing Services, 1975.   **305**

Descriptions of American firms, from colonial times forward, with drastically abbreviated (but surprisingly sufficient) citations of their catalogues, including locations. The most useful amplifications of Annenberg's citations are probably those in the Wing catalogue (968), or in the *National Union Catalog: Pre-1956 Imprints* (London: Mansell, 1956-81), although the latter in particular makes one all the most appreciative of Annenberg's diligence in locating copies and pointing out the importance of particular ones. It may be too bad that music type is not specifically identified, although the many illustrations in this book should tell us why: the founders preferred to emphasize other items from their stock that were, if not more lucrative, certainly more spectacular reflections of the graphic tastes of the day.

Mayo (873) has also been a particularly helpful source on the American type specimens with music.

Other Countries

Albert BRUCKNER. *Schweizer Stempelschneider und Schrift-giesser.* Basel: Benno Schwabe, [1943].   **306**

Mentions a number of music type faces.

Christian AXEL-NILSSON. *Type Studies: The Norstedt Collection of Matrices in the Typefoundry of the Royal Printing Office.* Stockholm: Norstedt, 1983.   **307**

A set of 74 18th-century matrices ("NS 022") is shown on p. 165, with brief commentary there and on pp. 25, 40, and 77.

SPECIMEN BOOKS

My practice of collecting material of a bibliographical lineage, with comments on the later versions in the annotation, here may often result in a presentation that is particularly frustrating to its most important readers — namely those who attempt to trace the history of particular music type faces. Serving this audience with any authority, however, will not be possible until the different faces have been identified and their migrations figured out. This needs to be undertaken with recourse to three kinds of evidence: extant copies in which the particular faces appear, archival records, and specimen books. Locating contemporary apprearances is usually a prodigious virtuoso assignment, often made easier by gratifyingly clever search strategies, but always subject to surprising discoveries. Archival evidence is probably more abundant than one might suspect, but deriving inferences from it may be more problematical than one might wish. The specimen books deserve to be cited as evidence in their own right, although using them becomes all the more difficult when the early evidence is as sparse and scattered as it is and the nineteenth-century evidence as elusive as it is (see for instance the note on pp. 127-28 below).

Guillaume LE BÉ (I and II). [Accounts of early French typography. Paris, 1550s?, 1643? 1730-43.]   **308**
Early French music printing is the story not only of the Ballard monopoly but also of its Le Bé music type, handsome and capacious, also uncommonly well documented in its origins. Three surviving manuscripts provide the crucial evidence:

1. The "specimen" (Bibliothèque Nationale, MS. Nouv. acq. fr. 4528, No. IX), which reproduces type faces introduced in the 1550s. The music fonts are shown and discussed in part 2 of Henri Omont, "Spécimens de caractères hébreux, grecs, latins et de musique gravés à Venise et à Paris par Guillaume Le Bé (1545-1592)," *Mémoires de la Société de l'Histoire de Paris et de l'Île-de-France*, 15 (1888), 273-83.

2. The "inventory," prepared by the elder Le Bé (*d.* 1598), which is not extant but survives in a copy made by Jean-Pierre Fournier (l'aîné) between 1730 and 1742, with further commentary by Fournier and others (Archives Nationales). The document is reproduced, with an introduction by Stanley Morison, in *L'Inventaire de la fonderie Le Bé selon la transcription de Jean-Pierre Fournier* (Paris: André Jammes, 1957; Documents typographiques français, 1), in which matrices for seven plainchant fonts and seven fonts of "Musique venues de Lion" are cited on pp. 22-23, and eleven sets of punches on pp. 25-26.

3. The "memorandum" of the younger Le Bé, prepared just prior to his death around 1645, which survives in part in the original and in part in Fournier's copy (Archives Nationales). It is transcribed, with a discussion by Harry Carter, in *Sixteenth-Century French Typefounders: The Le Bé Memorandum* (Paris: André Jammes, 1967; Documents typographiques français, 3).

These documents have informed all subsequent studies in music typography (mostly for the better but in the noted case of Haultin for the worse), beginning with the 1765 *Traité* (44) by Fournier's brother Pierre-Simon ("le jeune").

Christopher PLANTIN. *Index sive specimen characterum.* [Antwerp, 1567].   **309**

The Plantin shop, producer both of books and type in the Renaissance and today pre-eminent as a typographic museum, claims punches and matrices that can be traced back to the 16th century. The 1567 specimen shows three music faces: "Grande Musicque" (no. 80, attributed to Hendrik van den Keere), "Moyenne Musicque" (no. 81, also by van den Keere), and "Petite Musicque" (no. 82, attributed to Robert Granjon). Dreyfus 17; Enschedé 1.

Plantin and his successors acquired additional fonts over the years, and detailed them in 15 extant manuscript inventories. These are described in Mike Parker, K. Melis, and H. D. L. Vervliet, "Typographia Plantiniana, II: Early Inventories of Punches, Matrices, and Moulds, in the Plantin-Moretus Museum," *De gulden passer*, 38 (1960), 1-139. Appendix II identifies 17 sets of extant music punches (ST 60-75, pp. 125-26) and 15 sets of extant matrices (MA 85-93, pp. 130-31), as well as the two sets of matrices that are today lacking (LMA 36 and 19, p. 134).

The music faces are widely reproduced, i.e., seven appear in Max Rooses, *Index characterum architypographiæ Plantinianæ: Proeven der lettersoorten* (Antwerpen: Museum Plantin Moretus, 1905), in which *f. 7^v*, following p. 14, shows three mensural fonts and four plainchant fonts, with black notes on red lines.

Fifteen music books using these fonts bear Plantin's own imprint. These are listed in Jean Auguste Stellfeld, *Bibliographie des éditions musicales plantiniennes* (Bruxelles: Palais des Académies, 1949; Academie royale be Belgique, Classe des beaux arts, Memoires, Tom 5, fasc. 3). For editions by other printers using Plantin's music type, 1602-57, see Rudi A. Rasch, "Noord-Nederlandse Muziekuitgaven met de Plantijnse Noten-typen," *Die Gulden Passer*, 51 (1973), 9-18.

The Museum has also been understandably happy to display its treasures in exhibitions. Its published catalogues include G. Persoons and H. D. L. Vervliet, *Muziekdrukken van de zestiende eeuw: De ontwikkeling van de musiek naar handschrift, prent en druk, voornamelijk in de Nederlanden* (Antwerpen: Museum Plantin-Moretus, 1963), also issued in *Antwerpen: Tijdschrift der Stad Antwerpen*, 9 (1963), 61-70; and *Muziek in Amsterdam: Catalogus van de Tentoonstelling, 15 november 1975-18 januari 1976*. The Museum's recognition of its musical heritage is also reflected in its handsome programs for early music concerts. A notable example is the one entitled *Christophori Plantini architypographi memoriam celebrat Antverpia MDXX-MCMXX*, with a facsimile from the *Encomium musices* of the 1580s and texts for vocal music sung on August 9, 1920 by the Chorale Cæcilia, directed by Louis de Vocht.

Georg Leopold FUHRMANN. *Typorum et characterum officinae Chalcographicae . . .* [Nürnberg, 1616].   **310**

Includes "notas item Musicas figuralis, quae vocant, et choralis."

Enschedé, 8. The specimen is also discussed in Robert Meldau, "Reichsfreiheit für den Frankfurter Schriftgiesser Jakob Sabon, 1575 and 1578," *Gutenberg Jahrbuch 1935*, pp. 205-12, where parts of it are reproduced, but not those that show music.

Andrea BROGIOTTI. *Indice de' caratteri, con l'inventori & nomi di essi, esistenti nella Stampa Vaticana & Camerale.* In Roma, 1628.   **311**

The Vatican's four music fonts (three plainchant and one mensural, for use in choirbooks), probably designed several decades earlier by Robert Granjon, are shown on leaves 69-72. They are also discussed in H. D. L. Vervliet, *The Type Specimen of the Vatican Press, 1628* (Amsterdam: Menno Hertzberger, 1967), pp. 39-40; also his "Robert Granjon à Rome, 1578-1589: Notes préliminaires à une histoire de la typographie romaine à la fin du XVIe siècle," *Bulletin de l'Institut historique de Rome*, 38 (1967), 177-32, also issued separately (Amsterdam: Menno Hertzberger, 1967); and *Cyrillic and Oriental Typography in Rome at the End of the Sixteenth Century: An Inquiry into the Later Work of Robert Granjon (1578-90)* (Berkeley: Poltroon Press, 1981), pp. 48-51.

The earlier presence of the type is documented in an archival transcript discussed in Alberto Tinto, "Di un inventario della Tipografia Vaticana (1595)," in *Studi di biblioteconomia e storia del libro in onore di Francesco Barberi* (Roma: Associazione italiana biblioteche, 1976), pp. 545-53.

Bartholomeus VOSKENS. *Proben van die fürnehmsten Matryssen und Schriften.* [Hamburg, ca. 1650?].   **312**
Includes "Cicero Noten." Dreyfus 6; Enschedé 14.

Music is also seen in the *Proef van Letteren, Die te bekomen zyn By de weduwe van Dirck Voskens, in syn leven lettersnyderengieter, op de Bloemgraft, tot Amsterdam*, issued by the widow of Dirck Voskens (Amsterdam, *ca.* 1695; Dreyfus 8; Enschedé 31, cf. also 32, 39-44, 56-61, etc.).

For background on the firm and its relationship to the Schmidt (316 below) see Gustav Mori, *Die Schriftgiesser . . . Voskens* (Frankfurt, 1923); also Douglas C. McMurtrie, "The Brothers Voskens and their Successors . . . ," *Inland Printer*, 88 (October 1924), pp. 59-66 (reissued, Chicago: Privately Printed, 1932), which includes illustrations of the above.

Broer JANSZOON. *Proeven der Letteren welke de naghelaten Weduwe en Erfghenamen van Zal. Brver. Jansz. van Meening zijn te verkoopen.* Amsterdam, 1653.   **313**
A font of "Groote Nieuwe Kanon Nooten" is mentioned in this auction catalogue, a copy of which is at the University of Leiden. Morison's *John Fell* (1967; 320 below), pp. 195-200, identifies this as a font sold by Jacques Vallet in 1672 to Thomas Marshall on behalf of Bishop Fell, discusses its subsequent use in Oxford, and shows several examples.

Balthasar KÖBLIN. *Costantzer Fractürlein* [and] *Noten auff Cicero Kägel.* . . . [Constance, ca. 1655].   **314**
Bruckner, pp. 152-53, assigns the date, shows a facsimile, and says it was commissioned by the Luther foundry in Frankfurt.

Cyriakus PISTORIUS. [Music type specimen]. Basel, 1673.
Shows "Kleine Noten." Cited in Jolles, p. 108, and reproduced by Bruckner as a *Beilage.*   **315**

Johann Adolph SCHMID. *Obgemelte schrifften Prob.* Frankfurt-am-Main, 1677. **316**
Includes "Gros Canon Nothen," "Bibel oder Parangon Nothen," "Cicero Nothen," and "Garamont Nothen"; Enschedé 23.
See also McMurtrie's essay on Voskens (312 above), p. 65.

Johann Erasmus LUTHER. [Specimen of Types]. Frankfurt-am-Main, 1678. **317**
Shows "Parangon und Cicero Noten." Mori, Tafel 9.
A 1718 Lutherische Schriftgiesserei specimen (Mori, Tafel 12) also shows these two fonts.

Christoffel VAN DYCK. *Proeven van Letteren, Die gesneden zijn . . . , soo als de selve verkoft sullen werden ten huyse van de weduwe Wylen Daniel Elsevier.* [Amsterdam], 1681. **318**
Broadside with "Mediaen Nooten" and "Descendiaen Nooten."
Enschedé 25, also discussed on pp. 77-75, with a facsimile; Dreyfus 12. A facsimile is tipped in at the end of the 1962 Carter-Davis edition of Moxon (160 above).
Another van Dyck *Proeven van Letteren*, undated but probably earlier, also shows these same two fonts.

Nicholas KIS. [*Specimen sheet, beginning with "Intramus mundum" in "Groot Canon Romein"*]. Amsterdam, [*ca.* 1685]. **319**
Shows a minuscule music face (3.2 mm tall, and designated as "Descendiaen Nooten"), which Kis took back to Kolozsvár and used there, mostly in Hungarian Calvinist psalmbooks. The music face also appears in Sámuel Telegdi Pap's 1723 sale catalogue, headed "Specimen typorum"; cf. Enschedé 27.
These faces are discussed and reproduced as Plates 1 and 2 in György Haiman, *Totfaluai Kis Miklós* (Budapest: Magyar Helikon, 1972), and translated and extended by Elizabeth Hoch, Mária Baranyai, and Sándor Bándy as *Nicholas Kis: A Hungarian Punch-Cutter and Printer, 1650-1702* (Budapest: Akadémiai Kiadó; San Francisco: Jack W. Stauffacher, 1983).

A Specimen of the Several Sorts of Letter Given to the University by Dr. John Fell. . . . Oxford: Printed at the Theatre, 1695. **320**

116

Includes the second music face devised for Bishop Fell by Peter Walpergen, with rounded note-heads. See Horace Hart, *Notes on a Century of Typography* (Oxford: Oxford University Press, 1900, pp. 58-59, 142; also the reprint, Oxford: Clarendon Press, 1970, with notes by Harry Carter discussing the music on pp. 185 and 191-92); Berry-Johnson, pp. 6-7; also J. S. G. Simmons on "The Fell Type Specimens," in Stanley Morison, *John Fell, the University Press, and the Fell Types* (Oxford: Clarendon Press, 1967; reprinted, New York: Garland, 1981), pp. 229-32 (with reproductions of the type on pp. 248-49); my *English Music Printing* (1975; 661), pp. 134-37; also Mores, pp. lxxvii, 33, and 42; and Reed-Johnson, pp. 143-46. See also the 1895 *Yattendon Hymnal* (929 below).

Jeremias STENGLIN. [Price-list for music type. Augsburg, [ca. 1700].   321
Mori, p. 9, reports this to contain four music fonts.

Claude LAMESLE. *Épreuves générales des caractères.* À Paris, Rüe Galande (*au milieu*) près la Place Maubert, 1742.   322
Includes specimens of two mensural and eight plainchant music fonts, the latter two of which are much older and likely came from Holland. I have not seen Lamesle's 1769 Avignon specimen (Audin 28; Howe, p. 36; Broxbourne 3.28).

Nicolas GANDO. *Épreuve des caractères de la fonderie.* Paris: Cloistre Saint-Julien le Pauvre, 1745.   323
Audin 28 a-b; see also Howe, p. 33.
    The Gandos' 1766 *Observations* (168 above) also includes a specimen showing six fonts from the Le Bé succession, with (per Howe) a four-page specimen of the Gandos' new music type.
    Later books include a Gando Frères *Specimen des caractères de plain-chant* (Paris: Adrien le Clerc et Cie., janvier 1837).

Isaak and Jean ENSCHEDÉ. *Épreuves de caractères que se fondent de la Nouvelle Fonderie.* Haarlem, 1744.   324
Includes music, as reproduced in Enschedé.
    The music faces are also seen in the 2nd ed., "augmentée & ameliorée jusqu'à l'An 1748" (Broxbourne 3.12) and in the 3rd

ed., to 1757 (Broxbourne 3.11). The music coverage is extended in the firm's 1768 *Proef van Letteren* (Broxbourne 3.15).

Widow of Johann Rudolff PISTORIUS. . . . *große und kleine Choral und Figural-Noten . . . in billichem Preiß.* Basel, 1747.   **325**

A broadside that shows no fewer than 23 (!) different music fonts. Bruckner, *Tafel* X, from Gustav Mori's collection (*Schrift-proben*, 12, no. 13). Bruckner, p. 60, also speaks of a 1704 speci-men (*Ecce specimen typorum variorum*) of Johann Pistorius, but which is said to contain no music.

Claude MOZET. Epreuves des caractères de la fonderie. Nantes, Rüe de Verdun, . . . , 1754.   **326**

This specimen shows no music, but it is still of interest here be-cause the absence is explained (or at least acknowledged): "Je n'ai pas mis des Notes de plein chant dans mes épreuves, quoique j'eusse tout ce que cette espece d'ouvrage demande, n'ayant pas cru que celle addition leur donnât beaucoup de relief" (literally: I have not shown plainchant notes in my specimen, for while I have everything needed for this kind of work, I do not believe that showing it here would be very useful).

Johann Gottlob Immanuel BREITKOPF. "Nachricht," in Johann Friedrich Gräfe, *Sonnet auf das . . . Pastorell Il trionfo della fedeltà* (Leipzig: Breitkopf, 1755), p. 2.   **327**

Breitkopf's brief announcement of his new music type, dated February 1755, appears in a specimen that precedes a four-page aria from the pastoral drama by the Saxon princess Maria Antonia Walpurgis, a work that Breitkopf soon issued in full.

Reproduced in facsimile as *Sonnet auf das . . . Pastorell Il trionfo della fedeltà* (Leipzig: Breitkopf & Härtel, 1919) to honor Oskar von Hase's fifty years with the firm.

The *Proben der Schriften in der Breitkopfischen Schriftgiesserei* of 1787 (Broxbourne 97.25) is much expanded and a very sub-stantial document well worthy of study in its own right, particu-larly for its price-list.

An ambiguous but promising *ATF* citation (vol. 3, p. 1615) actually identifies a copy of Friedrich Wilhelm Marpurg's *Rac-colta della più nuove composizioni di clavicembalo* (1756-57).

Pierre-Simon FOURNIER. *Essai d'un nouveau caractère de fonte, pour l'impression de la musique, inventé & exécuté, dans toutes les parties typographiques.* Paris, 1756. **328** Fournier's announcement of his new music type in the earlier double-impression form. Poole (141, p. 31*n*) locates the only known copy (Sohm 4° 99), and paraphrases the introduction.

Les caractères de l'imprimerie par Fournier le Jeune (Paris, 1764) also shows new "Petite Musique" (pp. 155-56), also the "Grosse musique, pour la Symphonie & pour le Chant" (pp. 161-63), followed by plainchant fonts (pp. 164-68; pp. 161*ff.* are double fold-out pages). Tome II of the *Manuel typographique* (1766; 166 above) reprints these same pages, pp. 155-56 now on pp. 172-73; a new example of the "Grosse Musique," on pp. 174-76; pp. 177-84 now on pp. 161-68; and further plainchant music on pp. 185-86. Tome I of the *Manuel* (1764) also discusses the fonts on pp. 36-37 and 280-91.

For more on Fournier's specimens see James Mosley, *An Introduction to Pierre-Simon Fournier's Modèles des caractères de l'Imprimerie* (London: Eugrammia Press, 1965); also pp. 63-64.

[Notices (*"Empfehlungs-Anzeige"*) of music type], *Gazette de Cologne*, 1757, nos. 28 (April 8) and 53 (July 5). **329** Two brief announcements, both of which appear on the last page prior to the *Suplement* of this bi-weekly journal, the former appropriately in large and elegant script, the latter in modest italic. Since finding these frequently cited texts may take more time than reading them, I summarize them here in translation:

The Enschedé foundry in Haarlem is improving daily, as one can see in this Gazette. In several weeks a new musical character will appear, surpassing anything of its kind. Printers who might want to see it should ask for an octavo book, which will be sent at once; please write to us.

The Luther foundry, in Frankfurt on the Main, reminds everyone, printers especially, that it intends to maintain its reputation and attempt to be even more illustrious in keeping everybody perfectly happy. Here you can obtain alphabets, flowers, and ornaments, also punches and matrices for printing vocal and instrumental music. This is a new invention, the cleanness, appearance, and beauty of which are not inferior to engraving, infinitely surpassing what one usually

gets these days, with the added advantage of low cost.[2] After
the next Fair [presumably the Michelmas Frankfurt book
fair] these can be seen at M. Desoer's shop in Liège, which
will be the first to be supplied. This new invention doubtless
owes much to the tastes of connoisseurs: orders may be
placed with Johann Becker, director of the foundry.
Frankfurt, March 30, 1757.

Jacques SANLECQUES.   *Épreuves des caractères du fond.*
Paris, De l'Imprimerie d'Aug. Mart. Lottin, 1757.   **330**
Includes four pages of specimens: a "Nottes qui se fondent
chacune sur quatre Moules," and another ". . . sur un Moule,"
both for plainchant, and two pages of mensural music, headed
"Trois Musiques qui se fondent sur cinq Moules," and "Suite de
la musique . . . Celli-ci se fait sur un Moule."

Jacques François ROSART.   *Épreuve des caractères, qui se
gravent & fondent dans la nouvelle fonderie.* . . . Bruxelles,
1761.   **331**
Rosart (1714-77) issued specimens as early as 1740 from his
shop in Haarlem (Enschedé 68, 71, 85-86, 87). The mosaic music
type that he had designed many years earlier is first seen in this
specimen, probably in response to Enschedé's decision to
promote Fleischman's version rather than Rosart's. Also seen
are a "Plainchant sur cinq, corps de Cicero," with black notes on
red lines, and a small "Double philosophie plain-chant."
    The "Deuxième édition augmentée" of 1768 (Broxbourne 3.31;
St. Bride 20227) is a considerably expanded specimen (43 to 70
pages), in which the plainchant types are shown on L_{3-4}, the mosaic music on M_1. This book is reproduced in *The Type Specimen
of Jacques-François Rosart* (Amsterdam: Van Gendt, 1973). Fernand Baudin and Netty Hoeflake trace the history of the shop
and discuss its fonts in the introduction: see in particular pp. 22-
24, also p. 66-67 and the charts on pp. 69-77. (Their essay does

---

2. C'est une nouvelle invention, dont la netteté, l'oeil & la beauté n'est pas
inferieure à la gravure au burin, qui surpasse infiniment tout qu'on a eu
jusqu'à présent en ce genre, & qui de plus a encore cet avantage, qu'un
quintal peut fournir à l'impression ou par delà de 3 quintaux des notes, qui
ont été en usage jusqu'à présent.

not mention Poole's major study of 1965-66, 141 above, but it generally agrees with his findings.)

The *Épreuves des caractères de la Fonderie de Mathias Rosart* (À Bruxelles, Rue Veuve, 1789; Broxbourne 103-28), shows another selection of music faces (pp. 110-15), four for plainchant (both roman and gothic, the latter not seen in 1768), one for mensural music (different from that seen in 1768), and one of blank staves ("Filets pour faire de papier de musique").

Jan ROMAN. *Proeven van Letteren, Die gesneden zijn door Wylen Christoffel van Dyck, welke te bekomen zyn op de Nieuwe Heere Gracht, over de Plantagie, in te Boekdrukkery.* [Amsterdam, ca. 1762].   332

Includes "Mediaen noten" and "Cicero noten."
Dreyfus 13; Enschedé 106.

[William CASLON]. *A Specimen of Printing Types.* London: Dryden Leach, 1764.   333

The most important music type faces of late 18th-century England and America, and the last important music font that was linear rather than mosaic in its conception. The specimen is reproduced in Carey S. Bliss, *A Pair for Printing . . . William Caslon and the First English Type Specimen Book* (North Hills, Pa.: Bird & Bull Press, 1982), with introductory comments on pp. 55-60. See also James Mosley, "A Specimen of Printing Types by William Caslon, London 1766," *Journal of the Printing Historical Society*, 16 (1981-82), 17-20.

Reed-Johnson (p. 73; cf. pp. 201, 237, 244) says that the matrices "came from Mitchell's foundry," which would date the face before 1739. But I have not seen the type prior to the 1764 specimen. (For a 1763 Caslon specimen that does not show the music see the *Signature* supplement to Berry-Johnson, p. 32, also Mosley, p. 25.) See also Mores, pp. 49*n*, 76. Berry-Johnson (pp. 21-28) traces the fonts through the Caslon specimen books of 1766, 1785, 1786, and 1805, but not thereafter.

At first the type seems to have been used mostly for songs in periodicals (e.g. *London Magazine, Gentleman's Magazine, Universal Magazine*). It was used in 1770 in Luckombe (169 above); and later in the second edition of Joshua Steele's *Prosodia rationalis* (London: J. Nichols, 1779). The type was imported to

America and is seen in the *Specimen of Isaiah Thomas's Printing Types* (Worcester, Mass., 1785). William M'Culloch in Philadelphia also began using it about the same time.

Its sudden disappearance around 1800, in both England and America, suggests that the Caslons withdrew it from circulation. Could popular tastes suddenly have turned fickle? Not likely. What may be its last appearance, in John Johnson's *Typographia* (1824; 179 above), could be just one more typographical affectation in a book conspicuous for anachronistic Regency sentiments. The history of this type face clearly promises rich prospects for study and conjecture.

For a brief discussion of Caslon's public concerts, based mostly on Hawkins, see William Bennett, *William Caslon, 1692-1766: Ornamental Engraver, Typefounder and Music Lover* (Birmingham: City of Birmingham School of Printing, Central School of Arts & Crafts, 1935), esp. p. 12.

Johann Thomas TRATTNER. *Characterum Russicorum, Turcicorum, Græcorum et Hebraicorum.* Wien, 1768.   **334**
Mozart's friend Trattner issued four specimens: a *Specimen characterum latinorum* for roman-letter printing, a *Deutsche Schriften* for gothic texts, this one, and an *Abdruck derjenigen Rüslein und Zierrathen* showing the ornamental stock. One page here is devoted to "Choral Noten," for plainchant, and one to "Nonparell Noten," for mensural music.

Louis VERNANGE. *Épreuves des caractères de la fonderie.* Lyon, Place de la charité, [1770?].   **335**
Five music fonts are seen: a "gros romain" (4 points), two "petit romain" (2 points, one with large and the other with small noteheads), a "cicero" (2 points), and a "Musique pour les Protestans."

La Veuve HÉRISSANT. *Épreuves des caractères ....* Paris, Rue Saint-Jacques, au coin de celle de la Parcheminerie, 1772.   **336**
"Article VI" consists of eight pp. of "Notes de Plainchant," progressing from "Deux points de Nompareille" on a 3.5 mm. staff, up to "Grosse note, rouge et noir," on a 34 (!) mm. staff.

Louis DELACOLONGE. *Les caractères et les vignettes de la fonderie.* Lyon, Montée & près les Carmelites, 1773.   **337**
Shows plainchant, pp. 118-21. Broxbourne 3:8; Enschedé 120.
Reprinted with introduction and notes by Harry Carter, as *The Type Specimen of Delacolonge* (Amsterdam: Van Gendt, 1969).

Joseph GILLÉ. *Épreuves de caractères de la fonderie.* Paris, Rue et petite Marché Saint-Jacques, 1773.   **338**
Includes "Notes de quatre points de nompareille" (plainsong), "Musique Gothique, à l'usage des Protestans" (small diamond notes), and "Musique portant ses filets sur le corps de petit Canon" (Fournier's type, actually the "grosse musique").
Poole has located in the Broxbourne copy (3.35) a four-page descriptive insert, giving prices for the type.
The 1778 specimen (*Caractères de la fonderie de J. Gillé*; Broxbourne d.5) shows the same three fonts, with more substantial texts on larger pages.

J. L. de BOUBERS. *Épreuves de caractères de le fonderie.* Bruxelles, Rue d'Assaut, près de Ste. Gudule, 1777.   **339**
Shows three pp. of plainsong and one p. of mensural (Rosart) music type, along with observations on the beauty of French music. Broxbourne 3.36; Enschedé 124.

Henry VAUSSY. *Épreuve des caractères de l'imprimerie.* Rouen, Rue Mamuchet, 1783.   **340**
Incudes a two-point "Cicero" music. Broxbourne 3.38.

PERRENOT & fils. *Épreuve des caractères de la fonderie . . . .* Avignon, 1784.   **341**
Includes a page of plainchant designated as "Note de deux Points de Cicero & de Philosophie." Broxbourne 103.24.

Gebroeders PLOOS VAN AMSTEL. *Épreuves de plusieurs sortes de caractères / Proef van . . . Letteren . . . welke gegooten worden by Gebr. Ploos.* Te Amsterdam, Op de Keizersgraft, tegen over 't Molenpad, [1784].   **342**
Four diamond-note fonts, labelled "Dubbelde Mediaan Psalmnooten," "Groote Mediaan Nooten," "Mediaan Nooten," and "Deszendiaan Nooten," appear after the Armenian letters.

Broxbourne 3.39; Enschedé 132. (For other Ploos specimens, 1765-1790s, see Enschedé 108, 111-12, 115, 121, 139, and 143.)

M. PIERRES. *Caractères de l'imprimerie . . . composés par Honoré-Théodore De Hansy.* Paris, 1785.   **343**
A rare instance of a music type compositor gaining due acknow-ledgment. Three pages are devoted to "Grosse musique" and "Petite musique" (Fournier's mensural fonts); "Plain-Chant de Gros-Canon" and "Plain-Chant de Petit-Canon;" and "Plain-Chant Rouge & Noir." Broxbourne 3.11.

IMPRENTA REAL. *Carácteres de la Imprenta Real.* Madrid, 1793.   **344**
Shows two music pages: "XLIV. Canto llano de Pradell" and "XLV. Orto canto llano." Broxbourne 3.43.

Antonio ZATTA e Figli. *Saggi dei caratteri, vignette e fregi de la Nuova Fonderia . . . .* Venezia, 1794.   **345**
Includes music. Broxbourne 3.44.

Pedro IFERN. *Muestras de los carácteres. . . .* n.p.: Fermin Thadeo Villalpando, 1795.   **346**
Includes a page of "Canto llano."

Johann Friedrich UNGER. *Schriftproben der Didotschen und gewöhnlichen Lettern,* Berlin [1798?]   **347**
Sohm 8° 101; Enschedé 143. See also Ernst Crous, *Die Schrift-giessereien in Berlin . . . bis Unger* (Berlin: H. Berthold, 1928), especially pp. 103-06.
The last page of the specimen, devoted to the song "Ich denke dein," is designated as a "Probe der neuen Noten in der Unger-schen Schriftgiesserei in Berlin." (Crous shows a facsimile as Tafel 3; this version, however, shows a different setting of type from what is seen in the Sohm exemplar.)
Unger also announced his type in two editions of music for a *Trauerspiel* on *Die Jungfrau von Orleans* by Bernhard Anselm Weber — in a *Krönungsmarsch* (Berlin, 1803, designated as a "Zweite Probe neuer Noten") and in a *Musikbegleitung zu dem Monolog* (Berlin, 1805, designated as a "Letzte Probe vollen-deter neuer Noten"). Unger's dedication of October 1803, on the last page of the *Krönunsgmarch*, speaks of great difficulties

and costs, but also promises to match prices with Breitkopf (whom he names specifically) and other dealers as well.

For all Unger's respected position in German typography, his music type is surprisingly little studied. Gustav Bogeng (*Die Unger Fraktur*, Heidelberg: Richard Weißbach, 1922, pp. viii-ix) insists that this type is a reflection of Unger's own type-cutting activities and not merely an imitation of Breitkopf. One respectfully defers to Bogeng, but finds it ironic that all three of Unger's *Proben* use roman text, in contrast to the *Fraktur* that is almost always seen with Breitkopf's. What Unger was groping for, one may speculate, is a lighter page. For several reasons his cause was ill-fated, we may conjecture: (1) his timing was bad, (2) Breitkopf was better known to musicians, and (3) Unger had no clear sense of the legibility of musical signs: his white notes were too long, and other signs seem idiosyncratic and distracting.

J. OOMKENS j. Zoon. *Proef van Letteren, Bloemen, enz.* . . . Groningen, 1807.   **348**
Two texts are set in "Mediaan Psalm Noten." Broxbourne 3.46.

Imprimerie Royale. *Spécimen des caractères,* . . . *Ière partie: Ancienne typographie.* Paris, 1819.   **349**
Shows an expanded version of Fournier's single-impression mosaic type, with a case layout, as discussed in Poole (141), part 2, p. 31.

Edmund FRY. *Specimen of Modern Printing Types.* London, 1820.   **350**
Three music faces—large and small plainchant and "psalm music"—are seen on *f.* [64-66], in the place in specimen books where one so often sees the music: after the exotic scripts and before the ornaments.

Reprinted, with an introduction and notes by David Chambers, London: Printing Historical Society, 1986.

Berry-Johnson, p. 49, also reports music in the Fry specimen books of 1823 and 1824.

Hugh HUGHES. *Specimen Sheet of Modern Music Types.* London, [after 1823].   **351**
A separate music specimen is mentioned specifically in Reed-Johnson, p. 364, but with no location; nor has Mosley seen it.

The music type does appear, however, in Hughes's *A Specimen of Book and Newspaper Printing Types* (London, *ca.* 1825), on *f.* [6] according to Berry & Johnson, p. 83; see also Reed-Johnson, pp. 358-59, also Savage (192).

J. Hancock, *Specimen of Music Types* (London, *ca.* 1845) shows two pages of "Nonpareil Music Type" and "Plain Church Chant Music," with an announcement that Hancock had purchased the type after Hughes's death, which was in 1841.

DIDOT, LEGRAND & Co. *Spécimen des caractères de la Fonderie Polyamatype.* Paris: Imprimerie de E. Duverger, rüe de Verneuil, no. 4, 1828.   **352**
A single paltry page of plainsong type, in anticipation of Duverger's spectacular assault on the world of music printing (see 184 above). Broxbourne 3.1.

James CONNER & Sons. *Specimens of Printing Types and Ornaments.* New York: Conner & Cooke, 1836.   **353**
Active between 1829 and 1892, according to Annenberg, the firm showed three music fonts in this specimen (which is designated as a "second edition"): Diamond Music no. 1 and Nonpareil Music nos. 1 and 2, in settings of "Hail Columbia!" Music type is not seen in the 1852 specimen. It reappears in the Conner specimens of 1854 and 1855, but not thereafter.

George BRUCE & Co. *A Specimen of Printing Types.* New-York, 1841.   **354**
Active 1813-1901 according to Annenberg, the firm showed music fonts in this book, and in its successors of 1848 and 1853 ("Nonpareil Section Music" 1, 2, and 3), but neither before nor later. Mayo (873 below) has interesting comments.

BÄR & HERMANN. *Schrift-Proben der Buchdruckerei.* Leipzig, 1842.   **355**
"Tertia-Noten" and "Text-Noten" are shown on p. 95.

Duncan SINCLAIR & Sons. *Specimen of Modern Printing Types.* Edinburgh, 1843.   **356**
Shows two music faces, "submitted to Mr. John Hullah, and sanctioned by his approval." The music type does not appear in the firm's specimen books of 1840 and 1842; but it is seen in the

one from 1846 — without the Hullah endorsement, however, and now spread over four rather than two pages.

Ch. LABOULAYE & Cie. *Épreuves de caractères.* Paris: Fonderie Générale de Caractères Français et Étrangers, [1851?].   **357**
The Newberry copy shows a page of "Plain-Chant" (in five sizes) followed by one of "Caractères de Musique," both near the end of an unpaginated volume. The Fonderie Générale is an amalgamation of the earlier firms of Firmin Didot, Dolé, Mion, Tarbé, Crosnier, Éverat, Laboulaye frères, and Biesta.

J. HADDON. *Specimens of Music Printing.* London, 1859.
[Davidsson 192.] I have found no music in any catalogues of John Haddon & Co. (The Caxton Type Foundry), which in any event flourished just after 1900.   **358**

We must now confront the specimen books of the great nineteenth-century corporate foundries. I have not examined all copies, most of which are today in very poor physical condition. They often consist of single leaves on coated stock, now very brittle, sometimes originally sewn as gatherings but more typically attached to thick fabric backing with glue that has now largely disintegrated, leaving fragile pages loose in their bindings. The extant copies are usually unpaginated, and their contents vary, so as to suggest that either (1) they were assembled intentionally for particular customers in mind, as "nonce" books; (2) they were assembled randomly, from whatever pages were at hand; (3) other circumstances applied that we do not know about; or (4) different explanations apply to particular copies. Most extant copies are undated, although some can be conjecturally dated from internal evidence (in ways and with levels of confidence not unlike that encountered in the dating of engraved music). Sometimes the dating evidence is contradictory, as with the Figgins title below, so that the latest date (assuming that even this much can be established) must be presumed to apply to the book as a whole.

The specimen books are in some ways functionally comparable to printed music itself. Both were intended for practitioners, trained in technical skills and aesthetic judgement, to be used as visual tools for guiding the mind in executing manual activities and then discarded. It is not quite correct to propose that an important difference was that the printers usually had dirty fingers. It is probably fair, however, to suspect that, whereas musicians loved their scores to death and disposed of them only with deep nostalgia, most printers knew paper only all too well and were happy to discard anything they suspected was no longer needed.

I have been further intimidated by the prospect of including here any of the single music specimen sheets that were made up and distributed, presumably as an alternative to the specimen books. Their survival is tenuous, since they are usually undated and fragile (although it is not surprising when a supply of several dozen copies turns up, in pristine condition, so as to suggest that they were never distributed at all. St. Bride has a nice collection of these). Locating them and studying their circumstances of intended use — which founders used them and why — should be a worthy challenge for future bibliographers.

With the nineteenth century, the proliferation of documentary evidence changes the research patterns of typographic historians. New type faces are more likely to be recorded not only in specimen books but also in extant copies, archival sources, and periodical announcements. As a result, scholarly expectations are usually all the greater and all the more generalized: instead of single evidences of survival (as with the Plantin and Caslon fonts detailed above), historians will more typically seek to uncover large-scale patterns. The extant evidence, in any event, has clearly proliferated, so as to justify the notion that the late nineteenth century represents the Golden Age of Music Printing.

Lawrence JOHNSON & Co. [*later*: American Type Founders Co., etc.]. *Minor Book of Specimens of Printing Types.* Philadelphia, 1853. **359**

Among the specimen books issued by the pre-eminent lineage of American typefounders, this is the earliest known to contain music. The lineage involves four names: Binny & Ronaldson (1796-1815; various Ronaldsons alone to 1833); Johnson (1833-45), later Thomas McKellar (1845-92, alone at first, later as MacKellar, Smiths and Jordan); and finally the American Type Founders Co., now relocated in New York.

The firm's jubilee book, *1796-1896: One Hundred Years*, p. 85, speaks of theirs as being at the time "the only type foundry in the country making music type." In addition to Annenberg, the *National Union Catalog* (London: Mansell, 1968-81; vol. 58, pp. 131-32, vol. 282, p. 257, and vol. 352, pp. 83-85) and John Bidwell's "Bibliographical Note" (pp. ix-xiii) in the "composite reprint" (*Specimens of Type*, with an introduction by Alexander S. Lawson. New York: Garland, 1981), provide an overview of the several dozen extant specimen books. MacKellar's *American Printer* (1866*ff.*; 202 above) is also part of this history. The music type associated with this lineage may be summarized thus:

1. Binny & Ronaldson probably sold music type, and it is historically of considerable importance, although none of it is seen in the specimen books of 1812, 1839, or 1841. The font devised around 1800 especially for the singing master Andrew Law, with shape notes at the appropriate height but with no actual staff lines, shown in Richard Crawford, *Andrew Law, American Psalmodist* (Evanston: Northwestern University Press, 1968), pp. 161 and 216 (curious in the extreme; see 383 below for the 1802 patent). The type probably came from Binny & Ronaldson, although there is no direct documentary evidence apart from extant correspondence from Law on other matters. Notes on staff lines were added to the font before 1810, and later, shape notes as well; and in these forms the type was widely used, effectively supplanting the Caslon forms almost at once. Binny & Ronaldson would seem to be the only known founders in America who could have supported this widespread usage.

2. Lawrence Johnson's 1853 specimen, cited above, shows "Diamond," "Agate" no. 1 and 3, and "Nonpareil" nos. 1 and 2 in the Houghton Library copy. Later specimens add "Excelsior" and other fonts, but erratically, so as once again to undermine their usefulness in tracing the history of the firm's inventory. The face is different from the one seen earlier in the century.

3. The MacKellar, Smiths & Jordan *Specimens of Printing Types*, its preface dated May 10, 1876, is a large folio (13 × 10", almost 4" thick). Pages 20-21 show seven music fonts, with optional patent notes. The appearance of music type in other specimens suggests a major promotion of the type to a wide market.

4. The American Type Founders Co. specimen books, variously entitled *Specimens of Printing Types* (with numbered supplements and numbered books — e.g. *Eleventh Book of Specimens*), also *Compact Book of Specimens*, *Printer's Handy Book*, and

running from 249 pages to 943 leaves (often unnumbered), serve mostly to confuse the record even further. The 1981 composite reprint, on pp. 16-20, shows nine music fonts (Tonic Sol-fa, Excelsior 1 and 2, Diamond 1-4, Agate 3, and Nonpareil 3).

The working relationship between this and other American firms (notably Gilson : see 365 below) is yet to be established.

Charles DERRIEY. *Spécimen-Album*. Paris, 1862.   **360**

A large and imposing folio, in which p. 127 shows "Musique & Plain-Chant" (four sizes of the former, five of the latter). Two pages are devoted to a layout of the four cases, with about 400 sorts. Bigmore & Wyman (vol. 1, p. 163-65) shows high respect for Derriey. For his music patent see 380; cf. also 191 above.

Derriey's 1844 *Spécimen* has no music.

V. &. J. FIGGINS. *Specimens of Type, Printing Materials*. London, [*ca*.1870].   **361**

Several undated specimen books were issued by Vincent Figgins about this time, with slightly different music pages. The four-page music section in St. Bride 2740 may be the earliest. Over the next decades music became more important; the 1895 "Centenary Edition" (St. Bride 2756) includes nine pages of music, preceded by a separate title-page that reads *1899* [sic] *Specimen of Music*. This unit also survives separately, some copies unpaginated, others with pp. 192-200 following the music title-page.

The numbered pages are also seen in the 1909 *Specimen of Printing Types* of Figgins's successor, R. H. Stevens & Co.; but the title-page is now replaced by a new p. 191, showing "Ruby Chant Music" and a synopsis of the music fonts. After 1909 the music section disappeared from the Stevens specimens, just as the books were beginning to be printed in a slightly larger page size. Still to be determined is whether the music type was abandoned, destroyed, sold to another distributor around 1910, or still available but no longer shown in the main specimen book in deference to earlier music specimens or new ones not extant.

PATENT TYPE FOUNDING COMPANY (Shanks, Revell & Co., Proprietors). *Specimens of Printing Types and Music Founts*. London, [1870s].   **362**

Three copies of this book at St. Bride serve to describe the problems of inference from type specimens. The three copies —

all undated, but the first two assigned to *ca*. 1873, on the basis of unspecified evidence — include music in the very final leaves, and show music type as follows:

copy 1: Ruby 3; Diamond 3; Semi-nonpareil 4; Plainchant
copy 2: Ruby 3; Diamond 1, 2, 3, 4; Semi-nonpareil 4
copy 3: Ruby 1, 3; Diamond 2, 3, 5; Semi-nonpareil 4; Plainchant

All nine of these fonts, and perhaps still others, were presumably available before and after these books were printed.

Bigmore & Wyman, vol. 2, p. 148, has a valuable annotation.

BEAUDOIRE & Cie. . . . *De caractères français & étrangers.* Paris, [*ca*. 1879?]. **363**

Théophile Beaudoire, whose *Manuel* (213 above) will be remembered for the divine wrath it earned in Solesmes, happily redeemed himself and, with the approval of Solesmes, now lay claim to the honor of "maître-fondeur." The specimen (its date suggested by the statement "Médailles d'Or aux Expositions de 1801, 1825, 1839, 1844, 1849, 1851, 1855, 1867, 1878," some of which exhibitions are of an obscurity that can be seen as either fascinating or disturbing) shows six pages of mensural and plainchant faces.

Around 1894 Beaudoire's type passed to the Paris firm of Deberny & Cie., active as typefounders since the 1830s. The Beaudoire plainchant is seen in many Deberny specimens (as traced through the Houghton Library holdings at Harvard University, for instance), beginning with *Les nouvelles créations* of 1895. The 1898 and 1904 specimens, entitled *Le livret typographique*, also show the type (p. 7) and add a case layout and accidentals. Further Beaudoire music faces are seen in the 1904 *Série Deberny* (no. 18); in the 1913 Deberny *Épreuves de caractères* (p. 19); in the books entitled *Le livret typographique* of 1910 and 1912 (pp. 97-107 and 131), 1916 (pp. 106-10 and 131), 1920 (confusingly paginated), 1921 and 1923 (pp. 205-14 and 138 [*sic*: 238]); and in a 1924 edition with a Deberny & Tuleu imprint. Around 1924 Deberny merged with Peignot, another great foundry dating from the early 19th century. Most of the subsequent Deberny & Peignot specimens show no music, although the huge two-volume *Spécimen général des fonderies* of 1935 includes an extended display of "Musique et plain-chant" (section 4 of vol. 1, pp. 33-44).

Jabez FRANCIS. "Universal-Musiktypen," in *Korrespondent für Deutschlands Buchdrucker*, 1884, no. 4.   **364**

Cited in Jolles, p. 109. I have not located this issue of the journal. Music is not mentioned in Francis's *Printing at Home* (Rochford, Essex, [1870]; 2nd ed., [1873]; 3rd ed., [1880]). Francis was an inventor and manufacturer of instruments of many kinds, particularly for use by hobbyists and amateurs.

F. H. GILSON Co. *Music Typography and Specimens of Music Types.* Boston, 1885.   **365**

I have not undertaken what promises to be a daunting and unrewarding task of sorting out the bibliographical history of this promotional booklet, which is usually cited in various abbreviated forms in deference to its modest appearance. The following later titles (probably in addition to still others) all run to about 32 pages and appear to be mostly reprints of the 1885 title, some with updatings: *History of Shaped or Character Notes, with Specimens* (1889); *Music-Book Printing, with Historical Notes of Music-Book Printing in America* (1897); *Music Book Printing [How it is done], with Specimens* (1897: *ATF*, vol. 3, p. 1615); and *Music Book Printing, with Specimens* (1915). See also "Printing of Music," *The Writer* (Boston), 2 (1898), p. 17.

In 1902 Gilson, America's leading music typographer, proudly announced that it had received permission to name its printing offices the Stanhope Press. The same type faces are thus seen in *The Book of Specimens: Stanhope Press* (Boston: F. H. Gilson Co. 1907), which is designated a limited edition.

Notenproben der Officin Breitkopf & Härtel in Leipzig, 1885.

A large folio with specimens of music "Notenstich" on pp. 1-74, "Autographie" on pp. 75-78, and "Typographie" on pp. 79-89, with lists of contents and prices on pp. ii-iv and descriptions of conditions and practices on pp. v-ix.   **366**

HENDERSON, RAIT, & SPALDING. *Specimens of . . . Printing Type.* London, 1886.   **367**

"Specimens of Music Types" (11 mensural and plainchant fonts, and two sol-fa) appear on eight unnumbered pages near the end, the last page showing a synopsis of all but the sol-fa.

These pages are not seen in the later *Specimens* of *ca.* 1894, which appeared under the imprint of Henderson & Spalding.

G. WILSON. *Specimens of Type-Music.* London, *ca.* 1890.
The only recorded copy (St. Bride 19408) has been missing since 1939. Wilson may be the printer named in 209 above. **368**

Noten und Schriftproben der Röder'schen Officin in Leipzig. [Leipzig: Röder, *ca.*1890?]. **369**
A sumptuous display of the available musical forms ("Notenproben," in six sizes) and letter forms ("Schriftproben," with 26 faces, roman, gothic, and cyrillic), with 25 sample page layouts. (A copy at the University of North Carolina, Chapel Hill, is the only one I know.)

BARNHART Bros. & SPINDLER. *Specimen Book of Types.* Chicago: [1900]. **370**
Herman F. Töpfer set up a type foundry in New York *ca.* 1850, according to Annenberg, moved it to Chicago, and in 1869 sold it to the Barnharts. Music, designated as Diamond and Agate, appears for the first time on pp. 668-69 of this edition.
The 1907 successor, even larger and designated as "Specimen Book No. 9," survives in several variants, which show two music fonts, now on pp. 722-23.

George BEAVERSON. *A Few Remarks on Music Typography.* New York: Published for the Trade, 1912. **371**
A 14-page pamphlet with samples of Beaverson's work, preceded by brief comments addressed to "users of music type plates." The comments are derived from Beaverson's "Some Bottom Facts on Music Typography," *American Art Journal,* 72 (March 18, 1899), 377-79, which includes illustrations of a compositor at work and of Beaverson's case layout.

HANDEL Bros. *Specimens of Music Engraving.* London, n. d. [1920s?]. **372**
This 16-page 8°, among the few specimens that were issued for music engravers, shows types for both music and words.

William CLOWES & Sons, Ltd. *Some Specimens of the Roman, Oriental, and Foreign Types.* London [Duke Street, Stanford St., S.E.], n. d. [1920s?].   **373**
Music fonts (Ruby Music, Diamond, Semi-nonpareil) are shown on pp. 39-45, also plainsong and three added pp. of sol-fa.

J. J. AUGUSTIN. *Schrift Muster.* Glückstadt, Hamburg, 1930.   **374**
Includes "15 Punkt Musiknoten" on p. 430.

"The Curwen Music Punches: A Descriptive Note," in *The Curwen Press Miscellany,* edited by Oliver Simon (London: Soncino Press, 1931), pp. 85-90.   **375**
Discussion of new punches designed by Paul Woodroffe, whose eye had told him that most music pages were "far too black. The Curwen music is an experiment in lowering the tone of the whole scheme." The essay is followed by an eight-page example of Rutland Boughton's "Guenever's Song."

AIRD & COGHILL, Ltd. *Specimens of Music Engraving and Printing.* Glasgow, 1932.   **376**
An imposing booklet, its hard-bound cover entitled "Music Engraving and Printing," with a five-page historical introduction and 15 pp. of examples.

Die Schriftproben der Offizin HAAG-DRUGULIN. Leipzig, 1936.   **377**
"Musiknoten" appear on p. 441.

BREITKOPF & HÄRTEL. *Schriftproben: Handsatz und Setzmaschinen Schriften.* Leipzig, [1939].   **378**
The brief "Musiknoten" section (pp. 391-98) shows nine fonts. Its appearance at the very end of a very large book testifies to the range of the firm's activities apart from music.

Stan NELSON. "Cutting New Music Type," *Matrix,* 8 (Winter 1988), pp. 47-54.   **379**
Stimulated by Fournier, the noted typographer at the Smithsonian Institution describes his work in cutting plainchant faces.

Paul Hayden Duensing has recently also designed and cast a face of diamond-shape type, more with a view to sustaining the craft than for commercial use.

Specimens are obviously the central documents for typographical study. But their existence is as tenuous as their evidence is inconclusive, forcing one to ask, "What are you really telling us about the tastes and practices of music printers?" Their greatest importance probably lies in the questions they raise, both of commercial distribution and aesthetic conception.

MISCELLANEOUS TECHNICAL LITERATURE

Other materials of special interest to printers include patent records, journals and organizational records, and writings on materials. Their sparseness suggests that there is much more that has not survived. What we have includes the following:

Music Printing Patents

The rise of modern protection of inventions generally coincides with the emergence of modern political states, as well as the Industrial Revolution. I have limited this survey to published records covering the nineteenth century (which for music printing was the period of most intense activity) or those parts of it that proved to be most readily available through published registers and indexes. I have made good use of Francis J. Kase, *Foreign Patents: A Guide to Official Patent Literature* (Dobbs Ferry, N. Y.: Oceana Publications; Leiden: A. W. Sijthoff, 1972).

The inadequacies of indexing militate against any claims to completeness. For now, however, even this list is useful as evidence of the wondrous ways in which music inspired the nineteenth-century inventive genius.

[**France.** Brevets d'invention]. *Description des machines et procédés . . . dans les brevets d'invention* Paris: [Madame Huzzard, etc.], 1811- . **380**

The French patent records were issued by the Ministère du Commerce (Office national de la propriété industrielle Brevets d'invention), usually under this title. From the first two series (1: covering 1791-1844, published 1811-63 in 93 vols., with 12,543 patents; 2: covering 1844-70, published 1850-74, in 116 vols., with 91,391 patents), the printing patents have been extracted and preserved at St. Bride. A subject index has been prepared, which includes the following entries:

November 28, 1800: sieur Bouvier, "pour des procédés de fabrication en cuivre ou bronze, de signes . . . propres à la composition des planches de musique vocale et instrumentale" (no. 430; vol. 6, pp. 124-26)

May 7, 1801: sieurs Reinhard & Mertian, "pour un nouveau système typographique", i.e., movable music type (no. 450; vol. 6, pp.177-208)

November 28, 1801: sieurs Duplat & George, "pour des procédés propre à imprimer la musique avec la press typographie" (no. 478; vol. 6, pp. 309-12 and *planches* 13-15)

July 6, 1802: sieur Ollivier, "pour les moyens de graver, fondre et imprimer la musique en le plein-chant, en caractères mobiles" (no. 269; vol. 4, p. 134)

December 21, 1825: Don Mario Carlotti, "pour l'application de la stéréotypie à la fabrication des planches de musique" (no. 4495; vol. 42, p. 405)

November 10, 1827: Jean-Henri Petitpierre, "pour une boîte mélotachygraphique servant à fondre les planches propres à la gravure de la musique" (no. 2918; vol. 30, pp. 340-41)

December 14, 1827: M. Petitpierre, "pour des perfectionnements apportés à la machine typomélographique de M. Carlotti, propre à graver de la musique" (no.2221; vol.24, pp.333-37)

August 20, 1828: sieur [Eugène Louis-Camille] Viellard, dit Duverger, "pour des procédés d'impression de la musique en caractères mobiles" (no. 6020; vol. 50, pp. 314-19; 184 above)

September 30, 1829: Jean-Marie Claude Duguet, "pour un procédé propre à composer et imprimer la musique" (no. 6724; vol. 54, pp. 231-37 and *planche* 16)

March 27, 1838: sieurs Busset & Leuillet, "pour des procédés d'impression de la musique" (no. 11278; vol. 81, p. 529, but with few further particulars)

July 23, 1840: Jacques-Charles Derriey, "pour l'impression typographique de la musique" (no. 5855; vol. 49, p. 383)

April 19, 1844: Henri Pape, "pour une machine propre à reproduire, par des signes ou de marques, l'écriture, les chiffres, la musique, etc." (no. 11583; vol. 84, pp. 66-67 and *planche* 1)

July 7, 1847: sieur Duverger, "pour des procédés de typographie musicale" (no. 2969; 2. ser., vol. 11, pp. 157-59)

March 15, 1851: sieur [Alphonse] Curmer, "pour des stéréotypes appliqués à l'impression de la musique" (no. 5523; 2. ser., vol. 18, p. 15)

[*Date not verified*]: sieur Serrière, "pour un nouveau procédé de fabrication de clichés servant à imprimer la musique au moyen de la presse typographique" (no. 8965; 2nd series, vol. 29)

In addition, the U. S. Patent Office issued a *Subject-Matter Index of Patents for Inventions . . . granted in France from 1791 to 1876 Inclusive* (Washington: Government Printing Office, 1883), in which the following additional entries are recorded:

Under "Printing Music" (p.632): Derrug (*July 23, 1840*; II, 49, p. 383); Quinet (*September 9, 1840*; I, 86, p. 474); Lopez-Vallejo (*October 4, 1844*; I, 85, p. 497); Knoderer (*March 7, 1856*; II, 54, p. 126); and three others cited above. Under "Printing Music, autograph process for": Laurent (*April 1, 1870*, no. 89525*), and "Printing Music, apparatus for": Lefman et Lourdel (*February 14, 1873*; III, 7, c.17, 4, p. 18). Under "Printing for Music" (p. 637): Knoderer (*February 25, 1871*; III, 2. c.17, 1-2, p. 1).

[Great Britain]. *Patents for Inventions. Abridgements of Specifications relating to Printing . . . .* London: Eyre & Spottiswoode, 1859- . **381**

The British counterpart is divided into sections and subject categories. Music printing is regarded as "Printing" up through 1866 (usually in Class 100: "Printing, Letterpress and Lithographic," but sometimes in 101: "Printing other than Letterpress or Lithographic"); beginning in 1867 it is under "Music" (Class 88).

1540-1857. The title cited above includes a brief overview of "Music Printing" (pp. 23-25) and indexes these music registrations:

December 24, 1767: Henry Fougt, for "Certain new and curious types . . . for the printing of music . . . " (no. 888; p. 87)

May 19, 1784: Samuel Arnold, for "Printing vocal and instrumental music . . . with types . . . " (no. 1435; p. 96)

February 26, 1810: Peter Stuart, for "A new method of engraving and printing maps . . . , music . . . " (no. 3307; p. 120)

June 12, 1841: Edward Palmer, for "Improvements in producing printing surfaces, and printing . . . music" (no. 8987; p. 229)

October 16, 1855: Lewis Normandy, for "Improvements in the mode of writing and printing music . . . " (no. 2307; p. 505)

January 18, 1856: Joseph Marzolo, for "a reproductive organ, printing . . . any musical fancies" (no. 145; p. 513)

April 11, 1856: Lewis Normandy, for further "Improvements in the mode of writing and printing music . . . . " (no. 868; p. 527)

May 17, 1856: Gustav Scheurmann, for "Improvements in printing music" (no. 1170; p. 531)

October 11, 1856: Gustav Scheurmann, for "Improvements in printing music when type is employed" (no. 2390: p. 556)

March 13, 1857: Edmond Joseph Nicolas Juvin, for "Improvements in producing printing surfaces . . . [relating to] letter-press and music printing . . . to supersede surfaces composed and set up in separate characters . . . ." (no. 725; p. 581)

In addition, p. 63 mentions the royal grant of February 17, 1623, to George Wither, "for fifty-one years, of the sole printing of the 'Hymns and Songs of the Church.'"

The 1859 text was reprinted, London: Printing Historical Society, 1969. The supplementary pages from the 1878 set that cover the pre-1858 period are included, along with an introduction to the reprint by James Harrison, which brings out Bennet Woodcroft's role in preparing the original set.

1858-66. (London: Commissioners of Patents, 1878; designated as Part II., but corrected in manuscript to I.a; also identified as a "second edition" of volume 18). This sequel includes five more music-related printing patents (as indexed on p. 375), along with a supplement to the 1859 set:

January 11, 1861: Paul Laffitte, for an "instrument for writing and printing music . . . . " (no. 76; p. 120-21)

February 21,1861: Joshua James Watts and Samuel Harton, for "manufacture of music plates" (seven parts lead, seven tin, and one antimony, not five lead and 14 tin: no. 434; pp. 124-25)

January 13, 1863: Joseph Beverley Fenby, for an "apparatus to be attached to . . . instruments, for printing the score of any music performed . . . ." (no. 101; pp. 184-85)

March 29, 1864: Thomas Bernard Harpur, for "an improved method of printing or representing musical characters . . . ." (no. 774; pp. 219-20)

December 31, 1864: François Joseph Endres, for "a new musical apparatus, printing on paper the music while being executed on . . . instruments" (no. 3257; p. 243)

1867-76 (published 1880):
January 15, 1868: John Lang, for "improvements relating to the printing of music," involving solfège letters placed inside the note heads, with white letters in the black notes and vice versa (no. 132; p. 7; pp. 7-8). *Shown at the left.*

FIGURE 2. John Lang's Solfège Music Type.

December 17, 1868: William Henry Lennox, John William Pearman, and William James Pearman, for "improvements in the apparatus used in the production of surfaces for printing music," intended to supersede the use of "engraved plates, music type, and the lithographic process" (no. 3840; pp. 14-15)

September 9, 1869: David Colville, for "an improved mode of and apparatus for producing printing surfaces . . . to facilitate the printing of music" with wax punches (no. 2658; p. 23)

May 11, 1870: Alexandre Amédée Rossignol, for "improvements in writing music . . . " i.e., a band of paper "impregnated with a solution that will decompose under the influence of an electric current . . . " (no. 1339; p. 28)

August 26, 1870: G.E. Morgan, for "musical notation," i. e., pitch names within the note heads (no. 2345; p. 29). *Shown at the right.*

December 24, 1870: John Lacey Davies, for "improvements in . . . producing and printing musical notation . . . " (no. 3369; p. 31)

April 25, 1874: William Morgan-Brown, for "improvements in

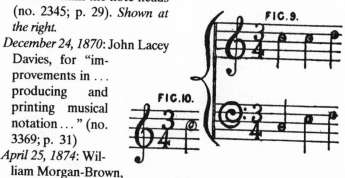

FIGURE 3. G. E. Morgan's Music Type.

printing music" i.e., four "processes for providing the printing surfaces" (no. 1445; p. 61)

April 30, 1874: Peter Martin Shanks, for "improvements in the production of raised surfaces or blocks . . . for use in letterpress printing, in printing music . . . " (no. 1517; pp. 61-62)

1877-83 (published 1893):

February 12, 1877: M. Alissoff, for printing music by photographic transfer (no. 591; p. 1)

August 16, 1878: H. Goodwin, for printing music (involving photographic plates; no. 3243; cited in the Appendix to the 1897-1900 volume, p.135)

1884-88 (published 1896):

June 20, 1885: D. Gestetner, for printing music (rollers for staff lines; no. 7536; p. 40)

June 4, 1886: M. A. Wier, for printing music (involving a roller frame for transferring signs from one copy to another; no. 7527; p. 63-64)

August 18, 1886: G. Becker and D. Monnier, for printing and copying music (involving gears; no. 10,558; pp. 68-69)

December 22, 1886: A. Chossefoin, for printing music (with loose-fitting mosaic type locked tight into the form; no. 16,802; p. 77)

December 1, 1887: G. G. M. Hardingham, for printing music (transfer from copy to zinc plate or stone; no. 16,547; p.105)

January 28, 1888: W. Howard, for music paper (with ledger lines added lightly for copyists; no. 1323; p. 111)

1889-92 (published 1898):

May 22, 1889: R. Tissington, for printing music (involving photolithography through glass; (no. 8504; p. 8)

June 6, 1889: C. A. Ker, for printing music (involving tracings; no. 9407; pp. 9-10)

August 6, 1890: E. Ball, for printing music (involving handstamps from vulcanized rubber; no. 12305; p. 33)

January 22, 1891: G. Royle, for printing music (involving rollers for staff lines; no. 1167; pp. 43-44)

May 2, 1891, improving E. Ball's earlier patent (no. 7620; p. 51)

January 6, 1892: S. E. Coppinger, for music notation, involving a "music printing process" (no. 274: a cross reference; p. 72)

February 11, 1892: W. A. Ker, for printing music (from coated plates; no. 2681; p. 74)

March 25, 1892: H. H. Lake, for printing music, involving a printing wheel and other mechanical devices (no. 5896; p. 76)

1893-96 (published 1900):

June 6, 1895: P. van der Haeghen, for printing music (with hand stamps; no. 11,182; p. 77)

October 14, 1896: A. A. Haylock, for music chord and note incidators (enabling words to be exhibited in close proximity to the music; no. 22,767; p. 122)

1897-1900 (published 1903):

July 20, 1897: H. Chossefoin, for printing music involving supporting plates (no. 17,121; p. 23)

September 7, 1897: A. Rivoire, for recording sounds from a piano onto a continuous staff roll (no. 20,589; p. 28)

March 28, 1898: W. H. Bolton and C. H. Bolton, for printing music, with hand-stamps for frequent signs (no. 7430; p. 44)

[**Italy**. Attestati di Privative Industriali]. *Descrizione della Macchine* (1855-64); and *Bolletino della Privative Industriali del Regno d'Italia* (1864-1882).   **382**

I have not seen these titles, but have worked instead from the U. S. Commissioner of Patents, *Subject-Matter Index of Patents for Inventions . . . granted in Italy from 1848 to May 1, 1882* (Washington: Government Printing Office, 1885). The following patents are indexed on p. 80, under "Printing, music":

December 31, 1855: Bianchi (*Descrizione*, vol. 1, article 195, designated as from Sardinia)

June 29, 1874: Loverdel (*Bollettino*, 2nd series, vol 6, article 317; also in the serially numbered vol. 14, article 426 and plate 75)

[**United States**. Patent Office]. *Subject-Matter Index of Patents for Inventions, issued . . . from 1790 to 1873 Inclusive.* Washington: Government Printing Office, 1874.   **383**

The indexes bring out music printing patents on pp. 953 (under "Music") and 1583 (under "Type"), chronologically as follows:

May 12, 1802: Andrew Law, for music printing (cf. 359 above)

February 7, 1812: U. K. Hill (of New York), for "music type"

February 28, 1816: George Webster (of New York), for "casting moveable type"

June 9, 1818: M. Elliot (of Boscawen, N. H.), for "arranging music to printed books"

June 18, 1829: W. C. Phillips (of Lunenberg Court-House, Va.), for "notes in music"

[*October 26, 1839*: T. Harrison (of Springfield, Ohio), for "writing music" (no. 1383): actually a system of notation]

November 27, 1830: G. Bruce (of New York), for "music type by combining printer's type"

August 11, 1830: G. B. Lothian (of New York), for "cutting and casting music type"

June 16, 1868: E. L. Balch (of Boston, Mass.), for "music type" (no. 78,855)

The Webster reference and several other facts have been kindly reported by Jean Bonin, whose forthcoming *United States Music-Related Patent Records, 1790-1874* will discuss many of these entries in further detail.

I have not included sources that began their coverage after 1860, such as Wolff's *Patenter udtagne i Danmark* (1875-95), in which the coverage extends back only to 1864), the Norwegian *Patenter* (1870*ff.*), the Canadian *Patent Office Record* (1873*ff.*), the German *Patentblatt* series (1877*ff.*), the Swedish *Register till patent* (1885*ff.*) and *Svensk tidskrift för industriellt rättsskydd*, the Spanish *Boletín oficial de la propriedad industrial* (1866*ff.*), the Swiss *Jahres-Katalog der Erfindungs-Patente* (1889*ff.*), or the *Oesterreichisches Patentblatt* (1899*ff.*).

Music Printers' Organizations and Journals

Journal de l'imprimerie et de la librairie en Belgique. Bruxelles: A. Floskin, Philippe Hen, 1854-68.   **384**

A semi-monthly journal, edited by Charles Hen. I have not examined this journal; Bigmore & Wyman (vol. 2, p. 174) mention its music coverage.

London Typographical Music Association. *Scale of Prices.* [n.p., 1861?]   **385**

A broadside (St. Bride, Trade Document Collection, 195) of a statement adopted at the Association's general meeting, March

1861. The scale applies to three categories (vocal music unaccompanied and accompanied, and instrumental music), with 16 additional "miscellaneous" conditions, some of them fascinating, e.g., jobs under 50,000 ems (however these were measured in the case of music) needed to be calculated at a higher rate because they were so small (!).

Further particulars on the music price scales are provided in Ellic Howe, *The London Compositor* (London: Bibliographical Society, 1947), esp. on pp. 183-84; see also pp. 58-60, 93, and 351. Note also Johnson and Hansard (179 and 180 above).

London Society of Music Compositors. *Rules of the Society ..., established January 9, 1872.*   **386**
Nineteen specifications, in a tiny booklet (St. Bride, 7834).

London Society of Music Engravers. *Annual Report*, 1901- .
Printed reports, 1949-56, most of them very brief, are in the Poole papers in Cambridge, along with manuscript archives and a *Music Engraving Price List* of 1913, another from January 1931.

At first the Society was known as the Master Music Printers and Engravers Association, Ltd.   **387**

National Music Printers & Allied Trades Association. *Open Price Reporting Plan for the Music Printing Industry.* [New York, 1934].   **388**
Developed by Project Group E6 (Graphic Arts Code), and put in effect by the Executive Committee of the Association as of December 28, 1934, the plan calculates the cost of transfer, make-ready, paper (including cutting and folding), and printing, in two colors or one, and on coated paper for the cover. The classes include 2TA (i.e., two pp. of music, title, and advertisements on the back cover), 4TA, 6TA, etc.; special prices for vocal and dance orchestrations; engraving of plates, by class (A-1 for "very simply music compositions," up to F, for methods and books with extra text matter, with ukulele, banjo or guitar "diagrams" extra); and flat-form printing, on small or large press.

Music Printing Plates and Metallurgy

Frank H. MASON. "Plates for Music Engraving," *Metal Industry*, 9 (1911), 260.   **389**

A brief technical note from the U. S. Consul General in Paris, responding to an inquiry from St. Louis regarding the kinds of metal plates used in Paris and in France for engraving music.

John T. Griffiths, the U. S. Consul General in London, adds a note on p. 461 on the lithographic stones used in London.

"Music Printing Plates," *Tin and its Uses*, no. 32 (July 1955), pp. 10-12.   **390**
A brief text in the quarterly journal of the Tin Research Institute, with information not easily found elsewhere, along with illustrations of engraving at the Augener shop in London.

Ernest S. HEDGES. *Tin in Social and Economic History*. London: Edward Arnold, 1964.   **391**
"Music" (Chapter 8, pp. 125-33) is mostly on organ pipes, but mentions music engraving, with pictures of the Augener shop.

Sandars (46 above), pp. 210-11, is among the few writings for a general audience to discuss the alloys used as printing surfaces.

Paper for Printed Music

Printing surfaces are one of the four requisites for printing, the others being ink, presses, and paper. There is little evidence to suggest that the inks and the presses needed for music were in any way different from those used for other kinds of printed matter. Paper, however, was occasionally prepared especially for use in printed music. The topic has three aspects: the special physical makeup of the sheets, the special folding and assembly of music gatherings, and the special binding constructions and other enclosures appropriate to musical editions. Writings on music paper are widely scattered. Stanley Boorman's discussion of "Paper" (*Grove P&P*, pp. 521-22) includes further points.

Special sizes and chemical constituency of music paper are described in the entries on "Music" in E. J. Labarre's *Dictionary and Encyclopædia of Paper and Paper Making* (2nd ed., Amsterdam: Swets and Zeitlinger, 1952), p. 169. (Music paper, for instance, should have "little or no rattle.") The famous historical instances include the music paper prepared in England under the Tallis-Byrd (1575) and Morley (1598) patents: see Fenlon and Milsom (662 below). The *Tablettes de Rénommées de Musique* (Paris,

1785), according to Brook (696 below, p. 25), speaks of four "Magazins de papiers rayés pour la musique": it is not clear whether this paper was intended for use by music manuscript copyists exclusively, or by music printers as well. There are also archival records of early 19th-century American papermakers that mention special orders for "music moulds" for wove paper.

Among the physical forms distinctive to music, oblong formats are perhaps the most widespread, the early occurences of which I have discussed (146 above). Indeed, early printers manuals often identify oblong forms in general as "music format." Much more curious, and very limited in their population, are the "Dutch-door" books discussed by Metcalf (142 above). With the ascendancy of engraving around 1700, and the concomitant preference for large-size pages, the imposition practices appropriate to the platen press become less relevant. As a result, however, music bibliographers have virtually ignored the matter of format in bibliographical descriptions, at least of editions after 1700. I know of no statements that are based on the directions of chain lines and the position of watermarks, at least in the most important music lists. By the nineteenth century, studies of format generally become all the harder, for, while almost all music continued to be printed from presses that were fed sheetwise rather than from a continuous roll, the emergence of wove paper around 1800 resulted in sheets that lack the critical evidence of the paper mould. Thus, in time, it was possible for format names to acquire the colloquial senses often affectionately used today, e.g., "song folios" for vocal anthologies in general; "band folios" for sets of parts; "quartos" for miniature scores; and "choral octavos" for ensemble vocal music typically on 9 × 6" sheets.

Music has most often been sold unbound: presumably in sheets before 1700, often in wrappers thereafter, optionally beginning in the nineteenth century in publisher's wrappers. Early music with added paper covers is seen in Michèle Valerie Cloonan, *Early Bindings in Paper* (London: Mansell, 1991), including such varied instances as a Paris 1663 part-book set (Plate 2; Samuel Pepys's copy) and a 1774 Breitkopf song-book (Plate 8; in Herrnhuter paste-paper covers). Plate 4 shows a painting of a "Scaffali con libri di musica," *ca.* 1720, while the book in the hands of Mme de Pompadour in Plate 1 is probably a music book as well. After *ca.* 1850 (perhaps beginning in the 1830s with opera vocal scores in

"Parisian format," i.e., with plate numbers in the lower gutter), musical editions of any thickness or distinction at all were distributed by the publisher in paper wrappers. These wrappers, usually printed by letterpress, are typically on thin, pastel-shaded, high-acid paper that was discarded by binders. The sheets that survive, however brittle their condition today, are much worth preserving as evidence of different printings.

Musicians will be delighted by the romantic sensibilities of the paper connoisseurs' adage, "Le papier chant." Indeed, the sound of paper on the music rack can understandably torment sensitive performers or listeners.

C. Aesthetics and Legibility

The study of musical notation itself is largely peripheral to the scope of this book. On the other hand, the layout of the music page, the design of music type faces, and the execution of music printing, with attractiveness and utility in mind, are clearly relevant, although the aesthetics are rarely discussed in print. Among the writings are these:

P. J. LASALETTE.   *Sténographie musicale, ou manière abrégée d'écrire la musique, à l'usage des compositeurs et des imprimeries.* Paris: Goujou, 1805.   **392**

Of those writings that describe innovative failures at improving our musical notation system, this one blames printing in particular: why haven't bright people been able to help us out of this mess? ("La typographie musicale est restée jusqu'à nos jours dans une imperfection qu'on a peine à concevoir, quand on considère que plusieurs hommes de génie ont fait de grands efforts pour la tirer de la barbarie dans laquelle des siècles d'ignorance l'avaient plongée": p. 32); and, the field is undeveloped mostly because printers have not talked enough with musicians ("Si la typographie musicale est restée si longtemps dans l'enfance, c'est peut-être à cause que les Musiciens ne se sont pas assez rapprochés des Imprimeurs": p. 33*n*).

Michel EISENMENGER. *Traité sur l'art graphique et la mécanique appliqués à la musique.* Paris: Gosselin, 1838.   **393**

An imaginative study, mostly on proposed enhancements of musical notation but implicitly on music printing as well, by an author who labels himself "Ingéneur-Mécanicien."

B. GUGLER. "Moden im Musikstich," *Allgemeine musikalische Zeitung*, 4 (1896), 34-36. **394**

Perceptive comments that argue for the ascendancy of music engraving. (Other writings on the subject are promised at the end of this article, proposed as the first in a series, "Musikstich und Musikalienhandel." I have found no successors, alas.)

Francesco BERGER. "On a changé tout cela," *Monthly Musical Record*, 46 (1916), 285-87. **395**

A brief but effective statement of the importance of graphic details in musical editions.

Hubert J. FOSS. "Modern Styles in Music Printing in England," *The Fleuron*, 3 (1924), 89-106. **396**

A major essay, perhaps the most important of its time and certainly the most important testament of Foss's aesthetic of music printing, with nine valuable facsimiles of different designs discussed with impressive insight (pp. 98-101).

Similar ideas are proposed for an audience of musicians in Foss's "The Printed Page of Music," *The Dominant*, vol. 1, no. 7 (May 1928), pp. 21-24, and in some of his other writings (see 239, 248, and 260 above in particular).

Walter Willson COBBETT. "Publishing of Chamber Music," in his *Cyclopedic Survey of Chamber Music* (London: Oxford University Press, 1929), pp. 246-48. **396a**

An "open letter" to publishers, slightly apologetic in its conservative truculence, which begins with admiration for continued improvements, and continues with a valuable list of the attributes that make a printed text useful to performers.

Also in the 2nd edition (*ibid.*, 1963).

Lorin Farrar WHEELWRIGHT. *An Experimental Study of the Perceptibility and Spacing of Musical Symbols.* New York: Columbia University, Teachers College, 1939 (Contributions to Education, 75). **397**

One of the few studies of music printing from the viewpoint of applied psychology, with discussions of "Typographical Factors" (pp. 13-15), "Reading Distance," and a "Visual Perception Test" (30 pp. after p. 116).
Doctoral dissertation, Columbia University, 1939.

W. O. WEISSLEDER. "Early Music Printing," *Print*, vol. 5, no. 2 (1947), 45-53.   **398**
A sermon to the wrong audience. It begins by describing the connoisseur of the graphic arts; then deems it "an indication of complacency, or lack of healthy self-criticism . . . that few of the important firms — and none in the United States — employ a competent typographical adviser or designer where the purely visual musical portion of their publications is concerned" (p. 50); and ends by seeing it "obvious that a need for improvement is felt by prospective buyers and users of printed music" (p. 52).

Antoine-Elisée CHERBULIEZ. "Die Lesbarkeit der Musiknoten," *SMG / Schweizer graphische Mitteilungen*, 68 (1949), 294-99.   **399**
"Kleine Beiträge zu einer prinzipiellen Stellungsnahme," with advice on layout, appropriate to the performers' needs.

Leonard FEIST. "Music as a Graphic Art," *Juilliard Review*, vol. 1, no.2 (Spring 1954), 26-31.   **400**
Brief but telling remarks on the importance of (1) the shape and size of the notehead and other elements, (2) the size and layout of the page, (3) the choice of type faces and sizes for texts, and (4) "design of cover, title-page, ornamental motifs."

Leonard SALZEDO and Peter E. M. SHARP. "Designs on Music: Changing the Score," *Design*, 222 (June 1967), 44-47.   **401**
Imaginative commentary on the "ergonomics of the score," i.e., the ways in which musical notation may usefully be improved, so as both to employ resources not available in the past and to serve the changing conditions of musical performance.

Music Publishers' Association. *Paul Revere Awards for Graphic Excellence*. New York, [1964-].   **402**

Annual announcements of the awards, with particulars on the aims, eligibility, publishing categories, and other matters, along with the judging criteria. The latter involve categories, slightly revised over the years, of note-setting (correctness, proportion and alignment, physical quality), printing and materials (quality, cover and paper stock, binding), artwork (especially covers) and typography, and overall use and practicality.

Kurt STONE. *Music Notation in the Twentieth Century: A Practical Guidebook.* New York: Norton, 1980.   **403**
A spirit of sensitivity and authority pervade this study, in which a highly respected music editor discusses his work with music that is often, by intent, as unprecedented and problematical in its presentation for performers to read from, as it is for its audiences to listen to.

Other writings of the author are concerned with similar matters, notable among them "Problems and Methods of Notation," *Perspectives in News Music*, 3 (1963), 9-31.

Also relevent are such pictorial anthologies as John Cage's *Notations* (New York: Something Else Press, 1969) and Eberhard Karkoschka's *Das Schriftbild der neuen Musik* (Celle: Moeck, 1972; translated as *Notation in New Music*, New York: Praeger, 1972), as well as the other major writings as cited by Gerald Warfield in *Writings on Contemporary Music Notation: An Annotated Bibliography* (Ann Arbor: Music Library Association, 1976; Index Series, 16), and H. Wiley Hitchcock's "Notation" article in *The New Grove Dictionary of American Music* (New York: Grove, 1986), vol. 3, pp. 396-97.

John SLOBODA. "The Uses of Space in Musical Notation," *Visible Language*, 15 (1981), 86-110.   **404**
While music printing itself is mentioned only in passing, this text (along with other writings by the author cited on p. 110) suggests considerations basic to music layout in general.

D. W. KRUMMEL. "Clarifying the Musical Page: The Romantic Stichbild," *Printing History*, 16 (1986), 26-36.   **405**
A call for scholarly studies of the history of the design and layout of music. Examples suggest that, mostly over the course of the early nineteenth century, the shapes and configurations of the musical signs were conceived in the interests of increased

legibility. This is perhaps the positive way of looking at a matter that fine printers have tended to view negatively, for instance Beatrice Warde's observation that Fournier's music type of the 1750s "is almost the last pleasant-looking music . . . soon afterwards the terrible perfections of lithography made irrevocable the ugliness of the modern note." See Paul Beaujon, "On XVIIIth Century French Typography and Fournier Le Jeune," *Monotype Recorder 212/13*, (1925), p. 32. Twyman (154) also reflects on the changing aesthetic in his discussion of the lettering in early music lithography, and the implications of his sentiments are rather less apocalyptic.

David WOODWARD. "Maps, Music, and the Printer: Graphic or Typographic?" *Printing History*, 16 (1986), 3-14.
A summary of the relationship between map printing and music printing, which ends by entertaining the prospects of talking of "a cartography of music or a music of cartography." (Indeed it does seem reasonable to see the score as a "mapping out" of the music, just as one might be thought to "perform on" a map, i.e., make practical sense out of it.)   **406**

Edward R. Tufte, *Envisioning Information* (Cheshire, Conn.: Graphics Press, 1990), also comments on musical scores as maps: see pp. 59, 82, 107, and 117.

Cummings's 1884 lecture (59 above), and especially the transcript of the audience response, are also important to this topic, as are the 1939 Philadelphia exhibition (433) and the bibliophilic editions cited on pp. 338-45 below.

Musicians will be fascinated by *Printing as a Performing Art* (San Francisco: Book Club of California, 1970), the title of Ruth Teiser's oral history of Bay Area fine printers. No less exciting is the anthology assembled by the printer-historian Charles H. Timperley, entitled *Songs of the Press, and other Poems Relative to the Arts of Printers and Printing* (London: Fisher, 1845), although, according to Bigmore and Wyman (vol. 3, p. 15), "there are French and German works of a similar character that much exceed it in scope and style." Meanwhile, Paul Hayden Duensing has turned up a socialist workers' songbook, *Vivat Polygraphia: Historische Lieder für Jünger der Schwarzen Kunst* (Leipzig: Gutenberg Verlag, n.d.).

IV.

Printed Music as a Graphic Art

THE DISTINCTIVE APPEARANCE of musical editions has been developed with performers in mind. Or so we should like to think: actually the matter is rarely discussed in print. We must assume that the appearance of the musical page involves conscious decisions, in hopes of eliciting the best efforts of performers or to distract the sales resistance of purchasers. The evidence of the former is more subtle than that of the latter, and its importance is often best conveyed by its absence. Visually, music can be impressive to look at; it can be exciting to acquire, and even gratifying to read — even if, when this happens, instinctively we thank the composer rather than the printer. By way of extending the previous discussion, this chapter deals with three groups of publications devoted to the visual aspects of music: exhibition catalogues, studies of music title pages and covers, and writings on other kinds of printed matter related to music.

A. Exhibition Catalogues

Music has often been shown in exhibitions, and printed music pervades the literature of music exhibitions, although the record of either the events or the catalogues is largely uncollected. The visual artifact of music can be a thoughtful complement to the experience of sound, however impressionistic the experience.

Admittedly the holograph manuscript is usually more richly senti-
mental in its evocation than the printed edition, the *verum corpus*
of the creative act that one worships. The publication, in contrast,
as the *sanctus spiritus*, which reaches out to conquer time and
space, is often the more provocative intellectual statement in its
many suggestions of the changing environment of music itself.

The list below is limited to exhibitions that either survey the history of music printing or otherwise reflect on printed music in a
general way. Four different kinds of events are involved: (1) exhibitions specifically devoted to the history of music printing, in libraries or elsewhere; (2) printing exhibitions, either historical or
current, with extensive or significant coverage to music; (3) music
exhibitions in which printed editions, historical or current, make
up a separate or particularly important part; and (4) world's fairs
and other international exhibitions, in which printed music, historical or contemporary, is significantly involved. Excluded are exhibitions devoted to particular composers, regions, periods, or musical genres; also current lists prepared individually or collectively
by music publishers in order to promote sales, for instance at conventions, rather than to celebrate their graphic presentations.

The coverage of world's fairs has benefitted greatly from two
sources. For calling my attention to this topic, I am particularly
grateful to Malou Haine, whose "Expositions d'instruments anciens dans la seconde moitié du XIXe siècle," *Revue belge de musicologie*, 42 (1988), 223-40, has provided both specific references
and a sense of purpose. Indeed the showings of printed music
complement the instrument exhibitions insofar as both help call
attention to changing tastes in and growing recognition of the historical artifacts of music. The second is the *Historical Dictionary of
World's Fairs and Expositions, 1851-1988*, by John E. Findling and
Kimberly D. Pelle (New York: Greenwood, 1990).[1]

Further studies may turn up even more music scattered through
these exhibits. What makes the large fairs particularly fascinating
is the overriding assumption that success required greater indus-
trialization, through more clever and sophisticated manufacturing
technology and distribution, as well as greater promotion efforts
in the international market. We assume that those aggressive pub-

---

1. References on pp. 153-62 are to the sectional bibliographies Findling.
The "General Bibliography" (pp. 411-17) has also been very useful.

lishers who exhibited, and who mobilized other publishers to exhibit, actually believed this, as did those who attended the fairs. To what extent were such attitudes shared by other publishers as well as by the many musicians who did not attend? Amidst the positivistic assumptions behind the nineteenth-century world's fairs, printed music proved increasingly awkward to exhibit. World's fairs may have offered desirable opportunities for public presentation, but also very expensive ones, at a time when music publishers were becoming increasingly specialized in their catalogues. (It may be no coincidence that social scientists at this time were coming to be attracted to their classic distinction between community and society, between *Gemeinschaft* and *Gesellschaft*, which underlies the justification for Chapter 6 in particular, as well as some of the perspectives implicit in Chapters 5 and 9.)

Occasionally (for the large-scale events in particular), several catalogues contradict one another in details; and often these involve great treasures. Did owners recall items that they feared might not be properly shown or protected, or did the documents simply not fit into the cases as planned? The annotation for 429 suggests the problem. Those who mount exhibits know such predicaments, along with other possible explanations, and can perhaps excuse my foregoing any further search in deference to exact dates of a catalogue's printing, publication, or introduction, when these are specified. In all events, the catalogues provide a valuable commentary on the changing role of printed music, from a commercial commodity with cultural implications to a cultural commodity with commercial implications.

Paris, 1834

François-Joseph FÉTIS. "Exposition des produits de l'industrie: caractères de musique gravés fondus et stéréotypés par les procédés de M. E. Duverger," *Revue musicale*, 8 (1834), 193-96.   **407**
The essay is easy to recognize as part of Duverger's advertising program; see 184 above. The title specifically mentions an exhibition, and around this time Duverger's music type was being shown to the public at every possible opportunity; but there are unfortunately no hints regarding the specific exhibit in question, or whether other music printing materials were exhibited.

London, 1851

Great Exhibition of the Works of Industry of All Nations. *Official and Descriptive and Illustrated Catalogue.* . . . London: Spicer Bros. (W. Clowes, Printers), 1851.   **408**
Displays of printed music were scattered through the Crystal Palace exhibition, and probably not all of them are accessible through the indexes at the beginning of most of the catalogues (i.e., on p. lxvi in the work cited above).

The British section (class XVII; vol. 2, p. 536-62) cites several musical editions; Jullien & Co., however, chose to show their "ornamental printed music" as "Plastic Art, Mosaics, Enamels, etc." (class XXX; vol. 2, p. 823). Among the foreign exhibits, only the "patent music compositor" of R. F. Bescher (vol. 3, p. 1174) is described in any detail.

The *Reports of the Juries* (London: Royal Commission, 1852), pp. 396-453, mentions none of these. *L'Imprimerie, la librairie, et la papeterie à l'Exposition Universelle de 1851: Rapport du XVIIe Jury* (2e. édition. Paris: Imprimerie Impériale, 1854), however, discusses "Musique éxecutée typographiquement" on pp. 34-40.

See Philip T. Smith's bibliographical note in Findling, pp. 8-9. I have not undertaken to sort out all the publications of the exhibition. Many of the British Museum copies of these publications were in a part of the stacks destroyed in World War II; while music printing was displayed, it was not among the highlights of the show. This may seem surprising, considering the importance of published music in 19th-century England. The years just prior to 1851, on close examination, may be suspected to have been lean or unsettled ones for most music printers and publishers.

Paris, 1855

Henri MADINIER. *Notes sur les principaux produits exposés de l'imprimerie.* Paris: Dupont, 1855.   **409**
Recent music typography (Duverger, Tantenstein, Cordel, Curmer) occupied a section of the Exposition Universelle as discussed on pp. 57-58 of this catalogue.

See also Jules Delalain, *La typographie française et étrangère, à l'Exposition Universelle* (Paris, 1856), pp. 33-34; also Barrie M. Ratcliffe's bibliographical note in Findling, pp. 21-22.

Paris, 1867

Oscar COMETTANT. "Les publications musicales," in *La musique, les musiciens, et les instruments de musique . . . à l'Exposition Internationale de 1867* (Paris: M. Lévy, 1869), pp. 466-515. **410**
The subtitle of the first section ("Coup d'œil historique sur l'impression de la musique chez les différents peuples du monde; Le commerce de la musique et les progrès de l'art") suggests the vacuous amiability of this discussion, filled as it is with rhetorical questions, dropped names, and pious respect for sponsors. A second section ("Les bibliothèques françaises . . . ," p. 483) pays special tribute to Georges Kastner (who, incidentally, was vice-president of the jury) and includes a sub-section, "Parémiologie musicale de la langue française" (p. 493*ff*.).

In vol. 2 of Michel Chevalier, *Rapports du Jury International* (Paris: Paul Dupont, 1868), "Caractères de musique" are discussed on pp. 13-15, "Publications musicales" on pp. 310-18, in a text that is more critical and thoughtful than Comettant's.

For general background see also Arthur Chandler's bibliographical note in Findling, p. 43.

London, 1871-74

Catherine Dibello (Findling, pp. 44-47) speaks of music as an important part of these exhibitions, but I have found no evidence of musical documents being shown, only instruments. General opinion has found these exhibitions less impressive than the earlier ones in London; see for instance the notice in the *Journal of the Society of Arts*, 20 (1872), 889-94.

Vienna, 1873

Carl B. LORCK. *Die graphischen Künste auf der Weltausstellung zu Wien.* Braunschweig: Friedrich Vieweg, 1874. **411**
"Autorisirter Abdruck aus dem 'Amtlichen Bericht über die Wiener Weltausstellung im Jahre 1873,' Band 1, Heft 6," with a summary essay on "Der Musiknotendruck" (pp. 71-73) that identifies contributions of several publishers and of C. G. Röder.

For general background see also Leila G. Sirk's bibliographical note in Findling, p. 54.

Philadelphia, 1876

Der Buchhandel und die graphischen Künste Deutschlands auf der Weltausstellung zu Philadelphia im Jahre 1876. Leipzig: Breitkopf & Härtel, 1876.   **412**
About a dozen German music printers and publishers are named among the exhibitors. For general background see also the bibliographical note by Alfred Heller, pp. 61-62.

London, 1877

Catalogue of the Loan Collection of Antiquities, Curiosities, and Appliances Connected with the Art of Printing, South Kensington, edited by George Bullen. London: N. Trübner, 1877.   **413**
For the 1877 "Caxton Celebration," according to Bigmore & Wyman (pp. 124-26), William H. Cummings, A. H. Littleton, and William Alexander Barrett prepared the catalogue entries on music printing (section F), for which Barrett prepared a fine introductory essay (pp. 247-50).

The exhibition of type specimen books (pp. 431-49) is also important as a major precursor of Berry & Johnson (298 above). See Robin Myers, "The Caxton Celebration of 1877: A Landmark in Bibliophily," in *Bibliophily,* edited by Robin Myers and Michael Harris (Cambridge; Alexandria, Va.: Chadwyck-Healey, 1986; Publishing History Occasional Series, 2), pp. 138-63 (esp. pp. 149 and 159).

Paris, 1878

Exposition Universelle Internationale. *Catalogue officiel.* Paris: Imprimerie Nationale, 1878.   **414**
Group 2, class 13 (vol. 2, pp. 85-93) lists about 30 musical editions, mostly French, along with about 170 instruments.

More interesting are the comments on the music printing awards (eight silver medals, ten bronze, and eight honorable mentions, with three bronze medals for collaborators) in Gustave Chouquet, *Rapport sur les instruments de musique et les éditions musicales* (Paris: Imprimerie Nationale, 1880), pp. 63-66. The introductory text is particularly stern: nobody deserves a gold medal, shame on opera publishers who issue only the vocal scores but not the full scores, and shame on all publishers who have their engraving done abroad.

For general background see also the bibliographical note by Arthur Chandler in Findling, p. 71.

London, 1885

International Inventions Exhibition. *Guide to the Loan Collection and List of the Musical Instruments, Manuscripts, Books, Paintings, and Engravings Exhibited in the Gallery and Lower Rooms of the Albert Hall,* edited by A. J. Hipkins. London: Clowes, 1885.   **415**
The show is a landmark event in the study of musical instruments, but printed music is also scattered throughout, and predominates in divisions 23 and 24 (pp. 80-105 in the catalogue). Manuscripts are also numerous in divisions 20-22 (pp. 69-79), portraits and playbills in division 23.

London, 1885

W. J. WEALE. *Historical Music Loan Exhibition, Albert Hall, London, June-October 1885: A Descriptive Catalogue of Rare Manuscripts and Printed Books.* London: Bernard Quaritch, 1886.   **416**
In addition to 37 manuscripts, some 161 printed editions, 1480-1773, drawn from collections other than the British Museum, are described in impressively detailed bibliographical citations.

London, 1885

British Museum. *A Guide to the Manuscripts and Printed Books Illustrating the Progress of Musical Notation.* London: Printed by Order of the Trustees, 1885.   **417**
An exhibition of 135 items shown in the Department of Manuscripts, followed by ten printed items (pp. 17-20) shown in the King's Library, presumably mounted so as to complement the Albert Hall exhibition. (As with many libraries, the loan of particularly impressive items for exhibitions has been precluded at the British Museum, whether because of formal rules, official practices, or something in between that it is counterproductive if not improper to question. This presumably is why so often there will be two London exhibitions at any one time.)

Internationale Ausstellung für Musik- und Theaterwesen. [*Various catalogues*].   **418**

A vast exhibition, complicated in its topical organization, which involved a classification scheme intended for use in the special presentations supplied by particular nations. The titles below all bear the imprint of the Kommission der Internationalen Ausstellung, unless otherwise noted.

The "zweite vermehrte Auflage" of *Führer durch die Ausstellung und Katalog der Gewerblichen Special-Ausstellung* shows the classification scheme on pp. 38-41: printed music is separated by period (pre-Bach, Bach to 1873, and modern, as located in Gruppe III, 18. and 19. Classe, and Gruppe IX, 56. Classe); the music literature, catalogues, and programs are separate (Gruppe IV, 20.-22. Classe, respectively). The modern music publishers who exhibited are listed on pp. 183-88.

In addition, several special catalogues were issued for the exhibits of particular countries. The *Fach-Katalog der Musikhistorischen Abteilung von Deutschland und Oesterreich-Ungarn* includes sections on music printing (pp. 89-97, 105-16, and 131-36, with 327 items between them). The *Katalog der Ausstellung des Königreiches Grossbritannien und Irland* designates several sections as "Musikdrucke" but actually shows printed music elsewhere as well. An extensive *Fach-Katalog der Abteilung des Königreiches Italien*, by Adolfo Berwin and Robert Hirschfeld, also describes a good deal of printed music. Adolfo Nossig's *Katalog der Polnischen Abteilung* has fewer printed items, as does the volume entitled simply *Russland*. Only the *Katalog der Ausstellung des Königreiches Spanien* follows the official classification scheme set forth in the *Führer*, with 95 items in classes 18-23 (pp. 23-27).

The publisher Ricordi, meanwhile, issued a catalogue of its own, a sumptuous folio of 178 pages of text and many illustrations, mostly of correspondence ("Brief Fac-simile"), with an attached *Album der Noten Fac-simili* with 32 items.

The *Spezial-Katalog der Fachausstellung des Männergesangvereins "Schubertbund" in Wien* also includes several small sections on printed music, as does Georg Thouret, *Führer durch die Fachausstellung der Deutschen Militär-Musik* (Wien: Im Selbstverlag,

1892), pp. 28-40. Finally, Siegmund Schneider's huge (16 × 12") book entitled *Die Internationale Ausstellung für Musik- und Theaterwesen, Wien 1892* (Wien: Moritz Perles, 1894) has many heliographic illustrations, along with promising essays (e.g., Robert Hirschfeld, on "Graphologische Studien," pp. 333-35), but little on printed music.

Chicago, 1893

The musical battles in connection with the World's Columbian Exposition, between Theodore Thomas and the piano manufacturers, are legendary, and music publishers and others interested in musical documents were no doubt well advised to run for cover. For background see Paul and Ruth Hume, "The Great Chicago Piano War," *American Heritage*, 21 (1970), 16-21; also Ezra Schabas, *Theodore Thomas* (Urbana: University of Illinois Press, 1989), Chapter 11 ("Debacle at White City," pp. 195-212).

The fact remains that the world of exhibitions, and of music printing displayed in them, was changing at this time. Heretofore most were industrial displays for a middle-class audience of merchants and the consumers of merchandise; hereafter, most were conceived for connoisseurs and those who seek to understand the workings of historical processes in art. Viewing the overall trend in music exhibitions, one can see that Thomas was losing another battle while he was witnessing the changing tide of civilized taste itself.

Paris, 1900

Lucien LAYUS. *La librairie, l'édition musicale, la presse, la reliure, l'affiche à l'Exposition Universelle de 1900.* Paris: Cercle de la Librairie (D. Dumolin), 1900.   **419**

The fair itself may have been a landmark event in the history of *Art nouveau* tastes, and while the "Musique" section (pp. 27-38) includes twelve illustrations, its text is thin, touching on history, current practices, and production statistics. Music covers are also discussed in the text on "Affiches" (pp. 96-97). Specimen pages from printers and publishers follow p. 100, unnumbered but arranged alphabetically by firm name, among them two music publishers, Lamoine (4 pp.) and Noël (6 pp.).

For general background see Richard D. Mandell, *Paris 1900: The Great World's Fair* (Toronto: University of Toronto Press,

1967), also the bibliographical note by Robert W. Brown in Findling, pp. 163-64.

London, 1901, 1913, 1926, 1939

British Museum. *A Guide to the Exhibition in the King's Library Illustrating the History of Printing, Music-Printing, and Bookbinding.* London: Printed by Order of the Trustees, 1901.   **420**

This catalogue was issued four times at intervals of roughly 13 years, essentially from the same setting of type but with several changes in 1913 and one in 1939.

The 1901 section on music printing (Cases 21-22) contains 43 items, as described on pp. 98-108.

The 1913 section (now in Cases 15-16) contains 46 items, described on pp. 105-14. (There are also about a dozen substitutions: in general the deletions are more famous than the additions, which however are more unusual than the deletions.) The titles retained are printed mostly with the same settings of type.

The 1926 edition is identical with that of 1913.

The 1939 exhibition was remounted (now in Cases 17-18), its music described on pp. 106-16. It shows 47 items (the South German gradual of *ca.* 1473 having been added; see 129 above). A few of the editorial changes are of some importance (e.g. newly established dates), but most are matters of lesser detail.

For commentary on historic "high spots" at the earliest of these exhibitions see W. J. Eden Crane, "The Evolution of Music Printing," *Caxton Magazine*, 7 (1905), 93-97.

Leipzig, 1902

Max KUHN. "Zur Geschichte des Musiknotendrucks," *Börsenblatt für den deutschen Buchhandel*, 69 (1902), 9020-22.   **421**

An exhibition at the Deutsches Buchgewerbehaus, which the author, partner in the respected music publishing firm of Lauterbach & Kuhn, describes in his address for the Verein der deutschen Musikalienhändler on October 31st, 1902. He evokes recent bibliographical studies (Riemann, Molitor, Mantuani), the *Paléographie musicale*, and the 1892 Vienna exhibition.

The text reportedly appears also in *Musikhandel und Musik-pflege*, no. 5 (November 1st, 1902). There is also an early five-page typescript *Ausstellung zur Geschichte des Musiknotendruckes*, stamped "Hug & Co., Leipzig, Export-Abt." (*NYPL*).

London, 1904

An Illustrated Catalogue of the Music Loan Exhibition ... by the Worshipful Company of Musicians at Fishmongers' Hall, June and July, 1904. London: Novello, 1909.   **422**
The "Music Printing" section appears on pp. 1-123. See my "An Edwardian Gentlemen's Musical Exhibition," Music Library Association, *Notes*, 32 (1976), 711-18. Also issued in connection with the exhibit was a visitor's guide entitled *A Special Loan Exhibition* (London: J. Truscott, 1904), of which there were apparently two editions: see *Notes*, p. 712 *n.*

The *Catalogue of 100 Works Illustrating the History of Music Printing from the 15th to the End of the 17th Century in the Library of A. H. Littleton* (London: Novello, 1911) was also derived from the exhibition, based on the treasures loaned by one of its main exhibitors, who was a director at Novello's. See also "Some Notes on Early Printed Music," in Littleton's *English Music, 1604 to 1904*, 2nd ed. (London, 1911), pp. 478-496; also Jeffrey Pulver, "Illustrations of the History of Music Printing in the Library of Alfred H. Littleton," *Musical Times*, 55 (1914), 650-51; 56 (1915), 21-22, 84-86.

St. Louis, 1904

Catalogue of German Music Exhibited at the St. Louis World's Fair. Leipzig: Breitkopf & Härtel, 1904.   **423**
An extensive (85-page) list with brief titles of recent publications, presumably intended for sales to the German community around St. Louis.

In addition, the Section Française issued their *Rapports des Groupes 17-18: Librairie, musique, reliure, et cartographie* (Paris: H. Le Suidier, 1906), in which a number of music publishers are described along with general publishers on pp. 51-112. The Deutscher Buchgewerbeverein in Leipzig also issued its *Katalog der Ausstellung für Buchgewerbe und Photographie in St. Louis*.

For background on the exposition see Yvonne M. Condon's bibliographical note in Findling, pp. 185-86; also Ernest B. Kroeger, "Music at the Louisiana Purchase Exposition," *The Musical World*, 3 (1903), 91-93, and "World's Fair Music," *Musical Courier*, 48 (1904), p. 21.

Berlin, 1906

Central-Verband Deutscher Tonkünstler und Tonkünstler-Vereine. *Offizieller Katalog der Musik-Fachausstellung, vom 5.-20. Mai 1906, in den Gesamträumen der Philharmonie, Berlin.* Berlin: Deutscher-Verlag, [1906].   **424**
Sections 9-17 (pp. 57-109) are devoted to music printing and publishing, in this rather unusual trade exhibition (which otherwise, for instance, includes displays by music binderies and of automatic music page-turning devices).

The *Katalog einer kleinen Sammlung wertvoller Musikalien und Bücher, als Beiträge zur Geschichte der musikalischen Notation* describes 77 items, most of them printed, shown by the music antiquarian Leo Liepmannssohn to complement the Philharmonie exhibit. The same items, except for two deletions, are reprinted with identical descriptions and prices added as the first part of the firm's Katalog 160.

Frankfurt, 1908

Ausstellung Schmuck und Illustration von Musikwerken, in ihrer Entwicklung vom Mittelalter bis in die neueste Zeit, 23. Dezember 1908 bis 24. Januar 1909. Frankfurt-am-Main: Kunstgewerbemuseum, [1908].   **425**
Of the 279 items that are briefly described, 239 are from Paul Hirsch's collection, 65 are from the Kunstgewerbebibliothek, while 67 are iconography and playbills from F. Nicolas Manskopf's Musikhistorisches Museum in Frankfurt.

Leipzig, 1909

Zweite Musik-Fachausstellung . . . : Katalog der Sonderausstellung aus der Musik-Bibliothek Paul Hirsch, Frankfurt-am-Main. Frankfurt: Englert & Schlosser, 1909.   **426**
Reproductions of the captions for 40 items shown at the Krystallpalast, June 3-15, 1909, to complement the main exhibi-

tion of the Central-Verband Deutscher Tonkünstler und Ton-künstler-Vereine, e.V.

The main exhibition, described in a catalogue entitled *II. Musik-Fachausstellung vom 3. bis 15. Juni 1909*, also covers many aspects of music, among them "Noten-Druck und -Stich" (Gruppe IX, summarized on p. 39), "Musikverlag" (Gruppe X, pp. 40-47), and "Bibliotheken" (Gruppe XI, pp. 48-56).

Leipzig, 1914

Oskar von HASE. "Der Musikalienhandel," in the Internationale Ausstellung für Buchgewerbe und Graphik, *Amtlicher Katalog* (Leipzig: Poeschel & Trepte, 1914), pp. 301-305. **427**

The Buchgewerbliche Weltausstellung took place between July and September 1914, at the time of the well-known guns of August. British books were shown (and, legend has it, eventually even with some difficulty returned), but apparently no music.

Hase's text is mostly historical. Among the exhibitors, a number of German music engravers and lithographers are listed in Gruppe X ("Der Hochdruck, der Tiefdruck," pp. 242-48); music publishers are in Gruppe XII ("Der Buchhandel"; see pp. 308-22). The Russischer Musikverlag and Breitkopf & Härtel also advertised (pp. 322-23). The catalogue for the Österreichisches Haus lists the work of major Viennese music publishers.

Plesske (no. 45) cites a 48-page booklet, *Der deutsche Musik-Verlag auf der Internationalen Ausstellung für Buchgewerbe und Graphik* (Leipzig: Pabst, 1914), which celebrates the achievements of German music publishing prior to the War.

Breitkopf & Härtel also issued an eight-page *Technischer Bericht 1914* (NYPL, *MPPS/Germany) in connection with the exhibition; it is not a summary of specifications, as its title may imply, but rather a promotional booklet, with photos of the recently expanded shop and examples of the pictorial work and bindings. The booklet was reissued, so as to assume a history of its own, which would be useful to trace as evidence of publishing practice. For instance, a copy at the University of Illinois, datable from *ca.* 1927, has been expanded to 48 pages, so as to accommodate a dedication to the staff members who died in World War I, several examples of famous editions published by the firm, and 17 photographs of activities in the plant.

Frankfurt, 1920

Eine kleine Bücherschau . . . im Oktober 1920 . . . im Hause Paul Hirsch . . . : Führer durch die Ausstellung. Frankfurt-am-Main: Privately printed, 1920.   **428**
Prepared for the Gesellschaft der Bibliophilien, the Maximilian-Gesellschaft, and the Gesellschaft Hessischer Bücherfreunde, with 214 annotated entries.

Frankfurt, 1927

Katalog der Internationalen Ausstellung "Musik im Leben der Völker," Frankfurt am Main, 11. Juni-28. August 1927. [Frankfurt: Werner & Winter, 1927].   **429**
The successor to the 1892 Vienna exhibition is similarly vast; not limited to but very strong in printed music, no doubt thanks in large part to Paul Hirsch; and enhanced by several guides, all of them valuable for — if contradictory in — bibliographical details. This official catalogue, prepared by Hirsch's librarian, Kathi Meyer, was available soon after the opening. A weighty book (340 pages and 49 added plates), its citations are actually rather brief. Printed music is scattered throughout; the contemporary publishers who exhibited are listed on pp. 322-24 (for Raum 62). Other catalogues include the following:

Max Bartsch, *Führer durch die Ausstellung . . .* (Frankfurt: Union-Druckerei und Verlagsanstalt, [1927]). A 47-page guidebook with a fold-out map, it was issued earlier than Meyer, and fails to correlate with Meyer in mildly disconcerting ways; e.g., "Raum 7" in the *Führer*, p. 7, is a "Musikraum um 1790," whereas in the *Katalog*, p. 2, it is a "Musikzimmer um 1800."

The *Catalogue de la Section Française* (Paris: Association Française d'Exposition et d'échanges Artistiques, Imprimerie de Vaugirard, 1927) extends pp. 152-204 of the *Katalog*, with fuller citations and descriptive annotations.

The *Catalogo della sezione italiana* (Roma: Ministerio della pubblica instruzione; Bestetti e Tumminelli, 1927) is a considerably expanded version of pp. 132-51 of the *Katalog*, with fuller citations and annotations, an introduction by G. Cesari (dated August 1927), 22 numbered plates at the end (and others earlier, unnumbered), and an index. The 508 numbered entries are somewhat rearranged in the *Katalog*; several items are new.

S. Bottenheim, *De Nederlandsche Afdeeling . . . : Catalogus* (Amsterdam: N. V. Van Munster, 1927). An expanded version in Dutch of pp. 249-54 of the *Katalog*, rearranged and annotated and with four plates. The introduction is dated July 12, 1927.

Antwerp, 1930

Exposition Internationale Coloniale, Maritime et d'Art Flamand. *Exposition . . . d'Art Flamand . . . Livre d'art, musique.* Anvers: Delaplace, Koch, 1930.   **430**
The music section (Salle 17), with 161 items, consists mostly of printed music, local (J. A. Stellfeld), nearby (Brussels), and distant (Danzig and Rostock), as acknowledged at the end of the above and in the *Catalogue* of the Section d'Art Flamand ancien, vol. 2 (Bruxelles: Veuve Monnom, 1930), pp. 99-122.

New York, 1937

[Exhibition of Printed Music, Grolier Club, December 17, 1937-January 16, 1938. Catalogue. New York: Recordak, (1938)].   **431**
Microfilm of selected pages from about 100 items from various collections. The captions suggest ties to the 1935 Meyer-O'Meara essay in *The Dolphin* (51 above).

Brooklyn (N. Y.), 1939

Marian Hannah WINTER. *Art Scores for Music: Historic Scores for Cabaret and Concert Hall Music, with Pictorial Decorations by Old and Modern Masters.* Brooklyn: Brooklyn Museum of Art, 1939.   **432**
Issued by the Brooklyn Institute of Arts and Sciences in cooperation with the Federal Music Project of New York City. The text is assembled from secondary sources, and twelve illustrations from the exhibition are included.

Philadelphia, 1939

The Story of the National Exhibition of Music Printing, March 28th to April 15th, 1939, at the Galleries of the Philadelphia Arts Alliance. Philadelphia: Philadelphia Graphic Arts Forum, 1939.   **433**

The exhibition was explicitly mounted in order to argue that "printed music . . . is a pretty sad-looking business," and, therefore, to "do something about it." In such blunt terms, Herbert Hosking's announcement asks readers to consider whether particular editions may give "an overall impression of having been produced by a printer who shared the publisher's preference that it would have been better to forget about the whole idea." No catalogue of the exhibition was planned, however, and this is unfortunate, since Section 4 ("Distinguished Modern Music Printing") was to consist of material "selected by a jury from the material submitted for Section 3" (which was "A Survey of the Field," consisting of "typical examples . . . from current lists of American music publishers.") Nor have I located Otto Kinkeldey's March 28 inaugural address on "The History of Music Printing." His copy of the booklet and invitation are in NYPL.

New York, 1950

New York Public Library, Music Division. "Music Printing in America: An Exhibition of Printing Methods, 1698-1950."   **434**

The Library's *Dictionary Catalog of the Music Collection* (2nd ed., Boston: G. K. Hall, 1982), vol. 13, p. 290, describes this as a microfilm of "specimen pages, portraits, proof-sheets, etc., with accompanying labels."

Williamstown (Mass.), 1950

Four Centuries of Music: An Exhibit. Williamstown: Williams College, Chapin Library, 1950.   **435**

Assembled by Joaquín Nin-Culmell and Mary L. Richmond, and showing several dozen treasures from the Chapin collections, with references to related holdings.

Toledo (Ohio), 1957

A. Beverly BARKSDALE. *The Printed Note: 500 Years of Music Printing and Engraving.* Toledo, Ohio: Toledo Museum of Art, 1957.   **436**

The compiler, later manager of the Cleveland Orchestra in the George Szell era, mounted three memorable music exhibits during his earlier tenure as curator at the museum. All have hand-

somely illustrated catalogues. The first (1953) showed medieval and Renaissance manuscripts; the second (1954) composers' portraits and autograph scores; and this one, the most extensive of all, printed music assembled from many libraries. The annotations serve as an introduction to the history of music printing itself. Their narrative may be encumbered by the sequence of the materials being shown, but the well-chosen illustrations are invaluable. See also Barksdale's essay, "On the Planning and Arranging of Music Exhibitions," Music Library Association, *Notes*, 10 (1953), 565-69 (reprinted in Bradley, pp. 217-20).
Reprinted New York: Da Capo, 1981.

Aldeburgh, 1972

J. M. THOMSON. *Notes and Embellishments: English Printed Music since 1500.* [Aldeburgh, 1972].   **437**
Catalogue of an exhibition at Grove Park, Yoxford, Suffolk, during the 25th Aldeburgh festival, June 2-19, 1972, with 91 items described by Thomson and H. Edmund Poole and an "Introduction" by A. Hyatt King.

Berkeley, 1977

Mary Kay DUGGAN. *Early Music Printing in the Music Library.* Berkeley: University of California, 1977.   **438**
Exhibition in honor of the 12th Congress of the International Musicological Society.

Lisbon, 1978

Arquivos musicais: musicografia, bibliografia, iconografia, discografia, instrumentos, varia; catálogo da exposiçao realizada na Biblioteca Nacional de Lisboa–Outubro 1978. Lisboa: Direcção-General do Património Cultural, 1978.
[Cited in *ABHBL*, 1978, no. 2815.]   **439**

Rome, 1985

Cinque secoli di stampa musicale in Europa. Mostra . . . Museo di Palazzo Venezia [Rome], *12 giugno-30 luglio 1985.* Napoli: Electa, 1985.   **440**
A handsome, illustrated catalogue edited by Silvia Cassani and Nerina Bevilacqua, with introductions by Francesco Siciliai and

Emilia Zanetti, followed by an encapsulation of his 1964 book (55 above) by Alec Hyatt King. The subsequent comments by notable scholars (Nino Pirrotta, Alberto Basso, Bruno Cagli, and Roman Vlad among them) are very brief, and altogether less impressive than the citations and glossy illustrations that follow.

England, 1986

Eye Music: The Graphic Art of New Musical Notation. London: Arts Council, 1986.   **441**
Catalogue of a travelling exhibition devised by Hugh Davies, Julie Lawson, and Michael Regan, shown at the Mappin Art Gallery, Sheffield, and elsewhere.

New York, 1986

Harmonizing the Arts: Original Graphic Designs for Printed Music by World-Famous Artists. New York: New York Public Library, 1986.   **442**
Checklist of 43 titles illustrated by noted French artists, 1851-1965, with an introduction by James J. Fuld. See also Frances J. Barulich and James J. Fuld, "Harmonizing the Arts: Original Graphic Designs for Printed Music by World-Famous Artists," Music Library Association, *Notes*, 43 (1986), 259-71.

Volkmann's 1910 essay (139), King's 1964 historical survey (55), and Tiersot's 1934 essay (126) are also important in the history of music printing exhibitions. See also the several Plantin catalogues (309); Wörthmüller's 1973 presentation detailing the Bach family's relationships with Nuremberg printers and publishers (584); the 1979 Speyer display; Stephan Zweig's 1934 address for the London *Sunday Times* exhibition (916); and several commemorative happenings in fond remembrance of Erik Satie (930), Volta in particular.

B. Music Covers and Title Pages

Writings on music as a graphic art usually concern mostly the covers, since the artists who designed them are often famous in their own right. Their lineage begins in the time of the elder Lucas Cranach in the Renaissance; extends through Gustave Doré, Currier & Ives, and Winslow Homer in the nineteenth century; and continues with Pablo Picasso, Hans Arp, and Jean Cocteau in the twentieth. Notable pictorial covers were also created by less celebrated artists, notable among them John Brandard and Alfred Concanen in nineteenth-century England. Often minor or anonymous artists have created images that cultural historians recognize as important, whether as ostensibly authentic illustrations or as symbolic statements.

As a result, the monetary value of musical documents often accrues to the cover more than to the music, so that private collectors have been known to save and frame the cover and discard the music entirely. (May God punish them in perpetuity.)

Josef HEIM. *Album Wiener Musiktitel, aus der Musikaliendruckerei v. Jos. Eberle & Co.* Wien, [188-?]   **443**
An anthology of nearly 100 facsimiles, the first in color, the rest mostly in monochrome, without text. The title is identified as "1. Ausgabe," but the pages are unbound and may have been collected as a "nonce" publication. The copy inspected (*NYPL*, *MC) has a bookplate that reads, "Bücherei J. G. Schleiter & Giesecke, Leipzig, 1902."

J. Grand CARTERET. *Les titres illustrés et l'image au service de la musique.* Turin: Bocca, 1894.   **444**
A notable collector of graphic materials shares his ardent but informed critical observations on design and context, and shows about a hundred facsimile illustrations. His emphasis is on French publications, and the arrangement is historical: from the beginnings to the Revolution (pp. 1-119), 1789-1817 (pp. 120-60), 1817-1830 (pp. 161-237), and 1830-1850 (pp. 238-96).

The text also appears in *Rivista musicale italiana*, 5 (1898), 1-63, 225-280; 6 (1899), 289-329; 9 (1902), 559-635; and 11 (1904), 1-23 and 191-227. (The text is identical, even the imposition, except for the last 36 pages, which are reset. The facsimiles, in soft pastel in the book, use black ink in the journal.)

A brief complementary piece devoted to the 19th century, with several illustrations, appears as "Titres de musique," in the author's *Vieux papiers, vieilles images: Cartons d'un collectionneur* (Paris: A. Le Vasseur, 1896), pp. 327-39.

Gabriel MOUREY. "The Illustration of Music," *International Studio*, 6 (1898), 86-98.   **445**

Enthusiastic commentary, with eleven illustrations, shown out of the context of their title pages as "vignettes."

Walter von ZUR WESTEN. "Moderne deutsche Notentitel," *Zeitschrift für Bücherfreunde*, Jg. 2, Heft 1 (April 1898), 1-12.   **446**
Extended descriptive and critical commentary on the work of Moritz von Schwind, Alexander Strähuber, Ludwig Richter, Adolf Menzel, Max Klinger, Bruno Wennerberg, Hans Unger, Karl Strathmann, and Hermann Hirzel, among others.

Maximilian RAPSILBER. "Künstlerische Notentitel," *Monatshefte für graphisches Kunstgewerbe*, 2 (1903), 17-22. **447**
On contemporary German covers, with 19 illustrations.

Jean LOUBIER. "Künstlerische Notentitel," *Kunst und Kunsthandwerk*, 9 (1906), 574-89.   **448**
The curator of the Buchgewerbemuseum discusses recent covers, with 17 illustrations.

Paul FLOBERT. "Les titres de musique et de romances illustrés avant 1870," *Bulletin de la Société archéologique, historique et artistique "Le vieux papier,"* 6 (1908), 267-74. **449**
Text read at a society meeting on April 28th, 1908, for which "Le menu du dîner était illustré d'un frontispice [sic] tiré en couleur de Caraffe, gravé par Ruotte."

I have not seen the author's "L'illustration des titres de musique," *L'art décoratif*, 6 (1909), 267-74. [Davidsson 145; the volume and date seem not to agree].

Walter von ZUR WESTEN. "Zur Kunstgeschichte des Notentitels und der Dekoration musikalischer Druckwerke," *Zeitschrift für Bücherfreunde*, 12 (1908), 89-107, 129-52.   **450**
The two parts of this extended essay, one on the era of woodcuts and copperplate engraving, the other on the era of lithography, anticipate the author's 1921 Röder Festschrift (459 below). Most of the 50 illustrations shown here also appear there, often enlarged and sometimes in color. The text was extensively re-

written, but the ideas are similar and in fact seem a bit more sharply focused in this earlier essay.

The author's "Die Graphik im Dienste der Musik," *Die Werk-kunst*, 5 (1910), 57-60, tells much the same story; his other writings cited in this section, however, are all essentially new.

H. von TRENKWALD. "Illustrierte Musikwerke," *Kunst-gewerbeblatt*, n. F., 20 (1909), 151-59.   **451**

A survey of a matter rarely discussed elsewhere: enhancement of musical notation itself with decorative effects, as distinct from illustrating its covers or attractively presenting the notation.

W. A. BRADLEY. "Some Attractive Music Titles," *Printing Art*, 19 (1912), 469-84.   **452**

Declining tastes, reflected in *passe-partout* practices, "antiquated job faces, and . . . grotesquely exaggerated hand lettering," together with a recognition of "the business advantage of . . . attention paid to the mere presentation of musical wares," led G. Schirmer and its affiliate, the Boston Music Co., to commission the design of new covers (13 of which are seen here), their aesthetic calling for simplicity of form and discretion of color.

William E. IMESON. *Illustrated Music-Titles*. London: Printed for the Author [1912?].   **453**

A *vade mecum* for collectors of music covers, with "A Dictionary of Delineators" (pp. 22-46). The "dates are invaluable, and it is full of chatty reminiscences of the artists, spiced by oblique reference to the private lives of those gay dogs of the Victorian demi-monde" (King, "English Pictorial Title-Pages," p. 262).

Schmidt-Phiseldeck also praises this book in "Ein englischer Privatdruck über Notentitel," *Philobiblon*, 6 (1933), 78.

Frank KIDSON. "Some Illustrated Music-Books of the Seventeenth and Eighteenth Centuries: English," *Musical Antiquary*, 3 (1912), 195-208.   **454**

A narrative account that mentions the major titles from *Parthenia* through Playford and Bickham and their contemporaries.

E. VALDRUCHE. *Iconographie des titres de musique aux XVIIIe et XIXe siècles*. Lille: Lefebvre-Ducrocq, 1912. **455**

Presented on July 23, 1912, at the meeting ("80ᵉ diner") of the Société archéologique, historique et artistique "Le vieux papier"; also issued in its *Bulletin*, 2 (1912), 139-59. Several choice items are selected from 14 bound collections and discussed. (A recreation and a critical analysis of the collections themselves would be informative.)

Walter von ZUR WESTEN. "Berliner Notentitel," in his *Berlins graphische Gelegenheitskunst* (Berlin: Otto von Hulten, 1912), vol. 1, pp. 111-32.   **456**
An elegant presentation with reproductions of paste-down vignettes of title-pages from Hummel forward, with running commentary.

Elizabeth LOUNSBERY. "Early Illustrated Music Titles," *American Homes and Gardens*, January 1914, pp. 22-25.
Appropriately gentle and delightful observations.   **457**

Arthur DOBSKY. "Alte und neue Notentitel," *Archiv für Buchgewerbe*, 54 (1917), 125-38, 159-74.   **458**
Historical and philosophical commentary on 24 illustrations, several of them full-page color insertions.

Walter von ZUR WESTEN. *Musiktitel aus vier Jahrhunderten: Festschrift anlässlich des 75-jährigen Bestehens der Firma C. G. Röder, G.m.b.H..* Leipzig, 1921.   **459**
An imposing folio volume, successor to the 1896 Riemann Festschrift (48 above). The presentation emphasizes music illustration as a reflection of changing tastes in the graphic arts, with 96 facsimiles.

—. "Notentitel," *Das Plakat*, 12 (1921), 146-71.   **460**
Commentary on 72 facsimiles (which for some reason start with nos. 37-72: nos. 1-36 follow, beginning on p. 161).

G. SERVIÈRES. "L'illustration romantique des titres de musique," *Revue de l'art*, 51 (1926), 301-12; 52 (1927), 79-88.   **461**
[Davidsson 474; also Schmidt-Phiseldeck (467 below), p. 185 *n*.]

M. VIMONT. "Visite de Paris à l'aide de chansons illustrées," *Bulletin de la Société archéologique, historique et artistique "Le vieux papier,"* 17 (1926-29), 404-40. **462**
Shows scenes from lithograph covers, quotes song texts, and relates anecdotes for a "causerie" of the society, March 15, 1927.

Otto BETTMANN. "Wesen und Wandlungsfähigkeit neuerer Editionstitel," *Offset-, Buch- und Werbekunst,* 4 (1927), 401-07. **463**
Special covers are often used to identify the special series under which music publishers emphasize particular works (usually standard classics) as part of their own special "edition." The author, displaying the imaginative critical and promotional eye that was later evident in his celebrated picture archive, discusses and illustrates the covers for "Edition Steingräber," "Simrock Volks-Ausgabe," "Universal Edition," "Collection Litolff," "Edition Peters," "Edition Breitkopf," and several of their successors.

Aaron DAVIS. "Music Covers," *Antiques,* 12 (1927), 394-96. **464**
Mostly on mid 19th-century American titles drawn from the author's collection, with six illustrations.

Wilhelm HITZIG. "Zur Geschichte des Notentitels," *Offset-Buch- und Werbekunst,* 4 (1927), 391-401. **465**
As one would expect, the distinguished Breitkopf & Härtel archivist addresses the question of "welches Kleid der Würde (oder Unwürde) des Stückes am besten entspricht" ("which cover speaks best for the value of the piece, or lack of value"). His heart of hearts, one hopes, has excused him for showing, among his illustrations, four late 19th-century color lithographs.

Alfred KALMUS. "Der mehrfarbige Notentitel," *ibid,* 4 (1927), 408-14. **466**
The concluding essay in this trilogy (with Bettmann and Hitzig above) works from the adage "Kleider machen Leute," in discussing colored covers — brightly colored ones especially — for popular songs from Italy, France, and Belgium as well as from Germany and Vienna.

K. SCHMIDT-PHISELDECK. "Om Nodetitler," *Bogvennen*, 1929, pp. 177-218.   **467**
Pays respects to the most important earlier writings (Zur Westen and Grand Carteret in particular) and reproduces 13 illustrations, 1699-1850s, mostly Danish.

Luigi PARIGI. "La música ornada," *La revista de música* (Buenos Aires), 3 (1930), 129-39.   **468**
On covers, mostly for Ricordi editions, with 16 illustrations.
Also issued as "La musica ornata, I: Le Edizioni," in *Musica d'Oggi*, 12 (1930), 343-51.

Bella C. LANDAUER. *Some Aeronautical Music*. Paris: Privately printed, 1933.   **469**
A keepsake describing the part of Landauer's personal collection that is now at the Smithsonian Institution.
The sequels (on items mostly now in the New-York Historical Society) are *My City 'Tis of Thee*, on songs about New York City; *Striking the Right Note in Advertising*, on promotional ephemera (both New York: Privately printed, 1951); and *Some Terpsichorean Ephemera* (New York: Privately printed, 1953), with portraits of dancers on sheet music and in other sources.

Edith A. WRIGHT and Josephine McDEVITT. "Early American Sheet-Music Lithographs," *Antiques*, 23 (1933), 50-53, 99-102.   **470**
First of a series of brief articles for this journal by the Washington, D. C., sheet-music collectors. Their later essays include "Collecting Early American Sheet Music," 29 (1936), 202-05, primarily on music covers; "What's in a Name Plate," 36 (1939), 182-83, on labels for binders' volumes of sheet music; and "Music Sheets for Stamp Collectors," 41 (1942), 183-85.

E. Beresford CHANCELLOR. "Early Lithographs on Sheet Music," *Connoisseur*, 93 (1934), pp. 258-61.   **471**
A brief effusion for frequenters of the auction rooms, with four Victorian illustrations.

Knudåge RIISAGER. "Nodeomslag," *Bogvennen 1934-37*, pp. 69-73.   **472**
On Danish covers in particular, with 13 facsimiles.

Kathi MEYER. "Die Illustrationen in den Musikbüchern des 15.-17. Jahrhunderts," *Philobiblon*, 10 (1938), pp. 205-12, 277-92.   **473**

A brief overview suggesting the range of graphic decoration of music, including hand rubrication and drawings, woodcut and engraved title pages, decorative initials, pictures and charts in books about music, and even the notation itself.

K. HÖCKER. "Notentitel und ihre Geschichte," *Die neue Gartenlaube*, 1940, p. 624.   **474**

[Davidsson 216]

Sacheverell SITWELL. *Morning, Noon, and Night in London*. London: Macmillan, 1948.   **475**

A slender tale, inspired by Victorian sheet-music covers.

Alec Hyatt KING. "English Pictorial Music Title-Pages, 1820-1885: Their Style, Evolution, and Importance," *The Library*, 5th series, 4 (1949-50), 262-72.   **476**

Still the major critical evaluation of Victorian music covers, with observations that honor the work of Brandard and Concanen.

"Some Victorian Illustrated Music Titles," *The Penrose Annual*, 46 (1952), 43-45, is a briefer essay, with eight plates.

James LAVER. "Music Titles," *The Penrose Annual*, 44 (1950), 54-55.   **477**

Comments on color reproductions of seven Victorian covers.

Alec Hyatt KING and François STAHLY. "Sheet-Music Covers, Yesterday and To-Day," *Graphis*, 9 (1953), 302-07, 330.   **478**

Appreciative remarks, by King on early covers in general, most of them English, and by Stahly on recent works, mostly French. Both texts appear in English, German, and French, and are enhanced by 42 greatly reduced but well presented illustrations.

[*Baseball in Music and Song.*] Philadelphia: Musical Americana (Harry Dichter), ca. 1954.   **479**

Color reproductions, reduced in size, of nine Americana "collector's items," 1860-94, this being the most substantial of several facsimiles prepared by the leading publicist of American sheet music collecting.

Eberhard HÖLSCHER. "Notentitel: 16. und 17. Jahrhundert," *Gebrauchsgraphik*, vol. 27 no. 2 (1956), pp. 44-49. **480**
A short paragraph of prose and eight half-tones.

Franzpeter GOEBELS. "Kleine Plauderei über Titelblätter der Klaviermusik," *Hausmusik*, 23 (1959), 158-64. **481**
An essay of some intellectual distinction, light in spirit but not patronizing, neatly illustrated, devoted to keyboard editions.

California Sheet Music Covers. San Francisco: Book Club of California, 1959. **482**
A keepsake, with 12 facsimiles, several in color.

Andrzej BANACH. "Lekcja z nut: une leçon des cahiers de musique," *Projekt 1963*, no. 1 (34), pp. 8-11. **483**
On 19th-century Polish music covers, with 16 illustrations, several in color. Abstracts (English, French, German, Russian) appear on p. 50.

Lester S. LEVY. *Grace Notes in American History: Popular Sheet Music from 1820 to 1900*. Norman: University of Oklahoma Press, 1967. **484**
All of Levy's writings grow out of his private collection of American sheet music, now at the Johns Hopkins University. All are handsomely illustrated, mostly from the American chromolithographs for which this collection is pre-eminent. Levy typically devotes most of his text to historical background that tells the tales behind the pictorial covers, usually with the song texts. His other titles include *Flashes of Merriment: A Century of Humorous Song in America, 1805-1905* (ibid., 1971); *Give Me Yesterday: American History in Song, 1890-1920* (ibid., 1975); and *Picture the Songs: Lithographs from the Sheet Music of Nineteenth-Century America* (Baltimore: Johns Hopkins University Press, 1976), along with the brief "Music Had Charms," *American Heritage*, April 1958, pp. 53-61.

Gottfried S. FRAENKEL. *Pictorial and Decorative Title Pages from Music Sources: 201 Examples from 1500 to 1800.* New York: Dover, 1968.   485

Illustrations with descriptions concerned mostly with the music, although the artists are usually identified. A neat, affordable, and informative book.

Doreen SPELLMAN and Sidney SPELLMAN. *Victorian Music Covers.* London: Evelyn, Adams, and Mackay, 1969; Park Ridge, N. J.: Noyes Press, 1972.   486

A small picture book built around illustrations, several in color.

Herbert C. ZAFREN. "The Value of 'Face Value,'" Hebrew Union College (Cincinnati), *Annual*, 40-41 (1969-70), 555-80.   487

On a late 17th-century title-page woodcut used by the Jewish bibliographer and printer Shabbathai Bass, with two rows of musical notes that may allude to Bass's earlier career as a singer in the Altneuschule in Prague.

Stefan C. Reif reports additional appearances of the woodcut in "Again the Musical Title Page," *Studies in Bibliography and Booklore*, 10 (1971/72), 57-61.

Ronald PEARSALL. *Victorian Sheet Music Covers.* Newton Abbot: David & Charles, 1972.   488

Comfortable reading, with 57 black-and-white reproductions.

The mood is anticipated in the author's "Victorian Music Covers," *British Printer*, 78 (1965), 98-101, built around six color illustrations.

Richard SCHAAL. *Musiktitel aus fünf Jahrhunderten.* Wilhelmshaven: Heinrichshofen, 1972 (Quellen-Kataloge zur Musikgeschichte, 5).   489

Essentially a republication of the 1921 Zur Westen volume (459), less lavishly produced and with a few deletions, some of them replaced by examples of recent work.

Nancy R. DAVISON. "The Grand Triumphal Quick-Step; or, Sheet Music Covers in America," in John D. Morse,

Prints in and of America to 1850 (Charlottesville: University Press of Virginia, 1970), pp. 257-89. **490**
A Winterthur Conference lecture in appreciation of 19th-century American music covers.
American Sheet Music Illustration: Reflections of the Nineteenth Century (Ann Arbor: William L. Clements Library, 1973) is a counterpart presentation issued as a booklet.

David TATHAM. *The Lure of the Striped Pig: The Illustration of Popular Music in America, 1820-1870.* Barre, Mass.: Imprint Society, 1973. **491**
A large boxed folio on the golden age of early and color lithography in America, evidenced in the output of the major Boston shops. (A "striped pig," whose "tale is unfolded" on p. 64, was the subject of events in the late 1830s in Dedham, Mass. On the enactment of a state law prohibiting the sale of spirits, a paid admission to the exhibit included the price of a drink.)
The author often discusses sheet-music covers in his other writings on the graphic arts in mid 19th-century America.

Marian KLAMKIN. *Old Sheet Music: A Pictorial History.* New York: Hawthorn, 1975. **492**
Very long on the pictures, very short on the history of old (i.e., early 20th-century) American covers.

Renate SCHUSKY. "Illustrationen in deutschen Liederbüchern für Frauen und Kinder," in *Die Buchillustration im 18. Jahrhundert* (Heidelberg: Carl Winter, 1980; Beiträge zur Geschichte der Literatur und Kunst des 18. Jahrhunderts, 4), pp. 317-34. **493**
A brief, well-illustrated analytical essay on the period 1770-1800, delivered at a colloquium of the Arbeitsstelle 18. Jahrhundert, Düsseldorf, October 3-5, 1978; also a bibliography of 21 women's and 25 children's songbooks, with comments on the illustrations.

Udo ANDERSOHN. *Musiktitel aus dem Jugendstil: 64 Beispiele aus den Jahren 1886 bis 1918.* Dortmund: Harenberg, 1981 (Die bibliophilen Taschenbücher, 250). **494**
Color facsimiles of 64 covers, mostly German, with annotations.

Catherine HAILL. *Victorian Illustrated Music Sheets.* London: H.M.S.O., 1981.   **495**
Color illustrations of 25 sheets, preceded by a brief text that reflects the quiet authority and enthusiasm of a public lecture at the Victoria & Albert Museum.

Tony LOCANTRO. *Some Girls Do and Some Girls Don't.* London: Quartet Books, 1985.   **496**
Fifty large-size brightly-hued title pages from sheet music, 1846-1925, mostly English, with vacuous drivel on the facing pages. The title of the book, actually taken from one of the covers reproduced, is obviously intended to attract purchasers rather than readers. Somewhat fewer than half of the titles in the book show what might reasonably be called "girls," and very few of the subjects seem to doing, or interested in doing, or not doing, much of anything at all. Seeing the book on a coffee table is sufficient basis for politely excusing yourself, the pursuit of music bibliography notwithstanding.

Giovanni FANELLI. *Musica ornata: lo spartito art nouveau.* Firenze: Cantini, [1988?].   **497**
Critical commentary on art nouveau covers for music and music periodicals, with 189 color illustrations from several countries.

Laurent GUILLO, with Jean-Michel NOAILLY. "Lettrines et ornements dans l'édition musicale aux XVIe et XVIIe siècles," in *Ornementation typographique et bibliographie historique*, edited by Marie-Thérèse Isaac (Bruxelles: Émile van Balberghe, 1988), pp. 107-28.   **498**
Paper at the Colloque de Mons, 26-28 août 1987, discussing the initials used in Ballard and Duchemin partbooks.

See also the 1986 Cullen *A-B Bookman's Weekly* essay (925), also the exhibition catalogues (432 and 442 in particular) and bibliophilic editions (pp. 338-46).

For all its very mixed history in print, the topic of music title pages is clearly not without intellectual excitement, essentially as part of the fascination with the "sister arts": those who are moved are often hard-pressed to assemble correlations that seem anything other than self-obvious: the few who have something new to say deserve respect as artists in their own right. The very purpose of music covers needs to be remembered. There is nothing wrong with advertising (nor even with coffee-table books), particularly when the interaction provides a living for deserving artists and when it serves to promote deserving music. At the same time, presumed innocence hardly exempts the topic from critical judgement. If one accepts the argument that art forms tell us things about ourselves that other means of communication tend to conceal, then it should follow that studies of the interaction of artist and musician have prospects of a circus that becomes the more admirable as it becomes the more disciplined and less patronizing.

C. Miscellanea and Ephemera

Music bibliography, like many studies, justifies its existence and finds significance at its peripheries. Printed music is useful to view in relationship to other graphic documents that concern music. But how far can the subjects studied by music bibliographers be meaningfully extended? Two criteria would appear to be useful: the peripheries should be manageable, and they should promise to be significant. Writings on music manuscripts would surely be both appropriate and useful to include in this book, as would writings on sound recordings, although including either one would double the size of this book, and no scrupulous bibliographer would dare to touch them without intending to spend the better part of a decade in order to do justice to the literature. With literary writings about music, on the other hand, there is very little that differentiates them from documents on other subjects. The same is mostly true of opera librettos as a form of printed literature, at least in terms of the present state of scholarship. Their special attributes, one might argue, probably make them more a part of the world of dramatic than of musical texts.

Musical ephemera and miscellanea can claim no prolific bibliographical literature, although the functions and appearances are often delightful and meaningful. They all employ one or another of the four processes discussed on pp. 4-6, although the diversity of functions certainly contributes to the variety of appearances.

The functions are mostly promotional or transactional and rarely involve musical performance (Braille music being the exception). These dictate not only the process of printing, but also the size (from postage stamps to posters), the use of color (from concert tickets in black and white to gaudy record jackets), and the distribution (from personal book plates, in small press runs, to mass-market advertising). Cumulatively they address, from different perspectives, the question of defining the proper domain of music bibliography.

Ephemera in General

H. Earle JOHNSON. "Notes on the Sources of Musical Americana," Music Library Association, *Notes*, 5 (1948), 169-77.   **499**

On source materials in general, emphasizing the uncommon forms these materials often take and their importance as historical evidence.

Reprinted in Bradley, pp. 90-96.

Vera B. LAWRENCE. *Music for Patriots, Politicians, and Presidents: Harmonies and Discords of the First Hundred Years.* New York: Macmillan, 1975.   **500**

A handsome pictorial treasury of historically important American musical documents of all kinds. (A coffee table is worth buying to have this book on it.)

James B. COOVER. "Musical Ephemera: Some Thoughts about Types, Controls, and Access," in *Foundations of Music Bibliography*, edited by Richard D. Green and Kären D. Nagy *(forthcoming)*.   **501**

Cogent arguments, with bibliographical references drawn from the literature of ephemera in general. Presented at the Conference on Music Bibliography at Northwestern University, October 9-12, 1986.

See also Landauer's 1953 ephemera catalogues (469 above). One of the best sources for other examples of music ephemera in general is pictorial biographies of famous musicians. Also of special interest are the catalogues prepared by F. C. Schang (in which the concept of "visiting cards" is usefully defined rather flexibly): *Visiting Cards of Celebrities, often illustrated by Memorial Postage Stamps, together with Photographs, Drawings, and Other Material*

(Paris: Fernand Hazan, 1971, reissued 1973; many of the celebrities are musicians); *Visiting Cards of Prima Donnas* (New York:
Vantage Press, 1974; reissued, New York: Joseph Patelson, 1977);
and *Visiting Cards of Violinists* (New York: Joseph Patelson, 1975).

Bookplates

The curious and engaging story of music bookplates is often useful in the study of provenance and the nature of musical ownership. One thinks here of the sentiment with which music-lovers
incorporated the imagery and the portraits that testify to their
great love; and specifically also of the memorable bookplates of
Otto Jahn, (which testify to the rise of music scholarship in nineteenth-century Germany), of James E. Matthew (which often
identify the pedigrees of musical rarities), and of Alfred Cortot
(which epitomize the character of early twentieth-century Parisian
culture), along with many less memorable examples.

[J. F. VERSTER.] *XL Muzikale boekmerken met eene opgave
van meer dan CCC sureupen, die op dit soort van boekmerken voorkomen.* [Title also in French and German].
*XL Musical Book-Plates, with a List of More than CCC
Mottoes to be Found on this Class of Book Plates.*
Amsterdam: Muller, 1897.   **502**
An anthology of bookplates showing musical instruments,
reproduced in rust-brown on hand-made paper, with a list of 343
mottos with names of the collectors on whose bookplates they
appear.

Sheldon CHENEY. "The Book-Plates of Musicians and
Music Lovers," *Musical Quarterly*, 3 (1917), 446-52.   **503**
The text is intelligent, imaginative, and critical, but the overall
effect is slightly mauve.

Herman T. RADIN. "On Musical Bookplates," *Musical
Quarterly*, 25 (1939), 135-41.   **504**
Radin's scholarship is more in keeping with the character of the
journal than Cheney's, with a distinctive "composerly" character
to it, as it discusses bookplates used by the masters or with their
portraits on them.

Irene VOISÉ-MACKIEWICZ. "Ekslibrysy muzyczne Edwarda Kuczyńskiego," in *Zeszyty Naukowe Uniwersytetu Mikołaja Kopernika: Naudi Humanistyczno-Społeczne*, 13 (1965), 53-97. **505**
[*BdMs*, 1965:289]

Motyw muzyczny w exlibrisie polskim: Wystawa ze zbióru Feliksa Wagnera, Poznań, marzec-kwiecień 1966. Poznań: Pozn. Tow. Muzyczne. 1966. **506**
An exhibit of "Music as a theme in Polish bookplates." [*BdMs*, 1966:313]

General bookplate bibliographies cite other writings; a more comprehensive study than is appropriate here would need to recognize, for instance, George W. Fuller's *A Bibliography of Bookplate Literature* (Spokane: Spokane Public Library, 1926), which cites "Ex-musicis," by Ferdinando Pasquinelli (the author of other book-plate writings around the 1910s) and "Beethoven ex-libris," by Emil Fickert. The index to Audrey Spencer Arellanes's *Bookplates: A Selective Annotated Bibliography of the Periodical Literature* (Detroit: Gale, 1981) cites over a dozen more English-language writings, 1896-1953.

Postage Stamps

Winthrop S. BOGGS. "Music and Stamps," *Musical Quarterly*, 24 (1938), 1-10. **507**
Details on a variety of special music issues, with illustrations.

James WATSON. *Stamps and Music.* London: Faber and Faber, 1962. **507a**
A descriptive account, arranged by topic, with 16 plates of black-and-white illustrations.

A. Herbert R. GRIMSEY. *Check List of Postage Stamps about Music.* London: National Philatelic Society, Philatelic Music Circle, 1974. **508**
Loose-leaf pages, to be updated (listing in 1977, for instance, about 2,500 stamps), with subjects and references to sources. The Circle also issues a journal called *The Baton*, vol. 8 of which dates from 1971.

Tamas UNGVARY. "Musikalische Grafik auf Briefmarken," *Melos: Zeitschrift für neue Musik*, 39 (1972), 341-43.

On Ingvar Lidholm's "stamp music," reproduced on Swedish commemoratives honoring the bicentenary of the Swedish Musical Academy, and purported to be the first postage stamps ever issued that could also serve as a musical score ("eine Briefmarkenpartitur für Jedermann").

This issue should be juxtaposed with Fr. Zikoff's musical potpourri, *Correspondenzkarten* (Breslau: Julius Haimauer, 1880), mentioned by Boggs. Perhaps both works could be scheduled on a concert devoted to music inspired by the postal systems.   **509**

Ethel BLOESCH. "Music Autographs and First Editions on Postage Stamps," *Fontes artis musicae*, 25 (1978), 250-63.

Citations of about 50 stamps with autographs and seven with first editions, with 29 illustrations.   **510**

Gerhard K. NEGLA.   *Musik im Spiegel der Philatelie.* Tübingen: Ernst Wasmuth, 1984.   **511**

A handsome book, showing (in color) 401 stamps, with name and subject indexes. The arrangement is topical: generalia, composers by period, performers by medium, opera and ballet, folk dance, and instruments.

See also the 1942 Wright and McDevitt essay on "Music Sheets for Stamp Collectors" (470 above); and Stanley Phillips's brief "Postage Stamps," in *Grove's Dictionary of Music and Musicians*, 5th ed. (London: Macmillan, 1954), vol. 6, pp. 890-93, with 12 reproductions on Plate 55. An article on "Philately, musical" in *The New Grove Dictionary of American Music* (New York: Macmillan, 1986; vol. 3, pp. 554-55) was prepared by Stephen M. Fry, who has called my attention to several more titles, perhaps most notable among them being Geoffrey Senior, *Music on Postage Stamps* (London: Orrell, 1979); and Alfredo Ragucci, *Músicos en el sello postal* (Buenos Aires: Centro Filatélico, 1955); in addition to a goodly array of journal articles. His study of this literature is forthcoming.

Postcards

Richard BONYNGE. *A Collector's Guide to Theatrical Postcards*. Sydney: Craftsman's Press Pty.; London: B. T. Batsford, 1988.   **512**

About 200 illustrations, many in color, mostly portraits, from ballet, circus, movies, and theatre as well as opera, based on the conductor's personal collection.

Also related to this genre is the material shown in Charles Osborne, *The Opera House Album: A Collection of Turn-of-the-Century Postcards* (New York: Taplinger; London: Robson, 1979).

Programs and Posters

Programs for musical events, as examples of graphic art, have changed significantly over the years, although their history awaits study. When this is done, printers' journals (*SGM / Schweizer graphische Mitteilungen* in the 1890s being a memorable example) should be a rewarding source. The reproductions of programs, on special paper as inserts and generally of high quality, are shown in these journals as models for other printers to imitate in their day; today they are evidence for later scholars of the history of taste.

Posters, on the other hand, probably have fewer models, but speak loudly for themselves. One has only to admire them, and pray that they may be preserved.

Lucy BROIDO. *French Opera Posters, 1860-1930*. New York: Dover, 1976.   **513**

Reproductions of 54 posters, 31 in color, assembled from operas published by Heugel and Hartmann, with brief notes.

Ladislav SABAN. "Neobjavljeni koncertni plakati i programi kao važna povijesna grada," *Arti musices*, 7 (1976), 101-31.   **514**

"Unpublished Concert Posters and Programmes as Valuable Historical Material," with summaries in English on pp. 131-33 and in German on pp. 133-35. On concert programs as historical and graphic evidence of musical life in 19th-century Croatia, Zagreb in particular.

Jean-Patrick DUCHESNE. *15 ans d'affiches musicales (1964-1979)*. Durbuy: Musée de Durbuy, 1980.   **515**
An exhibition of 59 posters by 39 named artists. (Durbuy, near Luxembourg, is said to be the smallest township in Belgium.)

James J. FULD. "Music Programs and Posters: The Need for an Inventory," Music Library Association, *Notes*, 37 (1981), 520-32.   **516**
Based on the author's personal collection, with a call for scholarly study and provision of bibliographical access.

L'Affiche d'opéra: du 10 octobre 1984 au 12 janvier 1985: Catalogue. Paris: Musée-Galerie de la Seita, [1984].   **517**
Citations from an exhibit of 114 opera posters from public and private collections in Paris, with 50 reproductions, 13 in color.

Frank HASKAMP. "Das Programmheft der Oper: Inhalt, Gestaltung and bibliothekarische Relevanz einer Publikationsform," *Bibliothek: Forschung und Praxis*, 13 (1989), 26-51.   **517a**
An extended library research report concerning post-1945 German programs, but with a brief account of the earlier materials.

Works devoted to posters in general often treat opera and concert posters, among them Catherine Haill, *Theatre Posters* (London: H. M. S. O., 1983), based on holdings of the Victoria & Albert Museum; James Laver and Henry Davray, *XIXth Century French Posters* (London: Nicholson & Watson, 1944).

The literature of playbills, even more elusive, similarly overlaps with the theatre. See, for instance, W. J. Lawrence, "The World's Oldest Playbills," *"The Stage" Year Book 1920*, pp. 23-30. Related printed musical ephemera are described in W. J. Davis and A. W. Waters, *Tickets and Passes of Great Britain and Ireland* (Leamington Spa: Courier Press, 1922; reprinted New York: Burt Franklin, 1973), in which tickets to musical events (mostly operatic) are cited on pp. 1-41, and *passim*.

Several of the exhibition catalogues, as noted on pp. 153-68, also include interesting portraits and playbills. The London 1885 International Inventions Exhibition (415) is a notable example.

Trade Catalogues

Lawrence B. ROMAINE. "Musical Instruments and Accessories," in *A Guide to American Trade Catalogues, 1744-1900* (New York: Bowker, 1960), pp. 243-50.   **518**
Cites about 200 catalogues, all but a few post-1870, with locations. The list, far from exhaustive, reflects mostly the author's experience as an antiquarian dealer in trade catalogues; it eloquently pleads the cause for further studies. The "Printers' Samples of Work Catalogues" (pp. 289-94) may include music type specimens, although their presence of music printing materials is not reflected in the citations.
Reprinted New York: Arno, 1976.

The topic of music advertising no doubt deserves a major history in its own right. I know of no descriptions of the historical literature on the music trades — of the production and merchandising of instruments, accessories, and other artifacts of performance and other musical activities. The materials relating to the world's fairs would be a part of it.

Record Jackets

Kurt WEIDEMANN. *Buchumschläge & Schallplattenhüllen / Jaquettes de livres et couvertures de disques.* Stuttgart: Gerd Hatje, 1969.   **519**
Also issued in two English-language versions, as *Book Jackets and Record Sleeves* (London: Thames & Hudson; André Deutsch, 1969), and as *Book Jackets and Record Covers* (New York: Praeger, 1969). Record jackets (and disc labels) are briefly discussed (English version, pp. vii-viii) and shown in black-and-white plates (nos. 27-32 on pp. xv-xvi, 301-427 at the end).

Walter HERDEG. *Record Covers: The Evolution of Graphics Reflected in Record Packaging.* Zurich: Graphis Press, 1974.
An anthology of 21 brief essays by notable designers. The 643 illustrations are greatly reduced but several of them are in color.
Further examples of record covers are seen in the Zurich annual *Graphis* itself, of which Herdeg was the editor.   **520**

Album Cover Album. New York: A & W Visual Library, 1977- .   **521**

A pictorial anthology, edited by Storm Thorgerson and Roger Dean, who provide a brief introduction and chapter commentaries. The covers, reproduced in color but variously reduced, range from "pristine photography" to "glorious frivolities."
    Volume 2 (1982) recognizes David Howells among the editors.

Brad BENEDICT and Linda BARTON. *Phonographics: Contemporary Album Cover Art & Design.* New York: Macmillan, 1977.   **522**
    A picture book with 128 pages of illustrations, mostly in color, and a swinging manifesto of an introduction by Charles Perry, editor of *Rolling Stone*, and Peter Plagens.

A number of other books (and series, many of them annuals) reproduce album covers; most of them are "downloadings" of graphic art copy, but, understandably, handsomely executed. The album cover may have affinities to the sheet-music cover of yore, but its design aesthetic is, one concedes with frequent regret, largely disposable. (Conversely, of course, one frequently must smile irreverently — or occasionally to laugh loudly — at the trappings of immortality that endow so much of the nostalgia of nineteenth-century published music).

Other graphic presentations of musical texts raise the question of whether or not printing is involved; in turn they beg the definition of printing itself. The forms include the following:

Braille Music

"Printing" acquires a special meaning in texts for the blind, one that covers the creation of embossed surfaces both singly and for purposes of duplication. See Elizabeth M. Harris, "Inventing Printing for the Blind," *Printing History*, vol. 8, no. 2 (1986), pp. 15-25. The system perfected by Louis Braille in 1834 was adapted for printing in Paris by Valentin Haüy, roughly a decade later. The writings on the printing of musical notation include the following:

Henry ROBYN. *Thorough Description of the Braille System for the Reading and Writing of Music.* St. Louis: August Wiebusch, 1867.   **523**

Ernst C. Krohn speaks of Robyn, during his tenure as teacher at the Missouri Institute for the Education for the Blind, having "invented a press and the Five-Type System which rendered it possible for the blind to set type and print text and music in the Braille point." See *A Century of Missouri Music* (St. Louis: Privately Printed, 1924; also in his *Missouri Music*, New York: Da Capo, 1971), p. 76.

Alexander P. REUSS. *Entwicklung und Probleme der Blindennotenschrift.* Schwetzingen: A. Moch, 1932.   **524**
Based on a dissertation (Heidelberg, 1933). An English translation was prepared by Ellen Kerney and Merle E. Frampton, as *Development and Problems of Musical Notation for the Blind* (New York: New York Institute for the Education of the Blind, 1935; Monograph no. 1).

I have not seen Reuss's *Systematik der Blindennotenschrift: Anleitung zur Übertragung von Musikstücken und theoretischen Werken aus der Schrift des Sehenden in der Blindenschrift* (Berlin: Notenschaffungszentrale für Blinde, 1938) [*BdMs*, 1938, no. 3669].

A *Manual on the Notation of Music: A Collection of Most of the Signs in Modern Music* (Philadelphia: N. B. Kneass, Jr., Printer for the Blind, 1884), by Napoleon B. Kneass, Jr., was recently called to my attention. I know neither how uncommon nor how significant such works may be.

Epigraphy

Bertha Antonia WALLNER. *Musikalische Denkmäler der Steinätzkunst des 16. und 17. Jahrhunderts.* München: J. J. Lentner, 1912.   **525**
Detailed descriptions of ten decorative etched stones, 1550-1610, with transcriptions of the music.
Originally a dissertation, Munich, 1910 (1911).
The stones have also been discussed again recently in Alois Kieslinger, *Kärntner Steinätzungen* (Klagenfurt: Geschichtsverein für Kärnten, 1965; Buchreihe des Landesmuseums für Kärnten, 51), with additional references.

Etching a musical text on stone is essentially different from etching a surface from which other copies will be drawn through the use of a printing press. Several bibliographies of music printing cite Wallner — I suspect erroneously. The book is probably not really concerned with printing, although it is useful in introducing the topic of printing surfaces, which in turn is important in defining the domain of music bibliography.

Music is almost always printed on paper (see pp. 124-26), although in fact almost any surface may be used. Indeed, of all the world's documentary treasures of music, one of the most marvelous is actually printed on linen: the "In gratiam" canon of Benedictus Appenzeller in the Bibliothèque Royale in Brussels, printed in 1548 from movable type (its font can be identified as one cut in the 1530s by Hieronymus Formschneider in Nürnberg, at this time in use mostly by Georg Rhau in Wittenberg). The document is not one that readers should wish to handle; happily it is reproduced between pp. 420 and 421 of vol. 7 of Edmund van der Straeten's *La musique aux Pays-Bas*, (Bruxelles: G. A. van Trigt, 1885; the plates are less clearly reproduced in the reprint, New York: Dover, 1969).

Parchment and vellum were becoming increasingly expensive at the time of the invention of printing, and while the earliest printed books were often on vellum, I cannot recall having handled music that was, although I await reports on its existence. Vellum was more durable than paper, but extremely costly, especially from the Renaissance onward, hence at first associated with high tastes; and the legendary poverty of musicians was in effect assumed by the time music was issued from the printing press.

Vellum may be the most common alternative to paper but it is not the only one; and music bibliographers, stimulated by the search for even more uncommon forms of textual transmission, could very quickly regret their imaginative instincts. "Happy Birthday," for instance, is often inscribed on birthday cakes. The icing, we presume, was written by hand rather than duplicated by a press that uses frosting rather than ink.[2] Music bibliographers, should they lack for anything better to worry about, may wish to be unsettled by the prospects that particular signs may have been mass produced, so as to amount to functional counterparts of the engraver's punch. Their fears are no doubt small beside those of

---

2. One reader of this manuscript, however, reports that there is now a machine that reproduces digitized photographs in frosting.

culinary decorators themselves, who may in fact be vulnerable to copyright infringement suits on grounds that theirs is indeed usually public and for profit, if of arguable status as a performance.

The stone etchings described by Wallner were probably no more intended for use in performance than "Happy Birthday." Both thus serve as symbolic rather than functional statements, although the intention behind the cake is consumption, so as to imply impermanence, while the stones aspire to immortality and the various forms of distancing that this implies. (One of the special virtues of the musical score is its aspiration to have it both ways: permanence through the most impermanent of events, which is performance: active consumption of sound through recourse to passive consumption of notation by the performer's eyes.)

An entire wall in downtown Minneapolis devoted to a page of the score of Ravel's *Gaspard de la nuit*, prepared by the Schmitt Music Co. to advertise its services, will remain to haunt many of us more than Scarbo himself. (One wonders how Harold Innis would have handled this in connection with his studies on oral and visual communication.) Comparable to Wallner's subjects, meanwhile, is the musical epigraphy that incorporates one chamber-music lover's dying wish to rest in peace under a cemetery marker inscribed with the second theme of the first movement of Schubert's quintet, opus 163. (The evidence is said to be in Vienna, but I have been unable to verify an exact location.) The mysterious ways of a more literal-minded Holy Comforter are wondrously revealed on p. 296 of *Better Homes and Gardens, American Patchwork and Quilting* (Des Moines, Iowa: Meredith Publishing, 1985), in which is shown a work exhibited at the "World of Quilts" show at Meadow Brook Hall, Rochester, Michigan, the blocks of which "consist of music scores and composers' signatures lovingly stitched in great detail. A quilted lyre design continues the theme in this music lover's patchwork."

One also recalls the stockings that William Gardiner arranged to have knitted for Haydn incorporating the composer's themes in the stitching. Presumably only one pair was knitted, and by hand; but knowing that early printers often ran off a few extra unauthorized copies for their own use, can one be sure they were not machine-knitted in several copies? No authentic evidence is known to survive, to my knowledge, apart from the legends; but should it appear, how might the scrupulous bibliographer go about arguing for its authenticity?

Alas, the zealous music bibliographer is clearly already in great trouble: what about the wide range of scarves, shirts, and carrying bags, and other fabrics and plastics, with music stencilled on them, for sale today in museums and high-culture gift shops? What insights await the scholarly community by studying them with the aid of extrapolations of the canonic methodologies suggested in the first three chapters above? One next awaits arguments that locks of a composer's hair (long resident in the inconspicuous attics of the libraries to which they had been tenderly bequeathed) are indeed bibliographic items by virtue of their containing encoded genetic information (and obviously of the purest kind), made multiform on the composer's head. And what technologies of sonar resonance may yet prove useful in probing the bathymetric depths in search of Prospero's drowned books, as exposed in the bibliographical wake of the Yellow Submarine that is celebrated in Barbara Fenick's *Collecting the Beatles: An Introduction & Price Guide to Fab Four Collectibles, Records & Memorabilia* (Ann Arbor: Pierian Press, 1982)?

For those fascinated by questions such as these, the metabibliographical future of music bibliography is indeed awesome to contemplate.

V.

Musical Commerce and Property

THE DIVISION OF LABOR between music printers and publishers has resembled that between book printers and publishers, at least in basic terms. We presume that most early music printing was financed by patronage, involving institutions of formal etiquette and informal trust, so as to leave us with few prospects of answering the meaningful questions of the dynamic relationships behind the recorded events. Slowly, mostly during the eighteenth century, the institutions of patronage came to be superseded by new institutions of commerce, so as to create the modern music publisher, who worked both as scout and editor in dealing with the composer, and as investor, accountant, distributor, and promoter in dealing with the public. If one result has been to render the music printer anonymous, another has been to make the music publisher conspicuously exposed.

The printer's practices thus come to enjoy a romantic aura, stimulated by the amateur's perennial fascination with how things work. Printing is a black art, not so much for the ink but because the skills of honest artisans are corrupted by forces dark and uncontrolled. Publishers may not always necessarily serve those forces as much as they personify them. The forces seem all the darker when, almost of necessity, they function covertly. Composers, on one side, are honor-bound to complain about being ill-served by publishers, since it is the artists' duty to bite the hand that feeds them. The public, on the other side, complains that music is too hard to find and too expensive: and, musicians' resources being limited, this is almost always the case. The music publisher's task is simple: keep everyone happy, and avoid bankruptcy. Under the circumstances it is truly wondrous that the literature of music publishing is as extensive as it is.

Scholarship aspires to objectivity, business and craftsmanship to success. Special pleading is usually easy to identify, after a passage of time if not always immediately. Furthermore, promotional materials are timely by intent, and survive mostly by happy coincidence. As a result bibliographers have felt duty-bound to pass harsh judgement on the literary output of publishers, the most successful ones in particular. The literature obviously needs its day in court.

Section A in this chapter covers publishing, section B copyright. In both sections, writings that describe present conditions are intermixed with historical studies. The effect is to embarrass both sides, the contemporary accounts for a tone that is either too sanguine or too earnest, the historical studies for a sterile detachment from the cultural forces that the publisher must grasp in order to survive and prosper. Writing about music publishing is no easier than succeeding in music publishing itself: for this reason the world of the music publisher needs all the more to be taken seriously. If Gutenberg's sometime partner Fust is indeed a prototype of Faust himself, it is the Faust of Goethe's part one; Goethe's part two deals with his career as a publisher.

It is in Section C below, as one surveys the publishers' dealings with their composers, that the texture of the publishers' predicament emerges. Here one gets a sense of the unpredictable crises that characterize the problem without ever defining it, along the way implying some of special rewards that justify the efforts to merge the worlds of art and business.

A. Music Publishing and Retailing

It is not easy to distinguish the promotional from the descriptive literature of music publishing. The descriptive literature, as it comes from publishers themselves, is almost necessarily self-serving, although this is easy to recognize, to evaluate, and ultimately often to respect. Since much of the practice depends on local, regional, and national considerations, the overlap with the next chapter is naturally quite considerable.

The writings below imply, but rarely analyze or rationalize, the separation of "popular" from "serious" publishing. This is clearly a major event that needs much further study, befitting its critical and generally painful importance to the art of music.

J. BORIES and F. BONASSIÉS. *Dictionnaire pratique de la presse, de l'imprimerie et de la librairie: Code complet.* Paris: Cosse & N. Delamotte, 1847. **526**

In this general survey of publishing, about a dozen entries (vol. 1, pp. 355, 550; vol. 2, pp. 40, 160-62, and 282; cf. vol. 1, p. 602) cite agreements and laws relating to music. (There may be still more references: the indexing of this book is among the most remarkable I have ever encountered.)

Reprinted, Westmead: Gregg, 1972.

Ernst WILHELM. "Der Berater im Musikverlage," *Caecilia*: *Mandelblad voor Muziek*, 62 (1905), 371-74. **527**

"Es ist Morgen in einem großen Musikverlage." An anecdotal re-creation of the quotidian activities of music publishers as they try to make enlightened decisions and survive in business.

Also issued in *Neue Zeitschrift für Musik*, 72 (1905), 694-96.

Wilhelm ALTMANN. "Die Notwendigkeit einer Stiftung zur Ermöglichung der Drucklegung umfangreicher Kompositionen: eine Anregung," *Die Musik*, 7 (1907-08), 98-100. **528**

Music of high quality is often unlikely to sell enough copies to justify publication. While the problem is well recognized in the literary statements of composers, this essay is one of the first of many that describes the problem.

Guide to Music Publishing. Private edition. Chicago: H. S. Talbot & Co., Music Printers, [1907].   **529**
A book of advice for amateur composers, with lessons on capturing the rhythm of the lyrics in the beat of the music; counsel to authors ("do not feel discouraged," along with hints on what and when to publish and the costs of publishing music); and assorted "Points to Remember" (no. 1: "Keep up-to-date and then some"; no. 14: "Do it NOW").

William Arms FISHER. "Song Sharks and their Victims," Music Teachers' National Association, *Proceedings*, 16 (1922), 118-20.   **530**
The concept of "song shark" has two definitions, one so broad as to include all publishers who exploit composers who should have known better (a large population), the other so narrow as to be identifiable through promises of various kinds, which the publisher never intends to fulfil. The shark of the latter sub-species contracts for printing and copyright, and occasionally even provides music itself to fit the victim's words (which, one can easily imagine, often leave us with mixed sympathies for everyone concerned). This much is almost always delivered. The shark is usually also expected to promote ("plug") the song, and make it into a hit; but while this hardly ever happens, the conditions are so vague as rarely to leave the publisher culpable.

"Sharking" is often thought to be a distinctly American phenomenon, although Wayne Shirley (to whom I owe thanks for many facts on this topic) cites the example of Malcolm Lowry, who describes his experience with a London shark in chapter 6 of *Under the Volcano* (1947). The practice is thought to have emerged around 1900. See Shirley's "The House of Melody: A List of Publications of the Gotham-Attucks Music Company in the Library of Congress," in *Black Perspectives in Music*, 15 (1987), 79-162, especially p. 88. Associated with Wilshire Boulevard in Los Angeles in the 1950s, "sharking" seems to have declined in recent years in deference to the sound-recording counterpart known as the "fake demo."

For another warning, see Sigmund Romberg, "So You've a Song to Publish," Music Library Association, *Notes*, n.s., vol. 1,

no. 4 (September 1944), 7-15, prepared especially for American music publishers as a warning about "song sharks."

Carl ENGEL. "Element of Gambling in Music Publishing," *Sheet Music News*, vol. 2, no. 2 (July 1923), pp. 9-11. **531**
A banquet address prepared by the Chief of the Music Division of the Library of Congress, for a dinner of the Music Publishers Association on June 12, 1923. (According to a footnote, however, instead of reading the prepared paper that is printed here, Engel spoke informally about the "need of a History of American Music Publishers, and urged the Association that it undertake and sponser [sic] the preparation of such a work along dignified and authoritative lines.")

The original text consists of the urbane and witty sermonizing that one would expect of its highly cultured author. He quite patronizingly distinguishes music publishers, for instance, as either "dairymen who . . . serve the public with clean and unadulterated nourishment," or "proprietors of racing stables, with a string of fast blood, who stake a fortune on a filly and run her to death in making the post." He continues by warning that "matters take a disastrous turn when one tries to encroach on the other." This distinction is announced as coming from "an article, some time ago," which I have not located under any explicit title in the author's prolific output of short articles, many cited on pp. 23-25 in *A Birthday Offering to* [*C. E.*], compiled and edited by Gustave Reese, New York: G. Schirmer, 1943. Many of them comment on music publishing in passing. Engel's concern for quality (witnessed, for instance, in his consignment of most of the copyright deposits to a category of "bunk and junk"), soon led him to leave Washington for the Schirmer firm in New York. The eloquence and altruism of his writings on music publishing, in all their diffuseness, justify a special study.

Jacques DURAND. *Édition musicale, historique et technique*. Paris: Durand, 1924 (Cours professionel de l'usage des employés de la musique, 1). **532**
Pious and somewhat engaging, without betraying many secrets.

Durand's *Abrégé historique et technique de l'édition musicale* (Paris: Durand, 1924) grows out of this text, as does the brief note on "L'édition musicale," in Albert Lavignac, *Encyclopédie de la musique et dictionnaire du Conservatoire*, vol. 6 (Paris: Delagrave, 1931), pp. 3834-35.

Wilhelm HITZIG. "'Pariser Briefe': Ein Beitrag zur Arbeit des deutschen Musikverlags aus den Jahren 1833-1840," *Der Bär*, (1929-30), 27-73.   **533**
Transcripts of the extensive and rich Breitkopf & Härtel correspondence to the Leipzig office from their Paris agent Heinrich Albert Probst, valuable in understanding both the practices of music publishing and the musical life of the day. Other studies that Hitzig prepared out of the firm's archive are listed in Plesske, pp. 163-66.
    Translated, with extended commentary by Hans Lenneberg, in *Breitkopf & Härtel in Paris* (Stuyvesant, N.Y.: Pendragon, 1990).

George E. DUNN. *Methods of Music Publishing: A Frank Explanation for the Consideration of the Tyro in Composition*. London: Office of "Musical Opinion," 1931.   **534**
A booklet with advice to composers on contracts: read the fine print very carefully.

Der Musikverlag und Musikalienhandel in der Welt. Leipzig: Bureau International d'Information et de Coopération des Éditeurs de Musique, 1938.   **535**
Brief reports on the music publishing activity in 19 countries, prepared as a keepsake for the 12th Conference of the International Congress of Publishers.

Paul BERTRAND. *L'édition musicale: caractéristiques, évolution, perspectives*. Préface de Roland-Manuel. Paris: Les Oeuvres françaises, 1947.   **536**
The first sections describe and defend the role of the reputable music publisher and trace its history in 19th-century France; the second suggest the impact of the new media, changing social conditions, and legislation; the third discuss the post-war setting.

Raoul CASTELAIN. *Histoire de l'édition musicale ou du droit d'éditeur au droit d'auteur, 1501-1793*. Paris: Lemoine, 1957.   **537**

The first part ("Historique des moyens de reproduction"), which is drawn mostly from secondary sources, argues that music publishing existed before the invention of printing. (A stronger case could have been made, even in 1957.)

The second part ("Historique du fondement juridique," pp. 47-89) treats the history of proprietary rights. A brief conclusion suggests the implications, more in philosophical principle than of quotidian practice, and completely evades any concession of the existence of performance rights.

Also issued in *Bibliographie de la France*, 146e année, 5e série, 2e partie ("Chronique"), N° 4-7 (Fascicules 1-8, 25 janvier-15 février 1957).

Richard SCHAAL. "Musikverlag und Musikalienhandel," *Die Musik in Geschichte und Gegenwart*, vol. 9 (Kassel: Bärenreiter, 1960-61), cols. 1169-92.   **538**

One of the most respected dictionaries that treats music publishing separately from music printing (108 above covers the music printing). The primary arrangement is geographical, with extensive lists of references and names, historical and current.

Erich VALENTIN. "'. . . verlegt bey': kleine Geschichte des Musikverlagswesens," *Musikalienhandel*, 14 (1963), 3-4, 36, 208.   **539**

[Davidsson 524; *BdMs*, 1963:249]

Sidney SHEMEL and M. William KRASILOVSKY. *This Business of Music*. New York: Billboard, 1964.   **540**

"A Practical Guide to the Music Industry for Publishers, Writers, Record Companies, Producers, Artists, Agents," with emphasis on the popular music business. Later editions appeared in 1969, 1971, 1977, 1979, 1985, and 1990.

In the 6th edition, Part 2 ("Music Publishers and Writers," pp. 133-337) consists of 19 chapters devoted mostly to trade practices and copyright. Other chapters are relevant as well (for instance, in the discussions in Part 1 on "Recording Companies and Artists," chapter 8, pp. 83-89, is on "Record Covers, Labels, and Liner Notes," while Part 3, on "General Music Industry Aspects," includes chapters on information sources, names and trademarks, and taxation). Several of the numerous appendices and forms also deal with music publishing.

Serious and specialized music publishing are treated more amply in the sequel, *More about This Business of Music* (1967, 1974, 1982, and 1989), for instance in chapters 4 ("Publishers and Composers," pp. 43-66 in the 4th edition) and 7 ("Production and Sale of Printed Music," pp. 95-111), as well as in other chapters and appendixes as accessible through the index.

Ernst ROTH. *Die Musik als Kunst und Ware: Betrachtungen und Begegnungen eines Musikverlegers.* Zürich: Atlantis, 1966.   **541**

English version as *The Business of Music: Reflections of a Music Publisher* (London: Cassell, 1969).

Anecdotes of the music publishing world in Vienna and London, delightfully related to suggest the music publisher as both *Macher* and *Mensch*. However personal, these are not to be confused with Roth's memoirs, *Von Prag bis London: Erfahrungen, Autobiographische Fragmente* (*ibid.*, 1974), and *Erfahrungen eines Musikverlegers; Begegnungen mit . . . Komponisten unserer Zeit* (*ibid.*, 1982).

Roth's title would better have been translated as "Music as Art and Business." Paul S. Carpenter, however, had previously written *Music: an Art and a Business* (Norman: University of Oklahoma Press, 1953) — an interesting book but not specifically on music publishing.

Klaus HORTSCHANSKY. "Pränumerations- und Subskriptionslisten in Notendrucken deutscher Musiker des 18. Jahrhunderts," *Acta musicologica*, 40 (1968), 154-74.   **542**
One of the few studies of the historical practice of seeking pre-publication subsidy for musical editions from purchasers.

—. "Selbstverständnis und Verantwortung des Musikverlegers," *Neue Zeitschrift für Musik*, 131 (1970), 295-300. **543**
A provocative attempt to define the modern role of the music publisher and to argue that Étienne Roger in Amsterdam should be seen as its first practitioner.

The Music Industry: Markets and Methods for the 70s. New York: Billboard Publications, 1970.   **544**

"Creative, technological, financial, and legal reports" from the Second International Music Industry Conference, at Palma de Mallorca, April 26th to May 2nd, 1970. Papers of special interest include "The Industry's *Music* Manager" by the Munich publisher Ralph Maria Siegel (pp. 22-24); "Coordination and Leadership" by Gilbert Marouani of Nouvelles Éditions Eddie Barclay, Paris (pp. 26-28); and "Sheet Music Income" by Frank Coachworth of Chappell & Co., London (pp. 161-64).

The trend in the music industries is clearly away from printed documents and toward the abstraction of musical property in performance rights. This may be implicit in these papers, although a disturbingly large number of the specific trends and products that are described or promoted here have proven to be of passing importance. Arguably among the more dated essays are those on "Serious Music for Profit" on pp. 119-29, by John Culshaw, James Frey, and Oliver Daniel (which however do not focus specifically on music publishing).

Of the papers of the previous conference, held at Nassau in the Bahamas on April 20-23, 1969, none deals specifically with printing and publishing. See Paul Ackerman and Lee Zhito, *The Complete Report of the First International Music Industry Conference: IMIC-1* (New York: Billboard, 1969).

Arnold BROIDO. "Publishing," in John Vinton, *Dictionary of Contemporary Music* (New York: E. P. Dutton, 1974), pp. 595-98.   **545**

This summary of conditions in 1971, by the director of the Theodore Presser firm, is even today probably the best brief introductory overview of the topic.

The British edition of this book (London: Thames & Hudson, 1974) bears the title *Dictionary of 20th-Century Music*.

Wilhelm MONKE and Horst RIEDEL. *Lehrbuch des Musikalienhandels*. Bonn: Musikhandel Verlaggesellschaft, 1971.   **546**

Instruction for aspiring music retailers and their employees, prepared for the Gesamtverband Deutsches Musikfachgeschäft. The four sections are devoted to generalities (including rudiments of music and music history), publications, musical instruments, and an *Anhang* of miscellany. Of these, the second

("Noten und Musikbücher," pp. 103-48) comprises seven sub-
sections: (A) *Formen des vertriebenen Musikalienhandels* (kinds
of businesses); (B) *Warenkunde* (the physical objects); (C) *Wege
zur Orientierung über den Inhalt der Noten* (the purchasers); (D)
Der Musikverlag (dealings with publishers); (E) *Die Einteilung
des Lagers* (managing and organizing the shop); (F) catalogues
and reference works (strong on literature guides and thematic
catalogues). The book is of particular interest as testimony to
how retailers define their work. From it emerge questions of
when and where circumstances may have been different, for
what reasons and with what effects.

I have located neither the predecessor to this book, Bernhard
Siegel's *Lehrbuch für den deutschen Musikalienhandel* (Leipzig:
Verlag des Verbandes der Deutschen Musikalienhändler, 1930;
cited in Plesske 33, but not catalogued in any of the American or
British libraries that I have used), nor what appears to be its suc-
cessor, the *Handbuch des Musikalienhandels* (Bonn: Gesamtver-
band Deutscher Musikgeschäfte, 1984), cited by Riedel in the
Festschrift Rudolf Elvers (Tutzing: Hans Schneider, 1985), p. 436.

Barry S. BROOK. "Piracy and Panacea in the Dissemination of Music in the Late Eighteenth Century," *Proceedings of the Royal Musical Association*, 102 (1975-76),
13-36.   **547**
On the visionary schemes of Christian Gottfried Thomas (1748-
1806) for disseminating music through his Leipzig warehouse.

Jim PROGRIS. *Language of Commercial Music*. New York:
Charles Hansen, [1975].   **548**
A dictionary of about 500 then-current terms in popular music
publishing. Many continue to be used; collectively they are of
continuing interest in studying the *mentalités* of popular music.

No. 6 in the "Commercial Music Bulletin" series. Others include Hank Kass, "What the Songwriter Should Know: Earning
a Living" (no. 1, 1975), Progris's "Writing Songs for Fame and
Fortune" (no. 5, [1976?]), and two pamphlets by Kass on music
engraving (283 above).

Handbuch des Buchhandels, edited by Horst Machill.
Hamburg: Verlag für Buchmarkt-Forschung, 1974-77. **549**

A four-volume encyclopedia of the book trade including, among the "Sonderformen des Verlags" in volume 2 (1975), "Der Musikalienverlag" (pp. 105-08) and "Musikvertrag" (pp. 252-54), also "Funkwerbung" (p. 539) and "Vertonung" (pp. 643-44).

"Music Publishing Today: A Symposium," Music Library Association, *Notes*, 32 (1975-76), 232-58. **550**
Essays by John Owen Ward, Joseph Boonin, Gary J. N. Aamodt, Claire Brook, and Geraldine Ostrove.

Leonard FEIST. *An Introduction to Popular Music Publishing in America*. New York: National Music Publishers' Association, 1980. **551**
A brief history of popular music publishing, assembled by a respected American publisher. Cf. 566 below.
Some of the ideas appeared earlier in "The Early History of Music Publishing," *ASCAP in Action*, Fall 1980, pp. 15-16.

Paula DRANOV. *Inside the Music Publishing Industry*. White Plains, N.Y.: Knowledge Industry Publications, 1980. **552**
On the business practices in American popular music publishing.

Carolyn SACHS. *An Introduction to Music Publishing*. New York: C. F. Peters, 1981. **553**
The work should be cited mostly because its title may mislead. For the Peters bicentenary, several dozen respected musical figures pay brief tribute, so as to leave readers with more of a cocktail-stained memento than any clearer understanding either of music publishing in general or of the Peters firm.

Ivo SUPIČIĆ. "Rani oblici 'masovne' glazbene kulture i izdavačka djelatnost," *Muzikološki zbornik: Musicological Annual* (Ljubljana), 17 (1981), 183-89. **554**
On the contribution of music publishing to the rise of "mass culture" in the 18th century.

"Music and the Censor." *Index on Censorship*, vol. 12, no. 1 (February 1983). **555**
Brief news reports on the suppression of music on political, ideological, or moral grounds. Also titled "Music is Dangerous."

The several dozen incidents are all recent, and drawn from around the world. Those that involve publication of physical objects, be they printed editions or sound recordings, all too easily lead to questions of motive: are the producers looking for trouble because it excites purchasers and thus makes money? Or is not the commercial medium the best way, perhaps the only way, to attract an audience to hear the argument? Above all, can the two viewpoints really be separated at all? A complementary anthology of historical confrontations will be equally important as a "theory of the music press" comes to be developed. Over the course of history censors have been damned to the role of villains, while clever publishers (beginning perhaps with Thomas Morley, or John Playford) have been quick to recognize the fact that mischief and prurience are not easily defined.

Horst RIEDEL.   "Der feste Ladenpreis im Musikalienhandel," in *Festschrift Rudolf Elvers zum 60. Geburtstag* (Tutzing: Hans Schneider, 1985), pp. 125-36.   **556**
A provocative first survey of the history of music pricing, with examples drawn from German sources. The larger story is vast, and filled with rumors. Kidson (656, p. 134), for instance, speculates that George Walker "may possibly be the first to institute the absurd practice of marking musical works at double the price intended to be asked." The recently prominent New York firm of Joseph Patelson got its start as the Half-Price Music Shop. The history of music publishing is surely filled with other evidence of special arrangements with performers, for purposes of promoting music, from the Victorian "royalty ballad" to "professional copies" of sheet music. Other serious-minded studies like Riedel's will be essential to any understanding of the economics of music publishing, although the specific evidence will be, if not necessarily bizarre, certainly obscure.

D. W. KRUMMEL.   "The Presence of the Note: Modern Music Publishing," in Alfred Mann (ed.), *Modern Music Librarianship: Essays in Honor of Ruth Watanabe* (Stuyvesant, N.Y.: Pendragon, 1989), pp. 41-56.   **557**
The present state of music publishing is proposed, and traced in terms of the music activities of the International Congresses of Publishers, 1901-65, with a list of the published reports.

PERIODICALS

The literature of general journals for printers and publishers is vast. (It presumably arises out of circumstances not unlike that of musicians performing for each other). Unfortunately, the extant runs are rarely complete, printers (unlike most musicians) having learned to throw out what they do not immediately need. Even more frustrating for music bibliographers are the practices well-known to serials librarians: changes of size and design, of periodicity, and above all, of titles, so as to accommodate mergers, retrenchments, and offspring.[1]

While I have cited many works from the journals below, I have not undertaken to read systematically through the journals themselves. The size of this book would no doubt be expanded considerably, mostly with timely brief articles that would bring out the details on what music publishers actually thought and did. (Coover, cited in the entry below, suggests what is lacking, why I desisted, and why I call attention to the decision without apologies.)

Musical Opinion and Music Trade Review. London, 1877- .

Fellinger 747 (p. 196). This journal served as the basis for Coover's *Music Publishing, Copyright, and Piracy in Victorian England* (1985; 682 below). **558**

American Music Journal (later *Music Publisher and Dealer*). New York, 1884- . **559**

Fellinger 941 summarizes the very complicated lineage. The journal was variously issued by the National League of Musicians and by the Musical Mutual Protective Union; at one time it viewed itself as "a trade paper devoted to the interests of music publishers, dealers and jobbers."

Musikhandel und Musikpflege. Leipzig: Verlag des Vereins der Deutschen Musikalienhändler, 1898-1944. **560**

Fellinger 1444 (p. 315). Later: *Musikhandel und Vereinswahlzettel*; *Musikalienhandel und Vereins-Wahlzettel*. In 1925 the Verein became the Verband der Deutschen Musikalienhändler.

---

1. References to *Fellinger* on pp. 205-07 are to Imogen Fellinger, *Verzeichnis der Musikzeitschriften des 19. Jahrhunderts* (Regensburg: G. Bosse, 1968; Studien der Musikgeschichte des 19. Jahrhunderts, 10), or, as specified, to her article on "Periodicals" in *Grove 6*, vol. 14, pp. 407-535.

Music Publishers' Journal. New York, 1946- .   **561**
   Grove 6, vol. 14, p. 442 (item 576). Also variously known as
   Music Journal, Music Journal Annual, Music Journal Anthology,
   Music Journal Annual Anthology.

The MPA Bulletin. New York: Music Publishers' Association of the United States, 1949- .   **562**
   Grove 6, vol. 14, p. 443 (item 642). Founded in 1895, the
   Association has come to serve American publishers of serious
   music, in contrast to the National Music Publishers' Association
   (566 below). In addition, an MPA *Newsletter* began in 1979.

Musikhandel.   Bonn: Deutscher Musikverleger-Verband,
Deutscher Musikalienwirtschaftsverband, 1949- .   **563**
   Grove 6, vol. 14, pp. 480-81 (items 808, 855). Successor to the
   Mitteilungen des Deutschen Musikalienwirtschafts-Verbandes
   (Celle, Bonn, 1946-49); with a supplement on educational music
   publishing, *Der Jung-Musikhandel* (1950-).

Der Musikalienhandel. Leipzig, 1955-68.   **564**
   Grove 6, vol. 14, p. 482 (item 966). In 1969 the journal was subsumed in the *Börsenblatt für den deutschen Buchhandel.*

MadAminA! A Chronicle of Music Catalogues.   Englewood,
N. J.: Music Associates of America, 1979- .   **565**
   A semiannual journal edited by George Sturm, devoted to news
   of serious music and its publication in America.

National Music Publishers' Association. *Bulletin.*   New
York, [1930s?]- .   **566**
   Founded in 1917 as the Music Publishers' Protective Association, the trade association serves the needs of American publishers of popular music, as distinguishable from the Music Publishers' Association above, its serious music counterpart.

Bigmore and Wyman, in its extensive list of "Periodical Publications" (vol. 2, pp. 153-95), cites several other titles that specify
music. I have not been able to inspect these periodicals fully
enough to describe their coverage of music printing with any sense
of authority. A few of the issues I have seen do include advertisements and brief notices relating to music, but mostly in their func-

tion as a current news medium. The prolixity of their titles suggests that music was specified mostly in hopes of a wider market:

Bayerischer Anzeiger, literarischer und merkantilischer, für Literatur, Kunstfreunde, Literar- und Kunst-Institute, Buchhändler, Buchdrucker, Antiquare, Kunsthändler, Musikalien-Verlerger .... München, 1829- , weekly.

Journal des artistes et des auteurs: peinture, sculpture, architecture, gravure, lithographie, poésie, musique, et art dramatique. Paris, 1840.

Annuaire de la librairie, de l'imprimerie, de la papeterie, du commerce de la musique, et des estampes.... Paris, 1860- .

Among other writings cited elsewhere, several of the general encyclopedia articles on pp. 49-54 comment specifically and provocatively on music publishing. Elsewhere the literature is vast indeed: the annual listings under "Publishing" in the *Music Index* (973 below) will suggest the highly selective nature of the coverage here. I have excluded many writings on "how to get your song published" (Dunn's 1931 booklet, 534 above, is an example), and on grass-roots initiatives (e.g., recent "desktop" music publishing).

A smaller but often very important topic is the role of publisher as impresario. Numerous and varied instances leap to mind, mostly from the nineteenth-century — Pleyel's Paris salon, Ricordi's heavy hand in Italian opera production, the "royalty ballad" in London. Willy Renz, "Verleger-Konzerte," *Die Musik*, 4 (1904), 169-70, is among the few articles to discuss the topic specifically.

Obviously publishers' catalogues are also very important. Some years ago a survey of the large general *Hauptkataloge* produced by many (but not all) major publishers was begun: see *Fontes artis musicae*, 24 (1977), 46-47. The plan needs to be revived: our best list is incomplete and now nearly 80 years old (Brenet, 962 below). George R. Hill has listed current music publishers' catalogues of all kinds in Music Library Association, *Notes*, beginning in June 1977, and, with Joseph M. Boonin, has also compiled annual music price indexes in the March issues since 1979.

Meanwhile, another lacuna in this literature — at least from the perspectives of today's fashions in cultural history — is any discussion of music as a "commodity" — as something to be "marketed" and "merchandised." The institutions of commerce may be well known, but the resulting changes in the nature of music itself are rarely addressed. Admittedly the notion of "musical commodity" needs to be defined in the first place: the evolving concepts are exactly what historical studies could elucidate. The "commodification" of music, beginning with the invention of printing in the Renaissance, and can be associated with several innovations:

1. the formulary nature of the editorial practices of Attaingnant around 1530 [*standardized presentation*];

2. the success, around 1540, of the firms that were established in major commercial centers [*strategic location*];

3. the popularity, after 1550, of specific books, like Arcadelt's "first book" (581) or the music of Lasso in general (531), so as, in a sense, to result in a kind of "canonization" through commercial objects [*recognition of demand*]; and

4. reprinting, involving Phalèse and other firms, mostly Dutch, beginning around the 1570s, allowing the publisher better access to the needs of purchasers, and, ultimately, freedom from the institutions of patronage [*management of venture capital*].

No doubt all of these conditions were in evidence in the work of Petrucci, and before. These practices have served to establish an imprint's reputation among modern scholars. The publishers' decision on particular musical compositions, in contrast, was what determined their character and the success in their own day.

Seventeenth-century music publishing was governed by different mercantile considerations: in an age of diminished patronage and unsettled political circumstances, publishers needed to publish less, cut corners with printers — when printing was even called for at all. [Thus, to the four Renaissance aspects of commodification, this century added a fifth: *calculation of costs*.]

The eighteenth-century rise of engraving coincided with the rise of musical professionalism, also of local retailing,[2] and in time

---

2. An example of an early English retailer's activity is suggested in Joseph Atkinson's announcement in the *Newcastle Chronicle* of June 15, 1771, as quoted by F. J. Mosher in *Direction Line*, 5 (Winter 1979), 28-29. In addition to books, prints, stationery, and small tools, Atkinson could provide:

music, operas, songs, sonatas, duetts, solos, symphonies, minuets, country dances, single songs, books of instruction for most instruments, ruled paper and books for music, of various sorts; all new music, songs, &c. as soon as published; musical instruments, &c. viz. violins, violincello [*sic*], guittars, French horns, trumpets, hautboys, amateurism. Recognizing the events as commodities may clarify their interrelationships. [No. 6: *market flexibility*.] A new form of standardized presentation also emerged, the periodical devoted to musical works. Imogen Fellinger cites many of the early titles, with detailed analytics, in *Periodica Musicalia, 1789-1830* (Regensburg: Bosse, 1986). For an overview of the genre, see my "Searching and Sorting on the Slippery Slope: Periodical Publication of Victorian Music," *Notes*, 46 (1990), 593-608. The nascent activity in Latin America (see 899-93 below) often also involved periodicals.

By 1800 several devices had become increasingly important to publishers: enhancement of editions with decorative covers devised to attract customers, and promotion through special catalogues and announcements. [No. 7: *strategic advertisement*.] The incorporation of selected titles into a publisher's special "edition" (see 463 above) reflects similar promotional considerations.

Finally, there is the distinction between musical sound and musical document, which began with musical notation itself. Their separation as commodities was no doubt appreciated well before the nineteenth century. By 1850, however, the distinction between the intellectual or artistic work and the physical book was coming to be recognized in a new and more powerful way: each had rather different legal property implications. This has led to the concept of performance rights (which proved to be very important with the advent of a new kind of musical document, the commercial sound recording), as it had also led to a redefined status of the printed musical edition as a distinctive commodity. The activity of British publishers in these events is nicely brought out in Cyril Ehrlich, *Harmonious Alliance: A History of the Performing Right Society* (Oxford: Oxford University Press, 1988).

---

clarinets, German flutes, common flutes, fifes, pitch pipes, mouth pieces for the easy sounding of German flutes; best Roman strings, violin, bass and tenor bows, bridges, mutes, pegs, rosin boxes, music desks, tuning forks, hammers for tuning harpsichords, wire for ditto of all kinds, hautboy and bassoon reeds, and every other article in the musical way. . . .

Further evidence is seen in the writings devoted specifically to some of the publishers who maintained their own retail outlets. A number of these writings are cited in *Grove P & P*; see for instance Doblinger in Vienna and Lyon and Healy in Chicago. For another example see *The Story of a Music Shop, 1857-1957*, an anniversary booklet on the Taphouse firm in Oxford.

B. Music Copyright and Performance Rights

Music bibliographers, like librarians, may often wish that copyright remain a periphery for lawyers to deal with. To today's publishers, driven by a need for timely profits, copyright has become increasingly important — often to the virtual discontinuation of producing graphic versions (i.e., printed copies) altogether.

Copyright enforcement practices vary with the political authority in question, however, and depend on the willingness and ability of that authority to enforce its regulations, which typically are more effective near the center of government and weaker in remote areas, and more effective under threat (cf. the *Index on Censorship* music issue, 555 above). The national emphasis is thus very important in the writings below, for although the trend toward international copyright seems inevitable and generally desirable, its enforcement is always crucial, and this can be effective only at a local level. Performance rights are today more lucrative for the largest music publishers than income from printed music. A historical overview can be extracted from sources like those below.

Alfred M. SHAFTER. *Musical Copyright.* Chicago: Callaghan, 1932; 2nd ed., 1939. **567**
An American law book, still valuable for the clarity with which it describes earlier legal perspectives on musical property.

American Society of Composers, Authors, and Publishers. *Copyright Law Symposium.* New York: Columbia University Press, 1939- . **568**
Essays submitted to the Nathan Burkan Memorial Competition, usually an annual event. Roughly half of them concern music copyright specifically, and most of them involve American practice, if not exclusively American precedents.

H. Wolfgang PHILIPP. "Notendruck oder — Notenraub?" *SMG/Schweizer graphische Mitteilungen*, 68 (1949), 303-05.
One of the most useful contemporary accounts of the widespread reprinting of German editions after World War II, with complaints about the impact. A scholarly re-examination of the event would by highly instructive. **569**

Erich SCHULZE. *Urheberrecht in der Musik.* Berlin: Walter de Gruyter, 1951. **570**

The standard description of German practice. 2nd ed., 1956; 3rd ed., 1965; 4th ed., 1972.

Stanley ROTHENBERG. *Copyright and Public Performance of Music.* The Hague: Martinus Nijhoff, 1954. **571**

American practices during a time of general stability. The relationship between ASCAP and BMI had become clarified, and formal copyright protection of sound recordings was still to be determined. European (i.e., British, French, and Dutch) conditions are summarized at the end.

Doctoral dissertation, Utrecht, 1954.

Hansjörg POHLMANN. *Die Frühgeschichte des musikalischen Urheberrechts, ca. 1400-1800; neue Materialien zur Entwicklung des Urheberrechtsbewußtseins der Komponisten.* Kassel: Bärenreiter, 1962. **572**

The most important history of early music copyright, focused on but not limited to practices in the German-speaking world and their economic and sociological settings. Extensive scholarly documentation supports a discussion of the evolution of the understanding of personal ownership of the musical work.

Melville B. NIMMER. *Nimmer on Copyright: A Treatise on the Law of Literary, Musical, and Artistic Property, and the Protection of Ideas.* New York: M. Bender, 1963- . **573**

The most respected account of American copyright practice, regularly updated, with commentary on music practice.

Gavin McFARLANE. *Copyright: The Development and Exercise of the Performing Right.* London: Offord, 1980. **574**

An overview of British practice, based on a London School of Economics dissertation.

The author's *A Practical Introduction to Copyright* (London: Waterlow, 1982) is a counterpart description of current practice. In the 2nd ed. (1989), chapter 4 (pp. 26-36) is on "The Music Industry," chapter 5 (pp. 37-44) on special problems, chapter 7 (pp. 53-63) on sound recordings, and chapter 16 (pp. 145-53) on copyright collecting societies, from British perspectives; chapter

17 (pp. 154-62) is on U. S. copyright, and 18 (pp. 163-72) on copyright in the European Economic Community. Also valuable is McFarlane's overview of "Copyright Collecting Societies," *Grove 6*, vol. 4, pp. 748-60.

William LICHTENWANGER. "94-533 and All That: Ruminations on Copyright, Today, Yesterday, and Tomorrow," Music Library Association, *Notes*, 35 (1979), 803-18; 36 (1980), 837-48.   **575**
Observations of a noted American scholar who, at the Library of Congress, worked closely with musicians, publishers, and the U. S. Copyright Office. The title refers to the number of the Public Law effective in the United States as of 1978.

In addition to these general writings, there are a number of dissertations, many of them German, and other writings on specific legal matters. I have cited elsewhere the writings that emphasize musical or cultural considerations. International copyright is discussed in writings on particular composers (e.g., Pincherle on Vivaldi, 651; Sachs on Hummel, 628; and Kallberg on Chopin, 610). Although it was very important to Stravinsky, his story is yet to be described. For Strauss see 931 below. (Prickly indeed!) Chapter 6 also has a good deal on copyright. The British history can be pieced together from my *English Music Printing* (661), especially Chapter 2 ("The Politics of the Music Patents," pp. 10-33), and from Fenlon and Milsom (662) for the sixteenth and seventeenth centuries, Hunter (673) for the eighteenth century, and Coover (682) for the nineteenth. For France, Lesure and Thibault (695) discuss the LeRoy and Ballard privilege; Devriès (699) describes the events of the early eighteenth century, while Brenet and Cucuel (689-91) transcribe the crucial documents of the latter part. Agee (738) discusses the early Venetian privileges. For German practices, Pohlmann (572 above) is the best overview; the 1907 Junker book (798) suggests how Austrian music publishers attempted to control themselves. Sanjek (874, his 1983 book in particular) elucidates the American titles above.

C. Composers and Their Publishers

Included here are (1) overview essays that discuss the role of the publishers in the composer's working habits; (2) collected correspondence between composers and their editors or publishers; and (3) studies in "reception history" that explore the publication of a composer's music[3] (the quintessential musicological form of meta-

---

3. In the "Bibliography" article in Grove 6 (vol. 2, p. 682), I suggest that bibliographers should look "for ways in which the physical form of the document may distort the intention of the composer." In "Zur Bibliographie von Musikdrucken der zweiten Hälfte des 16. Jahrhunderts" (see p. 7n), Horst Leuchtmann finds this an "uncommonly mistrustful method of approach." I would argue instead that it reflects on nothing more or less than what is expected of all scrupulous scholarship. My point is intended not primarily as a reflection on the negligence or mischief of music publishers, although they have sometimes been known to be negligent, mischievous, or both, whether thoughtlessly or intentionally. Instead, my aim was to propose that bibliographers are expected to look critically at their evidence, both of the physical object as an embodiment of the musical content, and of the content as it is embodied in the physical object.

The instances of textual corruption fall along a spectrum ranging from the specific and identifiable to the general and speculative, with enough speculative specifics and manifest generalizations to make the topic as stimulating and controversial as it is important. Here are examples of publishers who deliberately changed the text in the guise of editing it, without telling the composers; of composers who were grateful for the changes, or never noticed the difference, or, if they were told or noticed, never cared; of composers who discovered the changes and objected, prior to publication or afterward (from two hours to twenty-eight years), and publishers who then made the proposed changes, or said they would but didn't; and of printers who, whether knowingly or innocently, may have intermixed corrected and unbound gatherings before copies were assembled, which were tacitly or unwittingly accepted by the publisher — all of this perhaps understood by but more likely unbeknownst to the composer.

Somewhat less easily identifiable are instances of composers who denied their best musical instincts in order to appease their publishers' conceptions of what would sell (and this may or may not be different from the composers' appeasing of their performers' conceptions of what they could sing or play). Further along the spectrum are the instances of composers who sold their artistic souls to publishers, or who made their living (whether minimal or lavish) at the beck and call of their publishers. (Pickering, 643 below, attempts to face the question head-on.) The issue is bedeviled not only by the uncertainty of the evidence that the music would otherwise have been any better, also by the fact that the music is often very good. One thinks also of some of the very distinguished composers, from Guillaume Dufay through Johann Sebastian Bach, who did not work with publishers at all, having likewise sold their souls by writing music mostly to suit the tastes and resources of their patrons.

music-bibliography). I have cited writings on reception history that seem clearly bibliographical; but I must confess that I am very unclear as to what to include and exclude in this lively area.

I have excluded classic confrontations in print (often brokered by hungry music journal editors) between composers ("you owe us more than you give us") and publishers ("we need to make a living too, and if you don't like us, go somewhere else"). See, for instance, Albrecht Schneider's "Musikverlag und Autor," in *Das Orchester*, 29 (1981), 118-21, in response to Peter Jona Korn's earlier complaint, "Wozu braucht der Komponist einen Verleger?" Why does a composer need a publisher? Schneider's answer separates *Rechtliche Aspekte* (copyright, performance rights) from *Wirtschaftliche Aspekte* (handling financial details, promotion, distribution). Ralph Hawkes's "Composers and Economics," *Tempo*, 1 (1946), 10-11, provides a perspective on this classic relationship.

The recent rediscovery of self-publication may be an exciting event, but promoting it as a new development is clearly a sign of a "born yesterday" mentality, since the event is anything but new. Whether it is actually increasing is a question for statisticians. (As usual they will, or should, ask what precisely is meant by self-publication; and at this point the survey may well flounder.) For a lively and sensitive discussion see James Chute, "Publish or Perish?" *High Fidelity/Musical America*, January 1982, pp. 18-21. Jonathan Kramer, Edwin London, and Gunther Schuller speak as composers, Arnold Broido, Arthur Cohn, and George Sturm speak as publishers. (One hesitates to call this a tag-team event, since several participants wear two costumes, and all of them are quick to appreciate the predicament of the other side). This literature of confrontation bears remembering in juxtaposition to the citations that follow, most of which describe success stories and happy relationships fondly to be cherished.

I have also excluded many writings that treat small details, also the chapters, discussions, and individual references scattered through the biographical literature, in deference to subject bibliographies on the composer in question. Nor dare I fail to pay respect to the great thematic catalogues of composers, gold mines of bibliographical facts even when they do not focus primarily on composer-publisher relationships. I have included those few with extensive, and thus separately citable, discussions of the topic.

214

Preceding the composer list below are writings on the relationship between composers and publishers in general, and on the publishers who also composed and the composers who published (with whatever degree of success in either, or neither, or both).

Karl WESTERMEYER. "Tonkünstler als Verleger: Ein musikgeschichtlicher Rückblick durch vier Jahrhunderte," *Signale für die musikalische Welt*, 80 (1922), 777-85.   **576**
Calls attention to several dozen publishers who also composed.

Wolfgang SCHMIEDER. "Komponierende Musikverleger des 18. und 19. Jahrhunderts," *Allgemeine Musikzeitung*, 64 (1937), 147-49, 163-65.   **577**
On several Breitkopfs and Andrés, also Simrock, Nägeli, Hoffmeister, Haslinger and Litolff.

"Composer and Publisher, 1500-1850," *Bericht über den siebenten internationalen musikwissenschaftlichen Kongress, Köln 1958* (Kassel: Bärenreiter, 1959), pp. 340-43.   **578**
Report on a study-group session led by Alec Hyatt King, at which ten scholars briefly presented a wide range of observations. Two points emerge. First, the panelists' authority rests firmly, not on broad, elegant, and provocative theorizing, but on their biographical and bibliographical expertise. Second, most of the questions raised, especially the broadly defined ones, have yet to be answered. They continue to be very important, perhaps because they are unanswerable.

Hubert UNVERRICHT. "Autor – Komponist – Musikverleger: Ein Geschichtsabriß ihrer Rechtsbeziehungen," in *Musik und Verlag: Karl Vötterle zum 65. Geburtstag* (Kassel: Bärenreiter, 1968), pp. 562-76.   **579**
A thoughtful overview of the appropriate relationships between the composer and publisher, as developed out of a formal statement made on the founding of the Verband der Deutschen Musikalienhändler (1831) and published in early issues of *Cäcilia*.

Michael MÜLLER-BLATTAU. "Optionsbedingungen zwischen Komponisten und Musikverlegern," in *Zum 70. Geburtstag von Joseph Müller-Blattau* (Kassel: Bärenreiter,

1966; Saarbrückener Studien zur Musikwissenschaft, 1), pp. 201-11.   580
Working from a letter by Wagner to Schott's, dated January 17, 1862, six basic aspects of the relationship between composers and publishers are proposed: comprehensive agreements, options for the next work, borderlines of coverage ("Abgrenzungsfragen") for future works, contract violation, ethics, and changing copyright conditions.

Raynor (111a) is also very good on this topic. There is also a small literature of entertaining tales on composers and their music publishers. Kidson's 1917 essay emphasizes exploitation in recalling some eighteenth-century British incidents (656). The critic Felix Borowski comments on "Composers and Their Publishers," *Christian Science Monitor*, March 22 and 29, 1924 (beginning with the observation that "it is at once strange and regrettable that no one has written a book about music publishing"). I have not seen Wilhelm Hitzig's "Verleger und ihre Komponisten," *Musikalienhandel*, 40 (1938), 196-97 [Plesske 14], although it presumably views the topic from the perspective of Breitkopf & Härtel. Other points are made in August Spanuth, "Komponisten und Verleger," *Signale für die musikalische Welt*," 73 (1925), 556-58.

Jacques Arcadelt

Thomas W. BRIDGES. *The Publishing of Arcadelt's First Book of Madrigals.* Ph.D. dissertation, Harvard University, 1982.   581
Over the composer's last years and long after his death, *Il primo libro a quattro* was issued as a pedagogical anthology, across Europe but especially in Italy. The editions provide a basis for this survey of many aspects of music publishing.

Johann Sebastian Bach and his family

Hermann von HASE. "Carl Philipp Emanuel Bach und Joh. Gottl. Im. Breitkopf," *Bach Jahrbuch*, 8 (1911), 86-101. 582
Correspondence on publication arrangements, 1765-89.

Georg KINSKY. *Die Originalausgaben der Werke Johann Sebastian Bachs: Ein Beitrag zur Musikbibliographie.* Wien: Herbert Reichner, 1937.   583

Detailed discussion of the music published in Bach's lifetime, and a survey of other editions of his music before 1800.

The auspices and character of this book suggest an essay originally intended for the *Philobiblon* music series (8 above), but one that grew to a length better suited to a book.

Die Nürnberger Musikverleger und die Familie Bach. Zirndorf: Bollmann, 1973. **584**

"Materialien zu einer Ausstellung des 48. Bach-Fests der Neuen Bach-Gesellschaft." An exhibition catalogue, prepared by Willi Wörthmüller, with essays by Lothar Hoffmann-Erbrecht, Hans Klotz, and Christoph Wolff, with facsimiles and a list of titles.

Briefe von Carl Philipp Emanuel Bach an Johann Gottlob Immanuel Breitkopf und Johann Nikolaus Forkel. Tutzing: Hans Schneider, 1985 (Mainzer Studien zur Musikwissenschaft, 19). **585**

Transcripts of 181 Bach letters, edited by Ernst Suchalla, complementing the von Hase work above.

Gregory BUTLER. *Bach's Clavierübung III: The Making of a Print: With a Companion Study of the Canonic Variations on "Vom Himmel Hoch," BWV 769.* Durham, N.C.: Duke University Press, 1990. **586**

A meticulous investigation of the circumstances of the engraving and production of an edition that is as complicated historically as it is significant musically.

Béla Bartók

Ralph HAWKES. "Béla Bartók: A Recollection by his Publisher," *Tempo*, 1 (1946), 10-15. **587**

An appreciative sketch by a publisher who enjoyed high respect for his good working relationships with well-selected compoers. The text is important both for its impressions of the composer and for what it tells about Hawkes's efforts on Bartók's behalf.

Also in *Béla Bartók: A Memorial Review* (New York, etc.: Boosey & Hawkes, 1950), pp.14-19.

Ivan F. WALDBAUER. "Bartók's First Piano Concerto: A Publication History," *Musical Quarterly*, 51 (1965), 336-44.

A lucid account of the complicated circumstances that result when two ancient adages are overlooked: "haste makes waste" and "too many cooks."   **588**

John VINTON. "Hints to the Printers from Bartók," *Music and Letters*, 49 (1968), 224-30.   **589**
Correspondence with Universal Edition in 1921 and with Boosey & Hawkes, 1939-43, specifying details that would enhance the readability of the printed page.

Malcolm GILLIES and Adrienne GOMBOCZ. "The 'Colinda' Fiasco: Bartók and Oxford University Press," *Music and Letters*, 69 (1988), 482-94.   **590**
On the projected English edition of Transylvanian Christmas songs, based on correspondence with Hubert J. Foss, 1923-37.

László SOMFAI. "Nineteenth-Century Ideas Developed in Bartók's Piano Notation, 1907-14," in Joseph Kerman, *Music at the Turn of Century: A 19th-Century Music Reader* (Berkeley: University of California Press, 1990), pp. 181-99.   **591**
Study of Bartók's concern for details of the presentation in editions prepared for the publishers Rozsnyai (beginning with the *Bagatelles* and editions of works by other composers, e.g., Bach's *Well-Tempered Clavier*) and Rózsavölgyi, among others.

For Bartók's correspondence with Universal Edition see Victor Bator, *The Béla Bartók Archives, History and Catalogue* (New York: Bartók Archives Publication, 1963), pp. 16-17.

Ludwig van Beethoven

Alfred OREL. "Beethoven und seine Verleger," in *Ein Wiener Beethoven Buch* (Wien: Gerlach & Wiedling, 1921), pp. 168-203.   **592**
A general but basic summary.

Ludwig van Beethoven und seine Verleger S. A. Steiner und Tobias Haslinger in Wien, Ad. Martin Schlesinger in Berlin. Berlin, Wien: Schlesinger, 1921.   **593**
"Eine Erinnerungsgabe zum 150. Geburtstag des Meisters," with transcriptions by Max Unger of 102 letters from Steiner and

Haslinger and 23 from Schlesinger, some previously unpublished. Also reprinted, Berlin: Lienau, 1981.

Hubert UNVERRICHT. *Die Eigenschriften und die Original-ausgaben von Werken Beethovens in ihrer Bedeutung für die moderne Textkritik.* Kassel: Bärenreiter, 1960 (Musikwissenschaftliche Arbeiten, 17).   **594**
The state of bibliographical scholarship as of the late 1950s.

Alan TYSON. *The Authentic English Editions of Beethoven.* London: Faber & Faber, 1963.   **595**
A celebrated study of the early London editions, which persuasively argues that some of them are textually independent of, and comparable in authority to, the Viennese editions.

—. "Maurice Schlesinger as a Publisher of Beethoven, 1822-1827," *Acta musicologica*, 35 (1963), 182-91.   **596**
Mostly on the late piano sonatas and string quartets.

Anneliese LEICHER-OLBRICHT. *Untersuchungen zu Originalausgaben Beethovenscher Klavierwerke.* Wiesbaden: Breitkopf & Härtel, 1976.   **597**
"Textkritische Untersuchungen" of parts of opp. 33, 52, and 57, informed by fastidious "Stichtechnische-typographische Untersuchungen" (pp. 369-421), mostly on punch forms and layout.
Originally a dissertation, Bonn, 1971.

Beiträge zur Beethoven Bibliographie: Studien und Materialen zum Werkverzeichnis von Kinsky-Halm, edited by Kurt Dorfmüller. München: Henle, 1978.   **598**
Part 2 of Liesbeth Weinhold, "Erst- und Frühdrucke von Beethovens Werken" discusses terminology in "Zur Definition der Ausgabe-Typen" (pp. 245-68, with ten facsimiles), particularly valuable for its detailed examination of Beethoven variants. William S. Newman also writes "On the Problem of Determining Beethoven's Most Authoritative Lifetime Editions" (pp. 128-36).

Martin STAEHELIN. *Hans Georg Nägeli und Ludwig van Beethoven: Der Zürcher Musiker, Musikverleger und Musik-*

*schriftsteller in seinen Beziehungen zu den großen Kompo-
nisten.* Zürich: Hug, 1982. **599**
The perspectives of Nägeli's catalogue, the correspondence,
Weber's role, and Nägeli's recollection of Beethoven.

*Ludwig van Beethoven: Der Briefwechsel mit dem Verlag
Schott.* München: Henle, 1985. **600**
Annotated transcripts of 72 letters, 1824-27, edited on behalf of
the Beethovenhaus, Bonn.

Friedrich SLEZAK. *Beethovens Wiener Originalverleger.*
Wien: Franz Deuticke, 1987 (Forschungen und Beiträge
zur Wiener Stadtgeschichte, 17). **601**
Local archival sources provide evidence of musical life in general
and the work of 17 publishers.

Alban Berg

Rosemary HILMAR. " . . . nach den hinterlassenen end-
gültigen Korrekturen des Komponisten revidiert," *Gutenberg Jahrbuch 1983*, pp. 112-30. **602**
Reconstruction of the processes through which *Wozzeck* came to
be corrected and altered, with a chart listing nearly 100 discrep-
ancies between the various "original" sources of Act I, scene 1.

Hector Berlioz

Cecil HOPKINSON. *A Bibliography of the Musical and Literary Works of Hector Berlioz, 1803-1869, with Histories of the
French Music Publishers Concerned.* Edinburgh: Edinburgh Bibliographical Society, 1951. **603**
Recognized in its day for its elegant presentation and for its meticulous scholarship (also for what some saw as a bold assertion
that bibliography might not be beholden to musicologists: the
controversy with Richard S. Hill is provocative and unsettling.)
The "Introduction" (pp. xii-xvii) discusses publishing sources,
while Appendix F (pp. 194-200) is a preliminary version of the
author's 1954 directory of French music publishers (686).
   The 2nd edition (Tunbridge Wells: Richard Macnutt, 1980) incorporates the author's additions and revisions.

Johannes Brahms

Briefe an P. J. Simrock und Fritz Simrock. Berlin: Deutsche Brahms Gesellschaft, 1917-19 (*Johannes Brahms Briefwechsel*, 9-12). **604**
The four volumes consist of transcriptions of 939 letters from Brahms, 1860-97, edited by Max Kalbeck.
Reprinted Tutzing: Hans Schneider, 1974.

Briefwechsel mit Breitkopf & Härtel, Bartolf Senff, J. Rieter-Biedermann, C. F. Peters, E. W. Fritzsch, und Robert Lienau. Berlin: Deutsche Brahms Gesellschaft, 1920 (*Johannes Brahms Briefwechsel*, 14). **605**
Wilhelm Altmann's edition of 433 letters, 1853-96.
The correspondence with Breitkopf, and with others in other volumes, is the basis for Imogen Fellinger, "Brahms zur Edition Chopinischer Klavierwerke," *Musicae scientiae collectanea: Festschrift Karl Gustav Fellerer* (Köln: Arno Volk, 1973), pp. 110-16.

Johannes Brahms und Fritz Simrock, Weg einer Freundschaft: Briefe des Verlegers an die Komponisten. Hamburg: J. J. Augustin, 1961 (Veröffentlichungen aus der Hamburger Staats- und Universitätsbibliothek, 6). **606**
Transcripts of 166 letters from the Simrocks to Brahms, 1862-97, also an extensive introduction by Kurt Stephenson and a chart of Brahms's works by opus number, with Brahms' honoraria for each, and the prices of the different editions.

Robert PASCALL. "Brahms and the Definitive Text," in his *Brahms: Biographical, Documentary, and Analytical Studies* (Cambridge: Cambridge University Press, 1983), pp. 59-75. **607**
On the problems of a definitive edition of Brahms, who was, surprisingly, an erratic proofreader and who, not surprisingly, made changes that do not always appear in the printed editions.

Camilla CAI. "Was Brahms a Reliable Editor?" *Acta Musicologica*, 61 (1989), 83-101. **607a**
The proofs for Opus 116-19 reveal the sad answer to the question, also details on the workings of a large publishing house.

Developed out of a doctoral dissertation, *Brahms' Short Late Piano Pieces, Opus Numbers 116-119* (Boston University, 1986).

George S. BOZARTH. "Brahms as Editor," in *Brahms Studies: Analytical and Historical Perspectives* (Oxford: Clarendon Press, 1990), pp. 229-328.   **608**
Papers delivered at the International Brahms Conference, Washington, D. C., May 5-8, 1983. This section includes David Brodbeck, "Brahms's Edition of Twenty Schubert Ländler: An Essay in Criticism" (pp. 229-50, reflecting his 1984 University of Pennsylvania Ph. D. dissertation); Linda Correll Roesner, "Brahms's Editions of Schumann," (pp. 251-72, with quotations from unpublished letters of Brahms to Clara Schumann, mostly concerned with proof corrections, pp. 273-82); Robert Pascall, "The Publication of Brahms's Third Symphony: A Crisis in Dissemination" (pp. 283-94, with a useful chart detailing the relationships between the manuscript and the printed sources, p. 285, and facsimiles of Robert Keller's manuscript and Simrock's printed corrections, pp. 289-90); and Margit McCorkle, "The Role of Trial Performances for Brahms's Orchestral and Large Choral Works: Sources and Circumstances," (pp. 295-328, with a chart on pp. 289-99 that summarizes the place of the various printed versions in establishing the text).

Kurt Hoffmann's *Die Erstdrucke der Werke von Johannes Brahms* (Tutzing: Hans Schneider, 1975) is of special interest for its scrupulous detail, reflected in its many illustrations of title pages.

Frédéric Chopin

Maurice J. E. BROWN. "Chopin and his English Publisher," *Music and Letters*, 39 (1958), 363-71.   **609**
On the relationship with Christian Rudolf Wessel.

Jeffrey KALLBERG. "Chopin in the Marketplace: Aspects of the International Music Publishing Industry," Music Library Association, *Notes*, 39 (1983), 535-69, 795-824. **610**
Part 1: France and England, mostly on Troupenas, Schlesinger, and Wessel; part 2: Germany, mostly on Breitkopf & Härtel.

Other writings of the author deal with Chopin editions. "Are Variants a Problem? Composer's Intentions in Editing Chopin," *Chopin Studies 3* (Warsaw: Chopin Society, 1990), part 1, pp.

257-67 (a paper at the International Musicological Symposium "Chopin and Romanticism," Warsaw, October 17-23, 1986) has particularly good points on the theory of textual bibliography.

Claude Debussy

Lettres de Claude Debussy à son éditeur, publiés par Jacques Durand. Paris: A. Durand, 1923.   **611**
Transcripts of over 200 letters from Debussy, 1894 and 1902-17.

Karl Ditters von Dittersdorf

Jan LARUE. "Dittersdorf Negotiates a Price," in *Hans Albrecht in Memoriam* (Kassel: Bärenreiter, 1962), pp. 156-59. Correspondence with Artaria in 1778.   **612**

Antonín Dvořák

"Antonín Dvořák im Verkehr mit Fritz Simrock," *Simrock Jahrbuch*, 2 (1929), 84-151.   **613**
Wilhelm Altmann's transcriptions of and commentary on correspondence, 1877-1902, with Brahms as the intermediary.

Denis Vaughan's "Dvořák: Getting to the Truth," *Musical America*, November 1989, pp. 19-21, is captioned, "Errors in publishing have obscured many fine points in his symphonies."

Edward Elgar

Letters to Nimrod: Edward Elgar to August Jaeger, 1897-1908. London: Dobson, 1965.   **614**
Elgar's correspondence with his editor at Novello's (the "Nimrod" of the "Enigma" Variations), edited by Percy M. Young.

Elgar and his Publishers: Letters of a Creative Life. Oxford: Clarendon Press, 1987.   **615**
Correspondence, edited by Jerrold Northrop Moore, with Novello's, Breitkopf & Härtel, Enoch (Paris), Geidel (Leipzig engraver), Keith, Prowse & Co., Massina (Melbourne), Charles Tuckwood, and Joseph Williams, among others.

Stephen Foster

John Tasker HOWARD. "Stephen Foster and His Publishers," *Musical Quarterly*, 20 (1934), 77-95.   **616**

On dealings mostly with Firth, Pond, & Co. (New York); also Benteen (Baltimore), J. J. Daly, S. T. Gordon, and Horace Waters (New York), W. C. Peters (Louisville, etc.), and others.

Largely subsumed in Howard's *Stephen Foster, America's Troubadour* (New York: Thomas Y. Crowell, 1939; revised ed., 1953).

Stephen SAUNDERS. "A Publication History of Stephen Foster's 'Massa's in de Cold Ground,'" Music Library Association, *Notes*, 43 (1987), 499-521.   **617**

An examination of the earliest 1852 editions (New York: Firth, Pond & Co., and Boston: Oliver Ditson), with special concern for textual variations here and in manuscript sources.

Francesco Geminiani

Robert DONINGTON. "Geminiani and the Gremlins," *Music and Letters*, 51 (1970), 150-55.   **618**

On the scholarly confusion that results from the choice of a title for a publication, in this case *The Art of Playing on the Violin*.

Edvard Grieg

Briefe an die Verleger der Edition Peters, 1866-1907. Leipzig: Peters, 1922.   **619**

A handsome book, with notes by Elsa von Zschinsky-Troxler.

Based on his wide experience with Grieg editions, Dan Fog has prepared *Zur Datierung der Edition Peters auf Grundlagen der Grieg-Ausgaben* (Copenhagen: Dan Fog, 1990).

George Frideric Handel

Cecil HOPKINSON. "Handel and France: Editions Published There during his Lifetime," *Transactions of the Edinburgh Bibliographical Society*, vol. 3, pt. 4 (sessions 1953-54, 1954-55, issued 1957), pp. 223-48.   **620**

Background on the editions, with bibliographical citations.

William C. SMITH. *Handel: A Descriptive Catalogue of the Early Editions.* London: Cassell, 1960; 2nd ed., 1970.   **621**

The "Introduction," in its discussion of sources (pp. xiii-xx), summarizes the publishing history.

Other of Smith's essays, mostly bibliographical, are collected in two anthologies: *Concerning Handel* (London: Cassell, 1948) and

A Handelian's Notebook (London: Adam & Charles Black, 1965).

Hans Ferdinand REDLICH. "Georg Friedrich Händel und seine Verleger," *Musik und Verlag: Karl Vötterle zum 65. Geburtstag* (Kassel: Bärenreiter, 1968), pp. 493-501. **622**
A summary dealing mainly with Walsh, and with the musical variants in the editions.

Donald BURROWS. "Walsh's Editions of Handel's Opera 1-5: The Texts and their Sources," in *Music in Eighteenth-Century England: Essays in Memory of Charles Cudworth* (Cambridge: Cambridge University Press, 1983), pp. 79-105. **623**
An impressively detailed evaluation of the text with particular attention to the different engravers as identifiable through their engraving styles.

Cecil HILL. "Early Engravers of Handel's Music," Bibliographical Society of Australia and New Zealand, *Bulletin*, vol. 11, no. 4 (1987; issued 1989), 125-40. **624**
Further studies of engravers, extending (but not always agreeing with) Burrows. Emphasizes the "boxes of tools" the engravers used, as seen in extant copies, mostly in the Dalley-Scarlett collection in Sydney.

Joseph Haydn

Franz ARTARIA and Hugo BOTSTIBER. *Joseph Haydn und das Verlagshaus Artaria*. Wien: Artaria, 1909. **625**
A centenary tribute, with texts of letters, 1780-1803, commentary, and a chart of Artaria's 157 Haydn editions.

Hermann von HASE. *Joseph Haydn und Breitkopf & Härtel: Ein Rückblick bei der Veranstaltung der ersten vollständigen Gesamtausgabe seiner Werke.* Leipzig: Breitkopf & Härtel, 1909. **626**
Another centenary tribute, emphasizing the 1799 "Oeuvres complettes" edition.

Mark Arthur RADICE. "Haydn and his Publishers: A Brief Survey of the Composer's Publishing Activities," *Music Review*, 44 (1983), 87-94.   **627**
Early dealings with Artaria, Longman & Broderip, and Breit-kopf & Härtel. The "reliability chart" on p. 90 is particularly ingenious in its conception.

Haydn has proven to be a rich topic for bibliographical study. For instance, he is the only major composer with a special "Publishers" section in *Grove 6* (vol. 8, p. 403). Other studies include Georg Feder, "Die Eingriffe des Musikverlegers Hummel in Haydns Werke," in *Musicae Scientiae Collectanea: Festschrift Karl Gustav Fellerer zum 70. Geburtstag* (Köln: Arno Volk, 1973), pp. 88-101; also James Webster, "The Significance of Haydn's String Quartet Autographs for Performance Practice," in *The String Quartets of Haydn, Mozart and Beethoven: Studies of the Autograph Manuscripts* (Cambridge: Harvard University, Department of Music, 1980), pp. 62-90; and Poole's essay on Forster's London editions (671). Haydn's letter to Artaria of April 8, 1783, speaks of an engraver so bad as to deserve to have his arms cut off ("die Sinfonie . . . so voller fehler ware, daß man den kerl so es geschrieben die Bratze abhauen solle"): see the *Gesammelte Briefe*, edited by Dénes Bartha (Kassel: Bärenreiter, 1965), pp. 127-28.

Johann Nepomuk Hummel

Joel SACHS. "Hummel and the Pirates: The Struggle for Music Copyright," *Musical Quarterly*, 59 (1973), 31-60. **628**
As documented in extant correspondence, Hummel's activities in the 1820s, mostly in Leipzig, significantly fostered the international copyright legislation of the 1830s.
    See also the author's "Authentic English and French Editions of J. N. Hummel," *Journal of the American Musicological Society*, 25 (1972), 230-99.

Leoš Janáček

Ernst HILMAR. *Leoš Janáček: Briefe an die Universal Edition*. Tutzing: Hans Schneider, 1988.   **629**
Transcriptions of 351 letters, 1914-28, with commentary.

Nigel Simeone's bibliographical catalogue, *The First Editions of Leoš Janáček* (Tutzing: Hans Schneider, 1991) reproduces the most important title pages.

Zoltán Kodály

"Kodály és az Universal Edition," in *Magyar zenetörténeti tanulmányok Kodály Zoltán emlékére* (Budapest: *Zenemü*, 1977), pp. 136-50.   **630**
Transcripts by Rudolf Klein of passages from letters, 1937-81.

Orlando di Lasso

Wolfgang BOETTICHER. *Orlando di Lasso und seine Zeit.* Kassel: Bärenreiter, 1958.   **631**
On the wide dissemination of the composer's music during and just after his lifetime. Indeed, the sheer quantity of "Lasso-Drucke" (pp. 729-816), with several hundred monographic entries and analytic-level references, is not surpassed by any composer until the time of Handel: see p. 69 above.

[Special Lasso issue]. *Revue belge de musicologie*, 39/40 (1985-86).   **632**
Several articles are of bibliographical interest: Kristine Forney, "Orlando di Lasso's 'Opus 1'," (pp. 33-60, on the 1555 editions. See also 823 below); Henri Verhulst, "Lassus et ses éditeurs: Remarques à propos de deux lettres peu connues" (pp. 80-100, on 1581 letters of William V of Bavaria to Emperor Rudolf II); and Frank Dobbins, "Lassus, Borrower or Lender: The Chansons" (pp. 101-57, with good charts and commentary).

Franz Liszt

András KÜRTHY. "L'histoire du rapport de Liszt et de la Casa Ricordi reflétée par leur correspondance," *Studi musicologica*, 29 (1987), 325-42.   **633**
Letters, 1863-78, in facsimile and transcribed with commentary.

Felix Mendelssohn

Briefe an deutsche Verleger. Berlin: Walter de Gruyter, 1968 (Felix Mendelssohn Bartholdy Briefe, 1).   **634**
Transcriptions by Rudolf Elvers of 431 letters to German publishers (190 to Breitkopf & Härtel, 1830-47; 131 to Simrock,

1831-47; and 110 to other publishers, 1827-47), with notes and indexes.

Wolfgang Amadeus Mozart

Otto Erich DEUTSCH. "Mozarts Verleger," *Mozart Jahr-buch*, 1955, pp. 49-55.   **635**

Not so much a discussion of the relationships as a recitation of the basic facts, now largely subsumed in the vast Mozart litera-ture, in which Gertraut Haberkamp's *Die Erstdrucke der Werke von Wolfgang Amadeus Mozart* (Tutzing: Hans Schneider, 1986) is of special bibliographical distinction.

Giacomo Puccini

Suzanne SCHERR. "Editing Puccini's Operas: The Case of 'Manon Lescaut,'" *Acta musicologica*, 61 (1989), 62-81. **636**
Based on work in the Ricordi archives and with printed sources.

Gioacchino Rossini

Philip GOSSETT. *The Operas of Rossini: Problems of Textual Criticism in Nineteenth-Century Opera*. Ph.D. dissertation, Princeton University, 1970.   **637**

Includes three appendixes, on publishers of libretti (pp. 543-59), copyists (pp. 560-63), and publishers from Italy (pp. 564-80) and France (pp. 580-612), with plate-number lists and commentary on dating of mid-19th-century Italian music.

Erik Satie

Satie's concern for the graphic arts is discussed in 930 below.

Johann Hermann Schein

Adam ADRIO. "Die Drucker und Verleger der musi-kalischen Werke Johann Hermann Scheins," in *Musik und Verlag: Karl Vötterle zum 65. Geburtstag* (Kassel: Bären-reiter, 1968), pp. 126-35.   **638**

Details, often from Benzing, on the publishers in Leipzig and elsewhere, during the disastrous times of the Thirty Years' War.

Franz Schubert

Otto Erich DEUTSCH. "Schubert's Verleger," *Der Bär: Jahrbuch von Breitkopf & Härtel*, 1928, pp. 13-30.   **639**

Summarizes work with Sonnleithner, Diabelli, Sauer & Leides-dorf, the Artarias, and Haslinger in Vienna, and others else-where. Several letters to Probst in Leipzig are included.

Robert Schumann

Wolfgang BOETTICHER. "Robert Schumann und seine Verleger," in *Musik und Verlag: Karl Vötterle zum 65. Geburtstag* (Kassel: Bärenreiter, 1968), pp. 168-74.   **640**
Miscellaneous observations, mostly on dealings with Breitkopf & Härtel and Kistner.

Renata FEDERHOFER-KÖNIGS. "Die Beziehungen von Robert Schumann zur Familie André, mit unveröffent-lichten Briefen," *Gutenberg Jahrbuch 1988*, pp. 190-205. **641**
Transcriptions of several dozen letters, 1836-53, with commen-tary.

Anthony NEWCOMB. "Schumann in the Marketplace: From Butterflies to *Hausmusik*" in R. Larry Todd, *Nine-teenth-Century Piano Music* (New York: Schirmer Books, 1990), pp. 258-315.   **642**
Of particular interest to bibliographers are the comments on the relative merits of the early and late editions of the piano music, pp. 274 *ff*. The editorial implications are to be appreciated in Wolfgang Boetticher's *Robert Schumanns Klavierwerke: Neue biographische und textkritische Untersuchungen* (Wilhelmshaven: Heinrichshofen, 1984-). See also Linda Correll Roesner, "The Sources for Schumann's *Davidsbundlertänze*, op. 6: Composition, Textual Problems, and the Role of the Composer as Editor," in Jon W. Finson and R. Larry Todd, *Mendelssohn and Schumann* (Durham, N.C.: Duke University Press,1984), pp. 53-70.

Kurt Hoffmann's *Die Erstdrucke der Werke von Robert Schumann* (Tutzing: Hans Schneider, 1979) is of special interest for its scrup-ulous detail, reflected in its many illustrations of title pages.

Karl Stamitz

Jennifer M. PICKERING. "Printing, Publishing, and the Mi-gration of Sources: The Case of Carl Stamitz," *Brio*, 27 (1990), 59-66.   **643**

Argues that the character of Stamitz's six symphonies, opus 13 (1777) was influenced by the prospects of international dissemination through publication.

Also issued, with revisions, in *Fontes artis musicae*, 38 (1991), 130-38.

Richard Strauss

Alfons OTT. "Richard Strauss und sein Verlegerfreund Eugen Spitzweg," in *Musik und Verlag: Karl Vötterle zum 65. Geburtstag* (Kassel: Bärenreiter, 1968), pp. 466-75. **644**
Gives details on Aibl editions, 1889-1905, with special concern for the musical text of Mozart's *Così fan tutte*.

For Strauss's bibliophilic editions see 931-32 below.

Igor Stravinsky

Louis CYR. "'Le Sacre du Printemps': Petite histoire d'une grande partition," in *Stravinsky: études et témoinages*, edited by François Lesure (Paris: Jean-Claude Lattès, 1982), pp. 90-147.   **645**
A detailed analysis, amply undermining the conventional wisdom that textual variants are found only in earlier periods.

Karol Szymanowski

Między kompozytorem i wydawcą: Korespondencja Karola Szymanowskiego z Universal Edition. Kraków: Polskie Wydawnictwo Muzyczne, 1978.   **646**
A collection of 591 letters, 1912-87, in or translated into Polish, between the composer (or his assistant, Leonia Gradstein) and Universal Edition (mostly Emil Hertzka, B. Rothe, and Alfred Kalmus), and 28 letters involving other publishers, 1936-37.

Teresa Chylińska's *Karol Szymanowski: Briefwechsel mit der Universal Edition, 1927-1937* (Wien: Universal, 1981) is a selection of 187 of the letters, in German.

Georg Philipp Telemann

Martin RUHNKE. "Telemann als Musikverleger," in *Musik und Verlag: Karl Vötterle zum 65. Geburtstag* (Kassel: Bärenreiter, 1968), pp. 502-17.   **647**

Comments on the background of 47 publications, 1715-40. The implications of the difference between typographic and engraved editions are nicely developed.

Giuseppe Verdi

Pierluigi PETROBELLI, Marisa di Gregorio CASATI, and Carlo Matteo MOSSA. *Carteggio Verdi-Ricordi 1880-1881*. Parma: Istituto di Studi Verdiana, 1988. **648**
In documenting a famous productive relationship, the anthology begins in mid-course with this volume, largely in deference to the recent availability of documents previously unknown.

Luke JENSEN. *Giuseppe Verdi and Giovanni Ricordi, with Notes on Francesco Lucca: From "Oberto" to "La Traviata."* New York: Garland, 1989. **649**
Based on Ricordi archives and other sources, and developed out of a doctoral dissertation, *Giuseppe Verdi and the Milanese Publishers of his Music, from "Oberto" to "La Traviata"* (Ph.D., New York University, 1987).

Of perennial fascination to music bibliographers is the saga of Verdi textual scholarship that begins in the 1950s with the exposés by the Australian conductor Denis Vaughan. Music bibliographers, as they feel that their efforts are insignificant, may be reassured (and given pause to count their blessings) at the thought of the Italian parliamentary deliberations that occupy an intermediary chapter in the saga. A study — not so much of the media events themselves, as of the fact that the *New Verdi Edition* (Milano: Ricordi; Chicago: University of Chicago Press, 1985-) could come about despite the media events — would be nice, someday.

Giovanni-Battista Viotti

François LESURE. "Deux contrats d'édition de Viotti," in *Festschrift Albi Rosenthal* (Tutzing: Hans Schneider, 1984), pp. 221-26. **650**
On contracts with the Paris firm of Costallat.

Antonio Vivaldi

Marc PINCHERLE. "Note sur Estienne Roger et Michel Charles le Cène," in his *Vivaldi* (Paris: Plon, 1955), pp. 294-301. **651**

A respected study of both the dissemination and piracy of Vivaldi's music, and the workings of Amsterdam publishing, *ca.* 1700. See also Pincherle's "De la piraterie dans l'édition musicale aux environs de 1700," *Revue de musicologie*, 14 (1933), 136-40.

Richard Wagner

Richard Wagners Briefwechsel mit seinen Verlegern, edited by Wilhelm Altmann.   **652**
Three volumes were projected:
1. *Briefwechsel mit Breitkopf & Härtel* (Leipzig: Breitkopf & Härtel, 1911). 254 letters, 1831-74, mostly 1850s.
2. *Briefwechsel mit B. Schott* (Mainz: Schott, 1911). 274 letters, all but three of them from between 1859 and 1882.
3. *Briefwechsel mit verschiedenen Verlegern* (not published.)

Ludwig STRECKER. *Richard Wagner als Verlagsgefährte: eine Darstellung mit Briefen und Dokumenten.* Mainz: Schott, 1951.   **653**
Transcriptions of correspondence and commentary describing dealings not only with Schott (including later correspondence between Cosima and the Strecker family), but also with earlier publishers, notably Breitkopf & Härtel.

Cecil HOPKINSON. *Tannhäuser: An Examination of 36 Editions.* Tutzing: Hans Schneider, 1973.   **654**
Of special importance as an investigation of a famous instance of an evolving text.

Briefe Richard Wagners an Emil Heckel: Zur Entstehungsgeschichte der Bühnenfestspiele in Bayreuth (Berlin: S. Fischer, 1899) consists of letters to the Mannheim music publisher, 1871-83, edited by Karl Heckel, mostly on the erection of the Festspielhaus. William Ashton Ellis's translation, *Letters of Richard Wagner to Emil Heckel, with a brief History of the Bayreuth Festivals* (London: Grant Richards, 1899) adds a good index.

Müller-Blattau (580 above) uses a Wagner letter to develop a his taxonomy of composer-publisher relationships.

Carl Maria von Weber

Hans-Martin PLESSKE. " ' . . . so müssen die Kerls endlich zu Kreuze kriechen!' Carl Maria von Weber und seine

Leipziger Verleger," *Börsenblatt für den deutschen Buch-handel*, 143 (1976), 444-46. **655**
Mostly on dealings with Ambrosius Kühnel, with references to other publishers.

Section D ("Komponist und Musikverlag," pp. 213-22) of Pless-ke's bibliography (751) cites nearly a hundred titles discussing the relationships between composers and publishers, including several foreign composers' relationships with German publishers.

———

This is perhaps the best place to comment on a publishing activity that is very important but also rarely discussed: preparation of printer's copy. There is a substantial literature on scholarly editing and textual authentication; but copy editing is quite different. Terminology has not quite yet come into focus, although the concept of *historical editing* (i.e., what scholars or their assistants do involving early texts) and *manuscript copying* (i.e., what composers or their amanuenses do with contemporary texts) is perhaps the useful contradistinction to *copy editing* (i.e., what the publisher's staff does in preparing a copy for engravers or compositors to work from in creating into printing surfaces). The latter activity may be negligible: when there is a clean manuscript to work from, the engraver or compositor can make the decisions. Or it may require considerable attention: when the manuscript is problematical, as with Brahms, it may be necessary to design an interim *Stichvorlage*. Historical editing, like manuscript copying, is generally viewed as an activity undertaken with the performer in mind, copy editing with printers in mind, although those who actually do the work will likely insist that this oversimplification should almost be the other way around.

It is not that music copy editing has no history. Instead, like the crystal goblet beloved of book designers and typographers, the success of good music copy editing depends on its transparency. Its failure is easier to appreciate: ambiguous passagework, bad page turns, unclear conveyance of the sense of the music — many of the very matters that were touched on in theory in the discussion of aesthetics and legibility at the end of Chapter 3 above. In practice, decisions regarding copy would appear to be a simple matter of following the theory. But of course musical documents are far from being a homogeneous literature. One has only to look at, for instance, a Schubert song and a Broadway show tune, a medieval *conductus* and a Josquin motet, a Vivaldi concerto and a Bartók quartet, *Boris Godunov* and *Zauberflöte*, works by Duke Ellington and Aaron Copland, a hymnal and a choral anthology, a full score and a set of parts, to realize how specialized the different presentations really are, and how important the copy editor can be in making them usable by the specialized readers. The instinctive equating of manuscripts with originality and authenticity and respect, and printed copies with repetitiveness and corruption, is part of the problem.

Equally obscure is the practice of music proofreading, and for many of the same reasons. Of the printers' manuals cited in Chapter 3, a number have short discussions on music proofreading. They are useful in suggesting the basic nature of the activity — somewhat more so, of course, than the literature on general proofreading of literary texts. How, for instance, does one use a ruler in music? And what is the music counterpart to reading a prose text letter-by-letter, or backwards? The thought of such matters serves to suggest why music-printing and map-printing have followed parallel courses through history.

The elusive literature of music copy editing and proofreading probably contains more useful discourse than one might suspect, from the 1930s in particular. The *Festschrift Fritz Stein zum 70. Geburtstag* (Braunschweig: Henry Litolff, 1939), for example, in the five essays in section III ("Werkerkenntnis und Werkwiedergabe," pp. 137-95), includes such publishers' perspectives as Peter Raabe, "Über die Werktreue und ihre Grenzen" (pp. 153-60) and Adolf Sandberger, "Notenbild and Werktreue" (pp. 183-87). Among those primarily employed by publishers, Max Friedländer, who edited both German folksongs and with works by master composers, summarized his activities in *Über musikalische Herausgeberarbeit* (Weimar: Gesellschaft der Bibliophilen, 1912). Kurt Stone's "Music Editing," *MadAminA*, vol. 5, no. 2 (Fall 1984), pp. 21-23, is a succinct statement of the role of the editor in the publishing process.

VI.

National Literatures

DIFFERENT MUSICAL COMMUNITIES welcomed and were served by their printers and publishers in different ways. The communities are most often delimited geographically, whether as regions, nations, or cities. Language, laws, religion, and commercial institutions also shape their identity, as of course does the musical repertory. The latter in particular is what music publishers must discover or create, promote, and redefine. The communities may be small, by choice or necessity; or they may aspire to become world empires, but rarely with much success and seldom for very long; and they are always changing.

This chapter covers the literature that deals with music printers and publishers in particular geographical areas. It cites prose accounts that trace the history and describe the characteristics of the activity itself, ranging from surveys of the whole (an entity that usually turns out to be too vast to be all that convincing), to close examinations of events, persons, and editions (which usually prove to be fascinating). The literature also includes directories that variously identify the publishers, printers, engravers, copyists, and others involved in the arts and crafts of musical documents. Often one can substitute for the other: prose essays often incorporate the information that a directory would supply, and well-planned directories imply the contents of a prose study. I have included all of the prose writings except for brief, popular, or chauvinistic accounts, and all of the general directories except for those that require major efforts in extracting the relevant names, or that cover so limited a population as to be of interest only to the most diligent specialists.[1]

At the risk of inconvenience to those who are looking for references, each of the sections below is organized according to the patterns of its own history. The activity in Great Britain and France is largely concentrated in London and Paris, and thus each of these sections is subdivided by time period — Britain through explicit subdivisions, France through the introductory text. Activity in Italy took place in many locations, although one center was usually dominant, namely Venice in the sixteenth century and Milan in the nineteenth. For Italy, the general and miscellaneous

---

1. One useful way to view the developments is through the names of major printers and publishers. The lists at the end of each section of this Chapter suggest the local and chronological deployment of music printing, and also provide a basis for access to the extensive secondary literature on particular printers and publishers, which is included here only selectively. The names are drawn mostly but not entirely from the 1990 *Grove P & P* (57). Further references are found there, as well as in the writings cited here and in directories in Chapter 8 below.

I have excluded names of firms that began after *ca*. 1920. So remote a date may appear to reflect an embarrassing antiquarianism, until one looks for recent publishers whose production has been the subject of bibliographical study, or would appear to offer special prospects and needs for this study. Many new firms have clearly been very successful, although the ways in which historically minded bibliographers will study them, or even recognize their importance, are only now beginning to be understood.

Many of the founding dates assigned to individual printers and publishers are suggestive rather than definitive. Occasionally the very first publication is known and its appearance is well announced, or its date otherwise verifiable. Such instances are the exception. Many publication programs emerge gradually out of earlier activites in music or in the book trade, and understandably the activities were at first tentative. Sometimes the imprint developed out of an earlier partnership or association in ways that are obscure or covert. Few publishers are so fortunate as to have had their catalogue subjected to rigorous bibliographical reconstruction.

writings are followed by those delimited by city or region. For Germany the centrality has been more institutional than geographical, and the writings that describe the whole, of which there are not as many as one might expect, are followed by the many that describe regional activity. The rest of Europe is arranged by nation or region. The United States may have strong geographic elements, but as yet these are not reflected in the literature, perhaps because of the self-conscious concern for the unity of American music. Activities elsewhere are treated nationally and regionally. Within each subdivision the arrangement is by date.

A. Great Britain

As early as 1495, music was simulated in type in England. (This is the best verb to use in describing what Wynkyn de Worde produced at his press in Westminster. Its ingenuity will fascinate the casual reader as briefly as its simplicity will appall the trained musician.) Activity thereafter was at first spasmodic. Extensive music printing and publishing began to appear only around 1600 during the madrigal era, first explored in detail by Steele, and after 1650 with John Playford, for whom one still turns first to Day and Murrie. The burgeoning activity after 1700 is only beginning to be surveyed, although Kidson, followed by Humphries and Smith, have provided good groundwork for the later studies, many of which have been concerned with institutions and practices as much as with the music itself. Studies of later periods have also emphasized practices more than repertory. The directories are mostly very good ones.

DIRECTORIES

Frank KIDSON. *British Music Publishers, Printers and Engravers: London, Provincial, Scottish and Irish, from Queen Elizabeth's Reign to George the Fourth's, with Select Bibliographical Lists of Musical Works Printed and Published within That Period.* London: W. E. Hill, 1900.   **656**
An esteemed work, preceded by a historical summary. Its importance is attested to by subsequent studies, several by Kidson himself, as perhaps best suggested on pp. 40-41 of Humphries and Smith. Kidson's contributions to the second edition of *Grove's Dictionary* are also said to be something of a supplement

to his book. Most of the addresses and chronology may be embedded in Humphries and Smith, but Kidson often provides highly selective lists of titles and adds details and critical observations that are not included there.

Reprinted New York: Benjamin Blom, 1967.

J. H. MacMichael, in "Music Publishers' Signs," *Notes and Queries*, 9th ser., 7 (June 29, 1901), 507-8, innocently ventures into Kidson's domain, occasioning a response from Edward Heron-Allen on July 27th, to the effect that "Mr. MacMichael should refer to Mr. Frank Kidson's recent work."

Kidson's special interests in the early-18th century — like those of his successors Humphries and Smith — is suggested in "Composer and Publisher," *Musical Opinion & Music Trades Review*, 40 (1917), 353-54.

Charles HUMPHRIES and William C. SMITH. *Music Publishing in the British Isles, from the Earliest Times to the Middle of the Nineteenth Century: A Dictionary of Engravers, Printers, Publishers, and Music Sellers, with a Historical Introduction.* London: Cassell, 1954.   **657**

Based on Kidson, with considerably more entries and greater detail, but often more difficult to use.

The new edition (Oxford: Blackwell, 1970) reprints the text along with the authors' "Supplement: Addenda and Errata" (pp. 357-90) and additions to the "Index of Firms in Places Other than London" (pp. 391-92).

John A. PARKINSON. *Victorian Music Publishers: An Annotated List.* Warren, Mich.: Harmonie Park Press, 1990 (Detroit Studies in Music Bibliography, 64).   **658**

Brief entries for about 1,500 firms, 1830-1900, mostly extracted from current directories. Over 1,000 come from London; the rest are interfiled in the main alphabet but also identified in a "Geographical Index of Firms Outside London" (pp. 307-15). Names of frequent participants in the firm are useful, as are occasional particulars on the character of the catalogue of the firm (genres and sometimes titles, mostly reflecting holdings at the British Library).

PRE-1650

Edward F. RIMBAULT. "Early English Music Printers," *The Mirror*, 33 (1839), 349-51, 359-60, 373-75.   **659**
Working with his own and other collections and using Ames's *Typographical Antiquities*, the author identifies the landmarks of English music printing, from Wynkyn de Worde through *The Beggar's Opera*. Subsquent scholarship has generally agreed with his choices.

Robert STEELE. *The Earliest English Music Printing.* London: Bibliographical Society, 1903.   **660**
A bibliography of music printed in the British Isles before 1601, impressively sophisticated for its day, with well-reproduced facsimiles. Many of Steele's perspectives are reflected in the title below, but most of the particulars are not, nor are the bibliographical citations.
  Reprinted 1965, with two pp. of authorial corrigenda at the end.
  Steele and R. A. Peddie anticipate this major study in their brief "Early Printed Music to 1600," *Transactions of the Bibliographical Society*, 5 (1898-1900), 8-10.

D. W. KRUMMEL. *English Music Printing, c.1553-1700.* London: Bibliographical Society, 1975.   **661**
An interpretive study, extending the work of Steele. The focus is on the patents and the music type for the early years, on the rise of publishing and engraving during the latter years.

Iain FENLON and John MILSOM. "'Ruled Paper Imprinted': Music Paper and Patents in Sixteenth-Century England," *Journal of the American Musicological Society*, 37 (1984), 137-63.   **662**
The music patents of 1575 (Tallis and Byrd) and 1598 (Morley) included sole rights to produce music paper. By identifying extant exemplars, this study tells us exactly what the sheets looked like and suggests how the distribution was managed.

1650-1700

Cyrus L. DAY and Eleanore B. MURRIE. *English Song-Books, 1651-1702*. London: Bibliographical Society, 1940. One of the most respected of all music bibliographies, with model citations and detailed indexes. The introduction is an impressive essay in its own right. Further useful particulars are

FIGURE 5. A celebrated example of alteration of an engraved plate in an early music book. The Cawarden-Faithorne portrait of the gambist in copies of Christopher Simpson's *The Division Violist* (London: John Playford, 1659). (Better known to music bibliographers, admittedly, are those alterations that involve the notes themselves in a musical text.)

240

detailed in the authors' "English Song-Books, 1651-1702, and their Publishers," *The Library*, 4th series, 16 (1935-36), 356-401; and in Murrie's "Notes on the Printers and Publishers of English Song Books, 1651-1702," *Transactions of the Edinburgh Bibliographical Society*, 1 (1938), 241-76. **663**

Jennifer W. ANGEL. *Selections from Seventeenth-Century Songbooks*. Los Angeles: William Andrew Clark Memorial Library, 1984 (Augustan Reprint Society Publications, 46). **664**

FIGURE 6. The same portrait in copies of Simpson's *Chelys* (London: Printed by William Godbid for Henry Brome, 1667). George Somes Layard, *The Headless Horseman: Pierre Lombart's Engraving, Charles or Cromwell?* (New York: Frederick Stokes, [1922]) is a related essay that, as its title suggests, also deals with alteration in portraiture.

Facsimiles of 28 pages of music, 1611– *ca*.1713, with several modern handwritten transcriptions. (The transcriptions are arguably less easy to read than the originals.)

Peter MUNSTEDT. *John Playford, Music Publisher.* Ph. D. dissertation, University of Kentucky, 1983.   **665**
An overview of the activity of the most important music publisher of the day.

D. Ross HARVEY. *Henry Playford: A Bibliographical Study.* Ph. D. dissertation, Victoria University of Wellington (N. Z.), 1985.   **666**
A biographical account with bibliographical citations and transcriptions of archival sources.

Playford's dominant role in music publishing is such as to require anyone working in this period also to know the work on Playford by Margaret Dean-Smith and Nicholas Temperley, notably the latter's "John Playford and the Metrical Psalms," *Journal of the American Musicological Society*, 25 (1972), 331-78.

Eighteenth Century

W. H. Grattan FLOOD. "Music-Printing in Dublin from 1700-1750," *Journal of the Royal Society of Antiquaries of Ireland*, 38 (1908), 236-40.   **667**
A lecture, read May 26th, 1908, which identifies the main names.
    The author has expanded this essay in "Dublin Music Printing from 1685 to 1750," *Bibliographical Society of Ireland*, vol. 2, no. 1 (1921), pp. 7-12, and "Dublin Music Printing from 1750-1790," vol. 2, no. 5 (1923), 101-196.

William C. SMITH. *A Bibliography of the Musical Works Published by John Walsh during the Years 1695-1720.* London: Bibliographical Society, 1948.
— and Charles HUMPHRIES. *A Bibliography of the Musical Works Published by the Firm of John Walsh during the Years 1721-1766. ibid.,* 1968.   **668**
Walsh's shop produced a large share of the music printed in London between 1695 and 1766, making these two lists virtually tantamount to a British national music bibliography of the

period. The former cites 622 entries, arranged chronologically (undated imprints are located mostly through newspaper references), while the latter lists 1,564 entries, alphabetically by composer, in the absence of datable notices and transcripts.

Excluded from both volumes are the Handel editions, which are cited, along with editions by other 18th-century publishers, in Smith's 1960 Handel catalogue (621).

Also subsumed in or related to these lists are such articles as Smith's "John Walsh, Music Publisher: The First Twenty-Five Years," *The Library*, 5th series, 1 (1946-47), 1-5; "John Walsh and His Successors," *ibid.*, 3 (1948-49), 291-95; and "New Evidence Concerning John Walsh and the Duties on Paper, 1726," *Harvard Library Bulletin*, 6 (1952), 252-55.

William C. SMITH. "The Meaning of the Imprint," *The Library*, 5th series, 7 (1952), 62.   **669**
Stimulated by an essay by Allen T. Hazen, "One Meaning of the Imprint," *ibid.*, 6 (1951), 120-23, Smith suggests some of the circumstances specified in early 18th-century musical editions. See further in Hunter's 1991 essay (674), pp. 674-80.

Michael TILMOUTH. "A Note on the Cost of Music Printing in London in 1702," *Brio*, 8 (1971), 1-3.   **670**
Examination of an account of payments by Wriothesley, Second Duke of Bedford, to Thomas Cross, for the engraving of Nicola Cosimi's *Twelve Sonatas*.

See also David Hunter, "'A Note on the Cost of Music Printing in London in 1702' Revisited," *Brio*, 26 (1989), 71-72.

H. Edmund POOLE. "Music Engraving Practice in Eighteenth-Century London: A Study of Some Forster Editions of Haydn and their Manuscript Sources," in *Music and Bibliography: Essays in Honour of Alec Hyatt King* (London: Clive Bingley, 1980), pp. 98-131.   **671**
A reconstruction of the various activities in producing a musical edition. Working from the evidence, mostly in extant copies, the author builds persuasive arguments regarding the planning for the layout, the financing, the materials, and the engraving.

David HUNTER. "The Publication and Dating of an Early Eighteenth-Century English Song Book," *Bodleian Library Record*, 11 (1984), 231-40.   **672**
A discussion of the extant copies of *A Collection of the Choicest Songs & Dialogues*, a collection mostly of single song sheets also issued separately, assembled as a discrete edition by John Walsh in London, *ca*.1704, but subsequently altered in its contents so as to function as a "nonce" publication.

—. "Music Copyright in Britain to 1800," *Music and Letters*, 67 (1986), 269-82.   **673**
The complications of royal privileges to favored composers in the 18th century, and the extension of copyright protection to engraved editions in a period dominated by a book trade that worked primarily with letterpress editions.

The topic is a rich one, worth still further study in spite of a large literature, which includes John A. Parkinson, "Pirates and Publishers," *Performing Right*, 58 (1972), 20-22; and, on a celebrated controversy, Hunter's *"Pope* v. *Bickham*: An Infringement of *An Essay on Man* Alleged," *The Library*, 6th series, 9 (1987), 268-73, and Nancy Valpy, "Plagiarism in Prints: The 'Musical Entertainer' Affair," *Print Quarterly*, 6 (1989), 54-59.

—. *English Opera and Song Books, 1703-1726: Their Contents, Publishing, Printing, and Bibliographical Description.* Ph.D. dissertation, University of Illinois, 1989.   **674**
The basic study of the anthologies of the early engraved song-sheet era. Out of this work the author has developed several studies: "The Printing of Opera and Song Books in England, 1703-1726," Music Library Association, *Notes*, 46 (1989), 328-51; "Bibliographical Description of Opera and Song Books Issued in England, 1703-1726," *Papers of the Bibliographical Society of America*, 83 (1989), 311-35, with observations on the suitability of accommodating music within the classic framework of descriptive bibliography, in matters of title-page transcription, pagination statement, the concept of ideal copy, and bibliographical classification (edition, impression, issue, state); and "The Publishing of Opera and Song Books in England, 1703-1726," Music Library Association, *Notes*, 47 (1991), 647-85.

NINETEENTH AND TWENTIETH CENTURIES

[Series of 74 articles on contemporary music publishers], *Musical Opinion*, 1895-1942. **675**
The series falls into 4 parts: (1) 21 brief accounts by Arthur Pearson and others, 1895-1924; (2) 17 additional accounts by Charles G. Mortimer and others, 1938-40, entitled "Leading Music Publishers"; (3) Florian Williams, "After Forty Years: Recollections of a Music Publisher," in 23 parts, 1940-41, on the Joseph Williams firm; and (4) 13 brief accounts of other major British firms of the day, 1941-42, entitled "The Music Publisher of Tradition," by Arthur Pearson and others.

Percy H. MUIR. "Thomas Moore's Irish Melodies, *The Colophon*, vol. 15, no. 8 (1933), pp. 1-16. **676**
An early exploration of bibliographical variants in music. The set was issued in parts (1808-34) and marketed as literature, as music, and as nationalistic folklore scholarship, following George Thomson's precedent. Bibliographers are drawn to the set because it includes letterpress texts, engraved music, and pictorial engravings; because it was issued in fascicles over a period of many years, by the Power brothers in Dublin and London, who did not always agree with their contributors or with each other; and because the set was also pirated.

The *Notes from the Letters of Thomas Moore to his Music Publisher, James Power (their Publication Suppressed in London), with an Introductory Letter by Thomas Crofton Croker* (New York: Redfield, 1854) is neither scandalous, nor particularly interesting.

Cecil HOPKINSON and C. B. OLDMAN. "Thomson's Collections of National Song, with Special Reference to the Contributions of Haydn and Beethoven," *Transactions of the Edinburgh Bibliographical Society*, vol. 3, part 1 (Session 1938-39; issued 1940), pp. 3-24. **677**
A detailed examination of the publishing circumstances, followed by a thematic catalogue (pp. 25-64).

This text is often cited under the caption heading on p. 3, "Haydn and Beethoven in Thomson's Collections."

A brief list of "Addenda et Corrigenda" appears in vol. 3, part 2 (Sessions 1949-50, 1950-51; issued 1954), pp. 123-24, preceded by the authors' sequel, "Haydn's Settings of Scottish Songs in the Collections of Napier and Whyte," pp. 87-97, with thematic catalogues on pp. 98-120.

O. W. NEIGHBOUR and Alan TYSON. *English Music Publishers' Plate Numbers in the First Half of the Nineteenth Century.* London: Faber & Faber, 1965.   **678**
Lists for 25 firms suggest the uses and limitations of plate numbers.

John Francis WILBRAHAM. *Music Publishing in London during the Period 1800-1850.* M. A. thesis, University of Sheffield, 1977.   **679**
A narrative account, developed out of Humphries and Smith, with selected illustrations.

Michael HURD. *Vincent Novello — and Company.* London: Granada, 1981.   **680**
A pleasant account of Victorian England's most famous music publisher and one of the century's notable families. A number of earlier writings are in the same spirit, including *A Short History of Cheap Music* (1887) and *A Century and a Half in Soho* (1961), both isssued by the Novello firm, the former prepared by Joseph Bennett, the latter by Laurence Swinyard. Recent scholarly studies include Victoria Cooper-Deathridge, "The Novello Stockbook of 1858-1869: A Chronicle of Publishing Activity," Music Library Association, *Notes*, 44 (1987), 240-51.

D. W. KRUMMEL. "Music Publishing," in Nicholas Temperley, *Music in Britain: The Romantic Age* (London: Athlone, 1981), 46-59.   **681**
Summarizes trends in the proliferating output, the rise of performance rights, and the specialization of repertory.

James B. COOVER. *Music Publishing, Copyright, and Piracy in Victorian England: A Twenty-Five Year Chronicle, 1881-1906.* London: Mansell, 1985.   **682**
The *Musical Opinion & Music Trade Review* (558 above) serves to detail the circumstances of music publishers and the events

that led up to the Copyright Act of 1906, which "finished the pirates" (p. 141).

—. "The Dispersal of Engraved Music Plates and Copyrights in British Auctions, 1831-1891," in *Richard S. Hill: Tributes from Friends* (Detroit: Information Coordinators, 1987; Detroit Studies in Music Bibliography, 58), pp. 223-306.   **683**

An account of the "plate auctions," through which music publishers transferred to other members of the trade those copyrights, engraved plates, and/or copies of particular titles that they saw as superfluous. The plate auction seems to have been a distinctive London institution; most of the nearly 200 sales date from the 1860s up to just prior to World War I. Some of the auction catalogues cited here also appear in the title below.

—. *Music at Auction: Puttick and Simpson (of London), 1794-1971, Being an Annotated, Chronological List of Sales of Musical Materials . . . .* Warren, Mich.: Harmonie Park Press, 1988 (Detroit Studies in Music Bibliography, 60).

A list of 1,650 auction sales, with detailed analysis of the changing tastes that are reflected in the properties offered and the prices fetched. There is some overlap with the title above. This book also covers the transactions involving "music scores, manuscripts, books about music, portraits, documents, and letters relating to music and musicians, [and] musical instruments (keyboard, string, wind, percussion, and mechanical)," but its references to particular titles rarely include prices.   **684**

Many other writings on British topics are cited elsewhere in this book. Chapter 3, for instance, covers writings on English printing, among them several general manuals, patent registrations (381 above), and guides to the premises — notably those of D'Almaine and of Lowe & Brydone (193, 229) — as well as Gamble's treatise on music printing (240). English music typography is also documented in an array of specimen books, from the major forms of Fell, Caslon, Fry, Figgins, and Shanks (pp. 116-34 *passim.*), among others, as well as in a lineage of notable histories and bibliographies (296-98) and records of British crafts groups (385-87). London has hosted a number of impressive music printing exhibitions, beginning in the Victorian era. English cover-illustration is traced in studies by Imeson (453) and others, King notably. The fine-printing tradition of the Morris and Cobden-Sanderson era is reflected in the *Yattendon Hymnal* (929), also in the critical writings of Hubert Foss on graphic design (396, and elsewhere). Among the writings on composers' relationships with English publishers are Tyson on Beethoven (595), Brown on Chopin (609); and two books on Elgar (614-15). King's study of music bibliophily (918) also reflects a strong British predilection.

The growing literature on British music as a social institution, has increasingly recognized the role of publishers. Examples range from the popular to the scholarly, and include Leslie Marsh, "The Price of a Song," *Punch*, November 2, 1959, pp. 23-26; and Rosamond McGuinness, "Music and the Press: Songs for Sale," *Eighteenth Century Life*, 12 (1988), 139-48, also her "The Music Business in Early Eighteenth-Century London," *Quarterly Journal of Social Affairs*, 1 (1985), 249-59. J. H. Plumb's 1972 Stenton Lecture, *The Commercialisation of Leisure in Eighteenth-Century England* (Reading: University of Reading, 1973), adds little to the record of music publishing, apart from its title, although that is perhaps enough.

Further references will be found under in other sources under the names of British printers and publishers, of whom the following are among the most important:

1495-1700

WESTMINSTER					
1495	Wynkyn de Worde	1599	Morley	1683	Heptinstall
		1603	Adams	1687	Moore
LONDON		1604	H. Lownes	1688	Jones
		1608	Snodham	1695	Hare
1520s	Rastell	1610	Allde	1695	Walsh
1530s	Gough	1611	Stansby	1699	Pearson
1544	Grafton	?1612	Wm. Hole	1699	Young
1553	Seres	1612	M. Lownes		
1562	Day	1650	Harper	*ABERDEEN*	
1570	Vautrollier	1650	Playford	1662	Forbes
1575	Tallis & Byrd	1656	Godbid	*DUBLIN*	
1587	East	1681	J. Carr	1686	Thornton
1592	Windet	1679	Hudgebut		
1596	Barley	1679	N. Thompson	*EDINBURGH*	
1597	Short	1683	Cross	?1611	Hart (Andro)

1700-1920

BRIGHTON					
1874	Chester	1726	Watts	1811	Novello
	(1915: London)	1727	Cooke	1815	Keith
		1734	Simpson	1816	Boosey
DUBLIN		1736	Fortier	1816	Metzler
1721	Neale	?1737	Bickham	1818	Regent's (Royal)
1740s	Manwaring	1737	Roberts		Harmonic In-
?1750	Rhames	1738	B. Cole		stitution
1752	Lee	1740	John Johnson	1818	Williams
1795	M. Hime	1740	Phillips	1820	Paterson
1802	Wm. Power	1746	Thompson	1823	Cocks
1807	Holden	1760	Forster	1823	Ewer
1825	Bunting	1762	Bremner	1823	Knight
		1762	Welcker	1824	Cramer
EDINBURGH		1766	Randall	1824	Wessel
1736	Oswald	1766	Skillern	1827	Cowper
	(1741: London)	1767	Fougt	1833	Coventry & Hol-
1757	Bremner	1767	Longman &		lier
1772	James Johnson		Broderip	1842	Jullien
1779	Corri	1770	Preston	1842	Leader & Cock
	(1790: London)	1772	Napier	1844	Davidson
1791	George Thomson	1776	J. Bland	1858	Augener
?1807	Penson,	1779	Harrison	1860	Ashdown
	Robertson	1783	Birchall	1863	Curwen
1809	Purdie	1783	Dale	1866	Hutchings &
?1819	Paterson	1783	Wright & Wil-		Romer
			kinson	1873	Lucas (Stanley)
GLASGOW		1784	Bland & Weller		& Weber
1778	Aird	1786	Goulding	1877	Francis, Day &
1848	Muir Wood	1787	Monzani		Hunter
		1796	Lavenu	1880	Murdoch
LIVERPOOL		1798	Clementi	1892	Lowe & Brydone
1785	H. & M. Hime	1805	Button & Whit-	1893	Lengnick
			aker	1904	Harris
LONDON		1805	Purday	1906	Ascherberg
1709	D. Wright	1807	Power	1907	Stainer & Bell
1713	Meares	1808	J. Williams	1920	Associated
?1720	Cluer	1810	Chappell		Board ...
1727	Cooke				

B. France

French music printing, like French culture in general, has been dominated by Paris, beginning in the 1520s by Attaingnant, later briefly by du Chemin, then for nearly two centuries by the Ballards. The studies of these printers' work — by Heartz on Attaingnant, and Lesure and Thibault on later firms for the early (and best) part of the Ballard era, along with that of Pogue and Guillo on the activity in Lyons — thus cover most of the country's early production. The seventeenth-century activity is poorly explored, perhaps in part because the events are unexciting, appropriate to an age of effective monopoly. In contrast, the work of Devriès for the early eighteenth century, and of Brenet and Cucuel for later years, suggests that this century is more exciting for bibliographers. For the later years Johansson is essential. The directories by Hopkinson and by Devriès and Lesure cover the rest of the history; the latter in particular helps to recognize the rich tradition of French Romantic and post-Romantic music publishing.

BIBLIOGRAPHIES AND DIRECTORIES

Ernest COYECQUE. *Inventaire de la collection Anisson sur l'histoire de l'imprimerie et la librairie, principalement à Paris.* Paris: Ernest Leroux, 1900.   **685**
A guide to the manuscripts and printed materials assembled by Étienne-Alexandre-Jacques Anisson-Dupérron (1748-94, director of the Imprimerie Royale prior to his decapitation). The vast collection, now in the Bibliothèque Nationale (Mss. Fr. 22061-22193), includes documents on the Ballard privilege (vol. 1, pp. 174-76) and on punch cutters and type founders (vol. 2, pp. 80-83), some for music type. The studies of Brenet and Cucuel below are largely based on this collection.

Cecil HOPKINSON. *A Dictionary of Parisian Music Publishers, 1700-1950.* London: Printed for the Author, 1954. **686**
A directory, valuable in supporting much of the intensive work on French music publishing over the subsequent generation, now largely superseded by Devriès and Lesure.
Reprinted, New York: Da Capo, 1979, with a new introduction by Jacques Barzun.

Anik DEVRIÈS and François LESURE. *Dictionnaire des Éditeurs de musique français.* Genève: Minkoff, 1979-88 (Archives de l'édition musicale française, 4).   **687**
A monumental bibliographical *vade mecum*, rich and definitive in particulars (firm names, street addresses, plate numbers, etc.).

"Volume 1" ("des origines à environ 1820") is actually in two physical books, the first a directory (alas, oddly lacking the letter A), the second an anthology of catalogues (219 facsimiles of over 50 publishers, complementing Johansson below). As for "Volume 2" ("de 1820 à 1914"), of few works can one say so respectfully: this work truly deserves to be used to be appreciated.

The activity outside of Paris (cf. vol. 2, pp. 433-71) is also described in Lesure's "Ébauche d'un repertoire des éditeurs de musique dans les provinces françaises," in *Beiträge zur Musikdokumentation: Franz Grasberger zum 60. Geburtstag* (Tutzing: Hans Schneider, 1975), pp. 233-58.

DOCUMENTS AND ACCOUNTS

Arrêt du Conseil d'État du Roi, qui établit un Bureau de Timbre pour la Musique. Du 15 September 1786. Paris: Imprimerie Royale, 1786.   **688**
A list of 25 conditions, extracted from the Council's registers, intended to control the output of the music press.

Michel BRENET [*pseud.* of Marie Bobillier]. "La librairie musicale en France de 1653 à 1790, d'aprés les registres de privilèges," *Sammelbände der Internationalen Musikgesellschaft*, 8 (1906-07), 401-66.   **689**
Transcripts of several hundred privileges in Bibliothèque Nationale Mss. Fr. 16742 and 21944-71, with an introduction and many reference footnotes.

Georges CUCUEL. "Quelques documents sur la librairie musicale au XVIIIe siècle," *Sammelbände der Internationalen Musikgesellschaft*, 13 (1911-12), 385-92.   **690**
A continuation of Brenet, which extracts nearly a hundred more citations from Mss. Fr. 21995-22002, from the years 1726-83.

—. "Notes sur quelques musiciens, luthiers, éditeurs et graveurs de musique au XVIIIe siècle," *Sammelbände der Internationalen Musikgesellschaft*, 14 (1912-13), 243-52. **691**
Notes on eleven persons, of whom Mme Castagnery, Moria, and the Siebers are bibiographically important.

Élisabeth LEBEAU. "Le timbre fiscal de la musique en feuilles de 1797 à 1840," *Revue de musicologie*, 24 (1945), 20-28.   **692**
Discusses the duties on sheet music, with reproductions of twelve authorization stamps between pp. 24 and 25.

François LESURE and Geneviève THIBAULT. "Bibliographie des éditions musicales publiées par Nicolas du Chemin," *Annales musicologiques*, 1 (1953), 269-373.   **693**
A listing of the output of the major French publisher of the years around 1550, between the decline of Attaingnant and the rise of LeRoy and Ballard.
Supplements, *ibid.*, 4 (1956), 251-53, and 6 (1958-63), 403-06.

Cari JOHANSSON. *French Music Publishers' Catalogues of the Second Half of the Eighteenth Century.*   Stockholm: Almquist & Wiksell, 1955.   **694**
An analysis of the rise and changes of the modern French music trade, reflected in the "plate catalogues" that were commonly appended to editions of the day. Subsequent studies testify that this work had obviously captured the imagination of music bibliographers, beginning with my own inventory of Library of Congress holdings (*Fontes artis musicae*, 7, 1960, 61-64), and continuing with Brook and Benton (below), as well as Weinmann on Huberty (800, no. 7), Larsen (145), and the facsimiles in vol. 1 of the Devriès and Lesure directory (687).

François LESURE and Geneviève THIBAULT. *Bibliographie des Éditions d'Adrian Le Roy et Robert Ballard, 1551-1598.* Paris: Heugel, 1955.   **695**
Le Roy and Ballard having secured the monopoly for music printing in France, the story of their firm over the next two hundred years is mostly that of the whole country; their list of titles is virtually a national French music bibliography. This study lists the 319 known editions, with detailed citations, locations, and contents, and includes transcripts of the major early documents and indexes the incipits, titles, and personal names.
The music printing done outside the monopoly is naturally interesting for this fact alone, as evidence not so much of dissent but of commercial enterprise, and occasionally of musical tastes.

During the late 16th century these are mostly Calvinist psalm-books and other provincial repertories; during the 17th century the engravings of instrumental music are much more spectacular, both in their own right and as they suggest the increasingly pernicious influence of the monopoly.

Barry S. BROOK. *La symphonie française dans la seconde moitié du XVIIIe siècle*. Paris: Université de Paris, Institut de Musicologie, 1962. **696**

In the course of this wide-ranging doctoral dissertation (Paris, 1962), the author explores many bibliographical sidelines, notably in discussing "L'édition musical" (vol. 1, pp. 36-43).

Reprint (Stuyvesant, N.Y.: Pendragon) announced, 1990.

Daniel HEARTZ. *Pierre Attaingnant, Royal Printer of Music: A Historical Study and Bibliographical Catalogue*. Berkeley: University of California Press, 1969. **697**

One of the most impressive of all music bibliography studies, rich in its exploration of all aspects of the topic (with a convenient survey of music printing throughout Europe, pp. 139-68), and handsomely printed.

Of Heartz's several earlier articles on Ataingnant, "La chronologie des recueils imprimés par Pierre Attaingnant," *Revue de musicologie*, 44 (1959), 176-92, includes a chart that is still valuable as an overview of Attaingnant's production.

Samuel F. POGUE. *Jacques Moderne, Lyons Music Printer of the Sixteenth Century*. Genève: Droz, 1969. **698**

Moderne's editions are impressive to look at, and we are led to believe that "grand Jacques" was, too (although, for all of Pogue's good work, it is not clear why he was regarded as great).

Pogue's "A Sixteenth-Century Editor at Work: Gardano and Moderne," *Journal of Musicology*, 1 (1982), 217-38, explores some of the ways in which the same music was presented in different ways by the two shops.

Anik DEVRIÈS. *Édition et commerce de la musique gravée à Paris dans la première moitié du XVIIIe siècle: Les Boivin, Les Leclerc*. Genève: Minkoff, 1976 (Archives de l'édition musicale française, 1). **699**

An account, based on archival sources, of the events through which the Ballard monopoly for typographic printing came to be supplanted by publishers who issued engraved music.
Also a dissertation (Paris, École Pratique des Hautes Études).

Élisabeth FAU. "La gravure de musique à Paris des origines à la Révolution, 1660-1789." Dissertation, École nationale des Chartes (Paris), 1978.   **700**
[*ABHBL*, 1979, no. 3141; see also the *Positions des thèses soute-nues des élèves de la promotion de 1978 pour obtenir le diplôme d'archiviste-paléographe* (Paris, 1978), pp. 47-58.]

Rita BENTON. "Pleyel as Music Publisher," *Journal of the American Musicological Society*, 32 (1979), 125-40.   **701**
Surveys the publishing activity, by way of complementing Ben-ton's study of Pleyel's music in *Ignace Pleyel: A Thematic Cata-logue of His Compositions* (New York: Pendragon, 1977), and supplementing the indexes of the firm's output in *Pleyel as Music Publisher: A Documentary Sourcebook of Early 19th-Century Music* (with Jeanne Halley. Stuyvesant, N.Y.: Pendragon, 1990).

Hans LENNEBERG. "Music Publishing and Dissemination in the Early Nineteenth Century: Some Vignettes," *Jour-nal of Musicology*, 2 (1983), 174-83.   **702**
An exploration based on conjectural prices, sales figures, and press runs of Schlesinger's Paris editions in the 1830s, with a view to understanding the economics of music publishing.

Laurent GUILLO. *Recherches sur les éditions musicales lyonnaises de la Renaissance.* Dissertation, École Pratique des Hautes Études (Paris), 1986.   **703**
Cited in the author's "Notes sur la librairie musicale à Lyons et Genève au XVIIᵉ siècle," *Fontes artis musicae*, 36 (1989), 116-35, which includes a brief overview followed by a short-title list of several hundred titles (pp. 123-33), based on 22 contemporary catalogues and inventories. The dissertation and the article will presumably both be subsumed in the author's forthcoming book on musical life and music printing in Lyons.

Anik DEVRIÈS. "La 'musique à bon marché' en France dans les années 1830," in Peter Bloom, *Music in Paris in the Eighteen-Thirties* (Stuyvesant, N.Y.: Pendragon, 1987; Musical Life in Nineteenth-Century France, 4), pp. 229-50. On the efforts to produce cheap music, suggesting why these were less successful in this decade than in the 1840s.   **704**

Samuel F. POGUE. "The Earliest Music Printing in France," *Huntington Library Quarterly*, 50 (1987), 35-57.   **705**
On the books known, or likely, to have been printed in Lyons in the 1520s, prior to the time of Moderne.

The literature on French music printing begins with the typographical accounts of the families Le Bé (308), Fournier (44, 165), and Gando (168). The technical accounts of Jaugeon (161) and in the *Encyclopédie* (166), as well as in the French patent specifications (380), attest to an imaginative concern for technology. Barber (155-56) describes the early manuals; later landmarks include three *Manuels-Roret* (186, 200, 218). Audin and Howe (299) describe the specimens, among which Duverger's (184) is of particular interest. Weckerlin's 1864 survey (45) emphasizes this French contribution to the history, as do Guégan (50) and several others.

The French literature generally seems to approach the descriptive task with a sense of argument, more so than most of its English and German counterparts, for which description is itself the more important goal. One thinks here of Weckerlin (45) and, perhaps most of all, Audin (e.g., 124 in particular), as well as of Robert's book on music engraving (222), and of several writers on music publishing. Durand (532), Bertrand (536), and Castelain (537) are among the few authors who have been so bold as to write on the topic in general, naturally reflecting Gallic tastes. Farrenc (908) and Curzon (911) on music collecting, and the several nineteenth-century international exhibitions, cited in Chapter 4, embody a spirit of connoisseurship — a spirit that may also serve to explain (if anything should) Satie's delight in the graphic arts (930 below). The same penchant for the pictorial statement also informs the worlds both of cover illustrations, its literature extending from Grand-Carteret (444) through Stahly (478), and of printed musical ephemera (513 on posters being an example).

Further writings will be found in other sources under the names of particular French printers and publishers, of whom the following are among the most important:

1481-1700

AVIGNON
1531   Channey

CAEN
1562   Mangeant

GENEVA
1537   Du Boys
1550   Davantes
1553   Du Bosc
1570   Goulart
1582   Jean II de Laon

LA ROCHELLE
1572   Haultin

LYONS
1525   Du Ry
1532   Moderne
1542   Du Boys
1547   Beringen
1550   Gorlier
1555   Guéroult
1559   Granjon
1572   Tournes

PARIS
1481   Du Pré
1489   Higman

?1496   Michel de
          Toulouse
1490s? Guerson
1527   Attaingnant
1549   Du Chemin
1551   Le Roy &
          Ballard (1591:
          Ballard alone)
1551   Fezandat
1551   Granjon
1671   Bonneuil
1690   Baussen
1690   Foucault

1700-1920

LYONS
?1776   Guéra

PARIS
1704   Ribou
1721   Boivin
1728   J.-P. Le Clerc
1736   C.-N. Le Clerc
1740s   Le Menu
1762   Mme Castagneri
1755   Venier
?1756   Huberty
1758   La Chevardiére
1760s   Bailleux
1760s   Cousineau
1765   Bureau d'Abon-
          nement Musical
?1771   Sieber
1772   Lemoine
1773   Heina
1775   Leduc
1777   Nadermann

1783   Imbault
1794   Magasin de Mus-
          ique (Fêtes
          Nationales)
1795   Pleyel
?1802   Érard
1802   Magasin de Mu-
          sique (Chéru-
          bini et al)
1802   Isouard (Nicolò)
1805   Carli
1805   Choron
1808   Pacini
1810   Janet & Cotelle
1811   Frey
1816   Richault
1820s   Farrenc
1821   Schlesinger
1825   Troupenas
1830   Schonenberger
1839   Heugel
1841   A. Leduc

1842   Escudier
1844   Choudens
1846   Brandus
1847   Flaxland
1851   Maho
1866   Hartmann
1869   Durand,
          Schoenewerk
1877   Hamelle
1885?   Fromont
1894   Salabert
1895   Costallat
1897   Joubert
1905   Rouart-Lerolle
1907   Eschig
1908   Senart
1918   Éditions de
          la Sirène
1920   Éditions Russes
          (earlier in Ber-
          lin, Moscow)

C. Italy

In no other country does the history of music printing and publishing range from stimulating exuberance to cheerless dormancy.
The events begin with liturgical and theoretical incunabula, widely

scattered in their auspices. They continue with the romantic stories of the heroic Petrucci, the convoluted relationships between Antico and his associates, and the prolific Gardano (Gardane) and Scotto firms. Thanks to these printers, Venice was by 1600 the center of music publishing in all of Europe. The seventeenth-century decline is painful to recognize, as is the virtual absence of any activity at all in the eighteenth. The revival in the nineteenth century is built around the operatic world of Milan, with the name of Ricordi in the spotlight. Reconstruction of the bibliographical record of this activity has taken place both at home and abroad — Italy has never lacked for ardent friends. Often it also seems that the personal motivations behind Italian music publishers have occupied scholarly attention more than those of their counterparts from other countries — perhaps because we take pleasure in identifying them as the protagonists in Verdi operas.

REFERENCE SOURCES

Associazione Editoria Libraria Italiana. *Elenco degli editori, librai, e negozianti di musica d'Italia.* Milano: Associazione tipografico-libraria italiana, 1910. **706**
Includes statutes of the general Italian printers' and publishers' association (pp. 7-14), and of the Associazione Italiana degli Editori e Negozianti di Musica (pp. 15-21), followed by a directory of about 4000 (!) names, arranged by city and mentioning the specialities for the larger firms. At the end are names of "Principali librerie dell'estero," about 100 from areas on the Italian periphery (pp. 237-39), and about 200 more from the rest of the world (pp. 241-52). The latter is a very strange assortment.

Claudio SARTORI. *Dizionario degli editori musicali italiani.* Firenze: Olschki, 1958 (Biblioteca di bibliografia italiana, 18). **707**
This directory confirms the historical trends: of the several hundred names that appear in Italian music imprints, many are from the 15th and 16th centuries, fewer from the 17th, next to none from the 18th, but many from the 19th and 20th.

Oscar MISCHIATI. *Indici, cataloghi e avvisi degli editori e librai musicali italiani dal 1591 al 1798.* Firenze: Olschki, 1984. **708**

Transcriptions of about 50 catalogues, 1591-1798, with lists of contents indexed by composer and title. An imposing work, for which Sartori's *Notes* essay (26) is a precedent.

HISTORICAL STUDIES

Anne-Marie BAUTIER-REGNIER. "L'Édition musicale italienne et les musiciens d'outremonts au XVIe siècle (1501-1563)," in François Lesure, *La Renaissance dans les provinces du nord* (Paris: Éditions du Centre national de la recherche scientifique, 1956), pp. 27-49.   **709**
On the Italian printers, from Petrucci through early Gardane and Scotto, who issued the music of Transalpine composers.

James HAAR. "The *Libro primo* of Costanza Festa," *Acta musicologica*, 52 (1980), 147-55.   **710**
One of the first Italian single-impression music books, without imprint, proves to be datable from 1538.

Donna G. CARDAMONE. *"Madrigali a tre et arie napolitane*: A Typographical and Repertorial Study," *Journal of the American Musicological Society*, 35 (1982), 436-81. **711**
A formidable attempt to clarify the publishing circumstances of an elusive late-1530s partbook from southern Italy. Dorico type was used, but the book was probably not printed in Rome.

Tim CARTER. "Music Publishing in Italy, c.1580 – c. 1625: Some Preliminary Observations," Royal Musical Association, *Research Chronicle*, 20 (1986-87), 19-37.   **712**
A well-reasoned overview of changing tastes, supported with interesting statistical data, most of them shown in charts. Useful in their own right, the observations are amplified in the author's writings on Florentine music publishing (718-19 below).

LOCAL AND REGIONAL STUDIIES

Bologna

Francesco VATIELLI. "Editori musicali dei secoli XVII e XVIII," in *Arte e vita musicale a Bologna: Studi e saggi* (Bologna: Nicola Zanichetti, 1927), 239-56.   **713**

On Bolognese activity originally stimulated by Venice and involving the imprints of Monti, Silvani, and Dalla Volpe.
Reprinted, Bologna: Forni, 1969.

L. GOTTARDI. *La stampa musicale in Bologna dagli inizi fino al 1700.* Dissertation, University of Bologna, 1951.
[Cited (under Micheletti) in *Grove P&P*, p. 339.]   714

Franco PIPERINO. *Gli "Eccelentissimi musici della città di Bologna," con uno studio sull'antologia madrigalistica del cinquecento.* Firenze: Olschki, 1985.   715
Includes lists of published music by Bolognese composers and authors of texts set to music, pp. 44-56.

Brescia

Maria Teresa ROSA BAREZZANI. "La musica nelle antiche stamperie bresciane," in *La musica a Brescia* (Brescia: Grafo, 1979), pp. 138-48.   716
Discusses publishers between 1490 and 1750.

Emilia-Romagna

Francesco VATIELLI. "La stampa musicale," in Domenico Fava, *Tesori delle biblioteche d'Italia: Emilia e Romagna*, vol. 1 (Milano: Ulrico Hoepli, 1932), pp. 623-34.   717
Comments on about a dozen books, 1482-1700, with seven facsimiles, in a luxurious folio volume.

Florence

Tim CARTER. "Music-Printing in Late Sixteenth and Early Seventeenth-Century Florence: Giorgio Marescotti, Cristofano Marescotti, and Zanobi Pignoni," *Early Music History*, 9 (1989), 27-72 .   718
An essay developed out of archival sources (by way of supporting the "preliminary observations" suggested in 712 above) with a list of 45 "Florentine Editions with Printed Music, 1581-1641."
See also the author's essay for the 1988 Bologna congress (40).

——. "Music-Selling in Late Sixteenth-Century Florence: The Bookshop of Piero di Giuliano Morosi," *Music and Letters*, 70 (1989), 483-504.   **719**
Reconstruction of activities, based on one of the rare known survivals of documentary evidence of an early music retailer.

Fossombrone

Writings on Petrucci's later publications are cited under Venice.

Milan

Catalogo (in ordine numerico) delle opere pubblicate dall' I. R. Stabilimento nazionale privilegiato . . . di Tito di Gio. Ricordi in Milano. . . . 1857.   **720**
The great Ricordi plate number catalogue, beginning with no. 1 in 1808 and extending through 17693 in 1845, and (in vol. 2) through 29840 in 1857. Following each number is a brief entry and price; and preceding it is the date, which is of special value for cataloguing assignments as well as in attempts to understand the operation of the shop by reconstructing the flow of work.
    Vol. 1 is reprinted in *Il catalogo numerico Ricordi 1857, con date e indici* (Roma: Nuovo istituto editoriale italiano, 1984; Bibliotheca musicae, 8; Cataloghi editoriali, 1). Philip Gossett comments on the arrangement and its fascination in his brief "Prefazione" (pp. v-xii), reprinted as "The Ricordi Numerical Catalogue: A Background," Music Library Association, *Notes*, 42 (1985), 22-28). Agostina Zecca Laterza translates it (pp. xiii-xviii) and adds useful details in a strong "Introduzione" (pp. xix-xiii). Unfortunately vol. 2 has apparently not been published.

Mariangela DONÀ. *La stampa musicale a Milano fino all'anno 1700.* Firenze: Olschki, 1961 (Biblioteca di bibliografia italiana, 39).   **721**
A list of just over 200 titles, arranged by publisher, with locations and bibliographical commentary, and transcripts of important archival documents at the end.

Claudio SARTORI. *Casa Ricordi: Profilo storico, itinerario grafico editoriale.* Milano: Ricordi, 1958.   **722**

A jubilee book honoring the Ricordi sesquicentenary. Sixteen facsimiles of musical autographs suggest the firm's dealings with composers, while 32 color reproductions, mostly of illustrated covers of important works, provide evidence of Ricordi's well-deserved reputation for graphic design.

Preceding this work is the volume prepared by Ricordi for the 1892 Vienna exhibition (418), no less impressive in its monochromatic printing.

Musica, musicisti, editoria: 175 anni di casa Ricordi, 1808-1983. Milano: Ricordi, 1983.   **723**

An updated successor to the 1892 and 1958 books, more lavish and presumably costlier (e.g., the introductory statement is by Herbert von Karajan, and there are nearly 300 color illustrations). Fewer than 30 pages are given over to prose, but it is mostly well done, notably by Francesco Degrada on the historic opera firm ("Il segno e il suono," pp. 11-25), Maria Pia Ferraris on the graphic design of the covers (pp. 192-95), Mario Luzzatto Fegis on recent pop music (pp. 232-37), and Giorgio Fioravanti on music printing technology (pp. 260-67).

An English version was also issued simultaneously, entitled *Music, Musicians, and Publishers,* translated by Gabrielle Dotto, Anna Herklotz, and Kaye Singleton. (The Italian edition seems to be more widely available, however.)

Agostina ZECCA LATERZA. "Milanese Music Publishers in the First Half of the Nineteenth Century," *Fontes artis musicae,* 32 (1985), 80-81.   **724**

Summary observations on Ricordi and his associates.

Naples

Ulisse PROTA-GIURLEO. "Le prima calcografia musicale a Napoli," *L'arte pianistica,* anno 10, no. 11 (1 Novembre 1923), pp. 4-6.   **725**

On the Marescalchi controversy in the 1780s.

Angelo POMPILIO. "Editoria musicale a Napoli e in Italia nel cinque-seicento," in Lorenzo Bianconi and Renato Bossa, *Musica e cultura a Napoli dal XV al XIX secolo*

(Firenze: Olschki, 1983. Quaderni della rivista italiana di musicologia, 9), pp. 79-102.   **726**

The coverage of Italy in general is broad and statistical; that for Naples itself is specific and closely reasoned, and complemented by a "Cronologia delle edizioni musicali napoletane del cinque-seicento" (pp. 103-39) by Keith A. Larson and Pompilio.

Padua

Antonio GARBELOTTO. "Anche di musica pubblico: la ti-pografia del seminario di Padova," in *Libri e stampatori in Padova: Miscellanea di studi storici in onore di Mons. G. Bellini* (Padova: Tipografia Antoniana, 1959), pp. 95-106.

A survey of activity that extends from the era of Petrucci through the 18th century.   **727**

Rome

Emilia ZANETTI. "L'Editoria musicale a Roma nel secolo XIX: avviso di una ricerca," *Nuova rivista musicale italiana*, 1984, pp. 191-99.   **728**

A survey of the mid 19th-century activity in particular.

Suzanne G. CUSICK. *Valerio Dorico, Music Printer in Six-teenth-Century Rome.* Ann Arbor; UMI Press, 1981.   **729**

Clarification of a highly convoluted chapter in music publishing history, with a bibliographical list of several dozen titles. Based on a dissertation (University of North Carolina, 1975).

Bianca Maria ANTOLINI and Annalisa BINI. *Editori e librai musicali a Roma nella prima metà dell' Ottocento.* Roma: Torre d'Orfeo, 1988 (Cataloghi di fondi musicali italiani, 8).   **730**

Strong in its explanation of the lithographic processes and evaluation of the repertory, with a list of Ratti e Cencetti imprints (pp. 143-204) and a facsimile of Pietro Alfieri's *Catalogo* (pp. 205-12).

For a preview see the authors' "Music Publishing in Rome during the 19th Century," *Fontes artis musicae*, 32 (1985), 31-32.

Giancarlo ROSTIROLLA. "L'editoria musicale a Roma nel settecento," in Bruno Cagli, *Le muse galanti: La musica a Roma nel Settecento* (Roma: Istituto della Enciclopedia italiana, 1985), pp. 121-76.   **731**
Includes transcripts of archival documents and a directory of the Roman music trades.

Turin

Stefano AJANI. "Appunto per una storia dell'editoria musicale in Torino," *Graphicus Year*, vol. 52, no. 9 (September 1971), pp. 10-15.   **732**
On early 19th-century lithography, with illustrations and an "Elenco delle edizioni musicali esposte alla mostra 'Un secolo di attività litografica in Italia,'" with 41 titles from various cities.

Umbria

Nicoletta GUIDOBALDI. "Music Publishing in Sixteenth- and Seventeenth-Century Umbria," *Early Music History*, 8 (1988), 1-36.   **733**
Well researched background on activities in Perugia (mostly of Pietro Giacomo Petrucci, active 1577-1603 and not known to have been related to Ottaviano), Assisi (on Giacomo Salvi in 1620-21), and Orvieto (1620-44, with close ties to Rome).

Venice

The literature concentrates on the work of Petrucci and of his sixteenth-century successors. Writings on the former are listed here first, followed by those on the latter. The literature on Petrucci in particular has been understandably rich, with its beginnings dating back to Anton Schmid (1, 114), soon followed by several journal articles by Angelo Catelani in the *Gazzetta musicale di Milano* and the *Monatshefte für Musikgeschichte*.

Augusto VERNARECCI. *Ottaviano de' Petrucci da Fossombrone: Inventore dei tipi mobili metallici della musica nel secolo XV*. Fossombrone: F. Monacelli, 1881.   **734**
A biographical account, based on archival sources.

The 2nd edition (Bologna: Gaetano Romagnoli, 1882, with a slightly altered title) appends a bibliography (pp. 231-72), with contents of 13 anthologies.

Gustave REESE. "The First Printed Collection of Part-Music (The Odhecaton)," *Musical Quarterly*, 20 (1934), 39-76.   **735**
A survey of earlier Petrucci scholarship, stimulated by the *Bolletino bibliografico musicale* facsimile (Milan, 1932).

Claudio SARTORI. *Bibliografia delle opere musicali stampate de Ottaviano de Petrucci*. Florence: Olschki, 1948. **736**
Petrucci scholarship has been greatly extended in recent years, in studies that combine bibliographical and musical study. Much as Helen Hewitt's scholarly edition of the *Odhecaton* (Cambridge, Mass.: Mediæval Academy of America, 1946) is the respected modern edition from which musical study will be derived, so this bibliography, in spite of its shortcomings, will likely remain the canonic version, subject to updatings. Sartori's own corrections appear in his 1958 *Dizionario* (pp. 117-20); "Nuove conclusive aggiunte alla 'Bibliografia del Petrucci,'" in *Collectanea historiae musicae* (Firenze: Olschki, 1953), 175-210; also "Il 'povre omo,' Ottaviano Petrucci da Fossombrone, 'primo inventore' della stampa musicale," in *Commemorazione di Ottaviano de' Petrucci: Conferenza tenuta in Fossombrone, il 16 ottobre 1966* (Fossombrone: Città di Fossombrone; Bartola & Andri, [1967]), 9-27.

Stanley BOORMAN. *Petrucci at Fossombrone: A Study of Early Music Printing*. Ph.D. dissertation, London University, 1976.   **737**
Meticulously assembled arguments suggest how Petrucci managed his press, and what this may tell us about the music itself.
    Boorman's "Petrucci's Typesetters and the Process of Stemmatics," in *Formen und Probleme der Überlieferung mehrstimmiger Musik im Zeitalter Josquins Desprez* (München: Kraus, 1981; Wolfenbütteler Forschungen, 6), pp. 245-80, covers some of the same material and is generally more readily accessible. For a closer study of Petrucci's monumental first opus, see his "The 'First' Edition of the *Odhecaton A*," *Journal of the American Musicological Society*, 30 (1977), 183-207. See also his "Pe-

trucci at Fossombrone: Some New Editions and Cancels," in *Source Materials and Interpretation of Music: A Memorial Volume to Thurston Dart* (London: Stainer & Bell, 1981), pp. 129-53; and other titles cited in 132 above.

Richard J. AGEE. *The Privilege and Venetian Music Printing in the Sixteenth Century.* Ph.D. dissertation, Princeton University, 1982.   **738**
The basic study of the proprietary practices controlling the most fertile music publishing activity of the Renaissance. See also Agee's "The Venetian Privilege and Venetian Music-Printing in the Sixteenth Century," *Early Music History,* 3 (1983), 1-42.

—. "A Venetian Music Printing Contract and Edition Size in the Sixteenth Century," *Studi musicali,* 15 (1986), 59-65.
A survey of the evidence of press runs from the years 1516-1600, which range from 12 to 1,500 copies, based on ten extant records, including a newly-located Scotto document of 1565.

For the notable earlier discussion of the question of the size of press runs, see François Lesure, "Pour une sociologie historique des faits musicaux," in the International Musicological Society, *Report of the Eighth Congress, New York, 1961* (Kassel: Bärenreiter, 1961), vol. 2, pp. 341-43.   **739**

Jane A. BERNSTEIN. "The Burning Salamander: Assigning a Printer to Some 16th-Century Music Prints," Music Library Association, *Notes,* 42 (1985), 483-501.   **740**
Some 22 editions were issued without imprint, 1545-47, probably by Girolamo Scotto, although the arguments had not heretofore been assembled. The evidence is delightfully diverse and, if not totally conclusive, certainly persuasive. (The trip, in other words, is generally more exciting than the destination.)

Mary S. LEWIS. *Antonio Gardano, Venetian Music Printer 1538-1569: A Descriptive Bibliography and Historical Study.* New York: Garland, 1988.   **741**
A historical account of the activities between 1538 and 1549, with descriptions of the 143 anthologies (pp. 123-62) and a bibliographical list (pp. 165-666), along with detailed contents lists, extended appendixes, and indexes. (The imprint, incidentally, is

in French, as Gardane, up to 1555. The firm's early years are also clearly the most significant ones, although the Gardano imprint is seen as late as the 1680s.)

Based on a dissertation (*Antonio Gardano and his Publication of Sacred Music, 1538-55*, Brandeis University, 1979).

Italian topics are also treated in the incunabula study of Duggan (133). The indexes to the original Vogel (947) and Sartori (950) cover mostly Italian publications. Italian printing technology is identified in the work of Brogiotti in the 17th century (311), Castro in the 18th (167), Montanello in the 19th (194), and Arneudo in the 20th (232). The literature on Rossini, Verdi, and Puccini in the chapter above deals mostly with Ricordi, as do many writings on title pages: Fanelli (497) is an example. The catalogue of the 1985 Rome exhibition (440) is quite imposing.

Further references will be found in other sources under the names of Italian printers and publishers, of whom the following are among the most important:

Incunabula

MILAN		*PARMA*		*VENICE*	
1477	Pachel	1477	Moilli	1477	Giunta
1482	Valdarfer			1481	O. Scotto
1488	Zarotto	*ROME*		1482	Hamman
		1467	Han	1492	Emerich
		1482	Planck	1496	Torresani

1501-1770

BOLOGNA		*FLORENCE*		1603	Vitale
1584	Rossi	1580	Marescotti	1609	Gargano & Nucci
1627	Tebaldini	1614	Pignoni		
1639	Monti	1623	Cecconcelli	*PALERMO*	
1660	Pisarri	1739	Moücke	1592	Franceschi
1660	Silvani			*PERUGIA*	
1663	Dozza	*MILAN*		1577	P. Petrucci
1683	Micheletti	1583	Tini (1602: T.		
1720	Della Volpe		& Lomazzo)	*ROME*	
		1598	Tradate	1510	Antico
BRESCIA		1616	Colonna	1526	Dorico
1578	Sabbio	1619	Rolla	1539	Blado
		1648	Camagno	1555	Barré
FERRARA		1660	Vigoni	1581	Alessandro
1538	Buglhat, Campis,				Gardano
	& Hucher	*NAPLES*		1586	Verovio
1582	Baldini	1597	Carlino		

1593	Valesi	*VENICE*		1583	Vincenti & Amadino (1587: separately)
1596	Mutii	1501	Petrucci (1511: Fossombrone)		
1602	Zannetti			1587	Valesi
1609	Robletti	1516	O. Scotto	1606	Raverii
1615	Borboni	1517	Antico	1611	Magni
1615	Fei	1538	Gardane	1652	Bortoli
1619	Soldi	1539	G. Scotto	1685	Sala
1620	Mascardi	1561	Rampazetto		
1620	Poggioli	1562	Franceschi	*VICENZA*	
1630	Grignani	1566	Merulo	1618	Salvadori
?1657	Caifabri				

1770-1920

FLORENCE		1874	Sonzogno	*ROME*	
1812	Lorenzi	1887	Carisch	1821	Ratti, Cencetti
1844	Guidi	*NAPLES*		1852	De Santis
MILAN		1786	Marescalchi	*TURIN*	
1805	Artaria	1818	Girard	1859	Giudici & Strada (1897: Milan)
1808	Ricordi	1846	Clausetti		
1815	Scotti	1848	Cottrau	*VENICE*	
1820	Bertuzzi	1912	Curci	1770	Marescalchi
1823	Carulli	*PADUA*		?1775	Alessandri & Scattaglia
1825	Lucca	1908	Zanibon		
1835	Canti			1786	Zatta

D. Germany (and Adjacent Areas)

Considering the abundant output of German music publishing, it is perhaps excusable that the surveys of the whole should be more superficial than one would like: one's sympathies for the authors are in inverse proportion to the available space. Works that explore the topic in some detail confirm the break in tradition around 1700, during J. S. Bach's lifetime. For the period before this date, Benzing is the admirable reference source; Göhler provides many valuable perspectives, some of which may take coaxing. For the period after 1700, Plesske is still an essential starting point. Schumann, Richter, and Challier suggest the role of associations, as do Köster's dissertation for the years around World War I and Petschull's directory for the years after World War II.

German music and German publishing in general are effectively part of a *Deutsches Sprachgebiet*, a domain determined by the German language. Often limited to the geographical territory subsumed in the *Reich*, the domain can also extend virtually from Copenhagen to Zurich, from Amsterdam to Budapest, from Strasbourg to Riga, as its influence extends even further, to include the dominant activities in Moscow and Bucharest, in London and New York. It distorts the record very little to group the Austrian efforts with the German, so as to consider Vienna and Innsbruck among the German cities. Much of the literature covers at least the German-speaking parts of Switzerland as well, but there are also a few writings that need to be recognized as distinctly Swiss in their coverage, as cited on p. 288-89.

REFERENCE SOURCES AND GENERAL OVERVIEWS

[Karl] Albert GÖHLER. *Die Messkataloge im Dienste der musikalischen Geschichtsforschung.* Leipzig: C. F. Kahnt (Breitkopf & Härtel), 1902.   **742**

A discussion of the music in the semi-annual book-fair catalogues, 1564-1759, as recorded in the current lists out of which modern national bibliography was to emerge. Originally a dissertation (Leipzig, 1901), the text also appears in the *Sammelbände der internationalen Musikgesellschaft*, 3 (1901-02), 244-376.

Reprinted Hilversum: Knuf, 1965, along with the author's *Verzeichnis der in den Frankfurter und Leipziger Messkatalogen der Jahre 1564 bis 1759 angezeigten Musikalien* (Leipzig: C. F. Kahnt, 1902), which lists the titles, by centuries, so as to provide a basis for a retrospective national German music bibliography.

To be sure, only about a third of the known output was ever exhibited at the book fairs, more of it from the Protestant north than from the Catholic south. Curiously, titles are often listed in the *Messkatalog* from the year just before or just after the one recorded in the imprint statements of surviving copies. But this third part is the most important; and even the contradictory dates are useful to the extent that they offer potential insight into the nature of the publishing processes.

Ernst CHALLIER. "Der Stammbaum des Musikalienhandels," *and* "Der Musikalienhandel einst und jetzt," *Börsenblatt für den Deutschen Buchhandel*, 78 (1911), 7368-69, 10216-18.   **743**

[Plesske 27-28].

Max SCHUMANN. *Zur Geschichte des deutschen Musikalienhandels seit der Gründung des Vereins der Deutschen Musikalienhändler 1829 bis 1929.* Leipzig: Verband der Deutschen Musikalienhändler, 1929. **744**
A jubilee book, with informative statistics and a fold-out chart listing the officers.

Wilhelm ALTMANN. "Zur Geschichte des deutschen Musikalienhandels," *Die Musik,* 29 (1937), 485-87. **745**
A brief review of the major events, mostly since 1750.

Amtliches Verzeichnis der . . . zum Musikalienvertrieb zugelassenen Händler. [Berlin]: Reichsmusikkammer, Fachschaft Musikalienhändler, 1944. **746**
A directory of wartime German music dealers. The introductory sections (pp. 3-33) specify the rules and describe the practices of music distribution. These are followed by the directory itself (pp. 35-128), with about 4000 names and addresses in about 1500 cities, arranged alphabetically by city. A "Nachtrag" (pp. 129-30) covers German firms in Poland. (The introduction speaks of a 3. Aufl. of 1941, but I have not located any of its predecessors; nor have I seen any copies of this book designated as a "4. Aufl.")

Josef BENZING. *Die Buchdrucker des 16. und 17. Jahrhunderts im deutschen Sprachgebiet.* Wiesbaden: Harrassowitz, 1953 (Beiträge zum Geschichte des Buchwesens, 12). **747**
A massive general directory of the early printers of all kinds. Since one expects so much of this book, it seems almost churlish to mention that it covers only printers: publishers are included only if they were also printers. For the publishers see Benzing's "Die deutschen Verleger des 16. und 17. Jahrhunderts," *Archiv für Geschichte des Buchwesens,* 18 (1977), 1077-1322.
The second edition (1982) is slightly revised. If the sequel by David L. Paisey, *Deutsche Buchdrucker, Buchhändler und Verleger, 1701-1750* (Wiesbaden: Otto Harrassowitz, 1988; Beiträge zum Buch- und Bibliothekswesen, 26) may prove to be less important to music bibliographers, it is mostly because so little music was being published in Germany during its period.

Manfred RICHTER. "Aus dem Tagebuch des deutschen Musikalienhandels: Skizzen, Memorien, und Dokumente," *Der Musikhandel*, 16 (1955), 41-42, 89-90, 140, 189, 236, 294, 349; 17 (1966), 4, 44-45, 103.   **748**
[Plesske 43.]

Winfried HÖNTSCH. "Verlagsfragen auf der Tagesordnung," *Musik in Gesellschaft*, 12 (1962), 96-103.   **749**
A rationalization of music publishing in a socialistic economy, explaining the reassignments of particular broad repertories to the auspices of different imprints.

Musikverlage in der Bundesrepublik Deutschland und in West-Berlin. Bonn: Musikhandel Verlags G.m.b.H., 1965.   **750**
Descriptions, edited by Johannes Petschull, of about 400 firms in the Musikverleger-Verband, e.V., as of February 1, 1965, arranged by city with indexes to names of firms and their affiliates.

Hans-Martin PLESSKE. "Bibliographie des Schrifttums zur Geschichte deutscher und österreichischer Musikverlage," *Beiträge zur Geschichte des Buchwesens*, 3 (1968), 135-222.
An invaluable bibliography of 755 writings on music publishing in the German-speaking world, arranged under the following categories: (A) generalia and reference sources (25 titles); (B) historical studies (85 titles); (C) individual publishers (568 titles, with useful information on the publishers); and (D) composer-publisher relationships (77 titles).   **751**

Karl VÖTTERLE. *Zur Situation des deutschen Musikverlegers*. Bonn: Verlag Musikhandel, 1973.   **752**
A thoughtful description of present conditions, by the founder and director of Bärenreiter-Verlag.

Rudolf ELVERS. *150 Jahre (1829-1979) Musikverbände in Deutschland*. Bonn, 1979.   **753**
I have not seen this book (of 28 unnumbered leaves), cited in the *Festschrift Rudolf Elvers* (Tutzing: Hans Schneider, 1985), p. 564.

"Musik & Musikalienhandel," *Börsenblatt für den deutschen Buchhandel* (Frankfurt), 44 (1988).   **754**

A series of 14 popular articles in the February 12 issue:

Wolfram Göbel, "Wie findet das Musikbuch seine Leser?" (pp. 454-63)

Dietrich Berke, "Gegenwartsmusik kontra 'Papiergeschäft'?" (pp. 490-94: on marketable publishing)

Hanns Lothar Schütz, "Haus unterm Stern" (pp. 572-76: on Bären-reiter)

Ursula Rühenbeck, "Mit zeitgenössischer Musik in die Zukunft investiert" (pp. 578-82: on Breitkopf & Härtel)

Raoul Blahacel, "Haydn und Chopin,* Janácek und Bartók, Kodály und Křenek, Eisler und Weill, aber auch die 'radikalste Moderne' (pp. 588-93: on Universal Edition)

Marianne Menzel, "Der menschliche Faktor in der Musik, oder: Musik im Dienst einer humanen Gesellschaft" (pp. 594-600: on G. Bosse)

Marianne Menzel, "Die Farbe Blau" (pp. 600-05: on G. Henle)

Martin Walach, "Ein Musik-Verleger muß seine Ohren einfach überall haben" (pp. 607-11: on Boosey & Hawkes)

Sibylle Voss, "Musikverlag Schott: seit über 200 Jahren 'jung als Tradition' " (pp. 612-17)

Marianne Menzel, "Schon Liszt wußte: Ricordi ist Ministerresident der musikalischen Republik" (pp. 618-20)

Alexander Schmitz, "Mit Schmalspurigkeit wurde das Ansehen nicht erworben" (pp. 621-26: on H. Sikorski)

Ursula Rühenbeck, "Vom 'Bureau de Musique' zur Edition Peters" (pp. 626-28)

Marianne Menzel, ". . . vielstimmiges Orchester der Musikwissenschaft" (pp. 632-34: on Laaber Verlag, Regensburg)

Sibylle Voss, ". . . und abschließend ein schöner Schwung" (pp. 662-64: on the Schott engraving shop).

"Musikalien und Musikbuch." *Börsenblatt für den deutschen Buchhandel* (Leipzig), 155 (1988). **755**

There are three essays in the East German counterpart:

Hans-U. Rausch, "Wo Beethoven revidiert wird . . ." (pp. 605-09: on C. F. Peters)

Eva-Maria Hillmann, "Breites und interessantes Spektrum" (pp. 623-24: the rationalized diversity of socialized music publishing)

Gitta Große, "Bach-Wettbewerb, Festspiele und Sagittarius" (pp. 643-44: Musikalienhandlung "J. S. Bach").

GENERAL AND MISCELLANEOUS STUDIES

Erwin KÖSTER. "Der deutsche Musikalienhandel, insbesondere der Musikalienverlag, während des letzten Jahrzehnts." Ph.D. dissertation, Jena, 1923. **756** [Plesske 50.]

Wilhelm HITZIG. "450 Jahre Notentypendruck in Deutschland," *Der Musikalienhandel*, 33 (1931), 65-66.
Perfunctory observations on music typography.   **757**

Richard S. HILL. "The Plate Numbers of C. F. Peters' Predecessors," *Papers of the American Musicological Society*, 1938, pp. 113-34.   **758**
An explanation of the interlocking and overlapping workings of the Hoffmeister & Kühnel firms in Vienna and Leipzig. This essay probably did not greatly influence the work of Alexander Weinmann, although it did much to stimulate the development of plate-number files by American music library cataloguers.

Ulrich LACHMANN. *Die Struktur des deutschen Musikmarkts; unter besonderer Berücksichtigung des erwerbswirtschaftlichen Sektors.* Dissertation, Tübingen, 1960.   **759**
[Cited in Richard Schaal, *Verzeichnis deutschsprachiger musikwissenschaftlicher Dissertationen* (1963), no. 1384.].

Friedrich Wilhelm RIEDEL. *Quellenkundliche Beiträge zur Geschichte der Musik für Tasteninstrumente in der zweiten Hälfte des 17. Jahrhunderts (vornehmlich in Deutschland).* Kassel: Bärenreiter, 1960 (Schriften des Landesinstituts für Musikforschung Kiel, 10).   **760**
The story of music printing of the 17th century — discouraging most everywhere but in Germany in particular — calls out for a search for major trends and notable events. Of several musicological studies of particular repertories that suggest the main aspects, this exploration of the keyboard music makes important points regarding the emergence of music engraving. A similar study, Friedhelm Krummacher's *Die Überlieferung der Choralbearbeitung in der frühen evangelischen Kantate* (Berlin: Merseburger, 1965), while explicitly concerned primarily with manuscript sources, also touches on local music printing activities.

Liesbeth WEINHOLD. "Die Gelegenheitskompositionen des 17. Jahrhunderts in Deutschland," in *Quellenstudien zur Musik: Wolfgang Schmieder zum 70. Geburtstag* (Frankfurt: C. F. Peters, 1972), pp. 171-96.   **761**

On the flourishing output of occasional music" (for baptisms, birthdays, weddings, funerals, etc.), with lists of activity by city.

D. W. KRUMMEL. "Early German Partbook Type Faces," *Gutenberg Jahrbuch 1985*, pp. 80-99.   **762**
An overview of music typography in the 16th- and 17th-century German-speaking world.

LOCAL AND REGIONAL STUDIES

The extensive literature (cited here selectively) will be seen to be rich in short essays, including *Festschrift* contributions.

Augsburg

Hans RHEINFURTH. *Der Musikverlag Lotter in Augsburg* (ca. *1719-1845*). Tutzing: Hans Schneider, 1977 (Musikbibliographische Arbeiten, 3).   **763**
A history of the longevous firm, important for its association with the Mozarts, with a catalogue of the firm's 533 publications.

Bavaria

Adolf LAYER. "Notendrucker und Musikverleger in Bayern: ein Rückblick auf fünf Jahrhunderte," *Gutenberg Jahrbuch 1973*, pp. 329-36.   **764**
Generalizations, with several dozen references to writings on more specific aspects.

Berlin

Amalie ARNHEIM. "Zur Geschichte des Berliner Musikdruckes und Musikverlages: eine historische Skizze," in the Gesellschaft zur Pflege altklassischer Musik, *Bericht über die Tätigkeit . . . 1. Juni 1913 bis 31. Mai 1915* (Berlin: Albrecht Stahl, 1915), pp. 10-14.   **765**
A summary of activity in the 16th and 17th centuries.

Wilhelm HITZIG. "Ein Berliner Aktenstück zur Geschichte des Notendruckverfahrens," in *Festschrift Peter Wagner zum 60. Geburtstag* (Leipzig: Breitkopf & Härtel, 1926), pp. 81-86.   **766**
Negotiations among North-German music dealers in the 1780s.

Hans Ulrich LENZ. *Der Berliner Musikdruck von seinen Anfängen bis zur Mitte des 18. Jahrhunderts.* Kassel: Bärenreiter, 1933.   **767**
A dissertation (Rostock, 1932) on the city's early output, which included many editions of Johann Crüger's *Praxis Pietatis melica* from the Runge press. Of special importance is the concern for typographic particulars, such as the size of the page, description of ornamental stock, and identification and reconstruction of the different music type fonts through precise measurements.

Rudolf ELVERS. *Altberliner Musikverleger.* Berlin: Merseburger, 1961.   **768**
This work, issued as a publisher's Christmas gift, contains the best brief overview of modern activity in Berlin. Many of the author's later essays also deal with the topic, e.g., "Die bei J. F. K. Rellstab in Berlin bis 1800 erschienenen Mozart-Drucke," *Mozart Jahrbuch 1957*, pp. 152-67 (wider in scope than its title suggests); "Datierte Verlagsnummern Berliner Musikverleger," in *Festschrift Otto Erich Deutsch zum 80. Geburtstag* (Kassel: Bärenreiter, 1963), pp. 291-95; "Musikdrucker, Musikalienhändler, und Musikverleger in Berlin, 1750 bis 1850: eine Übersicht," in *Festschrift Walter Gerstenberg zum 60. Geburtstag* (Wolfenbüttel: Möseler, 1964), pp. 37-44; "Berliner Musikverleger," in Carl Dahlhaus, *Studien zur Musikgeschichte Berlins im frühen 19. Jahrhundert* (Regensburg: Bosse, 1980; Studien zur Musikgeschichte des 19. Jahrhunderts, 56), pp. 285-91; "Die Berliner Musikverlage im 19. Jahrhundert," *Bericht über den Internationalen Musikwissenschaftlichen Kongress Berlin 1974* (Kassel: Bärenreiter, 1980), pp. 379-80; and "Some Aspects of Music Publishing in Nineteenth-Century Berlin," *Music and Bibliography: Essays in Honour of Alec Hyatt King* (London: Clive Bingley, 1980), pp. 149-59. See also Elvers's edition of Mendelssohn's letters to publishers (635 above).

See also Zur Westen's essay on title pages relating to Berlin (456).

Büdingen

Hans Joachim MOSER. "Eine Musikaliendruckerei auf einer deutschen Ritterburg," Zeitschrift für *Musikwissenschaft*, 17 (1935), 97-102.   **769**

On a folio mass book, ca. 1560.

Caroline VALENTIN. *Geschichte der Musik in Frankfurt am Main*. Frankfurt: Völcker, 1906.   **770**
"Musik, Musikhandel und Notendruck von 1520-1620" (pp. 51-126), impressive in its day, is now largely superseded by Berz.

Friedrich LÜBBECKE. *Fünfhundert Jahre Buch und Druck in Frankfurt am Main*. Frankfurt: Cobet, 1948.   **771**
Chapter 8 ("Notendruck und Musikalienhandel," pp. 145-59) is a general survey, emphasizing major names.

Ernst-Ludwig BERZ. *Die Notendrucker und ihre Verleger in Frankfurt am Main von den Anfängen bis etwa 1630: eine bibliographische und drucktechnische Studie zur Musikpublikation*. Kassel, Bärenreiter, 1970 (Catalogus musicus, 5).
Includes about 40 biographical accounts (pp. 12-121), a meticulous discussion of their 11 typographic faces (pp. 122-43, extending the work of Lenz and Davidsson), and descriptions of 258 Frankfurt publications (pp. 144-280), with a list of 86 editions distributed by Frankfurt publishers (pp. 281-92).   **772**
Based on a doctoral dissertation (Frankfurt, 1967; 1,285 pp.).

Walther LIPPHARDT. *Gesangbuchdrucke in Frankfurt am Main vor 1569.* Frankfurt am Main: Waldemar Kramer, 1974 (Studien zur Frankfurter Geschichte, 7).   **773**
Primarily a philological study of the derivation of the repertory of about a dozen printed books.

Hartmut SCHAEFER. *Die Notendrucker und Musikverleger in Frankfurt am Main von 1630 bis um 1720: Eine bibliographisch-drucktechnische Untersuchung.* Kassel: Bärenreiter, 1975 (Catalogus musicus, 7).   **774**
A valuable survey, reflecting another Frankfurt dissertation (1981), which extends and considerably amplifies the work of Berz so as to cover the generally less handsome but somewhat more prolific and elusive editions of the later period.

See also Hüschen (791).

Frankfurt an der Oder

Heinrich GRIMM. *Meister der Renaissancemusik an der Via-drina.* Frankfurt/Oder, Berlin, 1942.   **775**
"Die Stadt Frankfurt/Oder als bedeutender Druck- und Verlags-ort von Musikalien vor dem Dreißigjährigen Kriege" (pp. 230-44) speaks of Eichhorn, Baumann, and other nearby shops.
    See also Grimm's "Der Verlag ... Hartmann ... (1588-1631)," *Gutenberg Jahrbuch 1960*, pp. 237-54, esp. pp. 251-53.

Hamburg

Hermann COLSHORN. "Vom Musikalienhandel in Ham-burg: ein geschichtlicher Rückblick," *Aus dem Antiquariat*, 4 (1969), 870-78.   **776**
A cursory survey that mentions the major names, 1555-1940.

Heinrich HÜSCHEN. "Hamburger Musikdrucker und Mu-sikverleger im 16. und 17. Jahrhundert," in *Beiträge zur Musikgeschichte Nordeuropas: Kurt Gudewill zum 65. Geburtstag* (Wolfenbüttel: Möseler, 1978), pp. 255-70. **777**
A chronological overview, with observations on the impact of music printing in other cities.

Hesse

—. "Hessische Gesangbuchdrucker und -verleger des 16. und 17. Jahrhunderts," in *Festschrift Hans Engel zum 70. Geburtstag* (Kassel: Bärenreiter, 1964), pp. 166-87.   **778**
On the work of several dozen printers, mostly in Frankfurt but also in Marburg, Kassel, Hanau, Grobenstein, and Darmstadt.

Innsbruck

Anton DÖRRER. "Hundert Innsbrucker Notendrucke aus dem Barock: Ein Beitrag zur Geschichte der Musik und des Theaters in Tirol," *Gutenberg Jahrbuch 1939*, pp. 243-68.   **779**
With comments on 16th-century religious works and lists of the imprints of Michael Wagner, 1640-68, and others, 1626-93.

Königsberg

Georg KÜSEL. *Beiträge zur Musikgeschichte der Stadt Kö-nigsberg.* Königsberg: Bruno Meyer, 1923.   **780**

"Die Buch- und Notendruckereien in Königsberg i. Pr." (pp. 74-76) surveys the flourishing 17th-century activity.

Leipzig

Oskar von HASE. *Breitkopf & Härtel: Gedenkschrift und Arbeitsbericht.* Leipzig, Wiesbaden: Breitkopf & Härtel, 1917-68. **781**

Rich in portraits and quotations of archival documents. Volume 1 (1917) covers "the Breitkopf era," 1542-1827 (the former date seems a bit euphoric), volume 2 (1919) the "Härtel era," from 1827 forward, reportedly to 1895 in the *3. Auflage* (although I have not seen any of the first three *Auflagen*), to 1918 in the *4. Auflage*. A *5. Auflage* (1968) was issued with volume 3, which covers the postwar years.

MAHN & KÖLLNER. "Leipzig – traditionsreiche Stadt der Musiknotenherstellung," *Der Aussenhandel*, vol. 10, no. 16-17 (1960), 57-58. **782**
[Davidsson 319]

Otto SÄUBERLICH. "Leipzig als Hauptsitz des Notenstichs und Musikaliendrucks," *Archiv für Buchgewerbe und Gebrauchsgraphik*, 59 (1922), 19-22. **783**
Brief summary of major events since the J. G. I. Breitkopf era.

Hans-Martin PLESSKE. *Das Leipziger Musikverlagswesen und seine Beziehungen zu einigen namhaften Komponisten: ein Beitrag zur Geschichte des Musikalienhandels im 19. und zu Beginn des 20. Jahrhunderts.* Dissertation, Leipzig, 1974. **784**

According to *RILM*, vol. 10 (1976), no. 7813, this dissertation discusses the relationships between 15 composers and 14 music publishers, using previously unstudied archival documents.

Some of this material is presumably seen in "Namhafte Komponisten des 19. Jahrhunderts und ihre Leipziger Verleger," *Beiträge zur Geschichte des Buchwesens*, 1 (1965), 253-94, a summary account of the major firms, with observations on composers from Beethoven to Grieg, with many references. See also Plesske's "'Wenn mich die Höhe der Honorarforderung auch überrascht hat': Leipzigs Musikverlage und ihr Anteil an den Erst-

ausgaben von Gustav Mahler, Richard Strauss und Hans Pfitz-
ner," *Jahrbuch der Deutschen Bücherei*, 14 (1978), 75-102; and
Leipzigs Musikverlage einst und jetzt (Leipzig: Internationales
Bachfest, 1966; Die Musikstadt Leipzig, Arbeitsberichte, 2).

Mainz

Hans-Christian MÜLLER. *Bernhard Schott, Hofmusik-
stecher in Mainz*. Mainz: B. Schott, 1977 (Beiträge zur
Mittelrheinischen Musikgeschichte, 16). **785**
A history of the early years of the firm (pp. 17-58; the concluding discussions of bibliographical problems are especially useful), with a list of 284 imprints (pp. 59-167) and halftone reproductions of 24 title-pages and the 8-page catalogue of 1785.

Mannheim

Hans SCHNEIDER. *Der Musikverleger Johann Michael Götz
(1740-1810) und seine kurfürstlich privilegierte Noten-
fabrique*. Tutzing: Schneider, 1989. **786**
Vol. 1 is a meticulously detailed history, proceeding annalistically and including citations of the output of nearly a thousand
editions. It also includes indexes — chronological (pp. 275-346)
and by composer and title (pp. 347-426) — and facsimiles of the
firm's plate catalogues and other original documents. Vol. 2
reproduces the large catalogues of 1780, 1784, and 1802, giving
us a work that is both lovingly done and also slightly extravagant.

Nürnberg

Paul COHEN. *Musikdruck und Musikdrucker zu Nürnberg
im 16. Jahrhundert*. Nürnberg: Zierfuss, 1927. **787**
This dissertation (*Die Nürnberger Musikdrucker im 16. Jahrhundert*, Erlangen, 1927) surveys a prolific and important activity in
general terms, and appends short-title lists.
For additions and corrections see Rudolf Wagner, "Ergänzungen zur Geschichte der Nürnberger Musikdrucker des 16.
Jahrhunderts," *Zeitschrift für Musikwissenschaft*, 12 (1929/30),
506-08, and "Nachträge zur Geschichte der Nürnberger
Musikdrucker im 16. Jahrhundert," *Mitteilungen des Vereins für
Geschichte der Stadt Nürnberg*, 30 (1931), 107-52, the latter
mostly a biographical essay.

Theodor WOHNHAAS. "Nürnberger Gesangbuchdrucker und -verleger im 17. Jahrhundert," in *Festschrift Bruno Stäblein* (Kassel: Bärenreiter, 1967), pp. 303-15.   **788**
A directory of the major firms, summarizing their relationships. See also "Zum Nürnberger Musikdruck und Musikverlag im 16. und 17. Jahrhundert," *Gutenberg Jahrbuch 1973*, pp. 337-43, with longer prose sketches and citations of selected imprints.

Offenbach

Wolfgang MATTHÄUS. *Johann André Musikverlag zu Offenbach am Main: Verlagsgeschichte und Bibliographie, 1772-1800.* Tutzing: Hans Schneider, 1973.   **789**
A bicentennial history of the firm with a catalogue of the early years, completed after the author's death by Hans Schneider.
The author's observations on bibliographical theory, based largely on this André study, are described in 24 above.

Regensburg

August SCHARNAGL. "Regensburger Notendrucker und Musikverlage," *Festgabe Hans Schneider zum 60. Geburtstag* (Tutzing, 1981), pp. 99-115.   **790**
On activity ranging from a 1485 missal to the Bosse firm today.

Rhineland

Heinrich HÜSCHEN. "Rheinische Gesangbuchdrucker und -verleger des 16. und 17. Jahrhunderts," in *50 Jahre Gustav Bosse Verlag* (Regensburg, 1963), pp. 51-79.   **791**
Notes on and bibliographical references for about 40 Catholic imprints, mostly from Cologne, and a dozen Protestant imprints, mostly from cities north of Cologne.

Karl Gustav FELLERER. "Rheinische Musikdrucker und -verleger im 17./18. Jahrhundert," *Mitteilungen der Arbeitsgemeinschaft für rheinische Musikgeschichte*, 49 (1976), 139-41.   **792**
A list of about 100 publishers' names, supplementing Hüschen.

Saxony

Walter HÜTTEL. "Zur Geschichte des Musikverlages im südwestlichen Sachsen: Beispiele verlegerischer Aktivität

außerhalb der großen Zentren," in *Quellenstudien zur Musik: Wolfgang Schmieder zum 70. Geburtstag* (Frankfurt: Peters, 1972), pp. 95-102.   **793**
On publishing in the summer estates around Schönburg in the early 18th century, *Selbstverlag* activity in the early 19th, and the firm of G. A. Petzoldt in Glachau after 1862.

Speyer

Speyerer Musicalia und Musica theoretica aus der Pfälzischen Landesbibliothek. Speyer: Pfälzische Landesbibliothek, 1979 (Pfälzische Arbeiten zum Buch- und Bibliothekswesen und der Bibliographie, 9).   **794**
Catalogue of an exhibition for a session of the Arbeitsgemeinschaft für mittelrheinische Musikgeschichte, June 23-25, 1979, showing three early liturgical books and several dozen editions from around 1800 by Bossler and his contemporaries.

For the Bossler editions, Hans Schneider's *Der Musikverleger Heinrich Philipp Bossler (1744-1812)* (Tutzing, 1985) provides an well researched overview.

Strasbourg

William YOUNG. "Music Printing in Sixteenth-Century Strasbourg," *Renaissance Quarterly*, 24 (1971), 486-501. **795**
Activities beginning with Protestant service books in the 1520s, extending to include several notable lute books in the 1570s and turn-of-the-century anthologies.

Thuringia

Günther KRAFT. *Die Grundlagen der thüringischen Musikkultur um 1600.* Würzburg: Tritsch, 1941.   **796**
"Die thüringischen Musikdrucker und Musikverleger bis 1630" (pp. 130-51) discusses printers in Erfurt, Jena, and Coburg.

Tübingen

Heinrich HÜSCHEN. "Tübinger Musikdrucker im 16. und 17. Jahrhundert," in *Festschrift Georg von Dadelsen zum 60. Geburtstag* (Neuhausen-Stuttgart: Hänssler, 1978), pp. 167-78.   **797**

An overview of the output of partbooks, hymnals, and academic music, with a list of titles.

Vienna

Karl JUNKER. *Korporation der Wiener Buch-, Kunst- und Musikalienhändler, 1807-1907: Festschrift zur Feier des hundertjährigen Bestehens der Korporation am 2. Juni 1907.* Wien: Franz Deuticke, 1907. **798**
Evidence of the workings of the music trade in relation to the city's book and art trade. The copyright status of arrangements, for instance, was debated as early as 1819 (see pp. 29-30).

Kathi MEYER and Inger M. CHRISTENSEN. "Artaria Plate Numbers," Music Library Association, *Notes*, 1st series, 5 (December 1942), pp. 1-22. **799**
Prepared mostly from files at the New York Public Library, where Christensen was music cataloguer and Meyer was pursuing her bibliographical studies.

Alexander WEINMANN. *Beiträge zur Geschichte des Alt-Wiener Musikverlages.* Wien, 1948-87. **800**
A lifetime's labor of love, with two parts, assorted addenda, new editions, and in time an *Anhang* series of its very own. (Is it really necessary for Viennese confusion to be intermixed with its glories? When affection is so dear, one forgives.) To the best of my knowledge, the complete record is as follows:

Reihe 1. "Komponisten":
1. *Verzeichnis der im Druck erschienenen Werke von Joseph Lanner.* Wien: Ludwig Krenn (Leuen-Verlag), 1948.
2. *Verzeichnis sämtlicher Werke von Johann Strauss, Vater und Sohn.* Wien: Krenn, 1956.
3. *Verzeichnis sämtlicher Werke von Josef und Eduard Strauss.* Wien: Krenn, 1967.
4. *Ferdinand Schubert: eine Untersuchung.* Wien: Krenn, 1986.
5. *Johann Georg Albrechtsberger: Thematischer Katalog seiner weltlichen Komponisten.* Wien: Krenn, 1987.

Reihe 2: "Verleger" (mostly built out of plate-number lists):
1. *Verzeichnis der Verlagswerke des Musikalischen Magazins in Wien, 1784-1802: "Leopold Kozeluch", ein bibliographischer Behelf.* Wien: Oesterreichischer Bundesverlag, 1950.

1a. *Verzeichnis der Verlagswerke des Musikalischen Magazins in Wien, 1784-1802: Leopold [und] Anton Kozeluch.* 2. ergänzte und vollständig umgearbeitete Auflage. Wien: Krenn, 1979.

2. *Vollständiges Verlagsverzeichnis Artaria & Comp.* Wien: Krenn, 1952.

2a. A "2. ergänzte Auflage" (ibid., 1978), with added pp. 178-200, consisting of a sequential layout of the "Raccoltà delle migliori Arie" series, much of which information had been listed earlier by plate number ("Nr. des Hauptb."). A "3. Auflage" (ibid., 1985) is identical with the second.

3. "Vollständiges Verlagsverzeichnis der Musikalien der Kunst- und Industrie-Comptoirs in Wien, 1801-1810," *Studien zur Musikwissenschaft: Beihefte der Denkmäler der Tonkunst in Österreich,* 22 (1955), pp. 217-52.

4. "Verzeichnis der Musikalien des Verlages Johann Traeg in Wien, 1794-1818," *Studien zur Musikwissenschaft: Beihefte der Denkmäler der Tonkunst in Österreich,* 23 (1956), 135-83; "Ergänzungen und Berichtigungen," 26 (1964), 213. [cf. Folge 16-17 below.]

5. *Wiener Musikverleger und Musikalienhändler von Mozarts Zeit bis gegen 1860.* Wien: Rohrer, 1956 (Österreichische Akademie der Wissenschaften, Philosophisch-historische Klasse, Sitzungsberichte, 230, 4).

6. *Verzeichnis der Musikalien aus dem K. K. Hoftheater-Musik-Verlag.* Wien: Universal Edition, [1961].

7. *Kataloge Anton Huberty (Wien) und Christoph Torricella. Huberty-Torricella.* Wien: Universal Edition, 1962. See also "Der Notenstecher Anton Huberty," *Das Antiquariat,* 12 (1956), 261-62.

8. *Die Wiener Verlagswerke von Franz Anton Hoffmeister.* Wien: Universal Edition, 1964.

8a. *Addenda und Corrigenda zum Verlagsverzeichnis Franz Anton Hoffmeister.* Wien: Krenn, 1982.

9. *Verlagsverzeichnis Tranquillo Mollo (mit und ohne Co.).* Wien: Universal Edition, 1964.

9a. *Ergänzungen zum Verlags-Verzeichnis Tranquillo Mollo.* Wien: Universal Edition, 1972.

10. *Verlagsverzeichnis Pietro Mechetti quondam Carlo.* Wien: Universal Edition, 1966.

11. *Verlagsverzeichnis Giovanni Cappi bis A. O. Witzendorf.* Wien: Universal Edition, 1967.

12. *Verzeichnis der Musikalien des Verlages Joseph Eder-Jeremias Bermann.* Wien: Universal Edition, 1968.

13. *Wiener Musikverlag "am Rande": ein lückenfüllender Beitrag zur Geschichte des Alt-Wiener Musikverlages.* Wien: Universal Edition, 1970.

14. *Verzeichnis der Musikalien des Verlages Maisch Sprenger Artaria*. Wien: Universal Edition, 1970.
15. *Verlagsverzeichnis Ignaz Sauer (Kunstverlag zu den Sieben Schwestern), Sauer und Leidesdorf und Anton Berka & Comp*. Wien: Universal Edition, 1972.
16. *Verlagsverzeichnis Johann Traeg (und Sohn)*, 2. vermehrte und verbesserte Auflage [cf. Folge 4 above]. Wien: Universal Edition, 1973.
17. *Johann Traeg, die Musikalienverzeichnisse von 1799 und 1804 (Handschriften und Sortiment)*. Wien: Universal Edition, 1973. ["Band 1": cf. *Wiener Archivstudien*, Folge 6, below].
18. [Several listings cite this as "Nicht erschienen."]
19. *Vollständiges Verlagsverzeichnis Senefelder Steiner Haslinger*. München, Salzburg: Katzbichler, 1979 (vol. 1: 1803-26), 1980 (vol. 2: 1826-43), 1983 (vol. 3: 1843-75). [Also comprises Band 14-16 of the publisher's "Musikwissenschaftliche Schriften" series.]
20. *Verzeichnis der Musikalien des Verlages Anton Pennauer*. Wien: Krenn, 1981.
21. *Verzeichnis der Verlagswerke J. P. Gotthard*. Wien: Krenn, 1981.
22. *Verzeichnis der Musikalien des Verlages Thadé Weigl*. Wien: Krenn, 1982.
23. *Verlagsverzeichnis Peter Cappi und Cappi & Diabelli (1816 bis 1824)*. Wien: Krenn, 1983.
24. *Verlagsverzeichnis Anton Diabelli & Co. (1824 bis 1840)*. Wien: Krenn, 1985.

Reihe 2, Folge 5, is a directory that provides a valuable overview of the whole. See also Weinmann's "Zur Bibliographie des Alt-Wiener Musikverlages," in *Festschrift Otto Erich Deutsch* (Kassel: Bärenreiter, 1963), pp. 319-26; and *Der Alt-Wiener Musikverlag im Spiegel der "Wiener Zeitung"* (Tutzing: Hans Schneider, 1976), which describes the plan and activities of his project as a whole and discusses the *Wiener Diarium* and *Wiener Zeitung* as sources.

—. *Wiener Archivstudien*. Wien: Ludwig Krenn, 1979-81.
A supplement to Weinmann's *Beiträge* series (not devoted to the catalogues, but clear evidence that Weinmann, even in his last years, had not lost his momentum for bibliographical projects):
1. *Philomele: Zwei Werkreihen von Anton Diabelli*, I . *Für das Pianoforte;* II . *Für die Gitarre*. 1979. With Ignaz Weinmann.
2. *J. P. Gotthard als später Originalverleger Franz Schuberts*. 1979. With an added gathering of illustrations laid in.
3. *Ein erster gedruckter Verlagskatalog der Firma Anton Diabelli & Co*. 1979. The catalogue probably appeared in 1825, the supplements in 1827 and spring 1828; all are undated.

4. *"Das Grab" von J. G. von Salis-Seewis: ein literarisch-musika-lischer Bestseller.* 1979. On 43 different settings of the poem by Johann Gaudenz von Salis-Seewis, four of them by Schubert, with facsimiles.

5, 5a. Anton Huberty, *Stücke für Viola d'amore mit und ohne Begleitung,* edited by Louise Goldberg and Alexander Weinmann. 1980.

6. *Die Anzeigen des Kopiaturbetriebes Johann Traeg in der Wiener Zeitung zwischen 1782 und 1805.* 1981. Identified as "Band II," so as to indicate its relationship to Folge 17 of the *Beiträge.*

Weinmann's series deserves to be respected as one of the major achievements of music bibliography. Although some people never found it difficult to disparage Weinmann as a "Briefmarkensammler" among music bibliographers, his series is as valuable as it is overwhelming.

Peter RIETHUS. "Der Wiener Musikdruck im 16. und 17. Jahrhundert," *Das Antiquariat,* 14 (1958), 5-9.   **801**

A tightly-written but richly detailed overview, with a list of 83 titles, 1499-1702, and three facsimiles. (The author also deserves to be remembered for his contribution to the holdings of central and eastern European musical editions in American music libraries, during the era when bravery and loyal friends were required to obtain them.)

Hannelore GERICKE. *Der Wiener Musikalienhandel von 1700 bis 1778.* Graz, Köln: Böhlau, 1960 (Wiener musikwissenschaftliche Beiträge, 5).   **802**

Based on a dissertation (Vienna, 1959), which traces the origins of Viennese music publishing in the activities of booksellers, copyists, and engravers, and cites the 79 known music publications from this period, along with six censored titles.

Rosemary HILMAR. *Der Musikverlag Artaria & Comp.: Geschichte und Probleme der Druckproduktion.* Tutzing: Hans Schneider, 1977 (Publikationen des Instituts für österreichische Musikdokumentation, 6).   **803**

This study of the firm seeks to reconcile information in archival sources with that in other sources so as to recreate a sense of the early publisher's problems and attitudes.

See also Heim (443 above) on Viennese title-page illustrations.

Würzburg

Joseph B. KITTEL. "Würzburg, die Wiege des Musiknotendrucks." [ca.1910].   **804**
An essay on the 1481 Missale Herbipolensis, in an unidentified
journal. [*Mainz GM*, 18.m.1935.]

German perspectives inevitably pervade the literature of music
printing and publishing, if not necessarily of music bibliography as
a field of study. Roughly half of the technical writings in Chapter 3
are German, for instance, including the specimens of Luther,
Breitkopf, and Unger among typographers, Breitkopf & Härtel,
Röder, and Brandstetter among the engravers. Among topics for
future study are details of how publishers in other countries
actually worked with Leipzig engravers and printers. The few
scattered details we know about suggest that the arrangements
were both complicated and important.

Of all the music exhibitions, two (Vienna, 1892 and Frankfurt,
1927) stand out as truly pre-eminent. They frame a number of
others that testify to the presence of Paul Hirsch. Zur Westen's
several works on title pages (of which 459 is the most impressive)
also reflect a widespread interest in the topic during the early
years of the century. In the world of fine printing, Richard Strauss
as composer (931-32) and Paul Koch as typographer (933-40) are
particularly fascinating.

For all its fecundity and world-wide importance, German music
publishing itself actually claims a very meagre literature; of special
importance are the works of Siegel and Monke and Riedel (546)
and, among the practitioners' works, several journals (pp. 205-07).
Of the composers and publishers whose interrelationships are discussed in the writings cited on pp. 214-33, many are German, and
even more worked basically within the German (and Viennese)
musical tradition, so as to identify, in Deutsch's plan for an
international bibliography of musical masterworks (4), a special
focus, if not in fact a bias implicit in the proposed world of international cooperation in the world of music bibliography.

Further writings are cited in other sources under the names of
German printers and publishers, among whom the following are
important:

Incunabula

AUGSBURG
1487   Ratdolt
BAMBERG
1481   Sensenschmidt

1491   Pfeyl
LÜBECK
1493   Arndes

NÜRNBERG
1491   Stuchs

WÜRZBURG
1479   Reyser

1501-1750

AUGSBURG
1502   Oeglin
1517   Grimm &
    Wirsung
1522   Ulhart
1525   Kriegstein
1581   Schönig
1611   Flurschütz
1694   Bencard
c1719   Lotter

BERLIN
1611   Runge

BRESLAU
1592   Baumann

COBURG
1596   Hauck
1619   Forckel

COLOGNE
1512   Aich

DILLINGEN
1603   Meltzer
1670   Bencard

DRESDEN
1570   G. Bergen
1625   Klemm

DÜSSELDORF
1555   Baethen

ERFURT
1573   Baumann

FRANKFURT am Main
1530   Egenolff
1559   Feyerabend
1602   Stein
1650   Wust

FRANKFURT *an der*
    Oder
1549   Eichorn
GRAZ
1585   Widmanstetter

HAMBURG
1590   Rebenlein
1597   Van Ohr
1609   Carstens

HERBORN
1585   Rab

INNSBRUCK
1639   Wagner

JENA
1605   Weidner

KEMPTEN
1660   Dreher

KÖNIGSBERG
1585   Osterberger
1623   Segebade
1639   Reusner
1642   Paschen Mense

LEIPZIG
1533   Faber
1545   Hantzsch

LÜNEBURG
1570   Stern

MÜHLHAUSEN
1567   Hantzsch

MUNICH
1564   Adam Berg
1584   Sadelar
1597   Henricus
1686   Wening

NÜRNBERG
1524   Hergot
1524   Petreius
1526   Formschneider
1527   Wachter
1534   Ott
1542   Johann Berg
1548   Neuber
1565   Gerlach
1593   Wagenmann
1594   Kauffmann
1620   Endter
1690   Weigel
1716   Rönnagel
1726   B. Schmid
1742   Haffner

PASSAU
1602   Nenninger

SALZBURG
1655   Mayer

STRASBOURG
1529   Schoeffer

VIENNA
1510   Wietor
1636   Cosmerovius
1721   Van Ghelen

WITTENBERG
1517   Rhau

WOLFENBÜTTEL
1607   Fürstliche
    Druckerei
1620   Stern

WORMS
1518   Schoeffer

1750-1920

AUGSBURG
1795	Gombart
1803	Böhm

BERLIN
1750	Winter
1770	Hummel
1785	Rellstab
1802	Werckmeister
1810	Schlesinger
1820	Trautwein
1835	Challier
1838	Bote & Bock
1864	Lienau
1868	Förstner
1881	Ries & Erler
1909	Russischer Musikverlag
1911	Birnbach
1912	Drei Masken

BONN
1793	Simrock
	(1870: Berlin)

BRAUNSCHWEIG
1791	Spehr
1828	Litolff

BRESLAU
1782	Leuckart

COLOGNE
1822	Tonger

DRESDEN
?1840	Meser

DÜSSELDORF
1821	Schwann

HAMBURG
1794	Günther & Böhme
1814	Cranz
1826	Schuberth
1907	Benjamin

HANOVER
1835	Nagel

LEIPZIG
c1750	Breitkopf
?1772	Schwickert
1801	Hoffmeister & Kühnel (Bureau de musique; after 1814: Peters)
1807	Hofmeister
1823	Probst
1836	Kistner
1846	Röder
1847	Senff
1849	Merseburger
1851	Kahnt
1862	Forberg
1870	Leuckart
1874	Eulenburg
1884	Rieter-Biedermann
1885	Belaieff
1889	Bosworth
1890	Steingräber
1893	Brockhaus
1902	Lauterbach & Kuhn

MAINZ
1780	Schott

MANNHEIM
1780	Götz
?1822	Heckel

MUNICH
1796	Falter
1796	Senefelder
1825	Aibl

OFFENBACH
1774	André

REGENSBURG
1826	Pustet
1912	Bosse

SPEYER
1781	Bossler

STUTTGART
1919	Hänssler

VIENNA
1756	Trattner
1777	Huberty
1778	Artaria
1781	Torricella
1784	Hoffmeister
1784	Kozeluch
1787	Löschenkohl
1794	Eder
1794	Traeg
1796	Hoftheater
1798	Mollo
1798	Sauer
1800	Cappi
1801	Kunst & Indust. Comptoir
1803	Chemische Druckerei (Senefelder, Steiner)
1803	Weigl
1807	Mechetti
1810	Maisch
1821	Lithogr. Instit.
1822	Pennauer
1824	Diabelli
1826	Haslinger
1852	Spina
1868	Pazidirek (Gotthard)
1857	Doblinger
?1877	Rättig
1885	Weinberger
1901	Universal

Georg Kinsky's *Geschichte der Musik in Bildern* (Leipzig: Breit-kopf & Härtel, 1929) shows portraits of nine German music pub-lishers on p. 288.

SWITZERLAND

Writings on music printing and publishing in Germany often apply to Switzerland as well, but there is also a Swiss literature that needs to be identified separately, along with writings devoted to activities in particular Swiss cities. Activity in Basel, Berne, and Zurich admittedly has obvious affinities to that in Vienna, Innsbruck, or Stuttgart. Geneva is quite different: its activity, dating mostly from the Calvinist era, is closely related to that in Lyons and Paris (cf. pp. 250-56 above). The Fribourg essay will be seen to intermix both French and German elements.

Verband der Musikalienhändler und Verleger der Schweiz. *Jubiläum zum 50-jährigen Bestehen des Verbandes.* Gurten/Bern, 1953.   **805**
A 22-page description of the society, which had grown from 17 founders to 166 firms. Brief essays discuss their audiences, edi-tions, and special concerns, among them copyright and perform-ance rights, particularly for radio.
   The existence of a comparable booklet from 1927 is suggested here, along with *Jahresberichte*, but I have not seen them.

Basel

Arnold PFISTER.   "Vom frühsten Musikdruck in der Schweiz," in *Festschrift Gustav Binz* (Basel: Benno Schwabe, 1935), pp. 160-78.   **806**
Well documented and supported by facsimiles, with detailed bibliographical descriptions.

Edgar REFARDT.   "Die Basler Choral-Inkunabeln," *Schweizerisches Jahrbuch für Musikwissenschaft*, 1 (1924), 118-37.   **807**
Detailed descriptions of 41 books with printed music or staff lines for music, followed by brief descriptions of 23 music books with no musical notation.

Berne

Adolf FLURI. "Versuch einer Bibliographie der bernischen Kirchengesangbücher," [*Schweizerisches*] *Gutenbergmuseum*, 6 (1920), 35-47, 117-20; 7 (1921), 22-24, 85-88; 8 (1922), 20-22, 94-97. **808**
An annotated list of 52 Berne sacred music imprints prior to 1752, with useful bibliographical annotations.

Fribourg

Jurg STENZL. "L'imprimerie musicale Fribourgeoise à l'époque baroque," *Schweizerische Musikzeitung*, 114 (1974), 160-63. **809**
Mostly on late 17th-century religious collections.

Swiss music typography is described in Bruckner (306). See also Thürlings on Swiss incunabula (116). The special issue of *SMG* (77) also testifies to interests in music printing. Further references may be found in other sources under the names of important Swiss printers and publishers, among them the following:

BASEL		LAUSANNE		ZURICH	
?1480	Richel	1865	Foetisch	?1550	Wyssenbach
?1485	Wenssler			1790	Nägeli (Hug)
BERNE		WINTERTHUR			
1539	Apiarius	1849	Rieter-Biedermann (1884: Leipzig)		

E. Elsewhere in Europe

THE LOW COUNTRIES

Extensive sixteenth-century activity, at first in Louvain and later in Antwerp, was followed by a concentration on Calvinist psalmbooks in seventeenth-century Holland; after that by entrepreneurial publishing, by Roger in Amsterdam around 1700 and by the Hummel family later in the century; and since 1800 by modest but occasionally distinguished efforts. In documenting this diverse history, the major writings are as follows:

Alphonse GOOVAERTS. *Histoire et bibliographie de la typographie musicale dans les anciens Pays-Bas*. Anvers: P. Kockx, 1880. **810**

A venerable study, including a list of 1,415 editions, arranged by date. While the coverage extends to 1841, it is very sketchy in the later years. An extended introductory text includes transcriptions of and quotations from original sources.
Reprinted, Hilversum: Knuf, 1963.

Daniel F. SCHEURLEER. *Het muziekleven van Amsterdam in de zeventiende eeuw.* s'Gravenhage: Martinus Nijhoff, n.d.   **811**
A handsomely illustrated folio, issued as part of a series on *Amsterdam in de zeventiende eeuw* (1901-04). Examples of printed and engraved music appear throughout, and Chapter 4 ("Muziekdrukkers en Uitgevers," pp. 79-85) cites the major names.

E. F. KOSSMANN. "Eenige haagsche muziekuitgevers der negentiende eeuw," *Die Haag jaarboek 1928/29*, pp. 227-72.   **812**
An account of the early shops. The Weygand plate number list (p. 255) is one of the first, and one of the least known, published responses to Barclay Squire's 1914 appeal (3 above).

Paul BERGMANS. "La typographie musicale en Belgique au XVIe siècle," *Histoire du livre et de l'imprimerie en Belgique des origines à nos jours*, vol. 5, part 5 (Bruxelles: Le Museé du livre, 1929), section 2, pp. 47-75.   **813**
Elegantly produced, with conspicuous facsimiles, well printed, colorful, and on yellow-tinted background. The text is stylish as well, but derived mostly from standard sources.
Also issued separately (as pp. 1-33).

Charles van den BORREN. "Manuscrits et impressions," in Ernest Closson and Charles van den Borren, *La musique en Belgique du moyen âge à nos jours* (Bruxelles: Le Renaissance du livre, 1950), 469-78.   **814**
Valuable descriptions, more on the appearance and importance of particular documents than on their printing and publishing.

Suzanne CLERCX. "Les éditions musicales anversoises du XVIe siècle et leur rôle dans la vie musicale des Pays-Bas," *De gulden passer*, 34 (1956), 238-49.   **815**

A portrait of the cultural setting for the music printer's work.
The text, prepared for the Plantin tercentenary events, also appears in the *Gedenkboek der Plantin-dagen 1655-1955* (Antwerpen: Plantin-Moretus Museum, 1956), pp. 364-75.

Albert DUNNING. *Joseph Schmitt: Leben und Kompositionen der Eberbacher Zisterziensers und Amsterdamer Musikverleger (1743-1791)*. Amsterdam: Heuwekemeijer, 1962 (Beiträge zur Mittelrheinischen Musikgeschichte, 1). **816**
"Der Amsterdamer Verlag" (chapter 3, pp. 30-37) needs to be viewed in the context of the whole study, all the more so considering the author's sound bibliographical orientation seen in the thematic catalogue of Schmitt's own music, pp. 64-126.

—. *De muziekuitgever Gerhard Fredrik Witvogel en zijn fonds: een bijdrage tot de geschiedenis van de Nederlandse muziekuitgeverij in de 18e eeuw*. Utrecht: A. Oosthoek, 1966. **817**
A well-documented essay, complemented by citations of the shop's five catalogues and 95 reported editions, many of which appear to survive in only one copy, if at all.

A. HEUWEKEMEIJER. "Amsterdamse muziekuitgeverijen van af de 18. eeuw tot heden," *Mededelingenblad Vereniging voor Nederlandse Muziekgeschiedenis*, 24 (1967), 39-48.
A brief survey of the major figures. **818**

Ute MEISSNER. *Der Antwerpener Notendrucker Tylman Susato*. Berlin: Merseburger, 1967 (Berliner Studien zur Musikwissenschaft, 11). **819**
An account of the work of the mid 16th-century composer-printer, with a catalogue of and index to the anthologies.
Originally a dissertation (Berlin, Freie Universität), 1967.

François LESURE. *Bibliographie des éditions musicales publiées par Estienne Roger et Michel-Charles Le Cène (Amsterdam, 1696-1743)*. Paris: Société Française de Musicologie; Heugel, 1969. **820**
A brief essay precedes a "Bibliographie chronologique," built out of the small early catalogues, and a facsimile of the great 1737 catalogue.

Cari JOHANSSON. *J. J. & B. Hummel: Music Publishing and Thematic Catalogues.* Stockholm: Almquist & Wiksell, 1972. **821**
Vol. 1 consists of a detailed analysis of the operation and repertories of the family's firms in Amsterdam, Berlin, and Rotterdam, along with indexes to the catalogues in vol. 2; vol. 2 shows the "Music-Publishing Catalogues in Facsimile."
Originally prepared as an Uppsala doctoral dissertation.

Susan S. BAIN. *Music Printing in the Low Countries in the Sixteenth Century.* Ph. D. dissertation, Cambridge University, 1974. **822**
[Cited in guides to doctoral dissertations and reflected in the author's articles in Grove P&P.]

Clemens von GLEICH. "Niederländische Musikalien in Holland: Wege und Umwege" in *Festschrift Franz Grasberger zum 60. Geburtstag* (Tutzing: Schneider, 1975), pp. 93-99. **822a**
On the local printing of music by Dutch composers during the 19th and 20th centuries.

Kristine K. FORNEY. *Tielman Susato, Sixteenth-Century Music Printer: An Archival and Typographical Investigation.* Ph.D. dissertation, University of Kentucky, 1978. **823**
Detailed arguments that reflect recent typographical studies. The findings are used and developed in the author's "New Documents on the Life of Tielman Susato, Sixteenth-Century Music Printer and Musician," *Revue belge de musicologie*, 36-38 (1982-84), 18-52, and "Orlando di Lasso's 'Opus 1': The Making of a Renaissance Music Book," *ibid.*, 39-40 (1985-86), 33-55.

Paul RASPÉ. "Les débuts de la gravure musicale à Bruxelles, à la fin de l'Ancien régime," in *Annales d'histoire de l'art et d'archéologie*, 2 (1980), 123-34. **823a**
[Cited by Huys (below)]

— and Henri VERHULST. "L'Édition musicale," in Robert Wangermée and Philippe Mercier, *La musique en Wallonie et à Bruxelles*, vol. 1 (1980), pp. 293-305. **824**

Comments on several dozen music printers of the 16th, 17th, and 18th centuries in five cities (Douai, Tournai, Valenciennes, Liège, and Brussels) and their work.

Marianne FLEURUS. *L'activité des graveurs, imprimeurs, éditeurs et marchands de partitions de musique à Bruxelles entre 1850 et 1914.* Bruxelles: Commission Belge de Bibliographie, 1985 (Bibliotheca belgica, 139). **825**
[Not available for examination.]

Paul KUIK. *De lithografische muziekdruk in Nederland in het begin van de negentiende eeuw.* n.p., 1988. **826**
[A study of early 19th-century Dutch music lithography; cited in *Fontes artis musicae*, 37 (1990), 77.]

Bernard HUYS. "Overzicht van de muziektypografie in de Zuidelijke Nederlanden voor 1800," in *De eodem et diverso: Bundel essays over diverse themata van het oude muziekonderzoek* (Peer: Alamire, 1990), pp. 21-42. **827**
An overview of the major monuments of Belgian music typography, with reference to, and several illustrations of, copies in the Bibliothèque Royale, Brussels.

Henri VERHULST. "La diffusion des éditions de musique polyphonique dans les anciens Pays-Bas à la fin du XVIe siècle," in *Musique et Société: Hommages à Robert Wangermee* (Bruxelles: Faculté de Philosophie et Lettres, 1988), pp. 27-51. **828**
A valuable survey, with useful references and conspectus lists.

Donna G. CARDAMONE and David L. JACKSON, "Multiple Former and Vertical Setting in Lassus's 'Opus 1'," *Music Library Association, Notes*, 46 (1989), 7-24. **828a**
Another survey of the Susato edition (see 823), of distinction as an example of classic bibliographical method.

Maria PRZYWECKA-SAMECKA. *Rozwój drukarstwa muzycznego w Niderlandach (XVI-XVIII w.)* Wroclaw: Wydawn. Uniwersytetu Wroclawskiego, 1989 (Acta Universitatis Wratislaviensis, 1062). **828b**
[Not examined].

Dutch music printing must also be seen in the light of the typographical scholarship of Enschedé (303) and Vervliet (304), which in turn reflects on the notable typographical lineage that extends from Christopher Plantin (309) through Rosart (331) and Enschedé. Dumond's treatise on typography (215) bears a Brussels imprint, while Hen's journal (384) is directed to Belgian printers. The 1930 Antwerp exhibition (430) reflects the tastes of several writings cited above, perhaps most conspicuously Bergmans and Van den Borren. The most impressive book on music bookplates also comes from the Netherlands (Verster, 502).

Further references will be found in other sources under the names of Dutch and Flemish printers and publishers, of whom the following are among the most important:

AMSTERDAM		DOUAI		LOUVAIN	
1640	Matthysz	1575	Bogard	1545	Baethen
1689	Le Chevalier			1551	Phalèse (1582:
1697	Roger	GHENT			Antwerp)
1731	Witvogel	1565	Manilius		
1753	J. J. Hummel	1698	Le Chevalier	MAASTRICHT	
1760	Schmitt			1554	Baethen
		THE HAGUE			
ANTWERP		1755	B. Hummel	ROTTERDAM	
				1656	Geertsom
1523	Remunde	LEIDEN		1778	Barth
1539	Cock	1583	Raphelengius	1805	Plattner
1542	Vissenaecken			1866	Alsbach
1543	Susato	LIÈGE			
1554	Laet	1740	Andrez	TOURNAI	
1578	Plantin			1880	Desclée
1613	Aertssens				

SCANDINAVIA

Scandinavian music bibliography is the story of two diligent scholars, the Uppsala librarian and polymath Åke Davidsson, studying early music typography, and the Copenhagen antiquarian Dan Fog, specializing in nineteenth-century Danish music publishing. Others have done important and useful work, but mostly so as to anticipate or complement the work of Davidsson and Fog.

C. NYROP. "Om Nodetrykning i Danmark," *Skandinavisk Bogtrykker-Tidende*, 2 (1870), cols. 149-51.   **829**
A brief summary, supplemented by the author's "Indførsel af Nodetyper i forrige Hundredår," 4 (1873), 58-59.

Niels MØLLER. "Om Nodetryk til danske Salmer før Hans Thomisson: Nogle bibliografiske Bemærkninger," *Danske Studier*, 1915, pp. 139-49. 830
On the psalm books printed in Odense in 1535 and 1539, and later books from Copenhagen and Lübeck.

Carl BJØRKBOM. "Svenskt musiktryck: några anteckningar om musiktrycket under äldre tider särskilt i Sverige," *Nordisk boktryckarekonst*, 38 (1937), 53-63. 831
A survey of Swedish printing to the mid-19th century.

Albert WIBERG. *Den svenska musikhandels historia.* Stockholm: Svenska musikhandlare föreningen, 1955. 832
Largely subsumes several earlier studies by the author, including "Stockholms första musikhandel," *Svensk tidskrift för musikforskning*, 26 (1943), 7-86; "Olof Åhlstroms musiktryckeri," *ibid.*, 31 (1949), 83-136; and others on Henrik Fougt.

Åke DAVIDSSON. *Studier rörande svenskt musiktryck före år 1750.* Uppsala: Almqvist & Wiksell, 1957 (Studia musicologica Upsaliensia, 5). 833
A study of Swedish music printing activity before 1750, with illustrations, a list of 124 titles with extensive annotations, a German summary, and a detailed bibliography.
Derived from the author's doctoral dissertation, *Studier i svenskt musiktryck före år 1750* (Uppsala, 1957).
Sten G. Lindberg, "Svenskt musiktryck 1483-1750," *Nordisk boktryckarekonst*, 58 (1957), 309-12, is essentially an epitome of this work. See also his title below, however.

Sten G. LINDBERG. "Nytt ljus över typsnitt och nottryck i Sverige 1483-1750," *Nordisk tidskrift för bok- och biblioteksväsen*, 45 (1958), 26-39. 834
A critical evaluation of two recent doctoral dissertations, one by Bengt Bengtsson on Swedish typefounding before 1700 (*Svenskt stilgjuteri före ør 1700*, Stockholm, 1956), the other Davidsson's text above. Not having adequately consulted the German and English literature, Bengtsson missed a few points, and Davidsson did not know of Bengtsson's work, so as to enable Lindberg to propose several revisions of Davidsson's assignments.

Åke DAVIDSSON. "Isländskt musiktryck i äldre tider," *Svensk tidskrift för musikforskning*, 43 (1961; *Studier tillägnade, Carl-Allan Moberg*), 99-108.   **835**
Overview of Iceland's music printing monuments, 1589-1800.

—. *Danskt musiktryck intill 1700-talets mitt.* Uppsala: Almqvist & Wiksell, 1962 (Studia musicologica Upsaliensia, 7.) Type faces are emphasized in this discussion of 139 Danish music books, 1555-1750.
"Korrektur till ett Danskt musiktryck år 1620" appear in *Nordisk tidskrift för bok- och biblioteksväsen*, 3 (1966), 97-103.   **836**

—. "Das Typenmaterial des älteren nordischen Musikdrucks," *Annales Academiae Regiae Scientiarum Upsaliensis*, 6 (1962), 76-101.   **837**
A detailed essay, with 17 illustrations, tracing the music type used in Denmark and Sweden prior to the 18th century.

"Nodetryk," in *Nordisk Leksikon for Bogvaesen* (København: Arnold Busck; Oslo: Dreyer; Stockholm: Forum), vol. 2 (1962), 140-41.   **838**
The brief general introduction (by Åke Davidsson) is followed by discussions of Denmark (by Erling Winkel), Norway (by Øylstein Jørgensen), and Sweden (also by Davidsson).

Svenskt Musikhistoriskt Arkiv. *Bulletin 4* (1969).   **839**
The Arkiv has collected data on all aspects of Swedish musical life. Its impressive record of Swedish music publishing is particularly evident in this work, prepared by Axel Helmer and often cited for its directory ("Litet förläggarlexikon," pp. 9-13).

Dan FOG. *Dänische Musikverlage und Notendruckereien: Beiträge zur Musikaliendatierung.* Copenhagen, 1972.   **840**
Dan Fog's contribution may be summarized briefly: he is virtually tantamount to Danish music bibliography of the 18th and 19th centuries — a topic that extends up into Norway and down to Leipzig. See also his essay on dating and terminology (1977; 33 above), and his 1990 booklet on Peters, based on his work with Grieg editions (1990; see p. 224).

Dänische Musikverlage, the earliest publication (cited above; all of them have appeared under Fog's own imprint) is a directory of 38 firms active since 1771, with brief histories and plate-number lists. It was prepared just prior to Fog's and Nanna Schiødt's discovery of Sigurd Hagen's vast archive and index on Danish music publishing in the Royal Library in Copenhagen.

The second publication, *Dansk Musikfortegnelse, 1. del, 1750-1854: En dateret katalog over trykte danske musikalier* (1979), is an inventory of titles, arranged alphabetically by composer; while the third, *Musikhandel og Nodetryk i Danmark efter 1750* (1984), is a two-volume treatise dealing with all aspects of Danish music publishing, with a number of valuable interpolations and appendices. The fourth, *Notendruck und Musikhandel im 19. Jahrhundert in Dänemark* (1986), is a revised abridgement in German of the third, which rearranges several sections, reconsiders a few details, and adds new facts. Redundancies notwithstanding, this is one of the major achievements of recent music bibliographiy.

— and Kari MICHELSEN. *Norwegian Music Publication since 1800: A Preliminary Guide to Music Publishers, Printers, and Dealers*. Copenhagen: Dan Fog, 1976. **841**
A brief directory, prepared for the 1976 Bergen convention of the International Association of Music Libraries.

Michelsen's "Music Trade in Norway to 1929," *Fontes artis musicae* 29 (1982), 43-44, also cites her *Musikkhandel i Norge inntil 1929: a Historical Survey* (Oslo, 1980).

Other writings on Scandinavia include the articles on music covers by Schmidt-Phiseldeck (453, 467) and Riisager (472); the typographic manuals of Täubel (171), Sørensen (214), Lippmann (206), and Selmar (230); the Forschhammer essay (282) and the Axel-Nilsson inventory (307); and other items in the Sohm collection (291). Schmidt-Phiseldeck's dating essay (5) is a landmark. Further writings on Scandinavian music printing and publishing will be found in other sources under the names of persons and firms, among which the following are perhaps the most important:

COPENHAGEN	1846	Horneman &	1871	Samfundet til
1598 Waldkirch		Erslev		Udgivelse af
1784 Sönnichsen	1853	Hansen		Dansk Musik
1802 Lose			1880	Kgl. Hof-Musikhandel

HELSINKI	1851	Warmuth	1829	Hirsch
1897 Fazer	1909	Norsk Musik-	1837	Lundquist
		forlag	1893	Gehrmans
OSLO (CHRISTIANIA)	STOCKHOLM		1915	Nordiska
1822 Winther	1764	Fougt		Musikförlaget
1847 Hals	1783	Åhlstrom		

POLAND

Maria PROKOPOWICZ. "Szkic z djiejów kultury muzycznej Warszawy w okresie przed Chopinem (do 1815)," *Rocznik Warszawski*, 3 (1962), 149-72.   **842**
On musical culture and publishers in Warsaw before Chopin. See also her "La musique imprimée de 1800 à 1831 comme source de la culture musicale polonaise de l'Époque," *Fontes artis musicae*, 14 (1967), 16-22; also her essay in the 1971 *Szkice y kultura* anthology below.

Maria PRZYWECKA-SAMECKA. "Z historii druków muzycznych Gdańska XVII wieku," *Roczniki biblioteczne*, 8 (1964), 393-97.   **843**
"On music printing in Gdańsk in the 17th Century," particularly involving Paul Siefert (whom the author views somewhat unsympathetically) and Georg Rhetus.

—. *Drukarstwo muzyczne w Polsce do konca XVIII wieku*. Kraków: Polskie Wydawnictwo Muzyczne, 1969.   **844**
On Polish music printing up to 1800, with 40 illustrations and citations of about 600 editions, under publisher and city, i.e., Brzeg (Brieg), Brześć Litewski, Częstochowa, Elbląg (Elbing), Gdańsk (Danzig), Góra Śląska, Kraków, Królewiec (Königsberg), Legnica (Liegnitz), Leszno, Lwów, Nieświez, Nysa, Oleśnica, Poznań, Raków, Swidnica, Szamotuły, Toruń (Thorn), Warszawa, Wilno, Wrocław (Breslau), and Zgorzelec (Görlitz).

Szkice o kulturze muzycznej XIX wieku: studia i materiały, edited by Zofia Chechlinsky. Warszawa: Państwowe Wydawnictwo Naukowe, 1971 (Z prac Instytutu Sztuki Polskiej Akademii Nauk: *Studia i Materiały z XIX wieku*).   **845**
Essays on 19th-century musical culture, of which two are bibliographical: Maria Prokopowicz, "Z djiałaności warszawskich

księgarzy i wydawców muzycznych w latach 1800-1831" (pp. 33-49)," on early publishers; and Krzysztof Mazur, "Polskie edytorstwo muzyczne powstaniem listopadowym a styczniowym" (pp. 51-89), on the activities during the periods of occupation and revolt, 1831-64.

Other Polish writings include two on musical bookplates (505-06).

CZECHOSLOVAKIA

Erwin RICHTER. *Geschichte des Musiknotendrucks in den böhmischen Ländern bis 1618.* Dissertation, Prague, 1933.
[Cited in Richard Schaal, *Verzeichnis deutschsprachiger musikwissenschaftlicher Dissertationen* (1963), no. 1973.]   **846**

Marie TARANTOVÁ. "Z dejin hudebních nakladatelstvi," in *G 69.5* [*novinky ze sveta hudby z zvuku*], vol. 2 (Prague, 1969), p. 3.   **847**
[*BmMS*, 69:372: a history of music publishing, in a news-sheet on the world of music and song.]

HUNGARY

Ilona MONA. *Hungarian Music Publication, 1774-1867: First Summary.* Budapest: International Association of Music Libraries, Hungarian National Committee, 1973.   **848**
A directory of the major firms, also issued in *Studia musicologica*, 16 (1974), 261-75. See also her "Magyar zeneműkiadas, 1774-1867," *Magyar zene*, 15 (1974), 59-72.

The editions themselves are listed in Mona's *Magyar zeneműkiadók és tevékenységük, 1774-1867* (Budapest: MTA Zenetudományi Intérzet, 1989), arranged chronologically by publisher, with indexes.

Maria PRZYWECKA-SAMECKA. "Z dziejów wegierskiego drukarstwa muzycznego (XVI-XVII wieku)," *Roczniki biblioteczne*, 29 (1985), 116-29.   **849**
On the scattered activity beginning in Kolozsvár (Klausenburg, Cluj) in 1541, through the several service books, both Catholic and Protestant, of the 18th century.

RUSSIA

Россійская библіографія. С.-Петербургъ, 1879-82.

The respected *Rossiiskaia bibliografiia* (weekly in 1879, twice monthly in 1880-82), included lists, essays, and news. Bigmore & Wyman (vol. 2, p. 161, under *Bibliographie de la Russie*) specifically mentions music-selling.   **850**

Д. Ф. ЮФЕРЁВ. "Музыкальная и нотоиздательская деятельность Академии наук и её типографы в XVIII в.," Вестник Академии наук СССР, 4 (1934), 37-44.   **851**

Daniel Frederick Iuferov (Juferov), on the music publishing at the state academy in the 18th century.

Борис Львович ВОЛЬМАН. Русские печатные ноты XVIII века. Ленинград: Государстбенное Музыкальное Издательство, 1957.   **852**

Boris Livovich Vol'man's extended and nicely illustrated survey of 18th-century Russian music publishing. Cf. his "О насале ноторесатания в России," «Советская Музыка», 5 (1953), 79-82.

Cecil HOPKINSON. *Notes on Russian Music Publishers.* London: Printed for the Author, 1959.   **853**

A pamphlet issued for private distribution at the congress of the International Association of Music Libraries, Cambridge, 1959, listing about 80 names with particulars based mostly on Jurgenson, whose nephew (I am told) assisted in the translation.

Михаил Ефимович КУНИН. Из истории нотонечатания: Краткие очерки. Москва: «Советский Композитор», 1963.

Mikhail Kunin's general survey of music printing.   **853a**

Георгий ИВАНОВ. Нотоиздательское дело в России: Историческая справка. Москва: «Советский Композитор», 1970.

Georgii Ivanov's brief history of Russian music publishing.   **854**

Борис Львович ВОЛЬМАН. Русские нотные издания XIX-начала XX века.   Ленинград: Издательство «Музыка», 1970.   **855**

Volman's successor to 852, also detailed but not illustrated, on Russian music publishers of the 19th and early 20th centuries.

Jurgenson's 1928 survey (49) is noteworthy. Other references may be found elsewhere under the names of Eastern European printers and publishers, of whom the following are important:

Poland

KRAKÓW		GDANSK (DANZIG)		1822	Brzezina
1503	Haller	1609	Hünefeld	1829	Sennewald
1516	Ungler	1619	Rhetus	1840	Friedlein
1519	Wietor			1857	Gebethner &
1539	Szarfenberg	WARSAW			Wolff
1540	Wirzbieta	1820	Klukowski	1900	Arct
1870	Kryzanowski				

Hungary

BRASOV		BUDAPEST			
1548	Honterus	1837	Wagner	1856	Heckenast
KOLOZSVÁR (CLUJ)		1844	Treichlinger	1868	Táborszky
1553	Hoffgreff	1850	Rózsavölgyi	1889	Rozsnyai

Czechoslovakia

PRAGUE		1809	Enders	1867	Star
1578	Nigrin (Cerný)	1811	Berra	1870	Urbánek
1686	Labaun	1841	Hoffmann	1871	Hudební matice

Russia

ST. PETERSBURG				MOSCOW	
1795	Gerstenberg	1850	Stellovsky	1859	Gutheil
1802	Dalmas	1869	Bessel	1861	Jurgenson

Other Parts of Eastern Europe

RIGA (Latvia)		BUCHAREST (Rumania)		TIMISOARA (Rumania)	
1760	Hartknoch	1843	Pann	1920	Morawetz
		1859	Gebauer		
		1914	Doina		

SPAIN AND PORTUGAL

Rafael BARRIS MUÑOZ. *El primer libro de música impreso en España: Notable impreso Sevillano (1494)*. Cádiz: Rodríguez de Silva, 1926.   **856**
A graceful booklet on the Ungut–Polonius processional (Meyer-Baer 233), with bibliographical and music transcriptions.

Higini ANGLÈS. "La música y la imprenta musical en Sevilla hasta el siglo XVI," in his edition of Juan Vásquez, *Recopilación de sonetos y villancicos a quatro y a cinco (Sevilla, 1560)* (Barcelona: Instituto Español de Musicología, 1946; Monumentos de la música española, 4), pp. 1-8.   **857**
Eleven books are cited and discussed at the end of the essay.

José María MADURELL. "La imprenta musical en España: Documentos para su estudio," *Anuario musical*, 8 (1953), 230-36.   **858**
Transcripts of five music printing authorizations, 1557-1684.

Antonio ODRIOZOLA. "Los tipografos alemanes y la iniciación en España de la impresión musical (1485-1504)," *Gutenberg Jahrbuch 1961*, pp. 60-70.   **859**
Technical aspects of the printing of Spanish music incunabula by German immigrants.

Higini ANGLÈS. "Der Musiknotendruck des 15.-17. Jahrhunderts in Spanien," in *Musik und Verlag: Karl Vötterle zum 65. Geburtstag* (Kassel: Bärenreiter, 1968), pp. 143-49.
An overview, which mentions about 50 titles.   **860**

Carlos ROMERO DE LECEA. *Introducción a los viejos libros de música.* Madrid: Joyas Bibliográficos, 1976. (Colección de estudios y ensayos, 4.)   **861**
A luxuriously produced essay on Spanish music books, concerned mostly with their musical contents and historical context. For discussions on music printing see pp. 16-18 ("La imprenta y las viejas canciones hispanas"), pp. 83-92 ("Problemática de la música impresa"), and pp. 93-114 ("Primicias de la música impresa en España").

Angel SAN VICENTE. *Tiento sobre la música en el espacio tipográfico de Zaragoza anterior al siglo XX.* Zaragoza: Institución Fernando el Católico . . . , 1986.   **862**
An informative and well documented survey of five centuries of Zaragosa music printing, from liturgical books through villancicos to sheet music. The book is notable for its many reproductions, greatly reduced but occasionally in color, with a

reprint of the complete *Opera laudatoria* for the Infanta María Antonia Fernanda at the end.

Other Spanish writings include the 1927 Castaneda essay in praise of printing (914) and the Espasa encyclopedia (97). Further references may be found in other sources under the names of printers and publishers, among whom the following are important:

BARCELONA		BILBAO		LISBON	
1906	Boileau Bernasconi	1900	Dotésio (Unión Músical Española)	1848	Sassetti
				1914	Valentim de Carvalho

F. United States

Diligent librarians, ebullient scholars, enthusiastic collectors, and gregarious publishers have infused the study of American music publishing with a distinctive polyglot character. They have also side-stepped such encumbrances of special pleading as might appear to suggest that their institutions were anything but indiginous. This may at first seem like a great blessing — the literature is less pretentious as a result — although the effect may also be insidious: America really expects very little of her music publishers, at least as agencies that might serve the best interests of her music. Major documents in the literature include the following:

REFERENCE SOURCES

Harry DICHTER and Elliott SHAPIRO. *Early American Sheet Music: Its Lure and Its Lore, 1768-1889.* New York: Bowker, 1941. **863**
A collector's *vade mecum*, with lists of the celebrated "collectors' high-spots," by period (pp. 1-163); a directory of music publishers' addresses, still invaluable today (pp. 165-248); a list of "Lithographers and Artists Working on American Sheet Music before 1870," prepared by Edith A. Wright and Josephine A. McDevitt (pp. 249-57), arranged by city; and 32 illustrations of famous American music covers.

Reprinted as *Handbook of Early American Sheet Music* (New York: Dover, 1977), with a few corrections by Dichter. The illustrations are rearranged and several are added.

Christopher PAVLAKIS. *The American Music Handbook.*
New York: Free Press, 1974. **864**
"Music Publishers" (pp. 624-46) provides brief but very useful sketches of about 150 major firms.

D. W. KRUMMEL. *Bibliographical Handbook of American Music.* Urbana: University of Illinois Press, 1987. **865**
Chapter 16 (pp. 211-27) cites bibliographical sources on U. S. music publishing, including minor titles not in the present book.

Thomas E. WARNER. *Periodical Literature on American Music, 1620-1920.* Warren, Mich.: Harmonie Park Press, 1988 (Bibliographies in American Music, 12). **866**
"Publishers, Publishing, and Publications" (pp. 553-61) cites 74 periodical articles, many from uncommon journals, including a number of minor titles not cited here.

HISTORIES AND ESSAYS

Oliver STRUNK. "Early Music Publishing in the United States," *Papers of the Bibliographical Society of America*, 31 (1937), 176-79. **867**
Few writings in this book convey less enthusiasm for their topic. One suspects that the author, in his capacity as Chief of the Music Division at the Library of Congress, saw this as an *ex officio* assignment. His impressive erudition may have prevented him from saying anything foolish, but his affinities for non-bibliographical forms of scholarship, and for other less profusely documented musical repertories, discouraged him from probing his subject with much concern for stimulating further efforts.

William Arms FISHER. *150 Years of Music Publishing in the United States.* Boston: Oliver Ditson, 1934. **868**
The account may be superficial, but previously the topic was scarcely imagined, making the book useful today mostly as a hasty overview. About two-thirds of this book appeared earlier in Fisher's *Notes on Music in Old Boston* (Boston: Ditson, 1918), a story of the Ditson firm, where Fisher was the respected editor. The 1934 book has somewhat more on publishers other than Ditson, also several new illustrations.
Reprinted St. Clair Shores, Mich.: Scholarly Press, 1977.

D. W. KRUMMEL. "Graphic Analysis: Its Application to Early American Engraved Music," Music Library Association, *Notes*, 16 (1958-59), 213-33. **869**
Early nineteenth-century Philadelphia musical editions suggest that publisher's catalogues might be organized chronologically, based on the changing appearances of the music, especially through different engraving punches.
Based on a Ph.D. dissertation, University of Michigan, 1958.

Dena J. EPSTEIN. "Music Publishing in the Age of Piracy: The Board of Music Trade and Its Catalogue," Music Library Association, *Notes*, 31 (1974), 7-29. **870**
A closely reasoned analysis of the actions of American music publishers in the late 19th century, in response to changing economic, social, and legal circumstances in particular.
An earlier version appeared as an "Introduction" to the reprint (New York: Da Capo, 1973) of the U. S. Board of Music Trade's 1870 *Complete Catalogue of Sheet Music and Musical Works* (pp. v-xxvi).

Richard J. WOLFE. *Early American Music Engraving and Printing: A History of Music Publishing in America from 1787 to 1825.* Urbana: University of Illinois Press, 1980. **871**
My great respect, along with some reservations, is conveyed in my review in the *American Book Collector*, 2 (1981), 64-66.
The study grows out of the author's *Secular Music in America, 1801-1825: A Bibliography* (New York: New York Public Library, 1964), which includes an "Index of Publishers, Engravers, and Printers," (pp. 1133-78, arranged by city), as well as a plate-number inventory ("Publishers' Plate and Publication Numbering Systems," pp. 1181-1200).

"Music Publishing in America." Special issue of *American Music*, vol. 1, no. 4 (Winter 1983). **872**
Includes articles by Paul R. Osterhout, Richard D. Wetzel, Diane Parr Walker, Rita H. Mead, and Lester S. Levy, with an introduction by the present author.

Maxey H. MAYO. *Techniques of Music Printing in the United States, 1825-1850.* Master's thesis, University of North Texas, 1988. **873**

An account of the typography (design, founding, and composition), stereotypography, engraving, lithography, and presswork, mainly concentrating on the period after Wolfe but with useful observations on earlier and later work as well.

Russell SANJEK. *American Popular Music and its Business: The First Four Hundred Years.* New York: Oxford University Press, 1988.   **874**
A vast narrative account, weak on the periods before 1791 (vol. 1), improving through vol. 2, and in vol. 3 (1900-1984) particularly helpful in sorting out the events after 1909. "Popular music" and "business" may be impossible to define precisely or convincingly, but the increasing importance of performance rights is particularly well documented.

Sanjek's earlier text, *From Print to Plastic: Publishing and Promoting America's Popular Music (1900-1980)* (Brooklyn, N.Y.: Institute for Studies in American Music, 1983: I. S. A. M. Monographs, 20), covers the 20th-century history more briefly but with useful documentation. *American Popular Music Business in the 20th Century* (New York: Oxford University Press, 1991) is "an abridged and expanded version of vol. 3," completed after the author's death by his son, David Sanjek.

Richard CRAWFORD. "Introduction" to *American Sacred Music Imprints, 1698-1810: A Bibliography* (Worcester, Mass.: American Antiquarian Society, 1990).   **875**
This major list of early tune-books was begun by Allen P. Britton and Irving Lowens. Sections 6-9 of Crawford's "Introduction" (pp. 26-42) discuss music publishers, engravers, printers and sellers. In the "Index of Prefatory Statements" about 180 entries under "Printing and Publishing" (pp. 737-38) provide first-hand evidence of the production process.

In "Early American Music Printing and Publishing," in *Printing and Society in Early America* (Worcester, Mass.: American Antiquarian Society, 1983), pp. 186-227, Crawford and I have contrasted the printing processes, audiences, and publishing activities for sacred music with those for sheet music in late 18th-century America, and discuss the subsequent fusions of the two.

Nicholas TAWA. "The Publishers of Popular Songs," in his *The Way to Tin Pan Alley: American Popular Song, 1866-1910* (New York: Schirmer Books, 1990), pp. 37-53. **876**
Tin Pan Alley derives its name from the publishers who worked there (i.e., at first around 14th Street near Union Square, later to West 28th Street, and finally to Broadway near 50th Street). The distinctive character and role of the publishers themselves will perhaps always remain a subject to be relished rather than rationalized. The basic facts are set forth here, along with references to the important earlier sources (of which the writings of Isaac Goldberg, Charles K. Harris, and Edward B. Marks in particular suggest the publishers' perspectives: "it's all happy anecdotes, since happy anecdotes sell, and that's why we're here").
 The romantic images of Tin Pan Alley immortality — of composers who boasted of (and often lied about) their musical illiteracy — suggests the impact of music publishers on a later institution known for its slightly less self-consciously disreputable New York street address, i.e., Madison Avenue.

LOCAL AND REGIONAL STUDIES

Mabel Almy HOWE. *Music Publishers in New York City before 1850*. New York: New York Public Library, 1917. **877**
A directory of about 50 publishers, based largely on imprint citations and city directories.

Virginia Larkin REDWAY. *Music Directory of Early New York City: A File of Musicians, Music Publishers and Music Instrument-Makers Listed in New York Directories from 1786 to 1835, Together with the Most Important Music Publishers from 1836 through 1875*. New York: New York Public Library, 1941. **878**
In early America as elsewhere, few musicians could survive in one line of work. This successor to Howe separates entries according to the specialty under which the firm chose to be listed in the city directories. Part I covers "Musicians, Music Teachers, etc."; Part II, "Publishers, Printers, Lithographers, and Dealers;" Part III, "Instrument Makers and Dealers;" and Part IV, "Dancers and Dancing Teachers." Appendix 1 is a "Chronological List of All Firms and Individuals Connected with Music, 1786-1811."

Dena J. EPSTEIN. *Music Publishing in Chicago before 1871: The Firm of Root and Cady, 1858-1871.* Detroit: Information Coordinators, 1969 (Detroit Studies in Music Bibliography, 14.)   **879**
An analysis, with imprint lists, of the city's production prior to the celebrated fire. The text grows out of the author's master's thesis (University of Illinois, 1943) and subsequent articles on "Music Publishing in Chicago prior to 1871: The Firm of Root & Cady, 1858-1871," Music Library Association, *Notes*, n.s., 1 (1943), 3-11, 43-59; 2 (1944-45), 16-26, 124-48, 201-26, 310-24, and 3 (1945-46), 80-98, 101-09, 193-215, 299-308.

Ernst C. KROHN. *Music Publishing in the Middle Western States Before the Civil War.* Detroit: Information Coordinators, 1972 (Detroit Studies in Music Bibliography, 23).   **880**
Practices in the early Ohio River settlements (St. Louis, Cincinnati, Louisville) seen later in Detroit, Cleveland, and Chicago.

Karl KROEGER. "Isaiah Thomas as a Music Publisher," *Proceedings of the American Antiquarian Society*, 86 (1976), 321-41.   **881**
Thomas, recognized as a patriot during the American Revolution, later became the foremost publisher of the Federal period, and in time the first major historian and collector of American printing. This study is of special bibliographical interest for its meticulous conjectures on the movement of the music type that Thomas used in printing tunebooks in his middle career.
Developed out of the author's dissertation, *The Worcester Collection of Sacred Harmony and Sacred Music in America, 1786-1803* (Brown University, 1976).

Mary Kay DUGGAN. "Music Publishing and Printing in San Francisco before the Earthquake & Fire of 1906," *The Kemble Occasional*, no. 24 (Autumn 1980).   **882**
A brief summary, with sketches of five publishers, complementing the author's "A Provisional Directory of Music Publishers, Music Printers, and Sheet-Music Cover Artists in San Francisco, 1850-1906," *The Kemble Occasional*, no. 30 (Summer 1983).

[California Pioneer Sheet Music issue], *Inter-American Music Review*, vol. 8, no. 1 (Fall-Winter 1986).   **883**
Detailed and extensively illustrated commentary by Robert Stevenson, including sketches on "California Pioneer Sheet Music Publishers and Publications" (pp. 1-71); an inven-tory of 247 items in the "California Sheet Music Collection, 1104" at UCLA, with a bibliographical note (pp. 73-118); facsimiles of an 1882 guitar collection (pp. 119-30); and an index.

Ernst C. KROHN. *Music Publishing in St. Louis.* Warren, Mich.: Harmonie Park Press, 1988 (Bibliographies in American Music, 11).   **884**
Miscellaneous essays, partly from unpublished studies, posthumously assembled, completed, and edited by J. Bunker Clark.

Writings on music typography in America include the general manuals of Adams (188), MacKellar (202), and Devinne (224) and the specimen literature (see pp. 126-34, also in particular Annenberg, 237), as well as Driffield's essays (216, 220) and the Hackleman's engraving studies (235). The patent records are cited in 383. Recent writings on music engraving, including Gray (267), the M. P. A. standard (278), Ross (281), and Kass (283), have been prepared in hopes of receiving better copy for publication, or at least of explaining the problems of working with bad copy.

Since 1937 all but three of the major music printing exhibition catalogues have been American: see pp. 165-68. Krohn (25) discusses music bibliography in general mostly as a sheet-music historian, while Feist and Dranov (551, 552) address the business audience on pop music publishing. Romaine speaks of ephemera (518) as a dealer *qua* collector. The same spirit informs the *Antiquarian Bookman* music series (925) for collectors.

Further references will be found in other sources under the names of American printers and publishers, of whom the following are among the most important:

Pre-1787

BOSTON	GERMANTOWN (Pa.)	WORCESTER (Mass.)
1698 Green & Allen	1752 Saur	1785 Isaiah Thomas

1787-1920: East Coast

BALTIMORE
1794   Joseph Carr
1802   Cole
1822   Geo. Willig, Jr.
1838   Benteen
1853   Miller &
       Beacham

BOSTON
1798   Hagen
1801   Graupner
1825   Prentiss
1835   Ditson
1843   Elias Howe
1849   Russell
1876   A. P. Schmidt
1885   Boston
       Music Co.

CHARLESTON (S. Car.)
1819   Siegling

HARTFORD
1846   Gordon

NEW YORK
1792   Hewitt
       (also in Boston)

1794   Gilfert
1798   Paff
1811   Riley
1814   Geib
1815   Firth (later with
       Hall & Pond)
1817   Dubois
1833   Atwill (1849:
       San Francisco)
1845   Waters
1850   Schuberth
1853   Gordon
1853   Mason Bros.
1854   Schirmer
1869   Hitchcock
1872   Fischer
1881   Harms
1885   Witmark
1892   Von Tilzer
1894   Jung
1894   Marks
1895   Feist
1895   Shapiro,
       Bernstein
1906   H. W. Gray
1918   Belwin

1919   Mills

NEWTON CENTRE
      (Mass.)
1901   Wa-Wan Press

PHILADELPHIA
1787   Aitken
1793   Moller & Capron
1793   B. Carr (also
       N.Y.,Baltimore)
1794   Willig
1802   Blake
1803   Schetky
1834   Fiot & Meignen
1845   Winner
1848   Lee & Walker
1876   J. W. Pepper
1883   Presser

PROVIDENCE (R. I.)
?1824   Oliver Shaw
1842   Howe

ROCHESTER (N. Y.)
1857   Shaw

1800-1920: West of the Appalachians

CHICAGO
1855   Higgins
1858   Root & Cady
1864   Lyon & Healy
1888   Summy-Birchard
1891   Will Rossiter
1892   Hope (later Carol
       Stream, Ill.)
1896   Sol Bloom
1910   Rodeheaver (later
       Winona Lake,
       Ind.)

CINCINNATI
1859   Church
1870   Fillmore

CLEVELAND
1845   Brainard
1906   Sam Fox
      (later New York)

DALLAS
1926   Baxter

DAYTON (Ohio)
1864   Jno. Fischer
1890   Lorenz

DETROIT
1844   Couse
1857   Whitney
1868   Roe Stephens
1898   Remick (1904:
      New York)

GALVESTON (Texas)
1861   Sachtleben
1866   Goggan

LAWRENCEBURG
      (Tenn.)
1912   Vaughan

LOUISVILLE
1838   Wm. C. Peters
      (later in Cin-
      cinnati, St. Louis,
      Baltimore, Pitts-
      burgh, New York)
1854   Faulds

MILWAUKEE	NEW ORLEANS	SEDALIA (Mo.)
1851 Hempsted	1853 Werlein	1880 Stark (1900:
MINNEAPOLIS	1860 Blackmar	St. Louis; 1905:
1841 Augsburg	1870 Grunewald	New York)
MT. PLEASANT (Iowa)	SAN FRANCISCO	ST. LOUIS
1886 Barnhouse (later	1858 Gray	1848 Balmer & Weber
other Iowa towns)	1870 Sherman	1868 Kunkel

G. Other Areas

CANADA

Helmut KALLMANN. "Canadian Music Publishing," *Papers of the Bibliographical Society of Canada*, 13 (1974), 40-48.
An overview of the activity both before and after 1867. **885**
   Kallmann's other writings include the article on "Publishing" in the *Encyclopedia of Music in Canada* (Toronto: University of Toronto Press, 1981), pp. 782-83, as well as many brief entries there under particular names.

Barclay MCMILLAN. "Tune-Book Imprints in Canada to 1867: A Descriptive Bibliography," *Papers of the Bibliographical Society of Canada*, 16 (1977), 31-57. **886**
Examination of 25 books, 1816-66, with bibliographical citations that follow standards appropriate to letterpress practices. For a complementary study concerned with the content of this literature, see John Beckwith, "Tunebooks and Hymnals in Canada, 1801-1939," *American Music*, 6 (1988), 192-234.

Maria CALDERISI. *Music Publishing in the Canadas, 1800-1867 / L'édition musicale au Canada, 1800-1867*. Ottawa: National Library of Canada / Bibliothèque nationale du Canada, 1981. **887**
Dos-à-dos bilingually, detailing highly dispersed activities, from Latin plainchant books and songs for missionary work with the Indians from Québec, to singing-school books and songs in the Montreal newspapers, to sheet music from Toronto and its environs. See also Calderisi's "Sheet Music Publishing in the Canadas," Bibliographical Society of Canada / Société bibliographique du Canada, *Colloquium 3. / 3ᵉ colloque 1978* (Toronto: Coach House Press, 1979), pp. 115-31.

The Canadian Music Publishers Association has prepared several directories. Darch's essay (275) is interesting. Further references will be found in other sources under the names of printers and publishers, of whom the following are among the most important:

TORONTO	1844	Nordheimer
	1885	Anglo-Canadian Music Publ. Assn.
	1909	Gordon Thompson
	1910	Harris

LATIN AMERICA

Lota M. SPELL. "The First Music-Books Printed in America," *Musical Quarterly*, 15 (1929), 50-54.   **888**
On the activity in Mexico City, of Juan Pablos (1539*ff.*), Antonio de Espinosa (1551-76), and, eventually, Pedro Ocharte, Pablos's son-in-law.

Eugenio Pereira SALAS. *Historia de la música en Chile (1850-1900)*. Santiago: Publicaciones de la Universidad de Chile, 1957.   **889**
Includes references to the early activity, mostly under "La creación musical en Chile, 1850-1900," on pp. 357-63.

The author's *Los orígenes del arte musical en Chile* (Santiago: Imprenta Universitaria, 1941), includes good bibliographical details, *passim*. and in the "Inventario de la producción musical chilena de 1714-1860" (pp. 304-10), but mostly on early manuscripts and imported editions of the 19th century.

Vicente GESUALDO. *Historia de la música en la Argentina*. Buenos Aires: Editorial Beta S.R.I., 1961.   **890**
A massive source book, in which short prose introductions alternate with detailed inventories of publications, performances, and other events. Few publications come from the colonial period, 1617-1851 (pp. 152-55, 332-48, and 548-75). The chapter on "El comercio musical en Buenos Aires hasta 1851" (pp. 515-23) discusses early publishers, while "Las publicaciones . . . de 1852" concerns mostly periodicals. The vast inventory for the years 1852-1900 (pp. 929-1063) cites over 1,650 sheet-music editions, and includes many illustrations.

This book is valuable enough to deserve an index.

Robert STEVENSON. *Music in Aztec and Inca Territory.* Berkeley, Los Angeles: University of California Press, 1968.   **891**
The survey of music printing in the New World in the 16th-18th centuries (pp. 172-99) is still our most authoritative account.

—. "Brazilian Music Publishers," *Inter-American Music Review*, vol. 9, no. 2 (Spring-Summer 1988), pp. 91-103.   **892**
A survey of the earliest firms, active as early as 1834 and flourishing after the 1850s in Rio de Janeiro, later — and on a smaller scale — elsewhere. Includes illustrations of title-pages and music.

Susana FRIEDMANN. "The Special Situation Regarding Music Periodicals in Colombia," *Fontes artis musicae*, 38 (1991), 110-17.   **893**
As elsewhere in Latin America, the early activity concentrates in music published in periodicals. A list of 20th-century Columbian titles (pp. 116-17) concludes the essay.

See also Parigi (468) on title pages. Additional references will be found in other sources under the names of printers and publishers, of whom the following are among the most important:

Pre-1800   **Post-1800**

MEXICO CITY		BUENOS AIRES		RIO DE JANEIRO	
1556	Pablos	1850	Monguillot	1836	Laforge
1568	Espinosa	1850	Ortelli	1846	Filippone
		1882	Breyer	1857	Bevilacqua
LIMA				1896	Napoleão
1631	Bocanegra	HAVANA			
		1832	Edelmann	SAN JUAN (Puerto.Rico)	
				1880	Giusti
		MEXICO CITY			
		1840	A. Wagner	VALPARAISO (Chile)	
				1850	Niemeyer

SOUTH AFRICA

F. Z. VAN DER MERWE. *Suid-Afrikaanse Musiekbibliografie, 1787-1952.* Pretoria: J. L. Van Schaik, 1958.   **894**
Revised 2nd edition as *Suid-Afrikaanse musiekbibliografie: 1787-1952: En 1953-1972 bygewerk . . . deur Jan van de Graaf* (Kaap-

stad: Tafelberg-uitgewers vir die Instituut vir Taal, Lettere en Kuns, Raad vir Geesteswetenskaplike Navorsing, 1974).

AUSTRALIA AND NEW ZEALAND

D. Ross HARVEY. *A Bibliography of Writings about New Zealand Music published to the End of 1983.* Wellington: Victoria University Press, 1985.   **895**
"Music Publishing and Publishers" (pp. 196-97) cites five titles.

Other references may be found in other sources under the names of printers and publishers, including the following names:

MELBOURNE	1850	Allan	SYDNEY	1855	Paling
	1904	Chappell		1890	Albert

TURKEY

Bülent ALANER. *Osmanli Imparatorluğu'ndan günümüze belgelerle müzik (nota) y yayinciliği (1876-1986).* Ankara: Anadol Yavincilik, 1986 (Belgelerle türk müzik tarihi dizisi, 1).   **896**
Text in Turkish, with many illustrations and details on recent publishers, followed by a slightly abridged version in English ("Music Publications from Ottoman Empire up Today [*sic*], 1876-1976"), pp. 73-96.

JAPAN

P. Dorotheus SCHILLING. "Christliche Druckereien in Japan (1590-1614)," *Gutenberg Jahrbuch 1940*, pp. 356-95.
Printed music appeared in a *Manuale* issued in Nagasaki in 1605, as mentioned on p. 390.   **897**

Kazuo FUKUSHIMA. "Printing and Publication of Music in Japan, from the Beginning to the Meiji Restoration, 1868" (Report of the Research Archives for Japanese Music, Ueno Gakuen College, Tokyo, 1980).   **898**
A brief essay in English summarizes the history, which dates from 1472, and the content, function, and printing practices for the different bibliographical genres. See also the author's

"Source Materials of Music in Japan," *Fontes artis musicae*, 35 (1988), 129-34.

The 1983 *Index on Censorship* (555) also reveals details on activities throughout the world, such as one rarely sees in more officially sanctioned or circumspect writings. Among music dictionaries, UTET (110) deserves special respect for recognizing publishers outside Europe and North America.

The national literatures generally seem more diligent than critically perceptive, inspired mostly by familiarity with conveniently available materials and loyalty to friends or sponsors, rather than by a spirit of adventure and sharing. To be sure, there seems to be really very little blatant chauvinism. Nevertheless, it is in this literature that one should expect to learn best how music publishers have worked as intermediaries between the various communities they serve and the music that reflected their distinctive character and best aspirations. The evidence may lie a bit further beneath the surface than one might wish, although our hopes that it is indeed present almost always lead us to coaxing it out. We are still led to ask whether or not our inquiries are based on idealistic visions of demonstrating that music publishers are beneficial members of their communities, in ways heretofore undreamed of. For this reason we are particularly fascinated by the odd and unexpected evidence that occasionally does turn up in this literature to confirm our hopes.

VII.

The Custodial Setting

LIBRARIES, INSTITUTIONAL AND PERSONAL, have preserved the evidence of music. Thus while bibliography and library history may be separate topics, they also complement each other, much as printers and publishers do. Music bibliographers must understand this history — of institutions and affections, information policy and philanthropy, resources management and scholarly protocols — not only in order to consider the changing fortunes of music over the course of history, but often also if they are to find the evidence in the first place.[1]

It is not quite correct to propose that music libraries were born in the late Middle Ages, when works of and about music began to find their way into the early monastic, cathedral, and university libraries. Missals, antiphonaries, and other liturgical service books do indeed typically include plainchant; poetic texts often suggest the conditions under which they were intended to be sung; learned expositions and didactic summaries of the quadrivium usually discuss

---

1. An abridged version of this text will appear in the *Encyclopedia of Library History*, edited by Wayne A. Wiegand and Donald G. Davis, Jr. (New York: Garland, [forthcoming]).

the theory of music. The notion that these documents had any special identity as music, however, is mostly a figment of the evolutionary historicism of nineteenth-century academic historical musicology. However instinctively the human sense of order may have been attracted to the concept of subject arrangement, considerations of provenance, space, and use almost always took precedence over literary, artistic, or pedagogical functions in the scanty and generally neglected book repositories of the day. One must wait several centuries for libraries devoted especially to music, or in which any special identity was recognized.

More plausible beginnings may be found with the humanistic tradition of private collectors and musical academies. The Renaissance precepts of virtue associated with this tradition called for both musical and bibliophilic sensitivities and patronage: music was to be both supported as repertory and in performance, and collected as documents: the two fit together. (Why this should have occured at this particular time, and the ways in which the association of the two was unprecedented, must of course remain fundamental questions for cultural historians.) Holdings that clearly display a special musical identity, in any event, survive in the personal libraries of the Renaissance princes, at the Laurenziana in Florence as assembled by the Medici and at the Biblioteca Estense in Ferrara as collected by Alfonso II, among others. Equally notable were libraries of the German patricians of the Fugger and Herwart families in Augsburg, now mostly at the Bayerische Staatsbibliothek in Munich; and of Fernando Colombus (1488-1539), son of the explorer, whose detailed inventory is of special importance in that it far exceeds what survives today at the Bibliotheca Colombina in Seville. Among early music societies, the Accademia Filarmonica in late 16th-century Verona assembled a particularly important collection. Extensive holdings of performance materials for concerted sacred music also survive from dozens of chapels in the religious foundations of central Europe, notably Freising, Göss, Göttweig, Kremsmünster, Kremnitz, Litovel, St. Pauli, and St. Urban.

Pre-eminent among seventeenth-century music libraries is that of the bibliophilic King João IV (1604-56) of Portugal, rich in manuscripts — perhaps the autographs of Palestrina among them — and claiming to embrace all the world's printed music of the day — surely an exaggeration, although we shall never know, since the library was destroyed in the Lisbon earthquake of 1755. Its catalogue of 1649, the first separately published catalogue of a music collection, is thus all the more important to contemplate for this tragic history. Christ Church, Oxford, has the collection of its Dean, Henry Aldrich (1648-1710), which John Baptist Malchair (1727-1812) described so as to lay claim to the honor of being the first known music cataloguer.

Private music libraries proliferated greatly in the era of the Enlightenment. That of Abbé Sebastien Brossard (1655-1730) is now mostly in the Bibliothèque Nationale in Paris. Extensive English counterparts were assembled by the merchant and concert patron Thomas Britton (*ca.* 1654-1714); the learned scholar, teacher, and composer Johann Christian Pepusch (1667-1752); and the gentlemen historians John Hawkins (1719-89) and Charles Burney (1726-1814). None of their collections survive intact. Most significant of all the collections of this century was the library of the historian, theorist, composer, and pedagogue Giovanni Battista Martini (1706-84), the pre-eminent collection of Italian music of the Middle Ages and Renaissance, still maintained in quarters at the conservatory in Bologna.

The tradition of bibliophilic music collections has continued until today, reflecting changing tastes and contributing to the rise of modern musical scholarship. Aloys Fuchs (1799-1853) in Vienna may not actually have begun the critical study of music holography, although he is clearly the major figure in Mozart scholarship in the time between the auctions of the manuscripts by Constanze and the André firm and the 1856 index of Ludwig Ritter von Köchel. It is not surprising that his period coincides with the emergence of specialization as it anticipates the advent of the academic seminar. Whereas the earlier scholar-collectors could enjoy being generalists, their successors found it increasingly necessary to specialize. Fuchs's studies led him into looking not to the national library in Vienna, for instance, but rather to private and monastic collections; his close working relationship was not with Anton Schmid, but with the historian Rafael Georg Kiesewetter (1773-1850), who like Fuchs was for a time employed in the war ministry in Vienna. The separation of "old music" collecting and scholarship from that for "new music" (the early eighteenth century generally separating the two) is further evident in the events through which so many of the holographs of the Viennese classic composers were to end up in the national library, not in Vienna but in Berlin. These events would no doubt particularly have saddened Baron Gottfried van Swieten, who, as director of the imperial library in Vienna at the end of the eighteenth century, promoted concerts devoted to the music of the earlier era of music typography, and at the same time maintained affectionate and productive personal relationships with Haydn and Mozart.

Other music collectors were active elsewhere, often outside the celebrated musical hubs. The educator François-Joseph Fétis (1784-1871) assembled the vast collection that is now at the Bibliothèque Royale in Brussels. Karl Proske (1794-1861), by profession not only both a cleric and a physician, was also Kapellmeister in Regensburg, and it was in connection with the latter duties that he edited the large corpus of early music based on the notable collection he had assembled, which is now owned by his diocese. Great hymnology collections included those of Friedrich August Gotthold (1778-1858), bequeathed to the university library in

Königsberg (one prays that it may still prove not to have been destroyed in World War II, as official reports long insisted) and that of the court at Wernigerode, now in the state library in Berlin. The great Victorian and Edwardian collections — of the historian William H. Cummings (1831-1915), the organist and composer Sir John Stainer (1840-1901), the music publisher Alfred H. Littleton (1845-1914), and the bibliophile James E. Matthew (d. *ca.* 1910) — also inspired the great London music printing exhibitions discussed earlier.

The rise of modern academic musicology in the late nineteenth century seems to have stimulated the growth of seminar libraries more than of private collections of source materials. The several exceptions are indeed superb, reflecting on the high tastes of men of business who deserve comparison with the noblest Renaissance princes. The collections include those of the Cologne paper merchant Wilhelm Heyer (1849-1913), whose Musikhistorisches Museum, begun in 1906, included instruments and other memorabilia as well as music publications and manuscripts; of the lawyer Werner Wolffheim in Berlin (1877-1930), which was auctioned in 1928-29; of the industrialist Paul Hirsch (1881-1951), which was founded in Frankfurt but was moved to Cambridge during the Nazi era and is now in the British Library; and of the Dutch engineer and investor Anthony van Hoboken (1887-1983), whose studies under Heinrich Schenker in Vienna led to the founding of the Photogrammarchiv and to his private collection, maintained in Ascona in Switzerland and now in the Österreichische Nationalbibliothek. Crucial to the origins of modern music bibliography were not only the collectors but the librarian-scholars who were engaged to work in and for their libraries: Kathi Meyer (1892-) for Hirsch, Georg Kinsky (1882-1951) for Heyer and his heirs, and the art historian and journalist Otto Erich Deutsch (1883-1967) for a time for van Hoboken.

While printed music is not the exclusive province of these collections, it is clearly their strength, as it also reflects an outlook of mastery of the outer world — in contrast to other collections of the day, which specialized in autographs reflecting a quintessential romantic reverence for the spirit of genius. The collecting of manuscripts of master composers, its imagination fostered by legends of the Mozart autograph auctions and the Schubert rediscoveries, merges with general autograph collecting in the late nineteenth century, its spirit epitomized in the 1929 catalogue of Karl Geigy-Hagenbach and the prose of Stefan Zweig (1881-1942).

Notable collections of more recent times include those of the concert pianist Alfred Cortot (1877-1962) and the patron and scholar Geneviève Thibault, Comtesse de Chambure (1902-75), both of which included materials of all kinds but concentrated on printed works, and both of which are now dispersed, but with many of the choice items in the Bibliothèque Nationale, Paris. Among today's collectors, Paul Sacher in Basel recently began assembling the papers of major contemporary composers, many of whose works he had earlier commissioned; William H. Scheide in Princeton, New Jersey, was also a major patron of performance groups; while James J. Fuld in New York has worked from criteria of world fame in assembling a collection of first editions and other documents. (Two early twentieth-century music figures, world-famous in their own right, were also noted book collectors, although the violinist Fritz Kreisler did not make a specialty of music, while the musical comedy composer Jerome Kern was counseled to avoid it deliberately).

Among public institutions, the royal library in Berlin can apparently claim to being the first officially to establish a separate music collection, in 1824; Siegfried Wilhelm Dehn (1799-1858) was its director over the crucial years of the 1840s. About the same time, Anton Schmid (1787-1857) was first organizing the music collection of the imperial library in

Vienna. As with many institutions, the early growth of and services in these collections are sketchily understood, partly because the details of the operation, so crucial to the use of the collections, are all too often (wrongly) assumed to be of only local and passing interest. We suspect that in Vienna, Josef Mantuani (1860-1933) and Alfred Orel (1889-1967) were very important during their tenures of 1888-1909 and 1918-1940, respectively: our impressions may actually derive instead from the recognition of their names in connection with their many scholarly publications.

The situation was similar at the Preussische Staatsbibliothek in Berlin, thanks to the noted manuscript specialists Johannes Wolf (1869-1947) and Georg Schünemann (1884-1945), who were in charge of music, 1927-34 and 1935-45 respectively. The saga of this collection, from the 1930s to now, is a benumbing mixture of documented reports and fascinating legends, of thoughtful plans and unanticipated disasters involving dispersals in anticipation of bombings, followed by actual bombings and conflagrations; consignment in the name of reparations, followed by theft, clandestine dealings, and the spy-thriller setting of a partitioned society — all this in addition to the usual entropic predicaments to which all libraries can be liable.

The British Museum, blessed with its quieter setting, began acquiring its pre-eminence among scholarly collections toward the end of the nineteenth century, mostly through its lineage of keepers of the Music Room, beginning with Thomas Olifant (1799-1873) and later including William Barclay Squire (1855-1927). The several recent studies of its music collections by A. Hyatt King suggest the kinds of information on the history of bibliographical policy that are invaluable if one is to use the collections effectively. The reconstitution of the institution as the British Library may yet prove to have been a wise decision: the evidence to date suggests that the burden of greatness is heavy indeed.

322

Other major national libraries include the Bibliothèque Nationale in Paris, which today also subsumes the rare music of the Conservatoire and the Opéra; the Bibliothèque Royale in Brussels, which lays claim to Fétis's collection; and the Bayerische Staatsbibliothek in Munich. Their histories merge into the history of music scholarship itself. To be sure, the Paris Conservatoire may point with special pride to its roster of early librarians — Berlioz, Fétis, and Félicien David — than to Jean-Baptiste Weckerlin (1821-1910), who actually organized the collections between 1876 and 1909. Similarly the Opéra was proud to claim the composer Ernest Reyer (1823-1909) as its librarian, although it was Charles Nuitter (1828-99) who organized the collections and Théodore de Lajarte (1826-90) who prepared its great catalogue. It may seem sad that these are the best-known facts about the library during these periods, but perhaps this is about all that needs to be remembered. If so, the situation is not uncommon, although one hopes that future studies may show otherwise.[2] Similarly the story of the Bibliothèque Nationale between 1909 and 1930 is best known through its two librarians, Julien Tiersot and Henri Expert, and the many publications they wrote or edited.

Finally, among the great national libraries, the Library of Congress — its Music Division dating from 1897 — claims

---

2. It is not only in Paris that positions of music librarian have been conceived as sinecures. Perhaps the eeriest prospect is reflected in the well-circulated rumors of Leonard Bernstein's invitation, happily declined, to be Chief of the Music Division of the Library of Congress in the 1980s. Somewhat less celebrated and more sympathetic are the legends involving Noah Greenberg and the Newberry Library in the 1950s. Music clearly and understandably enjoys high regard in the cultural world of the library; and the best interests of the institution have on occasion been served by incumbents who work primarily in the political and social world' on the outside. But the odds are forbiddingly unfavorable, since the responsibilities require competences that benefit from personal experience in work with, and a compelling respect for, physical materials and intellectual services. Whether librarians today are being instilled with a sense of the importance of these values is of course another matter.

what is surely the most massive music collection in the world today, thanks largely to the deluge of American copyright deposits. That it should aspire to quality as well is evidence of the division's chiefs, notably Oscar Sonneck (1873-1928) and Carl Engel (1883-1944), later Harold Spivacke (1904-77) and Edward N. Waters (1906-91).

By 1900 the United States could of course already claim other remarkable music libraries. The Moravian repertory, beginning in the eighteenth century, was based on performance materials organized in their day and mostly still preserved at Bethlehem and Winston-Salem. Cuthbert Ogle in Virginia assembled a chamber music library listed in his will in 1755, while Thomas Jefferson (1753-1826) acquired music, mostly in Paris in the late 1780s, which is now maintained at the University of Virginia, separately from his several more celebrated book collections. The Harvard Musical Association, founded in 1837, published its library catalogue as early as 1851.

The 1850s emerge as a particularly important decade for American libraries and cultural activities in general, and music library activity was a conspicuous part of it. During this period Boniface Wimmer (1809-87) acquired most of the music for St. Vincent Archabbey in Latrobe, Pennsylvania. The decade also saw America's pre-eminent music educator, Lowell Mason (1792-1872), purchase the personal library of the German theorist Johann Christian Rinck (1770-1836) during his European travels. His collection was bequeathed to the Theological Department at Yale University, and is today the cornerstone of the School of Music Library. The philanthropist Josiah Bates, guided by the Beethoven scholar Alexander Wheelock Thayer (1817-97), acquired from Vienna in 1858 the collection of Josef Koudelka (1773-1850), which he presented to the new Boston Public Library. The Philadelphia music bibliophile Joseph Drexel (1826-93) purchased the library of H. L. Albrecht, on tour with the Germania company, as part of the collection that was bequeathed in turn to the Lenox Library in 1888 and is today the pride of the Music Division of the New York Public Library. The turn of the century also saw several other conspicuous events: in 1888 (its second year) the Newberry Library in Chicago acquired rare music from Pio Resse, a purported Florentine count; in 1894 the library of Allen A. Brown (1835-1916) was donated to the Boston Public Library. In 1902 the industrialist Hiram Sibley established a music library at the University of Rochester in New York, which in 1918 was moved to the newly founded Eastman School of Music.

Such events suggest the early history of American music libraries as one of decisive deeds. Other notable collections suggest slow, purposeful efforts over the years, among them those assembled at the Forbes Library in Northampton, Massachusetts, parts of it recently dispersed, and at the Grosvenor Library in Buffalo, New York, now part of the municipal system. As early as 1882 the Brooklyn Public Library was circulating scores, and by the 1930s most major public libraries had set up separate music departments.

Among American academic libraries, Vassar College early enjoyed a special reputation, thanks to its music professor, George Sherman Dickinson (1888-1964). Collections designed mainly to support historical research began to be developed in the 1950s, under the impetus of the new musicology programs then arising in this country, often through the work of World War II European expatriates. Otto Kinkeldey (1878-1966), at the New York Public Library and Cornell University and elsewhere in retirement, was crucial in fostering academic music libraries.

Among European public libraries whose special music collections are important to bibliographical scholarship, the Bibliothek der Stadt Leipzig is important as the repository of the C. F. Peters archives and other private collections.

325

Among European conservatory libraries the Svenska musikaliens Akademie in Stockholm, founded in 1771, is perhaps pre-eminent. The holdings of the Brussels conservatory, however distinguished, are still mostly inaccessible, in contrast to those in Paris, which were incorporated in 1965 into the Bibliothèque Nationale. Among collections maintained by musical organizations, the Gesellschaft der Musikfreunde in Vienna, founded in 1812, was enriched with the personal library of Johannes Brahms. Its affectionate ties to the musical community are reflected in its succession of librarians, beginning when Carl Ferdinand Pohl (1819-1887) was recalled from London to the post in 1866. His notable successors have included Eusebius Mandyczewski (1857-1929) and Karl Geiringer (1899-1989).

The history of music bibliography is one not only of libraries and their librarians. It is also a story of antiquarian music dealers, the most famous lineage of which extends from Leo Liepmannssohn (1840-1915) in Berlin, through Otto Haas (1874-1955), to Albi Rosenthal in London. (On one occasion in Washington in the late 1950s, Richard S. Hill told me that one of the most important facts any music bibliographer needed to know was PRImrose-1488, the phone number of the Belsize Park Gardens shop). The story also involves occasional music publishers and retailers who, however reluctant to glorify their work with any aura of antiquarianism, have rarely been averse to handling occasional special transactions or even maintaining a modest stock of antiquarian music. It is also a story of private scholars, not always of private means (Robert Eitner and Friedrich Chrysander, notable among those whose subsistence may forever remain a mystery); and of musicians, both professional and amateur, who may or may not have been collectors, but who recognized the fascination and the importance of the documentary evidence of music.

Since World War II, research collections have proliferated in the United States in particular, thanks in considerable part to the immigrant musicologists, as well as to the diligence of librarians who recognized the importance of documenting the musical activity associated with the communities whose special character determines their function. The wealthy private collectors who enriched our cultural resources may have become less conspicuous during the era of government-supported library acquisitions programs in the 1960s and 1970s. But they have never completely disappeared, and in fact are reemerging. We may never see another Fétis, Matthew, Wolffheim, or Hirsch, but personal music collecting continues to flourish. Most of the private collectors of today work in specially delimited materials that are not necessarily of great price. In an age vitally concerned with preservation and enriched by a burgeoning photocopying and reprographic technology, it seems inevitable that, for materials of artifactual importance, music libraries would be governed by the philosophies and practices of the reference collection, or "library of record," providing circulating performance materials through copies. The impact would surely be drastic. Responsible musicians will argue that they might wish to do without decorative covers but save the institutions of music publishing; publishers will argue the need for both, finding themselves in the company of many but not all bibliographers; librarians, predictably, will seek to define the compromise.

Through the interaction of collectors, librarians, antiquarian booksellers, and scholars, the materials and activities of music bibliography continue to be sustained. However broadly or narrowly they are defined and redefined, these activities will continue to be a prominent part of the consensus that sustains the heritage of Western music itself.

A. The History of Music Libraries

The titles below form the nucleus of the literature of the history of music libraries and librarianship, as they reconceptualize and amplify the history summarized above. In addition, the major directories of music libraries, as they describe the holdings of countless other collections, usually also cite writings of and about the collections that they cover.

Gottfried SCHULZ. "Musikbibliographie und Musikbibliotheken," in *Festschrift zum 50. Geburtstag Adolf Sandberger* (München: Zierfuss, 1918), pp. 129-34.   **899**
Argues the classic causes and names the famous scholars.

Carleton Sprague SMITH. "Libraries of Music," in Oscar Thompson, *International Cyclopedia of Music and Musicians* (New York: Dodd, Mead, 1939), pp. 1003-10.   **900**
In most reference books the article on "Libraries" is mostly a survey of the important and exciting holdings. Smith's essay deserves special respect as one of the few, and probably the earliest, to be attentive to historical trends. His article appears in later editions through the 11th (1964), often on different pages.

Wolfgang SCHMIEDER. "Die Rolle der Musik in wissenschaftlichen Bibliotheken," in *Bibliotheksprobleme der Gegenwart: Vorträge* (Frankfurt: Klostermann, 1951), pp. 76-82.   **901**
Lecture at the celebration of the 50th anniversary of the founding of the Verein deutscher Bibliothekäre, Marburg, 1950.

Karl-Heinz KÖHLER. "Zur Grundtypen historischer Musiksammlungen," in *Bericht über den siebenten internationalen musikwissenschaftlichen Kongress, Köln 1958* (Kassel: Bärenreiter, 1959), pp.162-64.   **902**
There are two kinds of collections: the historic residues of musical practice, and the products of intentional consideration of immediate scholarly needs. However provocative and important, the distinction is relevant less to intellectual and institutional history than to contemporary policy. Some libraries are today blessed with stunning residues of the past and at the same time cursed with tomorrow's problems of maintaining them. Others, blessed today with options for addressing current needs and with the means and encouragement to do so, will perhaps tomorrow

prove to be cursed by their successors for formulating policies that result in residual curiosities in their own right.

Guy A. MARCO. "Music Libraries and Collections: Historical Survey," in *Encyclopedia of Library and Information Science*, vol. 18 (New York: Marcel Dekker, 1976), pp. 340-58.   903
A useful essay, complemented by Carol June Bradley's "Historical Statements" for "Music Libraries in North America" (pp. 358-62) and my "Music Printing and Publishing" (pp. 482-93, now superseded by the Grove handbook, 57 above).

Carol June BRADLEY. *Music Collections in American Libraries: A Chronology*. Detroit: Information Coordinators, 1981. (Detroit Studies in Music Bibliography, 46.)   904
A list of institutions, with particulars on music library origins, major collections, catalogues, and descriptions of holdings. The arrangement by founding date is useful for browsing but difficult for access, although the index helps.

Hans LENNEBERG.   "Early Circulating Libraries and the Dissemination of Music," *Library Quarterly*, 52 (1982), 122-30.   905
Music rental libraries are a neglected but important institution of the late 18th and 19th centuries, mostly in northern Europe. See further Ballstädt and Widmaier (152), and also Fog (841).

Carol June BRADLEY. *American Music Librarianship: A Biographical and Historical Survey*.   New York: Greenwood, 1990.   906
A survey of 20th-century American music librarianship, built around 19 biographical sketches and a historical essay on the Music Library Association. Based on the author's dissertation, "The Genesis of American Music Librarianship, 1902-1942" (Florida State University, 1978), and oral history interviews now located at the State University of New York, Buffalo.
    Much of the text also appears in Music Library Association, *Notes*, 35 (1979), 822-46 (considerably revised here as pp. 83-108), 37 (1986), 272-91 (pp. 157-61); and 43 (1986), 272-92 (largely identical with pp. 137-55).

Pierre BOULEZ. "La Vestale et le voleur de feu," *InHar-moniques*, 4 (1988), pp. 8-11.   **907**
Translated by Susan Bradshaw as "The Vestal Virgin and the Fire-Stealer: Memory, Creation, and Authenticity," *Early Music*, 18 (1990), 355-58.

> "Must I once again sing the praises of amnesia? . . . By all means let there be a library, but a library as required . . . a 'library in flames' . . . perpetually reborn. . . . The documentary memory ought to be taken lightly, and even — like certain recent industrial products — treated as dispensable."

Tellingly, the translation in *Early Music* is introduced by the famous illustration of Étienne-Louis Boullée's 1785 visionary conception of a public library in Paris for the nation of France.

In addition, several of the essays in Chapter 1 include perspectives on the history of music libraries. The writings of Vincent Duckles (22, 29, 31 above) and François Lesure (18) are notably relevant.

B. Musical Antiquarians and Collectors

There is an extensive literature, but its most respected component consists of dealers' catalogues and memorabilia rather than descriptive writings. Dealers understandably must commit their best efforts to describing and promoting their stock; they will not wish to divulge such information as their sales devices, pricing practices, or — least of all — their sources of supply.

Writings on particular collectors, like those on particular printers or publishers, are excluded from the list below, except as they explicitly describe the activity itself in general terms.

For further references see Albrecht (922).

Aristide FARRENC. *Les livres rares et leur destinée: étude de bibliographie musicale*. Rennes: H. Vatar, 1856.   **908**
Commentary, in the tradition of French connoisseurship, on Tinctoris, the Philidor collection, music titles in the Bourret auction (Paris, 1735), Mozart autographs, Petrucci (with a list of 50 titles), Attaingnant (with titles), and Carpentras.

Also issued in the *Revue de musique ancienne et moderne*, August-Sept. 1856, pp. 465-78, 554-63, 669-77, and 730-36. This short-lived journal (12 issues only: Rennes, 1856; reprinted Scarsdale, N.Y.: Annemarie Schnase, 1968) shows a notable concern for bibliography. Adrien de la Fage's *Extraits du catalogue critique et raisonné d'une petite bibliothèque musicale*, also issued later as a book, first appears here (pp. 252-59, 356-64, 442-53). Numerous other entries, mostly by the editor, Théodore Nisard, are bibliographical, both historical (with transcriptions of texts) and current (mostly critical reviews of new scholarly studies. See p. 655 for a report on "Yankee Doodle").

Catalogue of the Extensive Library of Doctor Rainbeau, F.R.S., F.S.A., A.S.S., &c. . . . [London: R. Lonsdale, 1862?].   **909**

A preposterous catalogue of 116 frolicsome antiquarian music items, "which Messrs. Topsy, Turvy, & Co. will put up for public competition on Saturday, October, 1862." The collector is a thinly disguised parody of Edward F. Rimbault; the circumstances are appropriately obscure.

Reprinted Poughkeepsie, N.Y.: The Distant Press, 1962, with an introduction by James B. Coover.

The antiquarian bookseller's propensity for nonsense reaches into the world of music bibliography on other occasions as well. Who really perpetrated the bibliographical reference to a bass method book published in Cincinnati by "Litter, Rarey, & Hokes"? (Repeated citation of the title leads one to suspect that the perpetrator may in fact need to be damned among the gullible, at least until evidence emerges to absolve his sins.) Nor have I ever succeeded in locating a 1667 booklet by Sixt Boldrian Wurmschneider von Wurms, cited in a 1963 Swiss auction catalogue (Haus der Bücher 706-7, no. 1128) which James Coover called to my attention.

James E. MATTHEW. *The Literature of Music.* London: Elliot Stock, 1896.   **910**

An essay on important books about music, mostly in the author's personal collection, one of the largest and richest of its day. His text conveys the infectious joy of the bibliophile who not only owned and cherished but also knew books. The chapters cover twelve broad topics, the last being "The Bibliography of Music" (pp. 242-55), devoted to reference lists.

Henri de CURZON. *Guide de l'amateur d'ouvrages sur la musique, les musiciens, et les théâtres.* Paris: Fischbacher, 1901. **911**
The title is misleading. The *Guide* consists of a brief "Essai du classement d'une bibliographie générale de la musique," followed by a "Catalogue d'ouvrages," actually a list of about 1,000 in-print books about music for a collector, arranged by author with a subject index. The "2e fascicule" (1909) is in fact an updating of the "Catalogue."

Ludwig VOLKMANN. "Musikalische Bibliophilie," *Zeitschrift für Bücherfreunde*, n. F., 1 (1910), 121-36. **912**
A lecture, read in conjunction with an exhibition of the Zur Westen collection, that identifies the musical "high spots" that should be of interest to collectors.

Michel'angelo LAMBERTINI. *Bibliophilie musicale.* Lisboa: Typ. do Annuario Commercial, 1918. **913**
Essentially an adaptation of Curzon, with sections entitled, "Les bibliothèques portugaises," "Essai de classification," "Les livres d'un amateur," and "Cabinet iconographique."
The "édition abrège" (Viseu: Andrade, 1924) is a pathetic reprint of assorted pages on bad paper.

Vicente CASTAÑEDA y ALCOVER. *La imprenta: memoria: leída ante la Real Academia de la Historia en la Fiesta del Libro Español de 1926.* Madrid: Tipografía de la "Revista de Archivos," 1927. **914**
In this essay on printing, the Spanish bibliographer-polymath discusses music printing on pp. 106-10, in particular with respect to a *Colección de canciones patrióticas* (Valencia: Mariano de Cabrerizo, 1823) in his personal library.

Johannes WOLF. "Antiquariat und Musikwissenschaft," in *Aus Wissenschaft und Antiquariat: Festschrift zum 50-jährigen Bestehen der Buchhandlung Gustav Fock, G.m.b.H.* (Leipzig, 1929), pp. 167-70. **915**

Discusses early collectors, antiquarian dealers, and prices, in the context of present scholarly interest, with important names.

Stefan ZWEIG. *Sinn und Schönheit der Autographen.* Wien, Leipzig, Zürich: Herbert Reichner, 1935.　　　**916**
Printed by the Fachklassen für Typographie und Buchdruck at the Allgemeine Gewerbeschule in Basel, and issued as a supplement in the 1935 *Philobiblon* (Jahr 8, Heft 4). The essay was originally prepared for the 1934 Sunday Times Book Exhibition in London, "anlässlich der Ausstellung der Edward Speyer Collection gehalten." I have not located an English version. None is listed in Randolph J. Klawiter's *Stefan Zweig: A Bibliography* (Chapel Hill: University of North Carolina Press, 1964).

Zweig, one of the noted manuscript collectors of the Geigy-Hagenbach tradition, wrote often and eloquently of his collecting. See, for instance, Theodore Wesley Koch's anthology, *The Old Book Peddler* (Chicago: Caxton Club, 1938). The most specific discussion of his music is "Meine Autographen-Sammlung," *Philobiblon*, 3 (1930), 279-89, and in his autobiography, *The World of Yesterday* (New York: Viking, 1943), in passages near the beginning of chapter 6 ("Bypaths on the Way to Myself") and near the end of chapter 14 ("Sunset"). Zweig's collection, now in the British Library, is further memorialized in a newly instituted lecture and concert series.

It may seem ironic that the imprint in Zweig's book should also appear on the first edition of Elias Canetti's *Die Blendung* (*Auto da fé*). But this is surely no less odd than the appearance of another imprint from this same city and period, Universal Edition, on music of Hába and Schenker, Schoenberg and Janáček, and other such seemingly incompatible composers.

Percy H. MUIR. *An Autobiography: Minding my Own Business.* London: Chatto & Windus, 1956.　　　**917**
An eminent general antiquarian bookseller with special music interests (see 676 above) recalls favorite musical anecdotes in Chapters 16 ("Adventures in Search of Music", pp. 154-65), 17 ("Two Quests," pp. 166-77), and 21 ("The End of the Haffner Story," pp. 193-97), and passim.
Reprinted, Newcastle, Del.: Oak Knoll Books, 1991.

Albi ROSENTHAL. "The 'Music Antiquarian,'" *Fontes artis musicae*, 5 (1958), 80-89.   **918**

Historical background related by the venerable master among antiquarian music specialists of today, drawing on his wide erudition and delightful skills as raconteur.

   Reprinted in Bradley, pp. 81-89, also in Coover, *Antiquarian Catalogues*, pp. xv-xxiv.

Alec Hyatt KING. *Some British Collectors of Music, c.1600-1960*. Cambridge: Cambridge University Press, 1963.   **919**

Based on lectures by the 1961 Sandars Reader in Bibliography, with directories (notably "Appendix B: Classified Lists of Past Collectors," pp. 130-38). This work and Albrecht's list (922 below) are the high points of the scholarship on music collecting.

Hermann BARON. "The Musical Antiquarian of Today," *Brio*, vol. 1, no. 2 (Autumn 1964), pp. 1-3.   **920**

A respected dealer's experienced observations on current conditions, complementing Rosenthal's historical essay.

"Antiquarian Music Dealers." Music Library Association, *Notes*, September 1966 issue (Vol. 23, no.1).   **921**

Among the essays are Richard Macnutt, "Music-Dealing from Europe" (pp. 17-22), Gordon B. Wright, "Music Literature and its Dealers" (pp. 23-27), and a "Survey of Dealers Specializing in Antiquarian Music and Musical Literature" (pp. 28-33), with information on 11 American and 25 European dealers.

Otto E. ALBRECHT. "Collections, Private," in *The New Grove Dictionary of Music and Musicians* (London: Macmillan, 1980), vol. 4, pp. 536-58.   **922**

A valuable survey, rich in bibliographical references. The 64 entries for "existing collections," arranged by country and city, are followed by several hundred now deceased "individual collectors," alphabetically by name, with further particulars on the dispersal of their collections. Occasional addenda may still turn up: what, for instance, is known about the vast autograph collection in Bologna of Emilia Succi, the 1888 catalogue of which (*BL*, Hirsch 479) covers documents of some 886 different musicians? Other collections will be relocated and their contents rediscovered. Albrecht's landmark survey provides the basic evidence for all future study.

Lenore Coral's "Music Dealers and Antiquarians" (Grove 6, vol. 12, pp. 829-30) provides complementary perspectives.

Theodore FRONT. *An Antiquarian Music Dealer's Education*. Beverley Hills, Cal., 1981.   **923**

Personal reminiscences, "offered as a tribute to the 50th anniversary of the Music Library Association." Serious scholars, accustomed to sober, tightly organized prose, may not be impressed by so exuberant and discursive a parade of factual lore. Actually, a major part of the training of a bookseller involves many more such details: curious facts in abundance, flexible to the unpredictable circumstances of available stock and potential customers, to be promoted with honest and infectious delight.

See also the author's 1990 *AB Bookman's Weekly* text below.

Albi ROSENTHAL. "Gedanken zur Geschichte des Musiksammelns," *Aus dem Antiquariat*, 5 (1982), A170-75.   **924**

Shorter than the 1958 essay above, with a few of the same facts and observations, but also some not found there.

AB Bookman's Weekly. [annual music issues]. 1983- .   **925**

The series is anticipated in James J. Fuld, "Music: Books, Printed Scores, Autographs" (vol. 71, no. 8, February 21, 1983, pp. 1294-1316; reprinted in the 1984 *AB Bookman's Yearbook*, part 1, pp. 28-34). To date it has included the following:

vol. 72, no. 24 (*December 12, 1983*): James J. Fuld, "Fifty Years of Music Collecting" (pp. 4115-33); John and Jude Lubrano, "Antiquarian Printed Music: An Overview" (pp. 4134-46); Gene Bruck and Marianne Wurlitzer, "Some Notes on the Dealer Experience" (pp. 4147-54); Sylvia Craft, "G. Schirmer: The Music Publishing Experience" (pp. 4155-61); and Richard Jackson, "Americana Collection Focuses on Music" (pp. 4162-65; on the New York Public Library). (The Fuld article also appears in the 1984 *AB Bookman's Yearbook*, part 2, pp. 113-27, the Bruck-Wurlitzer on pp. 121-27, the Craft on pp. 128-34.)

vol. 74, no. 24 (*December 10, 1984*): Paul O. Pryor, "Collecting American Sheet Music" (pp. 4163-86); James and Constance Camner, "Buying and Selling Opera Autographs" (pp. 4187-90); John and Jude Lubrano, "Antiquarian Music: Highlights and Trends" (pp. 4191-98); Fran Lee Frank, "Music Publishing at Oxford University Press" (pp. 4199-4204).

vol. 76, no. 24 (*December 9, 1985*): John and Jude Lubrano, "American Popular Music, 1795-1920" (pp. 4267-90); D. W. Krummel, "American Music Bibliophiles and Their Collections" (pp. 4292-99: a revised version appears in the 1987 *Bibliographical Handbook of American Music*, 865 above, pp. 161-65); Kevin Kiddow, "Jazz Periodicals: Spreading the Gospel" (pp. 4300-4304); Peter Gradenwitz, "Music and Music Book Publishing in Israel" (pp. 4305-09); John B. Howard and Michael Ochs, "R.I.S.M. Project: Cataloguing Music Manuscripts in the U.S." (pp. 4310-14); and John E. Ingram, "Collecting Colonial Music Material" (pp. 4315-19).

vol. 78, no. 24 (*December 15, 1986*): Carroll M. Proctor, "Bicentennial Reflections of Mozart's *Don Giovanni*" (pp. 2425-31); Rosemary L. Cullen, "Twentieth Century Sheet Music Illustration" (pp. 2432-37); and Carol McKinley, "From Bach to Bop: Music Books Span the Genres" (pp. 2441-43).

vol. 80, no. 24 (*December 14, 1987*, with coverage now covering all of the performing arts): Gerald Kahan, "Collecting and Selling Books of the Theater" (pp. 2337-43); Gordon Hollis, "Dance Books and Prints as a Collecting Specialty" (pp. 2344-46); Carol McKinley, "Music and its History have Shaped His Life" pp. 2347-50, on James J. Fuld); and Carol McKinley, "New Books on Performing Take Center Stage" (pp. 2351-56).

vol. 82, no. 24 (*December 12, 1988*) and vol. 84, no. 24 (*December 11, 1989*): none of the articles in these sections is on music, although there are notices of new books about music.

vol. 86, no. 24 (*December 10, 1990*): Theodore Front, "Music as an Antiquarian Trade Specialty" (pp. 2289-97).

vol. 88, no. 24 (*December 9, 1991*): James J. Fuld and Beverly A. Hamer, "Collecting 20th-Century American Popular Music" (pp. 2289-90).

Siegrun FOLTER. *Private Libraries of Musicians and Musicologists: A Bibliography of Catalogs.* Buren: Knuf, 1987.

A listing of 392 titles, with useful particulars. Some of the collectors are musicians or musicologists only as very broadly defined, and several catalogues are only incidental and incomplete reflections of the owner's personal library; but the book is nonetheless useful for the interesting information it collects.   **926**

James B. COOVER. *Antiquarian Catalogues of Musical Interest.* London, New York: Mansell, 1988.   **927**

A listing of 5,531 catalogues, arranged by the dealer's name with indexes by subject, by type of material, and by city. The Preface (pp. vii-x), while brief, is invaluable. Albi Rosenthal's "The

'Musical Antiquarian'" (919 above) is also reprinted (pp. xv-xxiv). The list of "Sources and Related Readings (pp. xxv-xxviii) offers further guidance into the general bibliopolic literature.

John LUBRANO. "The Antiquarian Music Dealer and the Music Librarian," Music Library Association, *Notes*, 47 (1990), 21-27.   **927a**

Includes valuable particulars on how the transactions work.

Albi ROSENTHAL. "Tradition des Autographensammelns: Historisch," in *Internationales Symposium Musikerautographie, 5.-8. Juni 1989, Wien*, edited by Ernst Hilmar (Tutzing: Hans Schneider, 1990), pp. 15-26.   **928**

Music autograph collecting has historically been informed by four traditional conceptions of their value, (1) as expressions of the composer as a person, (2) as relics, (3) as revelations of the creative process, and (4) as sources for textual scholarship.

Other symposium papers are indirectly pertinent to music bibliography, among them Rudolf Stephan on promoting the cause of manuscripts, Theophil Antobiček on historicism, Georg Feder on editing, Ernst Herttrich on interpretation, Hans Schneider on prices, and Otto Biba on promoting private collecting.

See also Rosenthal's "Music und Antiquariat," *Musik in Bayern*, 37 (1988), 11-18.

Related to these topics are other specialized writings on American sheet music collectors, such as the Dichter and Shapiro directory (863) and Lester Levy's 1983 recollections in *American Music* (872). The collections at the Vereeniging ter Bevordering van de Belangen des Boekhandels te Amsterdam (968 below) and at the Grolier Club in New York are also noteworthy for their music content. The brief article on "Musikantiquariat" in the *Handbuch des Buchhandels*, vol. 4 (Wiesbaden: Gütersloh, Verlag für Buchmarkt-Forschung, 1977), p. 38, should be read along with the subsequent entry on "Autographenhandel," with almost an equal coverage of music manuscripts.

Georg Kinsky's *Philobiblon* essays (8 above) include "Musikbibliotheken: Ein Überblick über die wichtigsten öffentlichen und privaten Musiksammlungen," 6 (1933), 55-67, and "Die Handbibliothek des Musiksammlers," 5 (1932), 253-58, another brief list of reference sources recommended for collectors. Kinsky provided at least one other such list, in the *Lexikon des Buchwesens* (Leipzig: Hiersemann, 1936, pp. 504-06; see also an abridgement in the new edition, Stuttgart: Hiersemann, 1953, pp. 508-09).

C. Bibliophilic Editions of Music

Musical editions are usually intended for use in performance, and are expected to wear out. The thought of their being carefully handled seems almost odd. Perhaps as a result, as well as because of the legendary poverty of musicians, there have been very few editions designed specifically for the collector's shelves. Early examples of luxurious production do exist, but they reflect on circumstances of aristocratic music patronage more than any search for the Book Beautiful. Quick to come to mind among them are a handful of Renaissance Mass books (from Antico through Alessandro Gardano, many of them not surprisingly with Rome imprints); the great Lassus *Patrocinium musices* (Munich, 1574-1610); a high proportion of the seventeenth-century engraved music books; the pretentious scores of Lully operas (the large page size and stamped leather bindings usually blind one to their bad typography); Fortier's engraving of the Scarlatti *Essercizi*; and several typeset books from Trattner in Vienna. Since the rise of the modern fine-printing movement at the end of the nineteenth century, several musical editions or groups of editions have been designed for high bibliophilic tastes. Their varied purposes incorporate historical respect, social betterment, and control over performances, all in the name of an aesthetic statement. The most famous are probably the following:

The Yattendon Hymnal, 1899

The Yattendon Hymnal, edited by Robert Bridges and H. Ellis Wooldridge. Oxford: Printed at the University Press, 1899.   929

The four parts began appearing in 1895. The full text was also reissued in 1905 and 1920, with imprints that variously mention B. H. Blackwell in Oxford and Humphrey Milford at the Oxford University Press.

In its goal of combining social, aesthetic, and religious functions, the hymnal embodies the spirit of the English crafts movement. It was produced under the auspices of a group of Oxford book-arts enthusiasts: in addition to the poet Bridges (editor of the literary text, later Poet Laureate) and Wooldridge (editor of the music, also a noted ballad scholar and the Slade Professor of Art at Oxford), the group included Horace Hart, Controller at the Oxford University Press, who is still known today for his editorial style manual and who was particularly anxious for any opportunity to use Peter Walpergen's 17th-century music type; and the venerable hand-printer and promoter of private press work, Rev. Charles Henry Olive Daniel. See Hart's *Notes on a Century of Typography at the University Press, Oxford, 1694-1794* (Oxford: University Press, 1900), and especially Harry Carter's "Introduction" to the reprint (Oxford: Clarendon Press, 1970).

Erik Satie

Sports & Divertissements. Musique d'Erik Satie. Dessins de Ch. Martin. Publications Lucien Vogel, 11 rue Saint-Florentin, Paris, [1920s]. **930**
Satie's affinities to the graphic arts are reflected nowhere more exuberantly than in this large square-shaped (41 × 44 cm) book, printed in 215 copies as a complement to the performance edition from Éditions Salabert (Musique contemporaine). There are 42 leaves: a title page, then two leaves for each of the 20 piano pieces, and one leaf at the end for the index. The four-page gathering for each piece begins with a cover announcement of the title, in framed borders. The music appears on each verso, in brown ink on red staff lines, with Satie's date at the end of the holograph music. (According to the Salabert edition, "Ce recueil est constitué par les facsimilés du manuscrit de l'auteur.") Each musical setting is followed by a second leaf, with Martin's illustration on the recto (cubistic, mostly in soft but very rich pastels, and very happy), with each last page blank.

The celebrated introduction, on the verso of the title-page, deserves to be savored perhaps as much as the music and the visual design: indeed it is an indispensable part of the production. Appropriately it ends, "Je dédie ce choral à ceux que ne m'aiment pas. Je me retire." Now follows the "Choral in-appétissant," dated 15 Mai 1914. It is truly a splendid show.

Reprinted, New York: Dover, 1982 (reduced in size by about one third, and with the illustrations in black and white, but with useful translations and commentary).

Other Satie editions of interest for their graphic design include the *Relâche* (Paris: Rouart, Lerolle, & Cie., 1926), with another appropriately delightful lithograph, by Francis Picabia. For further particulars see Fuld and Barulich (442 above).

Satie's affinities with the graphic arts (involving Man Ray and Jean Cocteau, for instance) are surveyed in Ornella Volta, *L'Ymagier de Erik Satie* (Paris: Francis van de Velde, 1979). Also invaluable are several exhibition catalogues, including François Lesure, *Erik Satie: Exposition* (Paris: Bibliothèque Nationale, 1966); *Erik Satie: "Satie op papier"* (Amsterdam, Stedelijk Museum, March 27 - May 9, 1976; Catalogus nr. 598); *Erik Satie e gli artisti del nostro tempo*, edited by Volta (Roma: De Luca, 1981; for the 24th Spoleto Festival, June 26 - July 12, 1981); and *Erik Satie à Montmartre* (December 1982-April 1983; Musée de Montmartre, 1982). Still other Satie exhibitions are listed on p. 120 of Volta — which itself appeared in conjunction with events involving the Opéra in May 1979.

Richard Strauss

Richard STRAUSS. *Krämerspiegel; Zwölf Gesänge von Alfred Kerr, opus 66*. Berlin: Paul Cassirer, 1921. **931**

The colophon reads, "Die zwölf Lieder . . . erscheinen nur in dieser einmaligen Ausgabe von 120 Exemplaren. . . . Die Zeichnungen radierte Michel Fingesten auf den Stein, die Textschrift entwarf E. R. Weiß. Das ganze Werk wurde bei M. W. Lassally in Berlin auf der Handpresse gedruckt. Sämmtliche Exemplare sind von Richard Strauß und Michel Fingesten handschriftlich signiert."

For background see Hellmut Federhofer, "Die musikalische Gestaltung des 'Krämerspiegels' von Richard Strauss," in *Musik und Verlag* (Kassel: Bärenreiter,1965), pp. 260-67, where other writings are cited, including August Spanuth, "Strauss's 'Krämerspiegel,'" *Signale für die musikalische Welt*, 76 (1918), 641-43, which previously had been the landmark discussion of the work.

The music reconfirms the composer's wicked talent, as he attacks specific publishers (Bote & Bock, Breitkopf & Härtel, Drei Masken Verlag, Reinecke, Kahnt, Lienau, and Schott) in the first seven songs, and dismays, as, in the last five, he philosophizes on art and commerce. Recourse to a limited edition may perhaps have been intended to be seen as a means of controlling performances through access, although it also implicitly challenged and insulted music publishers as well, as it declared independence from them. The creation of a work of distinction as a graphic object, in the interests of inspiring either the performers who might perform from it, or others who design printed music, is harder to appreciate. The conception of the page itself is not kind: the margins are too extravagant, the notation too small for performers to read and too precise for them to delight in performing, the presswork and paper rather dandified. It is these graphic elements as much as anything that damn this as a profoundly self-indulgent production. Happily, the music itself is of a cleverness that makes one listen and enjoy as one recalls these odd, nebulous, and essentially petty circumstances.

Richard STRAUSS. *Sechs Lieder, nach Gedichten von Clemens Brentano*. Berlin: Adolf Fürstner, [1919].   **932**
The music is of standard Röder design, but on heavy 18 x 13" sheets, each preceded by the text and followed by its own illustration. The second colophon reads "Einband, Kupfer und Vignetten zeichnet F. Christophe. Die Kupferdrucke stellte A. Ruckenbrod her. Die Gedichte setzte und druckte Otto von Helten." Sixty copies were printed on handmade paper.

Paul Koch

Koch (1908-45), who died on the Eastern Front in World War II, was the son of Rudolf Koch (1876-1951), one of the great typographers of the twentieth century, who assisted in designing the music books and whose aesthetic is here amply in evidence. The most important of the books are:

Johannes [*sic*] Sebastian BACH. *Drei Menuette*. Wolfenbüttel, Berlin: Georg Kallmeyer, [1932].   **933**
In four oblong leaves: [1^r], title; [2^r], imprint; [2^v]–[4^r], music (four pages); [4^v], colophon ("Notenschrift und Satz von Paul Koch. Druck von Jahoda & Siegel, Wien 1932"). An inserted slip between the first two leaves explains the notation.
A prospectus is in the Poole papers in Cambridge.

Notenschreibbüchlein: eine Anweisung zum Notenschreiben mit einer kurzen geschichtlichen Einführung. Wolfenbüttel, Berlin: Georg Kallmeyer, 1939.   **934**
While the *Drei Menuette* was in its day Koch's best known music, this edition survives more widely, and is today the best known.
Reprinted, with a moving introduction by Hermann Zapf, Wolfenbüttel: Möseler, 1953.

Koch's music printing, sentimentally domestic in spirit, appeals to a warm, passionate amateurism. Musicians will more likely see it as at least unsettling, at worst threatening. As a romantic evocation of a Germanic homeyness, it reflects on gothic medieval manuscript models. Admittedly these used brilliant blacks, whites, and reds; but here they lend instead a sense almost of tribal arrogance. Delicate shades might have been more honest. Furthermore, while dramatic forms may appeal to a musician's need for precision, Koch's rough-hewn lines, those of a woodcutter, leave performers, in their search for perfection of execution, feeling rather exposed, especially after familiarization with the finely drawn detail of modern engraved music. If the aesthetic were ever to have been adapted for more complicated music, considerably more information would have needed to be accommodated on the printed page.
The descriptive literature about Koch's music printing is extensive and generally distinguished, and includes the following:

Paul KOCH. "Neugestaltung des Notenbildes in Handschrift und Druck," *Imprimatur,* 4 (1933), 174-76.   **935**
Koch's aesthetic of music printing, with a list of his two-color music books, 1923-33 (16 titles).
Other brief statements by Koch include "Die Musiknoten im Buchdruck," *Klimsch's Jahrbuch des graphischen Gewerbes,* 33 (1940), 61-66 [Davidsson 266]; see also *Volk und Schrift,* vol. 12, no. 3 (1941).

Hubert J. FOSS. "An Experiment in Music-Printing," *The Musical Times,* 73 (1932), 977-78.   **936**
Comments on the "Drei Menuette."

Georg HÄUPT. "Ein Notendruck," *Archiv für Buchgewerbe und Gebrauchsgraphik,* 70 (1933), 406-07.   **937**
Also on the "Drei Menuette."

Paul STERN. "Neue Versuche zur Gewinnung eines besseren Schriftbildes unserer Musiknoten," *Gutenberg Jahrbuch 1933*, pp. 232-36.   **938**
Includes a two-color example.

J. O. BRINGEZU. "Der Notenschreiber Paul Koch," *Archiv für Buchgewerbe und Gebrauchsgraphik*, 72 (1935), 456-57.
A brief appreciation, with three pages of music.   **939**

Helene DE BARY. "Notenschrift – Notendruck: Geschichtlicher Abriss ihres Werdens and Wesens," *Gutenberg Jahrbuch 1940*, pp. 85-92.   **940**
Koch's deference to a medieval aesthetic is especially well proposed in this critical essay.

F. H. Ernst Schneidler

Der Wassermann: Studienblätter für Schriftschreiben, Schriftentwurf und Schriftzeichen. Stuttgart: Julius Hoffmann, 1934.   **941**
"Über Forschungen im Bereiche des Schreibens und des Schriftentwurfes, des Setzens, des Bildgestaltung, der Bildwiedergabe und des Druckes." Schneidler's opus thus consists of research studies by artists on the graphic character of writing and sketching, shapes and images, reprography and printing. The modern Age of Aquarius may have come three decades later, but the "test of truth" of the "research" was even at this time nothing more or less than the critical sensibilities of the artist.

In vol. 2, examples 142-51 show calligraphed musical notation, one goal being to convey the temporal duration in spatial terms by spreading apart the long note values and crowding the short ones. The rationale is explained briefly on the last page of the typeset introduction to the volume.

In style the forms resemble those of Paul Koch, with large staves, squared note forms, and dramatic contrast. The staff lines are either red or black, and considerably thinner than most musicians would feel comfortable reading in performance. The conservative spirit of the work is guided by heavy tastes; other systems of the day are more radical in their disregard for conventional appearances. (*Klavarscribo*, for instance, turns the staff ler's last two pages are an experiment in typography that show music "mit einem Minimum an Einzeltypen anzukommen."

Hermann Zapf

Johannes BRAHMS. *Vier ernste Gesänge, opus 121*. Frankfurt am Main: August Osterrieth, 1939. **942**

Printed in 300 copies, for the associates of the Maximilian Gesellschaft. With black notes on red staves printed on yellowish paper, the spirit is that of Paul Koch (at whose workshop, "Haus zum Fürsteneck," the type was designed). The rounded notes, in movable type, compromise Koch's gothic woodcut angularity, as they become more accommodating to musicians in performance.

See Zapf's reminiscences, *About Alphabets: Some Marginal Notes on Type Design* (Cambridge, Mass.: M.I.T. Press, 1970; a revised edition of Typophile Chap Book 37, 1960), p. 15 on his apprenticeship under Koch, and p. 22 on the design of the "Alkor-Notenschrift" for Bärenreiter-Verlag. The type was destroyed in a bombing on March 9, 1945, Zapf's "Musica Roman," for Voggenreiter in Potsdam and Röder in Leipzig, having been destroyed on December 4, 1943. [*See p. 380.*]

The Harrow Replicas

"A series of facsimiles of memorable books, autographs, and documents," all but one on music. The series was inspired by Sydney Walton of Harrow (Middlesex), perhaps on the advice of Otto Erich Deutsch. The editions were printed by the Chiswick Press in London and made available through the Heffer bookshop in Cambridge. The printing is well done, on handsome, heavy paper, but it is the distinctively bright bindings, on heavy soft boards, that lend the set its distinctive character of bourgeois musicological connoisseurship. The volumes are as follows: **943**

1. *The Autographs of Three Masters: Beethoven, Schubert, Brahms.* 1942.

2. *Purcell and Handel in Bickham's Musical Entertainer.* With notes by Otto Erich Deutsch. 1942.

3. *Parthenia, or The Maydenhead of the first musicke that euer was printed for the virginalls.* 1942.

4. Johann Sebastian Bach. *Prelude & Fugue in B Minor.* Facsimile of the autograph in the Fitzwilliam Museum, Cambridge, with notes by Otto Erich Deutsch. 1943.

5. *Selected Plates from the Universal Penman, engraved by George Bickham the Elder*. With notes by Otto Erich Deutsch. 1943.

6. *Encomium musices: by Philippe Galle, Jean van der Straet, & Johannes Bochius*. Notes by Otto Erich Deutsch. 1943.

7. *St. Cecilia's Album* [Holograph facsimiles of 43 composers]. Notes by Otto Erich Deutsch. 1944.

8. *Selections from the Original Manuscript of the "Messiah": An Oratorio by G. F. Handel*. With notes by Henry Havergal. 1945.

The concept of "artist's books," meanwhile, has been redefined over recent decades, and while the implications on music are obviously exciting, unfortunately I see little evidence that anyone has become very excited. For an introduction to the new genre see Joan Lyons, *Artists' Books: A Critical Anthology and Sourcebook* (Rochester, N.Y.: Visual Studies Workshop Press, 1985).

All of these works beg the question of what fine music printing ought to be. Most of them represent attempts to modify the visual image of music in major or minor ways, in the interests of defying convention, upgrading the experience of reading music, or distancing themselves from the music publisher — but always necessarily through the institution of the bibliophile.

Many other examples of high-quality workmanship deserve to be cherished by musicians, merely by virtue of their being legible. These are editions that aspire to the Paul Revere Awards in the United States, or the RSA/Radcliffe Awards in Great Britain, or prizes at exhibitions, mostly by reflecting a traditional aesthetic. A bibliophilic tradition is clearly evident in the lavish *Choix de chansons* (1772-75) of Jean-Benjamin de La Borde. Among scholarly editions, those issued by L'Oiseau-Lyre in Paris and Monaco in the 1930s deserve to be remembered for much more than their "alligator" bindings. Some pedagogic editions use graphic means to foster and defend pedagogic ends, such as those from around 1900 by Bern Boekelmann in which the various structural elements of the Bach inventions appear in notes of different colors to reflect the editor's conception of the musical structure. Claude Terrasse's *Petit solfège illustré* (Paris: Quantit, 1893) may appear to be simply another sight-singing method, although in fact it includes the earliest lithographs of Pierre Bonnard. On the other hand, the original edition of *La boîte à joujoux*, a "ballet pour enfants" by André Hellé with music by Debussy (Paris: Durand,

1913), may be a delight to own, but its illustrations are unsigned and the modest price suggests mass production.

The thin line separating the effective from the affected, the well-done from the over-done, is usually defined by a graphic rather than a musical aesthetic, and probably quite properly. The ideal bibliophilic edition ought to make its artistic statement primarily through graphic presentation, but with an appropriate respect for the music as conveyed through the special character of the presentation and with as few compromises as possible to the tastes or financial means of the intended audience.

There are also some lavish and expensive editions, usually attractive graphically but unimaginative musically or commercially, conceived with a specific market of passionate music lovers in mind. To see these as bibliophilic seems rather to stretch a point. Most of them are either special presentation copies prepared individually for patrons, or small limited editions for those to whom the ownership of an ordinary copy could not possibly be sufficient expression of their great love of the music. The limited editions for aficionados are typically vocal scores of celebrated operas, printed on handmade or especially heavy paper with deckle edges, with added color illustrations (protected by a sheet of vellum paper so as to discourage the very thought of use in performance) and brightly stamped decorative bindings that look more expensive than they really are. Nor can one forget (although one perhaps should) the less elegant cultivations of nostalgia and idiosyncrasy, for instance the Ray Thomas and Gil Kane comicbook editions of Wagner's *Ring des Nibelungen* (New York: DC Comics, 1990), or the Europäischer Verlag editions of Beethoven's piano sonatas issued in Vienna around 1900, with original words to the music added by Theodor von Zeynek (the introductory *Vorwort* ending, "Also sprach Beethoven!"), specially to be beloved by collectors of Kitsch. Those who delight in such objects should of course be neither censured not pitied, but rather recognized as the most distressfully moved among those of us whose affections have sustained the arts of music and printing, and who are willing to sacrifice taste in one for the sake of delight in the other.

VIII.

Reference Works

BIBLIOGRAPHERS, who may seem odd for using reference books as their professional reading, are surely no stranger than their associates who use prose scholarship mostly for purposes of finding references. The Bibliographers' Heresy perhaps confesses that reference books are often more fascinating and informative than prose scholarship. The sources below, whatever their fascination, deserve their special corner in the literature of music bibliography.

A. Directories

General international lists of the names of music printers, engravers, and publishers may be selective (in which case the credibility depends on an explicit statement of who is included or not, and why), or comprehensive (in which case a tacit acknowledgement of the criteria for inclusion is a sign of good manners). The major directories include the following:

Franz PAZDIREK. *Universal-Handbuch der Musikliteratur aller Zeiten und Völker.* Wien, 1904-10.   **944**
     The main set — a bold attempt to list briefly all the world's music that had been published and was then available — opens with a list of about a thousand publishers active at the time, arranged

alphabetically with names of their cities and countries. The list, on pp. ix-xxix in vol. 1, is repeated in most copies of later vols.

Also issued in a French version. The German version was reprinted Hilversum: Frits Knuf, [1966?].

Robert EITNER. *Buch- und Musikalien-Händler, Buch- und Musikalien-Drucker nebst Notenstecher* .... Leipzig: Breitkopf & Härtel, 1904 (*Monatshefte für Musikgeschichte, Beilage*).   945

A printer-publisher index to Eitner's *Quellen-Lexikon*, not as meticulously edited as that work, but often today still the only general source for many minor names before *ca*. 1850.

Ray H. ZORN. *A Guide to the Music Publishers: Check List of Music Publishers of U.S.A. and British Empire.* Troy Grove, Ill.: Rayco, 1939.   946

Names and addresses of about 250 firms, followed by brief essays directed to a general audience of amateur songwriters. "Music Market Information" (pp. 17-29) provides particulars on how to work with the firms. Like most books on how and where to get your music published, this is not an auspicious source. (But it is better than others.)

———

Active music publishers are listed in current directories: general music directories are likely to be more useful than those for the printing and publishing trades, although often not as up-to-date. Very much used today, and conceivably of interest to future scholars, are the names of publisher's agencies in different countries.

The ostensibly comprehensive international directories listed above have generally proved to be less comprehensive and less detailed than those that cover particular regions, countries, and cities, as cited in Chapter 6. The most important of these, of varying degrees of reliability and currency but still highly respected, include Kidson, Humphries and Smith, and Parkinson for Great Britain (656-57); Devriès and Lesure for France (687); Sartori for Italy (707); Helmer for Sweden (839); Fog for Denmark (840) and Fog and Michelsen for Norway (841); Mona for Hungary (848); Jurgenson (49) and Hopkinson (854) for Russia; and Dichter and Shapiro and Pavlakis for the U.S. (863-64).

Other national directories of current publishers have covered Italy, in 1910 (706), and Germany, in 1965 (750).

Directories of publishers also frequently appear in performance lists and repertory guides, usually with current addresses or agency names. Consortia of publishers and performance rights organizations have also issued membership and advertising lists. The index to the Grove *Handbook* (57) covers many names mentioned in the text that do not receive separate entries. Extensive lists of major publishers of all countries also appear in several general music dictionaries, *MGG* (108, 530) and UTET (110) being the most extensive and respected.

Meanwhile, one asks: how many different music printers and publishers have there been, since Gutenberg's day and across the world. How many names would there be in a comprehensive directory? A total approaching a hundred thousand may seem surprising, although I suspect it is about right. The vast majority are likely to be of interest only to the study of very limited and localized topics.

For practical purposes, it may be useful to view the total of a hundred thousand as fitting in five concentric circles. At the center are firms of major significance through the course of history, of which there are perhaps a dozen. (My choice would be Petrucci, Attaingnant, Gardano, Ballard, Playford, Walsh, Breitkopf, Artaria, Ricordi, and Universal Edition: I name these with misgivings about Scotto, Phalèse, Peters, Novello, Ditson, Schott, Schirmer, and Bärenreiter; no doubt there will be other nominations and many protests). Beyond these dozen names lies a second circle of perhaps several hundred more that are close behind; a third circle with four or five thousand more of some eminence; and a fourth circle with perhaps close to ten thousand more that deserve recognition for modest efforts. Beyond this are the thousands of casual and one-time music publishers, along with a few of the engravers and printers whose work is signed or attributed, and who might enjoy greater respect if they were known. The names of a few publishers who issued much bad music in great quantities may live in infamy among those who would deny the need for anything but the best and would presume to define it. Of the names known for only one or a very few titles, in contrast, a few can actually lay some claim to high esteem: B. Fortier for engraving the superb London edition of the Scarlatti *Essercizi* around 1739, for instance, or the Philadelphia bookseller Nicolas Gorien Dufieff, who sponsored one of the earliest political songs honoring Thomas Jefferson. Most, however, are forgotten.

A directory of the directories may appear some day. It would certainly be used, and it might even be respected as an intellectual achievement.

INDEXES TO EARLY PRINTERS AND PUBLISHERS
IN MAJOR BIBLIOGRAPHICAL WORKS

Several reference lists are of special importance to music bibliographers for their indexes to printers and publishers.

Emil VOGEL. *Bibliothek der gedruckten weltlichen Vocalmusik Italiens aus den Jahren 1500-1700.* Berlin: A. Haack, 1892. **947**
Index of printers, pp. 527-43.

Alfred Einstein's supplement appeared in 13 installments in Music Library Association, *Notes*, n.s., vols. 2-5 (1945-48). It was reprinted with the main set (Hildesheim: Olms, 1962), although unfortunately the index is not updated; nor was a printer index prepared for Vogel's successor by François Lesure and Claudio Sartori, *Bibliografia della musica italiana vocale profana, pubblicata del 1500 al 1700* (Genève: Minkoff, 1977).

Rafael MITJANA. *Catalogue critique et descriptif des imprimés de musique des XVIe et XVIIe siècles conservés a la Bibliothèque de l'Université d'Upsala.* Uppsala: Almqvist & Wiksell, 1911-51. **948**
Åke Davidsson, who completed the set, prepared a printer index in vol. 3, pp. 185-87, and an arrangement by city, pp. 188-91.

Åke DAVIDSSON. *Catalogue critique et descriptif des imprimés de musique des XVIe et XVIIe siècles conservés dans les bibliothèques suédoises.* Uppsala: Almqvist & Wiksell, 1952. **949**
Index of printers, pp. 448-50; arranged by city, pp. 451-54.

Claudio SARTORI. *Bibliografia della musica strumentale italiana, stampata in Italia fino al 1700*. Firenze: Leo S. Olschki, 1952 (Biblioteca di bibliografia italiana, 23). **950**
"Indice degli editori e stampatori," pp. 647-50.
The supplement ("Volume secondo," ibid., 1968; Biblioteca di bibliografia italiana, 56) includes an "Indice degli editori, tipografi, incisori e librai" (pp. 257-61), covering both volumes.

Répértoire internationale des sources musicales / International Inventory of Musical Sources. München: G. Henle; Kassel: Bärenreiter, 1960- . **951**
The vast "RISM" project updates Eitner's *Quellen-Lexikon*, but primarily as a locating device rather than a bio-bibliographical guide, citing both manuscripts and printed music to around 1800, sometimes to 1850. The indexes to printers and publishers in the set are deployed thus:
Einzeldrucke vor 1800 (Series A). Kassel: Bärenreiter, 1971-81, with supplements in progress. An index is projected.
Recueils imprimés: XVIᵉ-XVIIᵉ siècle, edited by François Lesure. München: Henle, 1960 (Series B-I). Index on pp. 597-606.
——. *XVIIᵉ siècle*, edited by François Lesure. *Ibid.*, 1964 (Series B-II). Index on pp. 411-18.
Écrits imprimés concernant la musique, edited by François Lesure. *Ibid*, 1971 (Series B-VI). Index in vol. 2, pp. 1039-69.
Das Deutsche Kirchenlied ("DKL"), edited by Konrad Ameln, Markus Jenny, and Walther Lipphard. Kassel: Bärenreiter, 1975-80 (Series B-VIII). Index in vol. 2, pp. 119-48.

Deutsches Musikgeschichtliches Archiv. *Katalog der Filmsammlung*. Kassel: Bärenreiter, 1963- . **952**
The indexes appear at the end of each volume, following a plan developed mostly by Harald Heckmann. They are international, insofar as the Archiv includes films both of rare German materials and of rare materials of all kinds that were preserved after World War II in German libraries.

Howard Mayer BROWN. *Instrumental Music Printed before 1600: A Bibliography*. Cambridge, Mass.: Harvard University Press, 1965. **953**
Publishers are included in the name index, pp. 481-95.

Bernard HUYS. *Catalogue des imprimés musicaux du XVe, XVIe et XVIIe siècles: Fonds général.* Bruxelles: Bibliothèque Royale Albert Ier, 1965.   **954**
Indexes of publishers, pp. 418-22.

Wolfgang SCHMIEDER. *Katalog der Herzog-August-Bibliothek, Wolfenbüttel, Band 12: Musik, Alte Drucke bis etwa 1750.* Frankfurt: Klostermann, 1967.   **955**
Register III: "Namen, Titel, Sachen und Orte," pp. 219-310.

Marie H. CHARBON. *Haags Gemeentemuseum: Catalogus van de muziekbibliotheek, Deel II: Vocale muziek van 1512 tot ca. 1850.* Amsterdam: Frits Knuf, 1973.   **956**
Index IV: "Uitgevers en drukkers," p. 241.

Bernard HUYS. *Catalogue des imprimés musicaux du XVIIIe siècle: Fonds général.* Bruxelles: Bibliothèque Royale Albert Ier, 1974.   **957**
Indexes of printers, publishers, and engravers, pp. 504-12.

Bibliographical Inventory to the Early Music in the Newberry Library, Chicago, edited by D. W. Krummel. Boston: G. K. Hall, 1977.   **958**
Systematic arrangement based on a bibliographical classification scheme set forth on p. 17, with an "Index to Printers, Engravers, Artists, Copyists, and Publishers," pp. 565-87.

David A. WOOD. *Music in Harvard Libraries.* Cambridge, Mass.: Harvard University Press, 1980.   **959**
Printers and publishers are included in the general index on pp. 291-306.

Guy A. MARCO. *The Earliest Music Printers of Continental Europe: A Checklist of Facsimiles Illustrating their Work.* Charlottesville, Va.: Bibliographical Society of the University of Virginia, 1962.   **960**
An index to about 300 photographic reproductions of the music of about 100 printers and publishers before 1600, as seen in major secondary sources.

B. Sources of the Literature

Several earlier bibliographies have covered the topic of this list, directly or indirectly. Citing them serves both to acknowledge my indebtedness and to suggest some of the different conceptions of what the literature contains and how it fits together.

E. C. BIGMORE and C. W. H. WYMAN. *A Bibliography of Printing.* London: Quaritch, 1880.   **961**
A curious, learned, and thoroughly admirable anthology of early book lore and its sources. Among the works of musical interest not always easily located elsewhere, for instance, are references to numerous editions of music issued in honor of the 1840 Gutenberg centenary (most of which admittedly sounds dreadful; Falkenstein, 91 above, is an example), along with others for Gutenberg's putative harbinger, Laurens Janszoon Coster.
Reprinted New York: Duschnes, 1945; also London: Holland Press, 1969.

Michel BRENET [*pseud.* of Marie Bobillier]. "Bibliographie des bibliographies musicales," *L'Année musicale*, 3 (1913), 1-152.   **962**
Section V (pp. 140-52) lists about 200 "Catalogues d'éditeurs et de libraires." The earlier sections cover generalia, personal bibliographies of musicians, institutional library catalogues, and catalogues of personal libraries.
Reprinted New York: Da Capo, 1971.

Åke DAVIDSSON. *Bibliographie zur Geschichte des Musikdrucks.* Uppsala: Almquist & Wiksell, 1965 (Studia musicologica Upsaliensia, n.s., 1).   **963**
The third edition of a work that first appeared as "Litteraturen om nottryckets historia: En översikt jämte bibliografi," *Svensk tidskrift för musikforskning*, 29 (1947), 116-30; 30 (1948), 137-88; later as "Die Literatur zur Geschichte des Notendruckes," in his *Musikbibliographische Beiträge* (Uppsala: Lundquist, 1954; Uppsala Universitets Arskrift, 1954:9), pp. 91-115. The three successive versions include 145, 268, and 598 entries respectively, in one alphabet with useful introductory observations.
A number of titles cited in Davidsson's lists are omitted in the present work. Most are articles on particular printers, or entries

for them in music dictionaries, usually *Die Musik in Geschichte und Gegenwart.* A few omissions are general or very brief regional surveys, of some interest in their day in the absence of specialized studies, but now superseded.

Davidsson numbers for works that I have cited here but have not examined refer to the 1965 edition. Several authors' names, listed by Davidsson with initials only, have been verified and expanded here; and several publishers' names have been provided with the help of national bibliographies and other sources.

Arthur D. WALKER. "Music Printing and Publishing: A Bibliography," *Library Association Record*, 65 (1963), 192-95.   **964**
An annotated list of just over 100 titles. Most are standard works. A few citations have minor errors; but several are elusive references I had not seen cited elsewhere.

Carol June BRADLEY. *Reader in Music Librarianship.* Washington, D.C.: Microcard Editions, 1973.   **965**
An anthology of important writings for music librarians, the book also includes thoughtfully conceived bibliographies of other writings, of which those on pp. 73-75, 100-01, and 205-07 are of particular relevance here.

Vito BRENNI. *The Art and History of Book Printing: A Topical Bibliography.* Westport, Conn.: Greenwood, 1984. **966**
Chapter 8 ("Music," pp. 59-69) lists 160 items: 11 "Reference Works" and 9 "Manuals"; 26 "General Works"; 18 more under "Early History to the Twentieth Century" and four under "Twentieth Century"; and 72 entries sub-classified under "Individual Countries."

Ivo SUPIČIĆ. *Music in Sociology: A Guide to the Sociology of Music.* Stuyvesant, N. Y.: Pendragon, 1987.   **967**
The first half of this book consists of essays on various aspects of the topic and includes "Copying, Printing, and Publishing" (pp. 245-48) as part of a larger section on "Music and Economics." The second half consists of citations from the current bibliography sections from the *International Review of Aesthetics and Sociology of Music*, of which the compiler has been the editor.

The citations in the "Music and Economics" section (pp. 434-38) include a very odd assortment of writings on music printing and publishing. The citations in other sections appear to be much more promising, if curious in their commonalities. One may speculate that the general concept of music sociology usually proves to be irrelevant to the needs of bibliographers, insofar as it attempts to address their subject directly, but surprisingly provocative as it tries to do so indirectly.

CATALOGUES OF COLLECTIONS
ON THE HISTORY OF PRINTING

Vereeniging ter Bevordering van de Belangen des Boekhandels te Amsterdam. *Catalogus der Bibliotheek.* s'Gravenhaag: Nijhoff, 1920-34.   **968**

The most important coverage of music is in vol. 4 (1934) and consists of entries for catalogues ("Fondscatalogi", pp. 215-420). These are accessible through the classified index that follows, in which the music section (pp. 474-76) identifies about 200 entries, most of them antiquarian catalogues. The set also includes 24 general and bibliographical music titles in vol. 1 (1920), pp. 354-46; and 11 secondary sources in vol. 3 (1928), pp. 958-59.

Of the supplements, vol. 5 (1940) includes 24 music entries on pp. 263-64; vol. 6 (1949) 18 entries on pp. 177-78; vol. 7 (1965) about 80 entries on pp. 453-59; and vol. 8 (1979) about 300 entries on pp. 552-54.

St. Bride Foundation Institute. *Catalogue of the Technical Reference Library.* London, 1919.   **969**

Citations of writings on music printing are scattered throughout, arranged alphabetically by author with no subject coverage. The work remains invaluable, since the library itself is centrally important; a good deal of the technical literature cited here (mostly in Chapter 3), for instance, is uniquely held at St. Bride's.

The library's *Catalogue of Periodicals Relating to Printing and Allied Subjects* (London, 1951) is also useful, although for many of the most interesting and elusive titles one must turn to the classed subject catalogue, on cards at the library.

Newberry Library (Chicago), John M. Wing Foundation. *Dictionary Catalogue of the History of Printing*. Boston: G. K. Hall, 1961.   970

Writings about music printing, along with an assortment of significant exemplars of notable music printing, may be found under Library of Congress subject headings ("Music engraving and printing," "Music printing – bibliography," "Music printing – history," "Music printing – plate numbers," "Music printing – specimens – facsimiles," "Music manuscripts – facsimiles", "Music publishing," and "Music title-pages") in vol. 3, pp. 2633-37 of the main set (about a hundred items).

The First Supplement (1970), vol. 2, pp. 171-72 adds about 50 items; the Second (1981), vol. 3, pp. 5-6, about 30 more.

Columbia University (New York), American Type Founders Company Library. *The History of Printing from the Beginnings to 1930: Subject Catalogue . . . .* Millwood, N.Y.: Kraus, 1980.   971

See the introduction by Kenneth A. Lohf. The collection itself, assembled by Henry Bullen, is now dispersed through the Butler Library's rare book, library science, and graphic arts collections. About 40 "Music Printing" entries are in vol. 3, pp. 1615-17.

CURRENT BIBLIOGRAPHIES

Bibliographie des Musikschrifttums, 1936- . Leipzig (Frankfurt am Main, Hofheim am Taunus): Friedrich Hofmeister, 1938-68; Mainz: Schott, 1969- .   972

Music printing and publishing have been covered in various places over the years: up to 1955 mostly in class I (or A, as "Bibliographien," usually at the end of the section), and from 1956 to 1961 mostly in class 6-C ("Notendruck"). After 1961 "Verlagswesen und Urheberrecht" fit in at the end of class A or the beginning of class B, "Notendruck" usually at the end of class IX.d. In recent years, "Stich- und Sachregister" entries, such as "Notendruck" (or, the latest preference, "Musikdruck") and "Musikverlag" often turn up additional references, mostly but not exclusively to German publications.

The Music Index: A Subject-Author Guide to Music Periodical Literature. Detroit: Information Coordinators; Warren, Mich.: Harmonie Park Press, 1949- . **973**
Music printing and publishing are covered under such subject headings as "Composer-Publisher Relationship"; "Lithography"; "Periodicals – Music Published in"; "— Printers and Engravers"; "Printing and Engraving", and "Publishers", as well as under the names of particular publishers and printers.
Recent years are also now available on CD-ROM (Arlington, Va.: Chadwyck-Healey, 1991-).

RILM Abstracts. New York: Répertoire Internationale de Littérature Musicale, 1967- . **974**
Writings primarily about music printing and publishing are entered mostly in section 89, "Printing, Engraving, Publishing," and also occasionally in sections 01-10, among the Reference and Research Materials. Other works on music printing are classified elsewhere but accessible through the Author-Subject Index under headings such as "Copyright", "Dealers", "Dating Aids", "Publishers and Printers", and "Publishing and Printing", as well as under the names of particular publishers and printers.
Also available online and on CD-ROM.

Annual Bibliography of the History of Printed Books and Libraries. The Hague: Nijhoff, 1973-. **975**
Many of the annual volumes include music citations in section M7 ("Arts, Entertainment, Sports").

Bibliographie der Buch- und Bibliotheksgeschichte (BBB), 1980/81- . Bad Iburg: [Horst Meyer], 1980/81- . **976**
Entries under "Musikdruck" in the indexes to the annual volumes often cite writings that do not appear in any of the other four sets above.

IX.

Epilogue

THIS ACCOUNT has been designed as a bibliographical list intermixed with prose narrative, mostly in the hopes that it will be both read as a text and consulted as an index. The aim, like that of all bibliographies, is to respect and encourage the readers' privileges and responsibilities in developing arguments out of the literature. The writings themselves, of course, have their own privileges and responsibilities, which are always usefully described, and sometimes most honestly evaluated, in a bibliographical presentation.

Prose, if it is to be effective and of any consequence, may need to be selective and interpretive; but it does not necessarily follow that bibliographical lists (even un-annotated ones) are entirely objective and free from tendentiousness. Arguments, in fact, are inevitably embedded in bibliographical presentations — the most basic always being that the topic needs and deserves readers in the first place.

Let me thus comment on several other conclusions that may emerge from this list, so as to concede that they are in fact assumptions. My comments reflect a dialogue that has been, certainly not lacking in the literature, but largely assumed, and understandably: the amount of relevant detail is prodigious and ambiguous, feelings always run high where music is concerned, and the arguments often, unfortunately, look most attractive when the details are blurred.

One often proposed argument, attractive but vague, holds that music on paper is today a dead duck. Born of Gutenberg, it grew strong and prosperous by 1900, but is said to have been shot in mid-flight by a conspiracy that includes the sound recording (there are indeed some persuasive correlations); the computer (which still enjoys the heady power of getting blamed for many of today's evils); the photocopy machine (music publishers point to it as the villain); new and more competitive patterns of distribution, promotion, transportation, and retailing, which institutions of modest dimensions are ill-equipped to comprehend; and, finally, the demise of Western civilization itself. For better or worse, this is not exactly what is happening. As one examines our overflowing library collections, one admires Hamlet's resolve to "wipe away all trivial fond records." Lamenting the disappearance of the world's forests into the paper mill, one almost wishes for the unbearable lightness of paperlessness.

Instead, auditory documents — sound recordings, also live performances, which are still proliferating, even as formal events — have actually served to foster a society that now probes all the more diligently in search of textual authenticity and standardization, and does so with all the more trusting recourse to the paper copy. Computers have made it possible to generate documents, more easily if not ultimately more cheaply, and hence in greater profusion. Photocopies are clearly a godsend to performers, in a day when music publishers have failed to cope with a market that is increasingly specialized in its audiences, scattered in its locations, and harrassed in its scheduling. (Photocopies have also been a godsend to bibliographers, and scholars in general, in that they make possible the side-by-side comparison of original documents from widely-disparate repositories.) Academic instincts, as they come to enjoy special respect, naturally direct our attention even more deferentially toward the written text as arbiter of the musical experience. What yesterday's performers marked in black pencil or heavy crayon, creased at the corners for a faster page-turn, and pawed desperately on the music rack in the split seconds when their hands were free, today's readers view in the exhibit case in the rare book room, with humble respect and reverent critical imagination, and with hands held quietly at their sides.

Slowly the printed text has come to be recognized as an artifactual statement in its own right, something more than a conveyor of factual particulars. The notes have always been there, whether correct or corrupt, along with other indications of how and how not to perform them. Reading the notes, whether for purposes of executing them in performance or imagining their silent execution, is admittedly a demanding and engrossing experience that makes it very difficult to think of anything else. Yet we really know very little about the history of musical literacy, no doubt in part because the transformation of signs into musical sound is in itself so magical. One stops short of arguing that the single most important event over the history of Western music has been the emergence of the printed musical text itself,[1] beginning tentatively with the typeset artifacts of chant, its impact becoming manifest only after 1700 with the engraved editions that could stimulate the imaginations of increasingly skilled performers and of composers who understood the musical potential that is latent in the visual algorithm.

The transformation of signs into sound is at once self-evident, magical, and natural, so as to make it hard to be specific about the act of reading music. It is not easy to separate the evidence of a printer's respect for the muscular demands from other thoughtful details that enhance the

---

1. One also awaits an extrapolation of the basic argument in Enrico Bellone's *A World on Paper: Studies on the Second Scientific Revolution* (Cambridge, Mass.: MIT Press, 1980; a translation of his *Il mondo di carta*, Milano: Mondadori, 1976).

reading experience. What exactly is the "affecting presence" of a musical edition? Does the rich, creamy paper used in some Ricordi vocal scores really inspire singers to produce a more opulent tone, or conceive of a more passionate and sensitive performance? Did the performers of *Parthenia*, of the Borboni editions of Frescobaldi, and of other seventeenth-century engraved editions, actually touch the keys with greater sensitivity for not having to suffer the ugly and unforgiving typographic presentations of other repertories of the day? What different sense of conformity and individuality, of comparability of interpretation, might musicians have felt, knowing that others could be working from identical presentations of the same printed notes? What difference in performance practice might have accrued over the course of time, thanks to the different experiences of work with manuscripts and printed editions?

Amenities for the performer in recent editions are no easier to imagine than to discuss, nor are they even always separable from the amenities that paid respect to the composer's or publisher's patron of earlier days, or the purchaser of more recent times. We can more readily appreciate the fact that different statements are being made, for instance by the composer's lifetime editions of Lassus and Lully; of J. S. and J. C. Bach; of Stephen Foster and George Gershwin; of Erik Satie and Richard Strauss. We can also recognize that some publishers had an eye for the visual statement (Petrucci, George Bickham, and Ricordi among them, not to mention the publishers of Tin Pan Alley), while others did not. A few may even have been more successful because they chose to concern themselves with the content more than the appearance of their music. Attaingnant, Playford and most of the seventeenth-century Italian publishers come to mind, along with Breitkopf & Härtel and C. F. Peters in late nineteenth-century Germany, all of whom enjoyed an audience that was as captive as it was impecunious. Buried in the literature, and I hope suggested by the annotations to this book, may be an outline of an aesthetic of the printed musical document, although the panorama seems rather too vast to admit of any persuasive over-riding arguments.

A second assumption involves the proliferating specialization among the producers of musical documents. New functions emerged in time, often in response to new printing technology, but just as often serving to address the needs and inspire the tastes of different intended users. The event is both external and internal. The role of music publishers in developing new audiences, particularly during the nineteenth century, has been suggested earlier, and clearly deserves further study. It seems simplistic to see the music printer as a replacement for the copyist, as intermediary between composer and performer; yet this must remain the basis for our understanding, until Renaissance scholars can propose models that recognize the greater technical ingenuity required, along with the greater prospects for profit, and the greater entrepreneural challenges and risks.

Divisions of labor understandably very soon became evident. The printer became separated from the publisher; the printer opted for the use of either the platen press and typography, or the rolling press and engraving. Each method required one specialized craftsman to prepare the printing surfaces and another to run off copies. For the printing surfaces, either engravers were needed (and those who executed the music and the covers are often different, beginning notably in eighteenth-century France), or compositors (and those who set mosaic type were presumably more highly regarded than those who worked with linear or nested type). Also necessary were punch-cutters (for both movable type and engravers) and typefounders (for movable type); ideally, competent musical editors as well; occasionally even a special music papermaker; and binders to produce a sturdy cover to lie flat on a music rack.

On the publisher's side a sequence of specialties has in turn emerged: contact agents, accountants, copyright lawyers, advertising and promotion specialists, distributors, even impresarios, not to mention the sadly neglected but nonetheless essential network of retailers. Industrial models have no doubt been declining over the course of the present century. Recalling the pictures and descriptions of the vast factories of yore — the dark mills of Röder, Brandstetter, and Engelmann in Leipzig, of Lowe & Brydone and Röder too in London, of Schirmer in Long Island City, with tall smokestacks on the outside and very heavy machinery on the inside — it is hard to weep at their departure. One may even rejoice at the prospect that industrial amalgamation and corporate raiding may serve mostly to kill off both the already dying ducks and the new voracious vultures.

Small eggs are still being hatched, however. Music publishing may indeed be a cottage industry in a post-industrial society. The litany of all the activities that are entailed, as recited above, may serve to warn and deter some; others may be invigorated, and even sustained, by the great variety. Indeed, one of the lessons of this book ought to be that music printing and publishing are anything but dull, especially when quality is the goal.

Into this world, meanwhile, the music bibliographer arrives, at first to take inventory and to figure out how things were done, but along the way also to imply the verdict of history. The task of passing judgment is rarely encountered in the literature of music bibliography, perhaps out of fears of embarrassment and inadequacy: how can one possibly reconcile musical art and graphic art, let alone art and business? Practitioners generally avoid the question, having already answered it in their own minds and by their products. Still, knowing that there is no final answer, they entertain righteous hope that they may survive to have the privilege of continuing to re-formulate their answer. Body and spirit need to be accommodated, and music printing, even more than music publishing, offers particularly exposed settings in which to accommodate them.

What then should one respect in an imprint? Why should anyone wish to publish music? Tendinitis, or a poverty of creative musical imagination, have often indeed led to music publishing careers, although other considerations are no doubt usually in evidence as well. There are even a few music publishers who became very wealthy (J. Alfred Novello's forty years' retirement at his Mediterranean villas perhaps being the crowning example). Surely artistic ideals are also to be presumed, over lean years in particular, although the evidence is usually most profound when it is most implicit. The most successful music printer may be the one who produces the truest and most beautiful copy; but must the most successful music publisher be defined as the one who laughs the loudest on the way to the bank?

Across the panorama, one looks for praiseworthy achievements, the well done and the badly done, and the role of human intelligence in accommodating them, even as one seeks to define them. There have been instances of money thrown profligately into undeserving music, of kind words and deeds extended by well-meaning music publishers to some very curious composers and audiences. Less easily discernable are examples of the reverse: instances of promising efforts that can be argued to have failed because of a publisher's stinginess or lack of capital. Clearly a special shrine should be reserved for those publishers who were blessed to be able to recognize music of artistic merit, to encourage creative talents, and to help create audiences that would recognize the quality of the music — and at the same time to avoid bankruptcy.

The success rate obviously cannot be high. Being in the right place at the right time is crucial. I would give special honors to several Ricordis in the nineteenth century (in the Italian opera marketplace of their day, success no doubt bred chaos), and Emil Hertzka in the early twentieth (there are few losers in the early Universal catalogue, and the sheer diversity of the winners is nothing short of amazing). Attaingnant in the sixteenth century and Walsh and Breitkopf in the eighteenth also deserve special respect, (their successes having been determined in each instance by technological expedients) and also (there are obviously very important and interesting lessons here) by the complicated and creative ways they developed music publishing programs around those expedients. So too, for their impact on society in general in behalf of the art of music, honorable mention goes to the Venetians Gardane and Scotto, at least in the mid-sixteenth century, and to John Playford in the seventeenth. One must reserve a special lament for Petrucci, whose visions were probably too ambitious ever to have succeeded; perhaps too for Oliver Ditson in the 1890s, whose decision to upgrade its catalogue failed to recognize the changing audience. In all events, music bibliography must recognize its critical responsibility if it is to consider its mission at anything higher than a technical level.

At this point we must consider those writings that argue or assume that music publishing as a whole, and music printing in its wake, have worked to the detriment of musical quality itself. However desirable, it was not really possible to discuss the matter earlier in this book, since these ideas invariably seem to find themselves not only vaguely defined, but also well concealed in a polemical literature in search of larger and more dangerous game. Here, blended into dark and shadowy arguments, the music publisher and printer lie cowering, in innocence, guilt, or indifference. The basic complaints are frequently echoed, for instance by those who, often justifiably, decry the high prices, bad editing, slovenly production, and unavailability of copies.

Unfortunately, these sentiments rarely become very specific in their consideration of music publishing. The few writings that come close to the topic rarely venture close to the evidence of the printed artifacts themselves: they are difficult to recognize as part of the literature of music bibliography. (Supičić, 554 above, is among the few exceptions.) The accusations generally fall under five rubrics (closely interrelated and overlapping, so as perhaps to be not really separable at all):

1. Publishing renders the art of music anemic, less exciting and less imaginative. The notion applied to publishing in general finds its classic statement in Alexander Pope's *Dunciad* of 1729. But are there any writings from this period concerned with music (i.e., on Queen Dullness masquerading as St. Cecilia)? The closest candidate is probably Arthur Bedford's *The Great Abuse of Musick* (1711). Bedford shows himself to be remarkably sensitive to bibliographical matters. His sermonizing may strike us as redundant and confused, but it is also clear that he recognized the basic different processes of printing, and the way in which each produced a slightly different kind of musical edition — typographic anthologies as distinct from engraved song sheets, for instance. His bile is stimulated mostly by the "immodesty" and the "profaneness" of published music,[2] and he is, alas but predictably, totally serious — but still learned and perceptive enough to make his work still worth reading.

For a time recently, German scholarship was greatly concerned with the concept of musical trivia, culminating in the *Studien zur Trivialmusik des 19. Jahrhunderts*, an anthology of essays edited by Carl Dahlhaus (Regensburg: G. Bosse, 1967; Studien zur Musikgeschichte des 19. Jahrhunderts). Ballstädt and Widmaier (152 above) persuasively identify the role of music publishers in the history of "salon music." As the study of the phenomenon of Kitsch may become more scholarly, music publishers may be expected to be swept into the festivities.

Wilfrid Mellers[3] specifies several basic themes that he sees as characteristic of "the genesis of entertainment music" in Europe.

---

2. I have developed these points in a lecture on "Printing, Publishing, and the Rise of the Musical Canon in Eighteenth-Century England," at the William Andrews Clark Library of the University of California, Los Angeles, February 16, 1990.

3. *Music in a New Found Land: Themes and Developments in the History of American Music* (New York: Alfred A. Knopf, 1965), p. 244.

Some will argue that they are applicable to the output of the music press in general:

> dedication to the passing moment; a strain of cruelty that comes from denying the complexity of human passion; an awareness of lost innocence and a complementary desire to recover the immediacy of a child; an adolescent instinct to evade reality in a dream.

Powerful sentiments, impossible to certify with any exactitude, but none the less attractive to imagine, especially in moments of fatigue. Mellers continues his discussion with comments on the music of American "art" composers, proposing that it took them "longer to realize what these impulses were." He stresses the blending of elements of both art and entertainment in composers like Edward MacDowell ("pseudo-celtic dream-music . . . approximate to highly sensitive 'entertainment music'"), and others like Foster, Gottschalk, and Sousa, who "hardly claimed to be art-composers, but were content to be considered as popular entertainers." The distinction between art and popular music, if not demonstrably a music publishers' creation, is surely an event that has been fostered by their search for markets, as it has provided more specialized markets for their publications.

2. Music publishing is corrupted as it comes to be preoccupied with "big money." The arguments are mostly of recent American vintage — one can detect, not too deeply beneath the surface, the kindly idealism of Ralph Waldo Emerson and Matthew Arnold, more than the angry contempt of radical Marxism — and if the major bombardment misses any music publishers, it is probably because they seem like such small targets. Cecil Smith, in *Worlds of Music* (Philadelphia: Lippincott, 1952), for instance, directs his assault mostly at the world that has arisen to cater to greedy performers, while Paul S. Carpenter's "ASCAP's Golden Legend" (Chapter 6, pp. 109-136), in his *Music: An Art and a Business* (Norman: University of Oklahoma Press, 1953), takes aim at the performance-rights lawyers more than at printed music. G. Wallace Woodworth's *The World of Music* (Cambridge, Mass.: Belknap Press, 1964) scarcely acknowledges music publishers, perhaps in the benign assumption that music and money are happier when they are not mixed. Other recent commentaries, including several polemics by Nicholas Tawa, also suggest that a well-paid piper plays a louder tune, if not necessarily a more beautiful one.

3. Music publishing, by virtue of its capitalistic objectives, is "regressive" in that it suppresses the noblest aspirations of society. Such notions pervade the writings of the Frankfurt Marxists. I can cite no specifics on music publishing and very few references at all to particular documents. Theodor Adorno and Herbert Marcuse once again prefer to hunt for bigger game, notably the radio and recording media (Arturo Toscanini, for instance, being Adorno's favorite target). Another promising commentator might appear to be Walter Benjamin, especially in the classic "The Work of Art in the Age of Mechanical Reproduction."[4] Benjamin's sympathies (reflected in another notable essay, "On Unpacking My Library") make his heavy prose well worth the battle, although once again music bibliographers are left longing for particulars. His few examples deal mostly with film.

4. Music publishing is misguidedly manipulative, to its detriment, since manipulation is destined to fail and to earn contempt. In contrast to the arguments from the artistic aristocracy above — that the tastes induced by publishers debase society by appealing to its lower instincts — these arguments speak from below in the name of the common man as timid conservative: music publishers corrupt public taste through special access to officially sanctioned power. Alois Melichar's "Verleger-Epistel" in his *Musik in der Zwangsjacke: Die deutsche Musik zwischen Orff und Schönberg* (Wien: Eduard Wancura, 1958), pp. 44-54, for instance, saw the firm of Schott as part of the mischievous and pernicious "Kartell" of German avant-garde music.

A more complicated variant of the manipulative argument works from the widely accepted proposal (quoted in Rothenberg, 571 above, p. 101n), that "a publisher of serious music *needs* the performance royalties and a publisher of popular music *earns* the money." There is an unevenly recorded history of music publishers sharing their wealth. Altmann and Engel (528 and 531 above) both reflect on this, with different practical objectives in mind. Sometimes the practice is justified as charity: the duty of the rich is to support their own poor. Elsewhere it is justified as invest-

---

4. "Das Kunstwerk im Zeitalter seiner technischen Reproduzierbarkeit" appeared originally in the 1936 *Zeitschrift für Sozialforschung*; a *Zweite Fassung* appears in the Suhrkamp edition of Benjamin's *Gesammelte Schriften*, vol. 7, part 1, pp. 350-84. The translation is published in his *Illuminations* (London: Jonathan Cape, 1950), pp. 219-53.

ment: those who lose money are privileged for being unencumbered by profit motives. Hence the losers are free and indeed have, if not special responsibilities to the future, at least special insights into it: they amount to a trade investment in "research and development." However difficult such sentiments may be to rationalize, one is generally happy to have faith in them, although the failure of the institutions does create special problems, not unlike those of addicts in general. In "Who Cares if You Listen,"[5] Milton Babbitt argues that the contemporary composer was supported by publishers whose money came from mass-market piano methods, choral octavos, and band parts. The composer needs to look to other sources of income (and who cares if you listen), mostly because the piano methods have fallen victim to the illegal and legal misuse of the copy machine, and, lacking sympathetic government support for culture in general, even the choral and band music may be disappearing.

An alternative option for the harrassed music publisher reflects another classic dictum: bad music is someone else's fault, since the publisher is merely an accessory. (Herbert von Karajan, for instance, has pronounced that "no music is vulgar, unless it is played in a way that makes it so." See Helena Matheopoulos, *Maestro*, New York: Harper & Row, 1982, p. 226.) Shifting the battlefield may relieve music publishers, composers, performers, and especially administrators, although not everyone will be happy with such an ethically slippery excuse.

5. Music, having been corrupted by printing and publishing, will be better off when these institutions are no longer around to encumber it. This nihilistic argument rarely finds any convincing focus, to be sure.[6] The argument can also be approached from the perspective of cultural history in general, as for instance in Jacques Attali's cacophonophilic *Bruits: Essai sur l'économie poli-*

---

5. Originally in *High Fidelity*, vol. 8, no. 2 (February 1958), pp. 38-40, 126-27, the essay is widely reprinted, for instance in Gilbert Chase, *The American Composer Speaks* (Baton Rouge: Louisiana State University Press, 1966) and in Elliott Schwartz and Barney Childs, *Contemporary Composers on Contemporary Music* (New York: Holt, 1967), pp. 244-50.

6. During my own wayward if belated youth in the late 1960s, even I attempted to defend the cause in "Music as Vibrations and as Flyspecks," *Transactions of the Wisconsin Academy of Sciences, Arts, and Letters*, 58 (1970), 15-26. Rereading the text today is both nostalgic and humbling.

tique de la musique (Paris: Presses Universitaires de France, 1977; translated as *Noise: The Political Economy of Music*, Minneapolis: University of Minnesota Press, 1985), although, once again, any focus on music publishing is lost in the mudslide.

In these writings, it should be noticed, the focus is typically on music publishing rather than music printing.

Bombarded by such damning sentiments, the poor music publisher seems scarcely defensible at all. What ought to be the criteria for admitting music publishers to heaven? To find our guidance from on high we must probably, not surprisingly once again, look slightly afield to statements directed mostly to other musical specialties but also appropriate to a critical evaluation of music publishing. Hans Keller, for instance, suggests that concert managers will further a particular repertory, "either because they think we want it, or because they expect us to want it once they have introduced us to it."[7] Oscar Sonneck earlier suggested that a librarian "ought not to content himself with giving to the public what it happens to want, but ought to help create a demand for what the public needs."[8] The critical process, of passing judgment on our publishers, on the role of music publishing in our society, and on the documents created by music printers, ought to be recognized as one of the music bibliographer's major responsibilities. Nothing more or less demanding of business skills, musical taste, or social responsibility, ought to be expected of those who assume the task of providing the documents for musical performance.

The panorama of five centuries of published music, as it resides in our libraries, begs to be laid out against the sky. Bibliographers' attempts to comprehend the vast prosopography, admittedly, can be all too easily encumbered by a mixture of fatigue and ideology. It is far easier — and really more satisfying — to look specifically to the historical record and to the music itself. A list of music dedicated by composers to their publishers (e.g., Mozart's "Hoffmeister" quartet), to my knowledge, has never been compiled; equally elusive would be a list of music that can be proven to have arisen out of a suggestion from the publisher. Celebrated instances can be recalled, among them the notorious composite

---

7. *Musical Times*, 123 (1982), 109. Cf. p. 212*n* above.
8. "Music in our Libraries," in the *Miscellaneous Studies in the History of Music* (New York: Macmillan, 1921), p. 290, as reprinted from *The Art World* (also in Bradley, p. 6).

sets of quasi-Festschrift variations, one instigated by Diabelli and best known to us because of Beethoven's good judgment (for once) in his social behavior. A counterpart is the set arranged by Belaieff, to which his enviable stable of Russian composers prepared character pieces on a favorite theme (a simplified version of "Chopsticks") and dedicated them to the talented pianists able to play the theme with one finger (*pace* Wilfrid Mellers) of each hand. The paraphrases (24 variations and finale) and 14 pieces are by Borodin, Cui, Liadov, and Rimsky-Korsakov, in the 1870s; for the second edition Borodin added a Mazurka, Shcherbachev a "Bigarrures: Petit supplément."[9] Juxtaposed against such bagatellia, one recalls Elgar's powerful "Nimrod" section in the "Enigma" Variations, in honor of his editor, August Jaeger. Less well known — in fact it is, to my knowledge, if understandably then at least ironically, unpublished — is the "Garland for Dr. K.," prepared by eleven composers in honor of Alfred Kalmus's eightieth birthday (London, 1969). Fitting somewhere into the discussion is another of Belaieff's productions, the *Quatuor sur le nom B-la-f*, for which Rimsky-Korsakov, Liadov, Borodin, and Glazunov each provided a movement in further respect for the chamber-music lover Belaieff. Adding still other titles to this list may be the best antidote to the record of discontent set forth above.

The most telling record of all, and also the most elusive, is the tantalizing argument (or is it an assumption?) that needs to be recalled: for the past five centuries, composers come to conceive their music with printing and publication in mind.

The nine topics introduced on p. 4, meanwhile, remain basic to the pursuit of music bibliography. Should it really aspire to the status of an autonomous discipline? In terms of any "critical mass" of practitioners, the prospect seems, if not

9. Liszt also added a kind musical endorsement, which may be instructive testimony to the workings of a clever music publisher. Whether because he misread his instructions or because he wanted the whole piano-bench for himself, Liszt prepared the only contribution that could not be performed as a duet. His text is printed not in an engraved presentation, but as a facsimile of the holograph — thus inspiring and distracting everyone, except those who knew music publishing well enough to appreciate what was going on.

undesirable, at least very unlikely. The field may be small and also diffuse, populated with an odd but diligent and enthusiastic assortment of printers and publishers, scholars, musicians, collectors, and librarians: indeed this diversity is hard to see as anything but a special strength. Notable contributions from occasional lonely soloists notwithstanding, music bibliography has generally been more comfortable with team-players than with empire builders.[10] So long as the evidence of music on paper is preserved, questions of interpretation will continue to be stimulated. The literature discussed in this book has served mostly to redefine the agenda of music bibliography. Mixing description, wish list, and prognostication, I should propose that the topics should now be reconceived as follows:

1. Description. Given on the one hand the many different directions in which bibliographical study is now moving, and on the other hand its persistent (and laudable) concern for (or at least its lip-service to) the convenience of its users (reflecting the dictum that citations must be "concise but sufficient"): can formularies be devised, and (very important today) reconciled with online practices and cost factors, so as to enable readers to locate particular details that are (a) significant, (b) formulated consistently and consensually, and (c) unencumbered by irrelevant particulars?

Identification of "best copies" is a related question, and clearly *the* single most important question of all. But how is "best" to be defined? Different answers will reflect the different needs of editors, biographers, bibliographers, reception historians, or those respon-

---

10. However clumsily, this discussion affords the opportunity to pay my special respect to several academics whose major contributions to music bibliography consist significantly in what they accomplished through their students. Charles Cudworth at Cambridge University, Thurston Dart, there and in London, and John M. Ward at Harvard University come to mind. I know of no way to cite any of their writings here without stretching my criteria to call for several dozen more borderline titles. This footnote will at least allow me to pay homage through an entry in my index.

sible for mounting an exhibition. (To this list, one hopes, must soon be added those persons responsible for decisions on preservation policy, involving both the original physical evidence and, secondarily, the surrogate media.) However crucial, this may be nothing that could — perhaps indeed should — ever be incorporated into cataloguing practice; it is hard to imagine that a data field could ever be assigned to it. The only points at which the question may reasonably be asked are (1) when a price is set, for instance by an antiquarian dealer; (2) when the document's special significance comes to the attention of a reader, whether through the citation, or through remarks by the owner or by others who know it; and (3) when an argument is based on its evidence, by a scholar in writing or by a musician in performance. Wise scholars are likewise frightened by the prospect of addressing it in any ostensibly comprehensive bibliographical system: Deutsch's experience (cf. 4 above) offers good reason to think twice.

The matter clearly should never be allowed to disappear from the bibliographer's agenda. Credibility depends on it, all the more so at a time when enhanced bibliographical access is likely to produce more widespread experiences of "information overload."

2. Dating. What models can be hypothesized in proposing the typical procedures and the different special circumstances for the production of musical editions; and from each activity, what can be inferred, and with what range and levels of probability, regarding the relative dates and operational function of the other activities?

The study of "printing house practices" perhaps needs to be undertaken in terms of some historically oriented extrapolation of modern operations research. Obviously the dates that emerge from such modelling ought to be assigned, and reassigned or at least re-examined, on a continuing basis. Ideally the decisions should be made by bibliographical specialists rather than in individual libraries by cataloguers with differing specialties and abilities, even if the results, in particular for scarce early materials, usually prove to be ultimately "copy-specific," so as to reconfirm the librarian's adage that there is no such thing as a duplicate.

A distinction between "dumb" and "smart" dates may even be useful. The former predominate, and for most purposes are all that is needed. Most library cataloguing can accept dumb dates, since the only readers for whom the dates matter are those who will want to make their own assignments. (Along the way, librarians may acquire a reputation for not having the interests of scholars in mind; the question becomes one of the cost of high-quality work.) Dumb dates are among Matthew Arnold's "stock notions and habits, which we follow staunchly but mechanically, vainly imagining that there is a virtue in following them staunchly which makes up for the mischief of following them mechanically." Smart dates, in contrast, are the stuff of culture, of truth and beauty; and those who need them have a rough time in their lives. The answers are inevitably complicated, and often as not, arguable if not inherently unambiguous.

Smart librarians and bibliographers are ones who know never to ask a scholar, "do you need a dumb or a smart date?" Smart scholars, on the other hand, must always ask whether they need to go to the considerable trouble of establishing a smart date, or whether a dumb one is sufficient (and then assure readers, without patronizing them, that the dumb date is sufficient for the needs at hand).

3. Plate Numbers. How can a publisher's catalogue be organized so as to convey its changing character, and the position of any particular publication within the whole?

Plate numbers are often the handiest way to do this. Being numerical, however, they acquire an almost magical fascination, even when there seems absolutely nothing useful to learn by multiplying, extrapolating from, or otherwise manipulating them mathematically. Pythagoras cries when he sees plate numbers.

Admittedly, as the numbers look up smilingly from their tidy sequential beds, they also inspire many questions that are worth asking: how many copies were there in a press run, and how many press runs? Lacking better evidence relevant to these important questions, plate numbers will continue to fascinate.

In many ways the most interesting questions of all involve the phenomenon of bibliographical variants, insofar as it suggests that, for whatever reason, the original presentation needed to be revised. The deployment of the printing surfaces or the size of the first press run turned out to be wrongly calculated: but why? To the bibliographer this is exciting stuff — often more exciting than the existence of the original edition in the first place, in that it offers prospects for bibliographical inference. (And never mind that the inferences are as often as not inconclusive.)

The sheer numerical data on printed copies and on the number of press runs, on the other hand, can only lead to even more impenetrable quantitative questions. How many of the copies were actually sold; and then read by musical performers; and then performed in public; and to how sizeable an audience, in which how many members were listening; and of these, how many were listening critically; and then (at which point we are on the edge of Marxist aesthetics, or behavioral psychology, or other such shoals) to what effect on society as a whole? There is a place for the study of the cultural impact of music printing, probably within the quantitative terms of modern *histoire du livre* studies. Credibility, however, is scarcely to be expected from any synthesis of conclusions based on coincidental numbers from a very limited sampling.

4. Other Internal Evidence. What strategies should guide bibliographers in their decisions to go to the trouble of learning highly complicated and expensive laboratory methods that may tell us more than we now know, and forego others that are likely to be unproductive?

Photocopies are increasingly and more readily accessible; paper history is flourishing; ink studies are just around the corner (and perhaps even affordable); and collateral evidence is more widely available and more readily understood for what it can and can not tell us. New technologies are a natural product of human curiosity, and for this reason their fascinating proliferation will no doubt continue, even if it is not specifically encouraged (i.e., subsidized).

What music should we send to the cyclotron? (My own choice: Bach's *Clavierübung*, part 3.) Will watermark studies of printed music ever be productive? (Most music bibliographers will say no, knowing full well, or at least hoping, that they will be proven wrong.) Out of such questions inevitably comes the conviction that original evidence *must* be preserved. Our various diasporas, of microfilm, photocopies, or optical discs, are invaluable today mostly as reassurance. They may fulfill their intended purposes, which are to provide for access and an alternative medium of preservation over the future. For bibliographical scholarship, however, the "best evidence" can only be the document itself.

An important difference between music bibliographers and music paleographer emerges. The paleographer works with the knowledge that each manuscript is unique; the bibliographer must be forever skeptical, remembering Falconer Madan's classic recognition of "the duplicity of duplicates." The purpose of printing may have been to create identical copies in the interests of circulation, although in fact any copy of an edition may preserve unique information, of whatever importance.

5. External Evidence. As colleagues inspect and index other kinds of materials, what should they be instructed to watch for on the bibliographer's behalf?

In a time when vast quantities of data are being converted to machine-readable forms, the experience of librarians and bibliographers in managing large quantities of bibliographical data promises to be a valuable resource in the management of non-bibliographical data as well — enough so to raise the question of what, in essence, really makes the difference.

6. Textual Criticism. What potentially meaningful details should bibliographers look for, in supporting the philological agenda of performers, editors, and biographers?

Once the literature and the concepts of music copy editing are codified, the textual bibliography of music should be ready for the level of scholarly theorizing that has characterized the textual bibliography of works of literature. Some day soon we may look forward, for instance, to "The Rationale of the Music Copy Text," by way of complementing W. W. Greg's classic essay on "The Rationale of the Copy Text," *Studies in Bibliography*, 3 (1950-51), pp. 19-36 (and reprinted several times). More familiar sentiments will be reconciled in the successor to another classic, James Thorpe's "The Aesthetics of Textual Criticism," issued originally in *PMLA*, 80 (1965), 465-82, and often reprinted.

The dialogue must continue to be very important, even if the questions and the answers are mismatched. Much as Tolstoy saw the historian as the deaf person answering questions that were never asked, so the bibliographer must continue to assemble the catalogues, plate-number files, indexes, watermark inventories, and even arguments that may never serve the needs of performing musicians and scholarly editors, collectively or individually.

7. Terminology. Should a "thesaurus of music bibliography" be prepared? Can definitions be constructed that are (1) consistent (it may be too much to ask them to be compatible with other such thesauri, for instance for general cataloguing, or even for rare books in general); (2) sensitive to the different characteristic practices of early printers and publishers; and (3) flexible in serving the changing needs of bibliographers today and tomorrow?

Viewing the history and anticipating the future of bibliographical terminology, one prays that some form of adrenalin might be introduced into the dialogue. Spurts of enthusiasm seem to alternate with long periods of depression. The next period of excitement should appear any day now, as music cataloguers come to appreciate the importance of terminology in their efforts involving "authority control." Predictably, a long period of depression will begin soon thereafter, growing for instance out of the logical implications of *Jahrgang* on automated record fields; or the multilingual implications of separative terminology (*edition, impression, issue, state,* vs. *Auflage* and *Ausgabe* vs. *tirage*); or, reflecting painful experiences in handling such musical genres as *motet,* or comparable experiences in defining such bibliographical genres as *piano score.* What really is "sheet music" — i. e., is any definition really worth the trouble to formulate and hope to enforce? What exactly is a *Stichbild?*[11]

The introduction (pp. 51-55) to the "Multilingual Glossary" in Michèle Cloonan's *Early Bindings in Paper* (London: Mansell, 1991) suggests the questions that lie ahead, as it implies some of the reasons why we need to address them and to remember how much the evidence can and cannot tell us. One is struck by the statement from Josiah Q. Bennett's *The Cataloguing Requirements of the Book Division of a Rare Book Library* (Kent, Ohio: Kent State University Library, 1969), p. 35: "some of the terms we [used as book binders] would have not been understood, or would have been taken otherwise, in other binderies in the same city."

---

11. It is also time to exorcise a ghost of music bibliography, one that has crept into several lists because of a misreading of terminology. *Die Notenpresse: Eine Chronik* (Leipzig: Poeschel & Trepte, 1924), by E. C. Banck (an appropriately named author) deals not with printing music at all, but with printing currency and its impact on inflation.

8. Impact. How can the activities of the music trades be critically evaluated, for purposes of understanding and redefining their contribution to society and its music?

The heritage of the printing press has ordained that, in Western civilization, what is committed to paper necessarily survives longer than what is not on paper; and what is printed usually survives longer than what is in manuscript. At the same time, survival also depends on use — not necessarily being consumed, let alone eaten (birthday cakes notwithstanding), but certainly realized in performance. It is part of our faith in the printed word that the strength of the written record should lie in its ability to survive the ravages of time; but it is part of our faith, all the more so in the environment of democratic capitalism, in music that justifies its presence by claiming the affection of its listeners. The existence of an edition must thus tell us something about the musical society of its day, just as its survival must reflect a belief that it speaks, or can speak, or ought to speak, to the needs of at least some listeners. These assumptions alone should justify the music bibliographer's activities. And yet, the more closely we look at both the text and its environment, the more confusing the message becomes. It is the precious life-blood of a master spirit, but it tells us exactly what we want it to tell us, since it must be re-born with every reader, and (herein no doubt lies the special key to the continued survival of music in particular) in every reconception by any performer for any listener. Under such circumstances the role of music bibliography itself will also change, although the nature of the changes will no doubt become clear only after they happen.

9. Motivation. Music bibliography requires handling documents. Photocopies make it possible to compare distant originals, but conclusions must always be verified in the originals. Equally important, a sense of context and meaning can usually be coaxed more easily and more authoritatively out of original evidence than out of photocopies.

Music may no longer claim the spectacular private libraries of a century ago; music collecting, however, inevitably goes hand in hand with documentary study, bibliophily with bibliography. Bibliographers today, however, require broad access to collections, even — indeed necessarily — in the random and serendipitous activities of sorting and browsing. This is becoming increasingly difficult in an age when conservation has emerged as extremely important and in a time when (security being a primary worry) readers are being increasingly separated, physically and operationally, from the materials they need.

———

In his preface to *Typefounding in America*, Rollo Silver warmly remembers advice from Clarence Brigham: "Don't worry about a work not being complete, because if it is complete, the next fellow won't have any fun." There are no doubt many additional titles that should have been included here, and some of them may be important. It is nice that my apologies can be tempered with the joy of not having deprived readers of the joys of uncovering and adding more entries to the record. Even happier, of course, is the prospect that the addenda and corrigenda might be pieced together so as to redefine the literature once again, in pursuit of further agenda.

Addenda

---

no. 942 (p. 344)

Examples of these music faces are seen in *Hermann Zapf and his Design Philosophy* (Chicago: Society of Typographic Arts, 1987), pp. 21 and 125. Zapf's work under Paul Koch is also described in Otto S. Fabricius, "Die Werkstatt 'Haus zum Fürsteneck' in Frankfurt," in *ABC-XYZapf: Fifty Years in Alphabet Design* (London: Wynkyn de Worde Society; Offenbach: Bund Deutscher Buchkünstler, 1989), pp. 30-33. Other essays in this Festschrift that mention the workshop include Will Carter, "It Started in Frankfurt in 1938" (pp. 113-15), which also shows the house, a sketch of Koch by Victor Hammer, and an example of Koch's music. Zapf's music faces appear on pp. 213 and 226. The latter page also shows a title page entitled, *Die Entwicklung der Notenschrift in Kopien nach Originalen und Drucken, 1938. Hermann Zapf, Nr. 17,* which is described on p. 245 as "A collection of brush and pen copies of examples to study the history of musical notation." (Zapf's music printing interests are poorly covered in music bibliography sources; for guidance to these citations I am again indebted to Paul Duensing as well as to Hermann Zapf.)

Chronology of the Early Literature

Major Writings

1550s LeBé's notes on music
    typography (308)

1567 First music type specimen
    (Plantin, 309)
_____

1765 First history of music print-
    ing (Fournier, 44); *cf.* his
    Manuel (165) and the
    Gandos' *Response* (168)

ca.1765 Music engraving discussed
    in the *Encyclopèdie* (166)

1790 Meusel looks at music
    incunabula (113)
_____

1834 Fétis's account in Duver-
    ger's *Specimen* (184)

1841-47 Schmid describes early
    music in Vienna (1; also
    his 1845 Petrucci, 114)

1840s D'Almaine pamphlet (193)
_____

1854 Bouchet's account (197)

1856 Farrenc addresses music
    bibliophiles (908)

1864 Weckerlin's history (45)

1875 Sandars on technology (46)

1877 Chrysander's sketch (47)

1880 Goovaerts on the
    Low Countries (810)

1891-94 Beaudoire's manuals (213)

1892 Vienna exhibition (418)

1894 Grand-Carteret on music
    covers (444)

1896 Matthew's *The Literature of
    Music* (910)

1896 Röder Festschrift (48)

1897 Squire on incunabula (119)

1900 Kidson's British study (656)

Other Writings

_____

1608. First printer's manual to discuss
    music (Hornschuh, 158)
    [*Other type specimens with music,*
    1616- , 310*ff.*]

1679. First layout of a music type
    case (Veitor, 159)
    [*Other early manuals,* 1683- , 160*ff.*]

1776. Burney and Hawkins
    histories (89, 90)

1786. French music censorship (688)

_____

1818. Senefelder's instruction book
    on lithography (178)

1834. Earliest exhibition of
    music printing (407)

1844. Earliest commentary on
    music publishing
    (Bories & Bonassiés, 526)

_____

1857. Ricordi plate-number
    catalogue (720)

1865. Bachmann instructions for
    music typesetting (203)

1870. Marahrens " (204)

1872. Dittrich " (205)

1877. Caxton Celebration (413)

1881. Nahuys on early rarities (2)

1881. Vernarecci on Petrucci (734)

1884. Cummings addresses the
    Musical Association (59)

1892 Molitor on German liturgical
    incunabula (117)

1897. Verster on music
    bookplates (502)

Author Index

The list covers personal names; corporate auspices are covered in the Subject Index. Editors and compilers are also included to the extent that their intellectual contribution to the work in question could be viewed as involving any of the nine agenda discussed in Chapters 1 and 9.

Subject Index

This index covers subjects specified in the entries. I have attempted to embed the most important concepts in the annotations, although inevitably many are hard to provide for. (Many of these are of timely interest: such, almost by the very nature of scholarly inquiry, is almost to be expected.) Personal and corporate names in this index identify the subjects of writings, or, in several instances, activities in production and sponsorship (i. e., as typographers, publishers, or claimants to music printing inventions). Also included are a number of entries for distinctive titles.

This book is partly self-indexing, through the classified arrangement as laid out in the Table of Contents and the many internal references. Those with little overview of the subject as a whole will probably work most productively by beginning in this index, and later considering the Table of Contents and exploring the cross-references. Specialists, on the other hand, will more often start with the Table of Contents and use the cross-references and indexes as their search may need to be enlarged.

France, Lithography of music. *See*
Lithography of music, France.
— music, duties on, 692
— music covers, 419, 444, 462, 478
— music printers
— — directories of, 686-87
— — list of, 256
— music printing
— — earliest, 705
— — history of, 44, 45, 50
— music publishers, 603, 620
— — directories of, 686-87
— music publishing, 637, 688; pp.
249-56. *See also* Paris, music
publishing.
— music typography, 299
— opera posters, 513, 517
— patent records, 380
— printed music, quantity of, p. 68
— printers' manuals. *See* Printers'
manuals, French.
Francesco da Milano, engraved lute
book, p. 62
Frankfurt-am-Main. *See also*
Hirsch Collection, Luther foundry, Staats- und Universitätsbibliothek.
— exhibitions, (1908), 425; (1920),
428; (1927), 429; p. 285
— music printers and publishers,
p. 286
— music printing and publishing,
770-74, 778; p. 61
— music typography, 302, 772
Frankfurt an der Oder
— music printers and publishers,
p. 286
— music publishing, 775
Freising (Bavaria), p. 318

Frescobaldi, Girolamo, Borboni
editions, p. 361
Fribourg, music publishing, late
17th century, 809
Fritzsch, E. W., 605
Fry, Edmund, 350
Fuchs, Aloys, and Mozart
scholarship, p. 318-19
Fugger family, p. 317
Fuld, James J., 925 (pp. 335-36);
p. 321
Fust, Johann, pp. vii, 194

Galveston, Texas, music printers
and publishers, p. 310
Gando *frères*, 44, 168, 323
"Garamont Noten," 316
Gardano, Alessandro, p. 338
Gardano, Antonio (Antoine Gar-
dane), 42, 698, 741; p. 365
— editions of Orlando di Lasso,
632
Gardano (firm), pp. 257, 349
Gaspari, Gaetano, catalogue of
music in the Liceo Musicale,
Bologna, 39
Gatherings, signature practices in
early part-books, 32
Gazette de Cologne, 329
Gdańsk
— music publishers, 844; p. 301
— music publishing, 843
Geidel (engraver), 615
Geigy-Hagenbach, Karl, p. 321
Geiringer, Karl, p. 326
Gelegenheitskompositionen. See
Occasional music.
Gelinek, Josef, quantity of pub-
lished music, p. 69

431

447